Christ & Empire

Additional praise for Joerg Rieger's *Christ & Empire*

"Joerg Rieger has plunged into the complex theological waters of politics, Christianity, and the future of globalization. Historically the spread of the gospel message included the cross, the flag, and the cannon. In the midst of a tidal wave of superpower empire drenched in patriotism, prosperity preaching, and neo-charismatic international missions, Rieger's work constructs a new understanding of Jesus Christ. Here we finally have an alternative to the empire. This text argues cogently for a truth and freedom for humankind that yields genuine international people-to-people solidarity and wholeness for all."

— Dwight N. Hopkins, University of Chicago
author of *Being Human: Race, Culture, and Religion*

Christ & Empire

From Paul to Postcolonial Times

Joerg Rieger

Fortress Press
Minneapolis

To R., H., and A.,

who are making

their own history

CHRIST & EMPIRE
From Paul to Postcolonial Times

Cover image: © Giraudon / Art Resource, NY. Used by permission.
Cover design: Abby Hartman
Book design: Julie A. Prindle and Timothy W. Larson

This book was set in Adobe Garamond and Friz Quadrata.

Library of Congress Cataloging-in-Publication Data

Rieger, Joerg.
  Christ and empire : from Paul to postcolonial times / Joerg Rieger.
    p. cm.
  ISBN: 978–0–8006–2038–7 (alk. paper)
    1. Jesus Christ—Person and offices. 2. Christianity and politics. I. Title.
BT203.R54 2007
261.8—dc22   2006038938

The paper used in this publication meets the minimum requirements of American National Standard for Information Sciences — Permanence of Paper for Printed Library Materials, ANSI Z329.48-1984.

Manufactured in the U.S.A.

11   10   09   08   07   2   3   4   5   6   7   8   9   10

Contents

Contents

Preface

FOR THEOLOGIANS THE TITLE *Christ and Empire* will be reminiscent of H. Richard Niebuhr's famous *Christ and Culture*. Yet *Christ and Empire* follows a trajectory that is different from Niebuhr's. In this book the challenge of Christ is rethought in an expanded and more complex framework. The primary context in which we think about Christ—or anything else, for that matter—is never "culture" as such. We are clearer today about the fact that whatever we might call "culture" is not one unilateral phenomenon, and we know that culture can no longer be conceived apart from issues of power.[1] The primary context in which we think about Christ—whether we realize it or not—is shaped by large and ever-changing conglomerates of power that are aimed at controlling all aspects of our lives, from macropolitics to our innermost desires: this is what I call "empire." *Empire* in this sense is a more comprehensive term than *culture* because it incorporates more complex notions of culture (including the constant tensions between dominant and subaltern forms of culture) and because it incorporates concerns of power that commend to our attention a closer look at other phenomena as well, not only politics but also economics, and the complex ways in which these phenomena impact each other.[2]

In this book, I trace how our images of Christ have been shaped by empire at significant turning points. The surprising insight in this regard is that despite constant pressure—whether open or sublime—Christ could never be co-opted altogether by empire. While there are no pristine forms of Christology, where Christ would be completely independent of the metamorphoses of empire, there are various forms of resistance to empire and fresh inspiration for alternative images of Christ. In the process, we discover a complex picture that does not allow for the easy typologies and classifications of Niebuhr's *Christ and Culture*. The complexity of the matter requires more in-depth studies of each approach and close attention to the various points of connection and attraction of Christ and empire before we can identify the ways in which Christ pushes beyond empire.[3] If the question of empire is not accidental, because empire shapes us whether we like it or not and because our lives are contained by it as fish are contained by water, we can no longer do theology apart from such detailed investigations of the powers that shape us consciously and unconsciously. Only when those powers are seen can we show what difference our subject matter makes as it pushes beyond the status quo.

While this project seeks to open new vistas in the study of theology and particularly in the study of Jesus Christ, it also seeks to be useful in the classroom. One common complaint is that students today come with less-well-developed theological backgrounds than the students of previous generations. Rather than dwelling in nostalgia, however, we now have the opportunity to develop theological background knowledge in more complex fashions that go beyond the ability to recite Paul, Nicaea, Anselm, or Schleiermacher. We need to develop broader horizons that include an awareness of the challenges that our theological forebears faced and addressed and that are still with us in one way or another in our own time. In this project, the readers are invited to engage in a process of constantly rethinking our theological heritage in relation to the flow of power—an effort that keeps sending us back to the drawing board.

The theological issue to be pursued in terms of Christ and empire is this: Throughout the history of Christianity, Christ has often been understood in terms of the ruling empires: the Christ of empire became the Christ of the church. Even if this identification is not explicit, our most common images of Christ are top-down images. Christ is on the side of those who are successful, who have made it. This attitude defines even the images of the Christ who cares about the downtrodden and the marginalized, as we imagine a Christ who lifts them up, who integrates them into mainline society so that they, too, can benefit from the powers that be and find their place in empire.[4] This has become the default position for our thinking about Christ to such a degree that it is hard to think about Christ in other ways. In this project, I want to show that the images of the top-down Christ have not managed to block out alternative visions of Christ completely. There is hope that Christ will once again assert a different reality that cannot be contained by the powers that be and that creates space for different ways of life in situations of empire where alternatives are systematically persecuted and blotted out.

* * * * *

I would like to express my gratitude to those who have been in conversation about various issues developed in this book. Kwok Pui-lan and Catherine Keller in particular have discussed matters of empire and postcolonialism with me for several years, as have many of the members of the Workgroup for Constructive Christian Theology; Don Compier, Jim Perkinson, Nancy Bedford, and my colleague at Perkins Karen Baker-Fletcher deserve special mention. Kwok Pui-lan and Don Compier have also helped me formulate insights about empire in the process of a book that we are editing on the relation of empire and theology in the work of key theologians across two millennia of Christian tradition. I continue to learn from many international colleagues, in particular from Néstor Míguez (Argentina) and Jung Mo Sung (Brazil). As we collaborate on a transnational project that seeks to describe the spirit of empire, Néstor and Jung have helped me to become more astutely aware of the global situation of empire and the limited perspectives that we in the United States and in Europe tend to bring to it. I would also like to acknowledge the comments on chapters of the manuscript by Mikael Mogren of Sweden and Michael Nausner of Germany, Sweden, and Austria. Liz Clark has put me on the right track on some of the issues discussed in chapter 2. David Brockman and Patrick Provost-Smith have also made helpful comments and Kristin Herzog has read the manuscript as a whole. A special word of thanks goes to Tammerie Day, my research assistant, who has contributed to the editing process and has compiled the index. Note that all translations in the text from resources that are not available in English are mine. Institutional support from Perkins School of Theology and Southern Methodist University has been provided not just by Tammerie's work but also by research leaves and an Academic Outreach Award. The members of the Progressive Reading Group that meets at our house have helped shape my thinking on many issues, providing a space that is truly transdisciplinary and transpolitical. My wife Rosemarie Henkel-Rieger and my daughters Helen and Annika provide not only inspiration but also the sort of probing questions that theologians often would rather prefer to avoid—as one of them wondered at the age of five, years ago: Why is the church always talking about "Jesus, Jesus, Jesus," but not about the things that Jesus cared about?

Notes

1. This is one of the major insights of the emerging field of cultural studies. This insight is not yet fully developed in H. Richard Niebuhr, *Christ and Culture* (New York: Harper, 1951), who assumes that culture is the overarching term that incorporates other specific developments, such as science and philosophy and even the matter of politics. "What we have in view when we deal with Christ and culture is that total process of human activity and that total result of such activity to which now the name *culture*, now the name *civilization*, is applied in common speech"; ibid., 32. The field of cultural studies investigates how the question of power functions in all of these processes and demands greater attention to the complexity of the phenomena that Niebuhr seeks to address.

2. Graham Ward has sought to develop more complexity while maintaining the notion of culture. See his book *Christ and Culture: Challenges in Contemporary Theology* (Oxford: Blackwell, 2005). Ward points out that the binary that Niebuhr assumed between Christ and culture is no longer valid: "The difficulty here is that Christ is already a cultural event. We have no access to a Christ who has not already been encultured"; ibid., 21. Theologically speaking, "the cultural is that through which God's redemptive grace operates"; ibid., 22. Yet even this more complex notion of culture could benefit from a sense that cultural developments are part of a battle that is broader.

3. Once again, this is different from Niebuhr's approach, which draws stark typological and theological lines but provides little historical or other detail and does not address the complex interactions of theology and its cultural settings. Once again, Niebuhr's neglect of the question of power limits his perspective; he is unable to see the constant negotiation that takes place where influence is asserted. Ward's *Christ and Culture* is more aware of the complexity, but the question of power still needs more attention; for this reason alone the notion of empire is more helpful than the notion of culture.

4. Both conservative and liberal attempts to address issues of poverty, for instance, aim at a successful reintegration of the poor into society, albeit by different means. The conservatives emphasize personal responsibility and the liberals promote public welfare programs. What is not discussed, however, is how poverty is produced in the first place and what kind of a critique Christ might offer of the status quo.

Introduction

FROM THE VERY BEGINNING, our images of Jesus Christ have developed in the context of empire. Jesus was born under the rule of the Roman Emperor Augustus, lived under the auspices of the Roman Empire, and was executed by a common means of punishment for political rebels in unruly provinces: the cross. Empire in one form or another has been the context in which some of the most important later images of Christ developed: the notion of Jesus' lordship gained prominence at a time when the Roman emperors would claim to be the only lords; the idea of Jesus' equality with God and with humanity developed at a time when the Roman emperors had become Christians and drew their authority from the Christian God; Christ's role as God-human in salvation was clarified during the early years of the Norman conquest of England; the way of Jesus Christ was further explicated in the midst of the Spanish conquest of the New World; Jesus' roles as prophet, priest, and king were picked up during the heydays of Northern European colonialism; Christ victorious was proclaimed in neocolonialist circumstances; and even the cosmic Christ is tied to another empire. Yet the images of the Christ of empire have not managed to block out alternative visions of Christ completely. Christ continues to assert a different reality.

Empire, Past and Present

The key word for the present is once again *empire*. Even though we do not always use the term, we are greatly fascinated by talk about related issues, such as power and its comparative forms such as superpower and hyperpower—the latter term coined to describe the unique position of the United States in the world today. We are captured by the fantastic wealth created by multinational corporations and their leaders, and by talk about the exploits of the global economy and processes of globalization—even though there may not be much in it for us. We are even fascinated by the dark underside of empire, although it scares us to death, particularly when it manifests itself in violence and terror and what is now officially called *blowback*: that is, the unintended consequences of the politics of empire.[1]

1

But *blowback* is simply a new term for an old reality: "No one can afford for long to practice atrocities and tyrannies overseas without the evil done seeping back to contaminate the homeland," as Montesquieu, reflecting on the Spanish violence in the Americas of the sixteenth century, and Alexis de Tocqueville, reflecting on French violence in Algeria in the nineteenth century, would have argued.[2] Perhaps more than anything else it is these unintended consequences that nudge common people in the United States to wonder about empire. The question "Why do they hate us so?" had to be repressed promptly and comprehensively after the terrorist attacks on September 11, 2001.

There is a long debate in the history of the United States about whether or not the U.S.A. is an empire. Nevertheless, our current status as hyperpower and the foreign policies of the most recent U.S. administrations support a growing pride in our global leadership position and have lowered dramatically people's resistance to adopt the term.[3] Despite constant setbacks in the war in Iraq and the resignation of Secretary of Defense Donald Rumsfeld after the elections in the fall of 2006, pride about our role as an empire is still being fueled.[4] Of course, while the United States is one of the key players, the structures of contemporary empire are not limited to the U.S.A. as a nation; transnational corporations and the interests of other powerful nations such as the G8[5] contribute to empire as well.

Concern about empire is even stronger and more pressing in many places outside of the United States and Europe, where the crushing weight of empire is often felt more immediately in people's lives. At present, the pressures of empire manifest themselves, for instance, in sanctions against nations that refuse to comply with norms established by the powers that be; in economic arrangements that exploit the labor power, the land, or other assets of less powerful nations; and in the stimulations of a seductive consumer culture that permeates more and more spaces around the globe through the media and the market.[6] All these pressures are often directly transmitted to the people.[7] In the aftermath of the terrorist attacks of September 11, 2001, the United States' ongoing involvement in Afghanistan and Iraq, and with mounting internal pressures at home, an increasing number of people are beginning to wonder what the implications of these events might be for the future of life around the globe and what shape the resulting life-and-death struggles will take.

Empire, in sum, has to do with massive concentrations of power that permeate all aspects of life and that cannot be controlled by any one actor alone. This is one of the basic marks of empire throughout history. Empire seeks to extend its control as far as possible; not only geographically, politically, and economically—

these factors are commonly recognized—but also intellectually, emotionally, psychologically, spiritually, culturally, and religiously. The problem with empire is not primarily a moral one—it is not that all empires are necessarily equally evil and wrong. Some empires and certain modes of colonialism claim to promote benevolent causes, as we shall see.[8] The problem with empire has to do with forms of top-down control that are established on the back of the empire's subjects and that do not allow those within its reach to pursue alternative purposes. The problem with this approach can be seen in Christology: in a situation of empire Christ becomes part of the system to such a degree that little or no room exists for the pursuit of alternative realities of Christ. Empire displays strong tendencies to domesticate Christ and anything else that poses a challenge to its powers.

In the course of history, the manifestations of power vary and empires have taken different shapes. The European empires of recent centuries, including those of the Spanish, Portuguese, British, French, Dutch, Belgians, and Germans, used to maintain colonies in one way or another. Of course, the ways of maintaining colonies differed considerably, spanning from conquest, war, and slavery to more enlightened efforts at civilizing and educating people who were seen as less developed; at times even economic development can be found on the agenda of empire. At the beginning of the twenty-first century we live in an age when empires based on formal colonialism have mostly disappeared. While some colonial structures are still around—as, for example, Native Americans in the United States continue to remind us[9]—contemporary empire is a more dispersed reality that is embodied in various dependencies maintained through less visible ties. Economic relations, for instance, have created a tight net around the globe that competes with, and often surpasses, the political power of nations. Transnational corporations often amass greater wealth than entire nations and enjoy a great deal of freedom from the control of even the most powerful national governments. On these grounds, it could be argued that empire is primarily an economic reality, tied to the growth of global capitalism. There is much truth to this, but the full picture is more complex. Empire also exerts power through cultural and intellectual webs that tend to work in even more hidden ways, surfacing only from time to time—for instance, in debates on education and popular culture.[10] All this is supported by the rapid development and expansion of communication and technology. Michael Hardt and Antonio Negri describe current manifestations of the power of empire as "biopower," which is "a form of power that regulates social life from its interior" and that welds together economic, political, and cultural forces. [11]

3

Empires have come and gone, and the most famous ones, from the Roman to the British Empires, no longer exist. There is no reason to assume that present empires will last forever, even though their main proponents would like us to believe just that. Former British Prime Minister Margaret Thatcher's famous claim that "capitalism is here to stay" and Francis Fukuyama's thesis that the recent state of affairs after the collapse of the Soviet Union represents the "end of history" and history's goal are among the most prominent and popular arguments claiming that the pillars of the current empire are no longer negotiable and will endure.[12] In fact, the power and influence of any empire might be measured by the degree to which it can make us believe that it is able to support such claims of endurance. Can we even imagine the demise of the current empire any more?

Inspiring Resistance

In the history of empire, one of the common features of the varying structures of empire has to do with the fact that they are so overpowering and so pressing that those living under their rule cannot remain neutral. They have no other choice than to develop forms of resistance, however small and insignificant, or surrender through acquiescent support, manifested often in the simple silence of a people about the reality of the various empires in which they live. In the history of Christianity, both attitudes have found expression in many different forms. Resistance to empire is manifest in the lives of Jesus, of Paul, and in parts of the early church. At the same time, acquiescent support of empire can also be found in some of the earliest traditions, and this support becomes more pronounced when the church begins to benefit more and more from the powers of empire. Today, faced with an empire that is more all-pervasive and thus in many ways more overpowering than anything in the past, the questions are whether anything other than acquiescence can still be imagined and—this is the christological question posed in this book—*whether there is something in the reality of Jesus Christ's peculiar refusal to acquiesce to empire that continues to inspire us in the broadest sense of the word.* This inspiration will be traced through some of the most massive historical manifestations of empire related to the history of Christianity, beginning with ancient Rome and continuing through the apex of medieval feudalism, sixteenth- and nineteenth-century forms of colonialism, neocolonialism, and current structures of empire that are often labeled as "postcolonial."[13]

In the process it will become apparent that the scope of empire continues to widen throughout history. Current structures of empire are more all-encompassing than anything that has gone before, not only in terms of their geographical reach and ability to enforce order but also in their ability to reach into cultural and even personal spheres and to redefine them. One of the things that distinguishes contemporary empire from past empires is that its pressures appear to be more overpowering, even as the structures of empire are less visible than ever before. In the present situation, those two qualities seem to go hand in hand. Where the Roman Empire built streets and highways, for instance, a praxis that was still crucial to the expansion of European colonialism centuries later, empire now is less dependent on such visible structures and moves through the superhighways of technology, which reach farther than ever before (all the way into people's minds) and which are mostly invisible at the same time. Imagine if the trillions of dollars that move around the globe every day on the superhighways of the Internet would need to be transported by road. Not even the transport of large sums of money by airplane would be as invisible as transport by virtual reality, and it would certainly be less effective.

Moreover, the invisibility of the broadening influences of empire, aided by rapid technological developments in the realm of virtual reality, makes resistance much more difficult since most people never realize what it is that shapes them, that reaches all the way into and creates their deepest desires. In the final analysis, the forces of marketing and cultural persuasion through entertainment and education, also transmitted through technological superhighways, appear to be more powerful and irresistible than highly visible military displays of power that have the added disadvantage of revealing the real face of the empire.[14] In chapter 7, this analysis of contemporary dynamics of empire will be continued, coupled with the search for sources of alternative inspiration and resistance.

Empire, Religion, and Theology

Even a cursory glance at the history of empire reveals that empires have often been justified and supported by theological means. Already at the time of Jesus the Romans could rely on a well-organized theology of empire that was able to assimilate other theologies to varying degrees—even those that would appear rather incompatible, such as traditional Jewish theologies of places like Palestine. Later, at the time of the councils of Nicaea and Chalcedon, Christian theology felt the pressures to assimilate to the force fields of the Roman Empire and to contribute to them. With the conversion of the Emperor Constantine in the fourth century, the theology of empire turned more directly to Christian sources. It is well known that the feudal empires of the Middle Ages and even the colonialism of the sixteenth through the nineteenth century enjoyed strong support from Christian theology. What is less clear, however, is that even today empire enjoys widespread theological support that goes beyond the most obvious conservative Christian positions that have supported the administration of George W. Bush. Some of the current theologies of empire sound more moderate than their predecessors; some merely promote ideas of "progress," for instance, or try to shore up broadly accepted values of Western civilization.[15] At the same time, however, there is not only a history of theological support of empire but also a history of resistance. Some of the strongest critiques of empires throughout history have come from theological developments.[16] That is the challenge developed further in this book, leading to the question of how empire might be identified and resisted by contemporary theology.

One of the marks of current debates about empire is that these debates are often transdisciplinary. Here, theologians find a twofold challenge that pulls us out of our monodisciplinary slumbers and that leads us beyond earlier interdisciplinary efforts where theology often merely conformed to the expectations of other disciplines.[17] The transdisciplinary atmosphere of the study of empire is not only open to new contributions by theological thinkers, it needs these contributions in order to develop the broadest perspective on empire possible. Just as empire itself can no longer be reduced to a few isolated factors such as economics, politics, culture, or religion, neither can the study of empire and the possibility of resistance be reduced to only a few factors. In the encounter of the various perspectives on empire, the horizon of all who participate in the debate will be broadened.

Theology developed in a critical encounter with empire charts a new future for the field, leading us beyond the basic categories and paradigms developed by modern theology. It transcends, for instance, the modern category of "religion." The subject of theological reflections can no longer be limited to terms that are classified as "religious" in the modern sense, since the theological study of empire includes social, cultural, economic, and political dimensions and any other dimension that describes life. As we are beginning to realize, the modern dichotomies of *religious* and *secular* no longer apply without reservation; such dichotomies limit our understanding of the powerful impact of theological categories both in support of empire and in resistance to it. These limits of the religious/secular dichotomy can be seen, for instance, in the limits of the separation of church and state—a separation that is constantly undermined by the all-encompassing nature of empire, despite the general affirmation of this principle in the United States. In this context, assuming the universal validity of the separation of religious and secular or the separation of church and state severely limits one's ability to deal with the constant interplay of these categories in the ongoing history of empire and to consider alternative forms of resistance. It would never occur to nonmodern readers, whether ancient or contemporary,[18] that the images of God and Christ addressed in this book could be limited to what we now commonly define as "religious"; the category of religion as a clearly distinct realm that is only loosely tied to other expressions of life hardly exists elsewhere. We are now beginning to realize the problematic nature of this category in our own setting and the need for a broader horizon due to the complex nature of empire.[19]

Theology developed in a critical encounter with empire also transcends the modern theological paradigm of "contextual theology." In its modernist liberal forms, contextual theology often suffers from two problems. One problem is that the context to which theology seeks to relate is the context that is most visible and appears to be closest to home. Here, the more pressing issues that are often less visible (because they are pushed from consciousness into the unconscious) are overlooked. Dominant contextual theologies of culture, for instance, usually try to "be relevant" to whatever is identified as the most important and visible aspect of dominant culture; but they often neglect to read between the lines and to deal with the gaps and the silences of cultures, where the pain is.[20] Paul Tillich's efforts to address the feelings of anxiety and meaninglessness of the modern middle class, for instance, did not consider that the deeper roots of these attitudes cannot be found in the middle class itself but need to be sought in broader systemic distortions that affect the lower classes in even more severe fashion. While there is now a growing realization of the many different manifestations of culture—a great improvement over early "contextual" theologies that simply universalized their own cultures—there is still too little awareness that context may not be what is closest to home, but that what needs attending is "what hurts" and what lies below the surface.[21] One of the great advantages of the various liberation theologies over contextual theology is that they are trying to deal with context as *that which hurts*; accordingly, feminist, African American, Latin American, and other critical approaches have opened new possibilities in the context of the Americas.

The other problem with contextual theology is that it is often understood as having to "respond" to its context. This means that theological resources are interpreted in "correlation" to contextual concerns in such a way that context comes to determine theology.[22] And even where theological resources are read in opposition to contextual concerns, the context often still controls what theology does. The game is thus set by whatever is defined as "context"; there is no way to shift it. Once again, various liberation theologies have developed possible alternatives when they identify context as that which needs to be overcome and subverted rather than affirmed; a stronger doctrine of sin has been a helpful tool in this regard.

Finally, the argument of this book will be based on historical observations and what is now called "historical theology." Here, too, new frontiers will need to be explored as much of historical theology is still pursued in an ahistorical fashion, as abstract theological reflection on historical texts. Many theologians are trained to approach texts, whether ancient or modern, at face value and according to some supposed general conceptual meaning. In this mode historical theologians discuss ideas of the past without much investigation of context and at face value, according to their conceptual meaning—as if an idea developed by Athanasius could easily be compared to an idea developed by Anselm or Aulén. In this situation, taking into account the context of theological ideas will lead to a more complex picture and a fuller understanding that will, ultimately, make for a deeper and more informed dialogue among these various historical positions as well. In this respect, historical theology would benefit from being brought up to speed with some of the basic lessons developed by conventional historical-critical research of biblical scholars.

At the same time, we also need to push beyond the limits of historical criticism, and in this sense historical theology (this time in sync with historical-critical biblical scholarship) needs to catch up once again. One of the problems of historical-critical research has been identified as the lack of a self-critical moment. Historical-critical scholarship has often proceeded as if the historian's perspective would somehow be objective, able to sort out disputes of the past as a neutral judge.[23] What we realize now is that such objectivity and neutrality is illusionary; yet this does not mean that history becomes simply a web of unreconstructed narratives, a position that has become fashionable among certain "postmodern" historians. In order to continue the traditions of critical historical work in our own times, we need to include our own perspectives and biases into our research and let them be reshaped by the engagement with the historical sources—thus the "self-critical" moment. History, as I have explained in more detail elsewhere, can no longer be merely a record of past events. History takes on new shape if it is understood as a reconstruction of the past in relation to the present through the reappropriation of the repressed parts of history. This is why, to use a formulation of Fredric Jameson, "history is what hurts,"[24] just as context is that which hurts. Historical theology reshaped in this way picks up the repressed moments of the past but is geared toward a reconstruction that affects the present and the future, asking questions like, What difference do those reflections make in the present and how do they help us shape what is to come?

Empire and the Resisting Christ

In this process, another look at Jesus Christ might lead us in new directions. Christ—despite all efforts to domesticate him—remains a "stumbling block" (1 Cor. 1:23). He never quite fits in, to the surprise of his contemporaries,[25] to the surprise of the supporters of family values and other status quo institutions,[26] and to the surprise of the ecclesial establishment.[27] Even the empires-that-be, not easily caught by surprise, are caught off guard by Jesus and find it necessary to get rid of him.[28] This Christ who never quite fits in—who creates a theological and christological surplus that pushes beyond the splendor of the status quo—is the subject of this book. His strange not-fitting-in might help us to get in touch with context not as what we consider closest to home but as "that which hurts" and thus to shift the rules of the game.

The notion of surplus that I am proposing here is related to not fitting in and being in touch with that which hurts; people who experience oppression and who are pushed to the margins have access to a certain "surplus enjoyment," as Jacques Lacan argued for the case of women in patriarchal society.[29] While those who represent the status quo are limited to whatever the system offers and demands, those who do not meet the demands of the status quo and are repressed by it—that is, who are relegated to the social and political unconscious—have a wider set of options that transcend the system. In being pushed to the margins of the system the repressed not only gain an alternative perspective—you see things from the underside that you cannot see from the top, especially the distortions of the system—but they also gain surplus energies and enjoyment that escape the powers that be in a twofold sense. First, surplus literally escapes them—they do not really "get it"; and, second, surplus escapes their control. Such surplus is subversive because it cannot ultimately be controlled by the system. Surplus, in this context, can be anything that points beyond the status quo. An observation by Walter Benjamin helps us to frame this surplus in terms of historical insight: "Not man or men but the struggling, oppressed class itself is the depository of historical knowledge."[30]

The complex and transdisciplinary reality created by empire (a reality that cannot be limited to religion, politics, economics, and so forth) finds a stumbling block in the complex and transdisciplinary *real* of Christ (a real that cannot be limited to religion, politics, and economics either).[31] The battle between *reality* (the commonly accepted version of the way things are, upheld not by correspondence to a referent anchored in people's lives but by power) and the *real* (that which has been pushed below the surface and repressed in the formation of the dominant version of reality) is as uneven as any battle between dominant and repressed forces: reality seems to win every time. But where the dominant view of reality intersects with the repressed view of the real, things will never be quite the same. The real of Christ (repressed and pushed below the surface on the crosses of the empire, a form of repression that continues and is being repeated in many ways into the present[32]) not only holds up a mirror to the reality of the status quo but also creates a christological surplus that cannot be captured by this reality and thus points beyond it.[33]

It is no accident that these are precisely the two things about which our contemporary form of empire is most apprehensive. First, the empire needs us to believe that "there is no alternative" (Thatcher) and therefore no ambivalence. A large number of people, especially those at the center, share this view; everything depends on whether the empire can continue to make people at the margins share it too. But while the belief that no alternative to empire exists translates into security for those who benefit from empire, this belief translates into insecurity for those who do not benefit, and herein lies the apprehension. What if this discrepancy is recognized? Second, the empire does not like the kinds of mirrors that reflect the realities of repression. The only mirrors that are readily available in empire are the two-way mirrors of its panopticons (those in power can see out, those without power cannot see in) and the gold-anodized exteriors of its skyscrapers, both of which deflect the view from that which hurts and from that which inflicts pain. Indeed, there seems to be hardly any "outside" left in contemporary empire—a point that is often proudly proclaimed by postmodernists oblivious to the dangers of this situation. But what if the reality of repression will not go away and is recognized for what it is—not simply as an exception to the rule, as some unfortunate white spot on the map that can be assigned to the integrating tasks of charity and social work, but as the truth about the way in which the current empire operates?[34] The empire has good reason to be apprehensive about this too.

In the midst of the pressures of empire, Christology has the potential to make a difference. Not only can it help us analyze what is going on; Christ as the one who does not fit in also points us in new directions and gives us new hope. Nevertheless, analysis and redirection take place in the midst of ambivalence. Throughout its history, Christology has been employed both in support and in critique of empire, and often there is only a thin line between the two.[35] The fact of ambivalence itself is a witness to the limits of empire; postcolonial theorist Homi Bhabha notes how this ambivalence is disturbing to colonial discourse and how it "poses an immanent threat to both 'normalized' knowledge and disciplinary powers."[36] The challenge, thus, is a "*double* vision, which in disclosing the ambivalence of colonial discourse also disrupts its authority."[37] While ambivalence is thus a welcome companion in the resistance against empire, in this project I seek to pursue more direct paths of resistance as well.

Structure of the Book

The following chapters engage the historical challenges with a focus on what difference the specific forms of Christ's resistance to empire have made in various contexts of empire. The purpose of the argument is constructive, focusing on the difference that Christ is making today. Where do these ancient concepts continue to provide inspiration and a christological surplus that cannot be assimilated by empire? A good deal of work needs to be done before the constructive perspective emerges in the final part of each chapter; some readers might want to begin there. But we can only come to those constructive conclusions if the embeddedness of theology in the status quo and its entanglements with empire are clearly grasped.[38]

The argument is not merely a functionalist one. There is no simplistic assumption that whatever works against empire is good in and of itself. The deeper question has to do with finding our way into the reality/the real of Christ, and dealing with the resistance factor is part of the process of moving into this direction. Can we see Christ at work in places where the dominant logic of empire would never expect to find him—in the midst of its struggles for dominance?

With this question we seek to move beyond the impasse the nineteenth-century critics of religion already sensed so well, namely, that religion is generally a human projection.[39] What these nineteenth-century critics did not realize, however, is that the religion they critiqued was empire religion, based on the projections of people at the top of empire. Thus, the nature of this particular religious projection has to do with the logic of top-down power and domination, which tend to operate in a mode of projection and assimilation of any and all subject matters. Empire, as we have seen, is not just a matter of economic and political domination; religious and other dominations are part of it. John Wesley had an inkling of this problem in his own way long before Ludwig Feuerbach when he wrote that "religion must not go from the greatest to the least, or the power would appear to be of men."[40] In other words, the success of religion that moves from the top down can easily be explained. But what would happen if religion goes the other way around—what if Christ is found in the midst of a different dynamic?

How do we keep ourselves in tune with this "extraordinary power" that we have in "clay jars" and that "does not come from us" (2 Cor. 4:7)? What is it in the reality of Jesus Christ's peculiar refusal to acquiesce to empire that continues to inspire us in the broadest sense of the word? Perhaps the greatest surprise of this study is that the seedlings of resistance and alternative living grow in the very soil of empire.[41]

Each of the following chapters represents an important turning point in the history of Christology, set in the context of key developments in the history of empire. Geographically, this means that we will move from the centers of the Roman Empire to medieval Europe, to modern Europe beginning with its moves into the Americas and beyond, and finally to the contemporary United States of America. The current developments are perhaps the most difficult to evaluate, but the other chapters provide the necessary background and help to put things in perspective. Recently, several helpful projects have addressed the current strategies and dynamics of the "American empire" under the administration of George W. Bush.[42] In this book, we will have to address some of these developments, but we will do so in a broader framework that deals with what I will call the postcolonial empire as it has been taking shape even before Bush came to power. In the United States, Empire will continue to develop in the next administration unless dramatic changes are introduced that go far beyond what current party politics are able to accomplish.

Chapters

Chapter 1 addresses the notion that "Jesus is Lord," one of the earliest christological confessions. In the context of the Roman Empire this title is ambivalent. The title *lord*, applied to the Roman emperors, was inextricably part of the empire itself.

At the same time, the title *lord*, applied to someone other than Caesar, could constitute resistance to empire. In the Roman Empire, the claim to lordship was the prerogative of the emperor. The fact that the early Christians took up this term and used it for Christ introduced a certain ambivalence that would produce uneasiness in the empire. In some cases, this ambivalence would amount to a full-fledged challenge, for the early Christian confession that Jesus is Lord could be taken as a challenge of the emperor's claim to be lord. Seen this way, Jesus Christ's life, death, and resurrection represents a logic that diametrically opposes and redefines the empire's notion of lordship. "Christ the Lord" does not fit easily within the categories of empire. It took a long process of assimilation to come to a point where the title *lord* could be used for Christ and the emperor in the same breath and without ambiguity, and where invoking the power of Christ would no longer be in tension with invoking the power of empire.

The ancient ecumenical councils of Nicaea and of Chalcedon, the subject of chapter 2, mark important turning points in early Christian thinking about Christ. The Council of Nicaea in 325 CE affirms the coequality of God and Jesus, that is, the first and second persons of the Trinity. The Council of Chalcedon in 451 CE once again affirms Jesus' coequality with God in terms of his divinity, but it adds the notion of Jesus' coequality with us in terms of his humanity. This notion of coequality, *homoousia* in Greek, is among the most famous terms in the history of Christian doctrine and is at the heart of the development of early Christian theology. Nevertheless, these notions of coequality are ambivalent in the context of the later Roman Empire out of which they developed. "Coequality" can provide resistance to empire; yet it also might need to be resisted and reframed in the struggle against empire. It must be remembered that the notion of coequality was first introduced by the Emperor Constantine. Does Constantine's influence on the Council of Nicaea, promoting Christ's coequality with God, draw Christ into the support of empire? Could it be that Christ as coequal with God is somehow identified with the emperor? Is the Christ who is coequal with God somehow removed from the messiness of life that is experienced more severely by the common people? Constantine notwithstanding, even the official Christology of the Roman Empire cannot be controlled completely by the interests of empire; ambivalence remains.

Chapter 3 deals with Anselm of Canterbury's investigation of the God-human (*deus homo*) or God-become-human, which has become a classic. This model for thinking about Christ is among the most influential of all time. Nevertheless, already in its own medieval setting Anselm's thought proves ambivalent. His conception of God-become-human has often been seen as repressive and might need to be resisted and reframed in the struggle against empire. At the same time, as we will see, it can also can provide resistance to empire. Anselm's claim that only a God-human can restore the violated honor of God and thus effect salvation is developed in the context of medieval empire formation—the Norman conquest of England, the first Crusade, the expansion of the lands of "Latin Europe," and the extension of the power of the pope. It is commonly overlooked that all of these factors leave their mark on Anselm's approach, as they leave their mark on other intellectual developments. Yet despite the entanglements with empire, the empire and its structures cannot contain the God-human. There is a christological surplus in Anselm's approach that can be located if we analyze the context of empire historically and theologically.

In the midst of the Spanish conquest of the Americas, the context of chapter 4, Bartolomé de Las Casas's reference to the "way of Christ" as "the only way" for the New World has often been seen as an expression of christological resistance to empire. Emphasizing compassion and peace, Christ's way resists the way of fire and sword, promoted by the Spanish conquistadors. Yet even Las Casas's way of Christ harbors ambivalence and needs to be examined in terms of its potential support of empire. While Las Casas did more to resist the worst manifestations of empire than most theologians, his christological approach nevertheless displays certain affinities with the presuppositions of empire. These affinities are, for the most part, not at a conscious level. There is no doubt that Las Casas resisted the atrocities of the conquest and saw his role as protector of the Amerindians. Nevertheless, there is an undercurrent that flows in a different direction and needs to be noted—not for the sake of diminishing Las Casas's achievements but for the sake of uncovering the reach of empire, which does not stop even at our best intentions to overcome it. Realizing this reach can strengthen our resistance and help us to identify those christological aspects of Las Casas's approach that cannot be controlled by the powers that be.

In chapter 5 I deal with modern theology, which has rarely been aware of its colonial underpinnings. Reformed theology has drawn together the christological titles of prophet, priest, and king, and Friedrich Schleiermacher, father of modern theology, follows that tradition. Nevertheless, in the colonial worlds of the nineteenth century, those titles prove to be ambivalent. The titles of prophet, priest, and king can provide resistance to empire in some cases; yet they might also need to be resisted and reframed in the struggle against empire in others. Schleiermacher's work serves as an example for Christology interacting with colonial attitudes; at one point he uses the three offices of Christ to endorse the progress of the so-called "Christian nations." Nevertheless, Schleiermacher's Christ does not stand for raw power. He redefines the power of Christ in terms of "attraction" rather than "coercion." What is the relation of this definition of power to the softer and more enlightened forms of northern European colonialism, which no longer proceed by fire and sword, as did the Spanish and Portuguese conquests?

Chapter 6 investigates the victorious Christ, made famous by Swedish theologian Gustaf Aulén. This notion, too, is ambivalent if one considers the global constellations of power at the beginning of the twentieth century. The assertion of Christ's victory over sin, death, and the devil pursues themes that appear to have to do with liberation. Nevertheless, even those themes can be used in support of neocolonial structures. Consideration of the following questions will help locate the resistance factor of Aulén's approach: What are the causes of sin and death? Who are the forces of darkness that Aulén describes as the devil? If the forces of evil are not specified, *Christus Victor* can be used for neocolonial efforts—for instance, by blaming the victims of colonialism. The historical context of Aulén's Christology is closer to our own than that of the previous chapters. What might be its contributions to Christian resistance of empire today? Without considering our close historical neighbors in the twentieth century, constructive theology and Christology in the twenty-first century cannot develop the alternative perspectives and visions needed today.

At the end of the twentieth century and at the beginning of the twenty-first, the horizon of Christology has been broadened by the notion of the cosmic Christ, the topic of chapter 7. In the broadening search for the "ever-greater Christ," this is about as far as we can get, but it also returns to some early Christian origins: the cosmic Christ is both an ancient and a contemporary theme. Nevertheless, even the cosmic Christ proves to be ambivalent. Talk about the cosmic Christ can provide resistance to empire; it might, however, also need to be resisted and reframed in the struggle against empire. Statements about the cosmic Christ, when connected, for instance, to the theme of evolution in a framework of social Darwinism, can be used to affirm ideas like the survival of the fittest. Nevertheless, even when the cosmic Christ represents a different spirit—that of mutuality and interdependence—empire can still be sustained:

emphasizing values like mutuality, interdependence, relationship, and equality in situations of great asymmetry of power can obscure the reality of empire and thus provide a welcome cover-up. On the other hand, the image of the cosmic Christ might resist postmodern and postcolonial forms of empire where it gives voice to precisely those elements of the cosmos that are most overlooked and that suffer most under the pressures and exploitation of empire. If the cosmic Christ relates to the environment under attack and to people who are forced to labor under inhuman conditions, Christology begins to break out of the status quo.

The reader will notice that there is no separate chapter on contemporary conservative theology. On the whole, the connections between empire and conservative theologies are more obvious than the connections between empire and certain strands of nonconservative theology; there is still little theological critique of empire in conservative positions and in many cases there has been active encouragement.[43] In this book, I have chosen the more difficult path by trying to identify the more covert connections between empire and a kind of theology that tends to presuppose its independence from empire. Nevertheless, some indications of possible problems with conservative positions can be found throughout the previous chapters, due to the fact that conservative theologies often seek to draw on the images developed by Paul, the creeds, and Anselm. By the same token, an indication of the potential theological surplus of these positions can be found in those chapters as well.

Conclusion: The Truth Shall Make You Free (John 8:32)

Empire presents its own claims to truth even if, as in contemporary forms of empire, mostly in hidden fashion. This claim to truth is related to one of the key features of empire: its efforts to control all aspects of life. While there are few strong claims to truth in our current cultural climate, so determined by postmodern sensitivities, there are commonly accepted truths that support empire and that are never open for discussion or question. In this context, search for a different truth needs to move through the netherworld of truth as that which is being repressed by empire and pushed below the surface.[44] This move is reminiscent of Jesus Christ's truth found and pronounced in solidarity with those confined to the netherworlds of the empire. This solidarity is manifest throughout Jesus Christ's earthly ministry but it is symbolized in its most extreme form by his descent into hell, confessed in the traditional versions of the Apostles' Creed. Resistance arises in unexpected reversals of Jesus Christ's perennial repression by empire through the resisting Lord, resisting coequality, the resisting God-human, the resisting way of Christ, the resisting prophet, priest, and king, the resisting *Christus Victor*, and the resisting cosmic Christ.

Notes

1. Chalmers Johnson, *Blowback: The Costs and Consequences of American Empire* (New York: Metropolitan, 2000), 8. "What U.S. officials denounce as unprovoked terrorist attacks on its innocent citizens are often meant as retaliation for previous American imperial acts." The C.I.A coined the term *blowback*. Note that this book was written before September 11, 2001.

2. Anthony Pagden, *Peoples and Empires: A Short History of European Migration, Exploration, and Conquest from Greece to the Present* (New York: Modern Library, 2001), 70.

3. Andrew J. Bacevich concludes that "although the United States has not created an empire in any formal sense"—we simply do not need colonies in the conventional sense—"it has most definitely acquired an imperial problem." *American Empire: The Realities and Consequences of U.S. Diplomacy* (Cambridge, Mass.: Harvard University Press, 2002), 243. In other words, the United States is "a nation engaged in the governance of empire" (ibid., 244) and the question is what we make of this reality.

4. Support for notions of empire is provided, for instance, by well-funded think tanks such as the "Project for the New American Century" and the "American Enterprise Institute."

5. The "Group of Eight" (G8) consists of Canada, France, Germany, Italy, Japan, Russia, the United Kingdom, and the United States. According to the United Nations, together these countries represent about 65 percent of the world economy.

6. Note, however, that not all refusals to comply with international treatises lead to sanctions; for instance, the U.S. refusal to sign the Kyoto Protocols had no such consequences.

7. Economic sanctions tend to be felt most strongly by the weakest members of society; exploitation of labor power is felt by the workers; expropriation of land leads to the displacement of peasant populations; and the lure of consumer culture puts exponential pressure on the lives of the poorest members of society.

8. Robert Bellah uses a moral argument to justify empire: "In human history empires are a fact of life; they have not been all wrong." "The New American Empire," in *Anxious About Empire: Theological Essays on the New Global Realities*, ed. Wes Avram (Grand Rapids, Mich.: Brazos, 2004), 22. The problem with this comes when, with reference to Lawrence Keeley, he praises both the Roman and the British Empires for promoting peace and tranquility in the world. Such moral categories miss the point when it comes to an evaluation of empire as a whole.

9. Ward Churchill discusses the situation of Native Americans in terms of "internal colonialism." *Struggle for the Land: Native North American Resistance to Genocide, Ecocide and Colonization* (San Francisco: City Lights, 2002), 25.

10. For the changing notion of empire and an attempt to define empire for our age, see Michael Hardt and Antonio Negri, *Empire* (Cambridge, Mass.: Harvard University Press, 2000).

11. Ibid., 23.

12. See Francis Fukuyama, *The End of History and the Last Man* (New York: Free Press, 1992).

13. The focus of this book is on empires related to Christianity. Other empires have existed, and among the most significant ones of the Common Era are the Arab and the Chinese Empires.

14. In this sense it remains to be seen whether the recent displays of military might by the United States might harm the purposes of empire in the long run. In any case, the discussion of empire must not be reduced to military interventions and other highly visible displays of power.

15. This fact is often overlooked. See, for example, one of the most prominent accounts of Christian missions, David J. Bosch's *Transforming Mission: Paradigm Shifts in Theology of Mission* (Maryknoll, N.Y.: Orbis, 1991). While Bosch helpfully clarifies the problems of historical colonial theology, as any theology of mission should, he seems to assume that in "postmodern" times theology and the church are finally free to do their own thing. Bosch gives little indication that we would still have to worry about the problems of colonialism and empire.

16. Hardt and Negri go so far as to argue that "Christian religion is what destroyed the Roman Empire." *Empire*, 373.

17. Due to this abortive history of many interdisciplinary efforts in modern theology, I prefer the term *transdisciplinary*.

18. The term *nonmodern readers* refers not only to readers prior to modernity but also to those who cannot be defined exclusively by the values of Western modernity, be it people in other parts of the world or people on the margins at home. It also applies to a certain degree to broader "postmodern" cultural sentiments.

19. Talal Asad offers a trenchant critique of the "modest view of religion" of modern religious studies, focused mainly on individual belief. *Genealogies of Religion: Discipline and Reasons of Power in Christianity and Islam* (Baltimore: Johns Hopkins University Press, 1993), 45ff. For examples of the modern definition of other religions and an argument to broaden the definition in relation to its involvement in matters of

empire, see Richard A. Horsley, "Religion and Other Products of Empire," *Journal of the American Academy of Religion (JAAR)* 71 (March 2003): 1.

20. See my description of nineteenth-century liberal theology and the phenomenon of *Kulturprotestantismus* in Joerg Rieger, *God and the Excluded: Visions and Blindspots in Contemporary Theology* (Minneapolis: Fortress Press, 2001), chap. 1.

21. The notion of context as that which hurts is developed in my essay "Developing a Common Interest Theology from the Underside," in *Liberating the Future: God, Mammon, and Theology*, ed. Joerg Rieger (Minneapolis: Fortress Press, 1998). Here is one of the fundamental points of distinction between liberal and liberation theologies. What lies below the surface, in this sense, are not metaphysical "foundations," but that which has been repressed and which continues to shape us in powerful ways.

22. This is a danger, for instance, in Paul Tillich's famous "method of correlation."

23. This insight is developed in its own way in biblical studies. Richard Horsley talks about a critical historical approach in contradistinction to the modern historical-critical method: "Analysis of contexts (both of text and interpreter) is therefore as important as analysis of texts." *Paul and Politics: Ekklesia, Israel, Imperium, Interpretation* (Harrisburg, Pa.: Trinity Press International, 2000), 14. The emerging differences and conflicts among readings, due to different locations and perspectives, are "to be valued rather than avoided" (ibid., 15).

24. This definition is informed by a reading of the work of Jacques Lacan; see Joerg Rieger, *Remember the Poor: The Challenge to Theology in the Twenty-First Century* (Harrisburg, Pa.: Trinity Press International, 1998), 168. For the Jameson quotation, see Fredric Jameson, *The Political Unconscious: Narrative as a Socially Symbolic Act* (Ithaca, N.Y.: Cornell University Press, 1981), 102.

25. Not only does Paul talk about him as "stumbling block to Jews and foolishness to Gentiles" (1 Cor. 1:23), the Gospels are full of reports of people being taken aback by Jesus.

26. Jesus certainly does not get caught up in family systems (Mark 3:31-35); he also criticizes the Temple and its normal mode of operating (Mark 11:15-19; 13:1-2). This refusal to fit in is what Karl Barth found so refreshing about the "strange new world of the Bible." See Rieger, *God and the Excluded*, chap. 2.

27. This seems to be one of the primary battles that shines through in the Gospel of John. When John's Jesus confronts "the Jews," he appears to be confronting the religious establishment.

28. Mark 3:6 reports that a strange alliance of people, who in their own ways each benefit from empire (the Pharisees and the Herodians), conspires to get rid of Jesus early on in his ministry. Ultimately, of course, Jesus is nailed to the cross by Roman soldiers

, under the command of Pontius Pilate. Later empires found a similar need to get rid of Jesus' challenges.

29. For the notion of "surplus enjoyment" see Jacques Lacan, "Seminar 20, Encore" (1972–73), in *Feminine Sexuality: Jacques Lacan and the école freudienne*, ed. Juliet Mitchell and Jacqueline Rose (New York: W.W. Norton, 1982), 143–44.

30. Walter Benjamin, "Theses on the Philosophy of History," in *Illuminations*, ed. and with an introduction by Hannah Arendt, trans. Harry Zohn (New York: Schocken, 1969), 260.

31. For the distinction between "reality" and the "real," borrowed from a reflection on the work of Jacques Lacan, see my book *Remember the Poor*, 75–77. The term *reality* stands for the dominant point of view; the "real" is the repressed view.

32. This is one way to read the confession of some Good Friday hymns that our own sinfulness is what brought Jesus to the cross.

33. In this sense, the search is not for the "reality" of Christ but for Christ's "real."

34. As Benjamin has pointed out: "The tradition of the oppressed teaches us that the 'state of emergency' in which we live is not the exception but the rule." "Theses on the Philosophy of History," 257.

35. This ambivalence is with us in all that we do. In a recent interview for ordination, several members of a United Methodist Church Board of Ordained Ministry chastised a candidate for confessing to the need to challenge the members of her congregation every now and then. My response to the candidate made use of the ambivalent nature of Christology by encouraging her to "think about being more like Jesus." The candidate started off as expected, saying that perhaps she really should try to be less challenging and more loving and caring. But in the middle of her response she paused. "Wait a minute," she exclaimed, "Jesus also posed challenges." She was passed, but the institution kept a close eye on her and got rid of her later.

36. For the notion of ambivalence, see Homi Bhabha, *The Location of Culture* (London: Routledge, 1994), 86. Bhabha connects this term with his more famous notion of "mimicry": "the discourse of mimicry is constructed around an *ambivalence*" (emphasis in original). By repeating colonial images with a slight difference, rather than representing them accurately, mimicry establishes a challenge to the colonial narcissism and fiction of self-identity (ibid., 88).

37. Ibid., 88. While Bhabha understands this ambivalence of mimicry as a surface effect and does not want to see this as too closely related with the Freudian notion of the "return of the repressed," I do not think that these matters are mutually exclusive. For an effort to read Bhabha's work in relation to the notion of repression see my

essay "Liberating God-Talk: Postcolonialism and the Challenge of the Margins," in *Postcolonial Theology: Divinity and Empire*, ed. Catherine Keller, Michael Nausner, and Mayra Rivera (St. Louis, Mo.: Chalice, 2004). Bhabha's reference to metonymy as "non-repressive productions of contradictory and multiple belief" (ibid., 90) might well be related to the notion of metaphor as the location of repression (for the relation of the notions of metonymy and metaphor see Rieger, *Remember the Poor*, 37-38; 78). Bhabha's suggestion that ambivalence and mimicry amount to a "strategic confusion of the metaphoric and metonymic axes" (ibid.) might help us bring together both non-repressive mechanisms and the phenomenon of repression.

38. Perhaps this is the truth of the Latin adage of unknown origin *per aspera ad astra*, "through rough ways to the stars," and the related "through darkness to light."

39. See, for instance, Ludwig Feuerbach, *The Essence of Christianity* (New York: Harper Torchbooks, 1957).

40. John Wesley, journal entry of May 21, 1764, in *The Works of the Rev. John Wesley*, ed. Thomas Jackson, 3rd ed., vol. 3 (London: Wesleyan Methodist Book Room, 1872; reprinted Peabody, Mass.: Hendrickson, 1986), 178.

41. This is also one of the key hopes developed in the recent works of Michael Hardt and Antonio Negri, *Empire*; and *Multitude: War and Democracy in the Age of Empire* (New York: Penguin, 2004).

42. David Ray Griffin, John B. Cobb Jr., Richard A. Falk, Catherine Keller, *The American Empire and the Commonwealth of God: A Political, Economic, Religious Statement* (Louisville: Westminster John Knox, 2006); Mark Lewis Taylor, *Religion, Politics, and the Christian Right: Post-9/11 Powers and American Empire* (Minneapolis: Fortress Press, 2005).

43. It should be noted, of course, that certain theological orientations that are generally considered to be conservative have produced diverse responses to empire. Most notably, some evangelical theologians have produced critiques of the powers that be, such as Jim Wallis, *God's Politics: Why the Right Gets It Wrong and the Left Doesn't Get It* (San Francisco: HarperSanFrancisco, 2005); and Brian McLaren, *The Secret Message of Jesus: Uncovering the Truth That Could Change Everything* (Nashville: W Publishing Group, 2006). Yet while these approaches are self-consciously evangelical, they can hardly be classified as conservative in the contemporary climate of the United States.

44. These different kinds of truth relate back to the distinction between "reality" and the "real."

1

Resisting and Reframing Lord

———⟶⊰●⊱⟵———

Christology and the Roman Empire

"JESUS IS LORD" is one of the earliest christological confessions. In the context of the Roman Empire this title is ambivalent. The Roman emperors claimed the title *lord* and thus made it part of the empire. At the same time, Christians took up this term and used it for Christ in a way that would at times produce uneasiness in the empire. In some cases, this ambivalence about the matter of lordship would amount to a full-fledged challenge, for the early Christian confession that Jesus is Lord could be taken as a denial of the emperor's claim to be lord. Seen this way, Jesus Christ's life, death, and resurrection represent a logic that diametrically opposes empire and redefines the notion of lordship.

This chapter explores the christological confession that Jesus is Lord, contained in the earliest writings of the New Testament: the letters of the Apostle Paul. Written as early as two decades after Jesus' death, Paul's letters make use of Christian traditions that were already in existence at that time. These letters, as is well known, predate all of the Gospels. While Paul's letters have often been read in support of the status quo, a challenge to empire seems to be reflected, for instance, in his comments about the foolishness of the cross (1 Cor. 1:22-25). If it is true that "God chose what is low and despised in the world, things that are not, to reduce to nothing things that are, so that no one might boast in the presence of God" (1 Cor. 1:28-29), the empire is in trouble.

And yet, in the long history of effects, the challenges that Paul poses to empire have often been ignored if not repressed.[1] Even in modern interpretations of Paul there is little awareness of Paul's broader challenges. Paul is often seen as the creator of a universal and spiritual religion, sometimes couched in opposition to the parochial spirit of Judaism.[2] This Paul is considered a religionist with little interest in nonreligious matters; even his ethics are limited to religion. This misapprehension of Paul is consistent with the most critical problem in regard to the lordship of Christ: the almost complete absence of discussion of the difference between the nature of Christ's lordship and the nature of the emperor's lordship. Only in more recent research have the conflicts between Paul's theology and the Roman Empire been identified.[3]

Although the main focus of this book is theological, historical research plays an important role in the following chapter, as it will throughout the book. As Richard Horsley has poignantly stated, "trying to understand Jesus' speech and action without knowing how Roman imperialism determined the conditions of life in Galilee and Jerusalem would be like trying to understand Martin Luther King without knowing how slavery, reconstruction, and segregation determined the lives of African Americans in the United States."[4] The fundamental concern of this chapter, however, is not the search for the "historical Jesus" or the "historical Paul,"[5] but an investigation of how the earliest references to Jesus were developed in the context of empire, in ways that interfered with empire and ultimately subverted or at least resisted it. History shapes theology and vice versa, and for this reason we will deal with it critically and self-critically (see the introduction, above).[6] Such critical and self-critical reflection should help us to draw out some lessons for the present as well.

A caveat: theologians often shy away from such questions, not because they would be of no interest to theology but because we are afraid of encroaching on the territory of so many other specialists—scholars of the New Testament in particular, but also historians. Although a broad spectrum of scholars has begun to focus on the question of the relation of Paul's theology and empire,[7] the study of New Testament and empire is very recent; the goal of this chapter cannot be to resolve the scholarly debates but to learn from them in order to develop a genuinely theological framework for considering empire.

The Early Church and the Theology of Empire

Jesus was born, lived, and died under the rule of the Roman Empire and its vassals in Palestine. In the years preceding Jesus' birth, Rome had moved from being a republic to being an empire. The emperor at the time of Jesus' birth was Augustus, only the second Roman emperor after Gaius Julius Caesar; both were considered either divine or "sons of God." Augustus's rule was widely regarded as the "Golden Age." From Jesus' birth until the death of Paul in the latter part of the first century the Roman Empire was at a peak of its power.

As Christianity moved beyond Palestine and westward, across the Roman Empire and toward Rome itself, encounters with empire intensified. While the Roman Empire's presence was well established in Palestine—Jesus' crucifixion displayed the authority of the empire—it was even more strongly felt in the cities of the eastern Roman Empire into which Christianity moved. In this context, empire was present at all levels of life—including the political, the economic, the cultural, and the religious, framing the development of early Christianity. As Catherine Keller has pointed out, "There is no pre-colonial Christianity."[8] From this observation follows the question to be pursued in this chapter and in the rest of the book: How is Christianity different from empire? Or, as Keller puts the question, "Is there a postcolonial Christianity?" She continues that "the postcolonial contribution properly comes from the peripheries, diasporas, and boundary zones of empire,"[9] and this is where we will have to look for the answer.

In Jesus' and Paul's times, the presence of empire was clearly visible to all. The image of the emperor could be seen on the coins (even Jesus, far away from Rome, knew this image [Mark 12:13-17]). Other visible representations of empire included statues, the architecture of public buildings, and the construction of new temples that celebrated the emperor and the goddess Roma, the official deity of the empire. These visible images were joined by other expressions of empire in rhetoric, literary production, and song, which further helped to envelop people in the spirit of empire.[10] Lavish festivals were yet another manifestation of empire, attracting large portions of the population and pulling the inhabitants of the empire together.

The presence of empire could also be felt in the communal and political structures of the cities. Not only did the local rulers adapt their personal style to the demands of the empire (instituted by Rome, their task was to please Rome), but the empire gave new shape and emphasis to the institutions of the people, such as the *ekklesiae*, the assemblies of male citizens of a Greek city-state. In this context, the Christian practice of admitting women to the Christian *ekklesia* introduced a certain ambivalence, if not an altogether different spirit. No wonder the empire sought to reduce the level of popular participation in government issues by groups who were not directly related to the rulers, such as the early Christian communities.[11]

It is easily overlooked today that in none of these manifestations of empire could the political, the economic, the cultural, and the religious be separated; separating the realms of politics, economics, culture, and religion is a modern idea, which would have been foreign to inhabitants of the ancient world. A sense of this integration is only now returning to our understanding in the context of cultural studies.[12]

Of particular importance in this world that was so suffused by the reality of empire is what has become known as the emperor cult; the titles used for Christ must be understood on this backdrop. The Emperor Octavian (later called Augustus) proclaimed the divinization of Caesar on January 1, 42 BCE, and, as his successor, was thus able to call himself *Divi filius*, translated into Greek as *hyos theou*, "son of God."[13] At the same time, these early emperors still acknowledged some limits. Augustus seems to have been careful not to present himself directly as God[14] and his successor, Tiberius, was even more reluctant to present himself as divine—although this made no difference to the fact that people honored him like a god. It was only the next emperor, Caligula, who was more emphatic about his divinity, as was Nero, who was emperor when Paul wrote his letter to the Romans.[15] In general, it was the eastern parts of the Roman Empire, where early Christianity outside of Palestine first developed, that were more saturated with the emperor cult,[16] posing a challenge for the churches' emerging understanding of Christ.

As we are becoming more aware of the all-encompassing nature of the Roman Empire and its ability to integrate all aspects of life, the emperor cult needs to be taken more seriously. Rather than being just a thinly veiled instrument of political propaganda, as has often been assumed,[17] the emperor cult touched a nerve and expressed deeply held sensitivities of the people. Starting with Augustus, emperors were revered as divine and gave orders to build temples and altars for themselves, often together with the goddess Roma. When Augustus died in 14 CE, the Roman Senate even decreed his ascension into heaven. Emperor worship ultimately took on a life of its own, independent of the self-presentation of individual emperors.[18] In this context, the proliferation of imagery and lavish festivals played an important role.[19]

The emperor was not only the object of the cult but also its subject—people saw him as a savior[20] who had healing powers and who brought "peace and security" (this was the formula introduced after Augustus's victory at Actium at the beginning of his career) and "good news" (literally: "the gospel"—*euanggelion*) to the world. Priests of the emperor cult came from the elite, the wealthiest and most influential families. The role of these priests provides a telling example for how the emperor cult cannot easily be grasped by modern categories of "religion"; they were among the most influential political figures.[21] The overall importance of the emperor cult and the fact that it transcends narrow categories of religion can also be seen in spatial terms: imperial temples and sanctuaries occupied the most prestigious locations of a city.[22]

We can now see more clearly that in this world the realms of politics, economics, culture, and religion, which are routinely separated in modern scholarship, all flow into each other. It is not possible to separate religion and politics or religion and economics, and sometimes even the modern analytical habit of making distinctions seems impossible. If the ethos of the Roman Empire thus includes all of life—this is one of the basic marks of empire throughout history—the emperor cult cannot simply be regarded as a secondary "superstructure." This cult was not just the legitimization of the emperor and his empire; it played an active role in the construction of empire. It was an integral part of the network of power and created a space for the influence "of local elites over the populace, of cities over other cities, and of Greek over indigenous cultures."[23] In the words of John Dominic Crossan and Jonathan Reed, it was the "glue" that held the "civilized world together"[24]; and even if it was not the only unifying element, it was a crucial one. If this is recognized, the ways in which Christian communities adapted or resisted this cult—and their thinking about Christ is a major indication of the degrees of adaptation or resistance—gains in importance and appears in a new light.

Nevertheless, the emperor cult was not received in the same way by all social classes and ethnic groups, nor was it an entirely uniform phenomenon since the Roman Empire did not directly regulate all its manifestations and there were no official doctrines.[25] The emperor cult was considered mutually beneficial for rulers and ruled, and thus no direct coercion to enforce participation in the cult seemed necessary. Those who had most to gain from pursuing and maintaining the emperor cult were, of course, the groups in power. They were eligible for the prominent and powerful positions of priest of the emperor in the important cities. But common people were also attracted to the emperor cult; the festivals in honor of the emperor were high points in the life of the community, and the people participated in large numbers. The cult even provided a certain opportunity for upward social mobility in an otherwise highly structured society.[26]

Even though Augustus and other emperors did not make personal claims to divinity, the connection between the emperor and the gods is at the heart of this cult. As P. A. Brunt has pointed out, "what was most novel in the Roman attitude to their empire was the belief that it was universal and willed by the gods."[27] This tradition was foreshadowed by an older belief that the empire was based in the laws of nature. In the words of Cicero: "Do we not observe that dominion has been granted by Nature to everything that is best, to the great advantage of what is weak?"[28] Grounding empire first in nature and then in the divine had significant political consequences: since the divine is present in the world and concentrated in the person of the emperor, he does not need the affirmation by the people.[29] This is reflected in the transition from the Roman Republic to the Roman Empire, from an earlier appreciation for democratic principles to an ever-stronger emphasis on the authority and power of the emperor. Nevertheless, although popular affirmation was required less and less, the empire was still seen as beneficial for its subjects. The belief in the beneficial nature of the empire is expressed, for instance, by Plutarch (45–120 CE), who argues that "an essential difference between [the Roman Empire] and other ancient empires is that the Romans govern free men, not slaves."[30] The Romans came to believe that the gods favored them because of their piety and justice and that an empire based on those values could only be a good thing.

This is the fabric of the society in which early Christianity developed its own reflections on Christ. Empire was everywhere, a part of life so essential and normal that it was frequently taken for granted. What is particularly interesting is not that Christians were influenced by the logic of empire—after all, the empire was like the air they breathed; what is remarkable is that some of them were able to recognize the ambivalence of empire and to develop resistance. Without achieving complete independence from empire—an illusionary goal then as now—some of the earliest theologies and Christologies managed to refuse conforming to the expectations of the empire. Does the theology of the Apostle Paul, despite the fact that he has often been considered a social conservative,[31] belong to this group?

Nevertheless, even if they initially developed as a critique, these earliest theologies and Christologies have also been used in the support of empire. References to Christ, who refused to go along with empire, were subsequently grafted onto other theologies that promised to be more supportive of the status quo. Paul's radical statements about unity and equality in Christ, for instance, as found in Galatians 3:28 and elsewhere, were later "balanced" by Deutero-Pauline comments on the necessary submission of women to men. In the history of interpretation up to the present, Paul's statements about freedom and equality were often read through the lens of other statements, also attributed to Paul, that promoted hierarchy or at least "complementarity." Complementarity in this context is a more insidious concept because, like the idea of hierarchy, it naturalizes differences but, unlike hierarchy, it tends to hide power differentials.

If women and men are seen in hierarchical relationships, the power differential is clear; if women and men are seen in complementary relationships, however, each appears to fulfill an important role as part of a larger whole and even the most subservient roles of women are justified. The question of power is thus covered up. A Paul domesticated along those lines could often be employed directly in the justification of empire.

Even where Paul was not domesticated in those more obvious ways, however, a widespread reading of Paul as merely interested in "religious" matters has led to the support of empire as well. This type of support of empire is hidden for the most part and thus even more difficult to identify: after all, if Paul is seen as having little interest in political statements, why should he be in support of empire? Yet empire in Paul's times, not unlike in our own, was all-encompassing and omnipresent. The empire thus represents the political, economic, cultural, and religious default position, and could not be avoided even if Paul were only interested in "religious" matters. Not putting up resistance, therefore, amounts to an implicit endorsement of empire.

With the same logic it can be argued that to question the ethos of such an all-encompassing empire at any one point might well amount to resistance of the whole reality of empire. One must seriously wonder why Paul would have been persona non grata in the Roman Empire, spending much time in its prisons and enduring constant harassment and repression including torture (not a thing to take lightly in any context), if he did not pose a challenge to empire and if all he wanted was to address some of the more intricate points of intra-religious discourse.[32]

That the Roman Empire was held together not simply through military control or imperial bureaucracy is one of the most crucial insights when it comes to understanding Paul and his Christology. Military conquest was primarily a means of expanding the empire and of controlling unrest that threatened to get out of hand. While in Judea military force was a constant threat that often found expression in mass crucifixions, in Asia Minor, where Paul was at work, the governors employed only a small military staff and the cities usually governed themselves.[33]

The Roman Empire was thus held together by cultural, political, and socioeconomic mechanisms. The emperor cult and rhetoric, both cultural phenomena, went hand in hand with the system of patronage, a socioeconomic phenomenon. The power of the empire was most secure when it was backed up both by the emperor cult and by the patronage system.[34] The patronage system provided a socioeconomic hierarchy where the property owners, who enjoyed higher social status, dispensed power to be received by the lower classes. Some historians have argued that this bond of loyalty between the classes was another cohesive force that held the Roman Empire together. This system was even more powerful due to the fact that, unlike in the contemporary United States, rich and poor did not live in separate neighborhoods but in contiguous areas.[35]

As the older democratic and republican ideals that had a broader base in the population vanished, the propertied oligarchies gained more and more control.[36] In this situation, "politics" proper became the domain of the powerful and was no longer in the reach of most people. This might help explain why we find little interest in matters of direct political engagement in Paul; common people had to find other outlets for contributing to the common good.[37] We are beginning to understand better why Paul, as Horsley notes, "was hardly a rabble-rousing revolutionary, fomenting provincial rebellion against Roman rule."[38]

Another reason for a certain lacuna in the realm of politics at the time of Paul had to do with the prominence of the emperor cult. Horsley offers a caricature of the situation in which the cult gained prominence at the expense of traditional political structures: "mystifying pomp and ceremony make administration (and an administrative apparatus) unnecessary."[39] A better way to think about this phenomenon, however, might be that the emperor cult provided an alternative way of producing order and of ordering social relationships and thus an alternative to traditional politics. Without awareness of this context, Paul's writings might indeed be seen as nonpolitical. Paul is political in a different way, however, not by challenging the administration and official politics but by resisting three of the most powerful mechanisms of control of the Roman Empire: the emperor cult, the system of patronage (built on Latin notions like *pietas*, trusting a father figure; and *fides* [Greek: *pistis*, "faith"], loyalty between rulers and people[40]), and the prominent themes of the empire's rhetoric. One of these prominent themes is the assertion that peace and security are established by the emperor.[41]

Paul seems to have taken each of these topics very seriously. One of his disagreements with a faction in the church of Corinth was precisely that the worship of other gods and participation in sacrificial meals were dangerous. Rather than "harmless social gatherings,"[42] these worship events were at the very heart of what held the empire together. Furthermore, Paul refused to enter into patronage relationships with Corinthian elites; the system of patronage is problematic because it destroys the horizontal bonds of the common people—their solidarity with each other—and ties them to the powerful and the wealthy.[43] In all these cases, there is a close connection between cult and political power: the elites exercise their power by sponsoring the emperor cult. What is often classified as "religion" was therefore inextricably tied up with political power. In Horsley's words, "the fusion of the religious system of sacrifices and emperor cult with the social-economic system of patronage served to veil as it constituted the imperial network of domination and power relations."[44] No wonder that those who had a sense of what was going on perceived Paul's theology as politically dangerous; he seems to have lifted at least the edges of the veil of empire theology.

The main problem that would have made Paul so dangerous to the empire was not that he proclaimed alternative religious ideas. Other religious alternatives were available in the Roman Empire, and the emperor cult did not presuppose monotheism; while the emperors were counted among the gods, there was room for other gods. Thus, merely worshiping another god was not a problem. The Roman Empire was not unfamiliar with religious tolerance.[45] Greek and Roman thinkers even had a certain appreciation for Jewish monotheism and its emphasis on a transcendent God. Likewise, other non-Roman gods and goddesses, such as the Egyptian goddess Isis who did not challenge the theology of empire (a fact that did not make her "more religious" and "less political"), were easily integrated into the Roman pantheon and into popular piety.[46]

If seen through the lens of the modern category of religion, Paul's discourse does not stand out at first sight. To the contrary, some of his theological concepts are suspiciously close to those of the empire. But there are differences in his usage that make us suspect that there is no easy harmony of Christianity and empire. It is in the midst of the resulting ambivalence that we find the kind of theological surplus that points us beyond empire. Ambivalence and surplus arise from Paul's use of terms like *ekklesia* ("church," used for the gathering of citizens), *euanggelion* ("the gospel," used for the imperial good news), *savior* (an official title of the emperor since Augustus), *dikaiosynē* ("justice," attributed to Augustus), *eirēnē* ("peace," used to describe the peace established by Augustus), and especially the christological *kyrios* ("lord," used for the emperors after Augustus). Even a seemingly harmless "religious" notion like the idea of Jesus' ascension into heaven might pose political problems: If only select emperors ascended into heaven— only those the Roman Senate considered deserving—could the proclamation of the ascension of Jesus have been harmless? The religious terms that Paul chooses come as another surprise. Religious and cultic terms that were used in Hellenistic-Roman religions of the time are mostly absent, particularly the usual language for worship. According to Johan Christaan Beker, what remains of cultic-sacrificial language is "transformed metaphorically and applied to the daily life-style of the Christians."[47] As Wayne Meeks has noted, "these Christian groups would not have looked like a *religious* movement at all to their contemporaries, for one did not go to cultic places and occasions to hear this kind of moral advice."[48] The fact that they met in ordinary houses, not seeking to imitate religion and cult, might tell us something important about the self-understanding of those early Christians. Meeks's reference to "moral advice" given in these settings points in the right direction, as it takes us beyond the narrowly cultic and religious, but why should the matter be limited to morality? Why not think of even more comprehensive expressions of life that include politics and economics as well?

While the terminology of Paul's theology and the theology of the Roman Empire are quite similar, Paul tends to turn this terminology on its head. What sounds like purely religious terminology to modern ears could be heard as a subtle challenge of the Roman Empire. There must have been some tension, and Crossan and Reed bluntly state the extent of the potential challenge, "to proclaim Jesus as Son of God was deliberately denying Caesar his highest title and to announce Jesus as Lord and Savior was calculated treason."[49] Nevertheless, there remains a very fine line: Paul can also be read as conforming to the empire (although he explicitly resists conformity in Romans 12:2), particularly if he is read through the Deutero-Pauline literature and the often-quoted passage in 1 Peter 2:17: "Fear God. Honor the emperor." This happened frequently enough in the history of the church and the reasons are quite understandable.

First, Paul often had to use coded language so as not to endanger the congregations,[50] and thus, for the uninitiated, there seemed little difference between his theology and the theology of empire: perhaps Christ's lordship was modeled after the lordship of the emperor after all? It is telling that the difference between Christ's kind of lordship and the emperor's kind of lordship has not been discussed much by mainline theology in two thousand years. Even today, neither liberal nor conservative Christians seem to worry about this matter, as I will demonstrate in the next part.

Second, Paul's theology is often adapted to empire theology by default if the deeper problem with empire is not understood. The problem with the Roman Empire is not first of all a moral one—that it was somehow more evil than all other empires. The problem with the Roman Empire is that it follows a different logic than the faith in Christ. As Crossan has pointed out, Roman logic assumes that the normal order of the world lay in the sequence of "piety, war, victory, and peace." Paul, on the other hand, follows a different logic according to which the sequence is "covenant, nonviolence, justice, and peace."[51] Whatever the more detailed differences between the two forms of logic, if those differences go undetected, one of the major features of Paul's theology is lost. Empire theology is, therefore, not always immediately obvious as a theology that justifies the empire. In a situation where the empire determines what is "normal" and what logic to follow, failure to identify this normalcy and to resist it means to support the empire. In other words, any theology in a highly politicized situation that claims to be nonpolitical deceives itself. In this context, the supposed "universalism" of biblical studies, claiming universal applicability and failing to distinguish between the two diametrically opposed perspectives of Paul and the Roman Empire, has only made the problem worse.[52]

In sum, while it is commonly known that the theology of the early church and the writings of the Bible were produced in the midst of empire, the deeper theological connections are usually not drawn out, apart from ubiquitous critiques of the later church after Constantine. But in order to come to a clearer understanding of the lordship of Christ as envisioned by Paul we need to ask to what degree the categories of these early theologies are different from the categories of empire.

Resistance to empire of many of the texts in the Bible is mostly hidden; if there is ambivalence and a surplus that points beyond empire, it is not always clear on the surface. The Gospels, for instance, do not openly blame the Romans for the crucifixion of Jesus. To a certain degree, they even seem to defend the Romans and blame a less powerful group, the Jews. We need to keep in mind, of course, that the political situation is always changing and that the Roman Empire had become more threatening toward the end of the first century when the Gospels were written.[53] Paul, too, has at times been read in those terms and identified as a social conservative, promoting at best a "love patriarchalism."[54] This view is borne out particularly in the post-Pauline literature, that is, the Deutero-Pauline 1 and 2 Timothy, Titus, Ephesians, and even Colossians.[55]

There is no need to portray early Christianity and the New Testament in unambivalent terms. It is not necessary to claim that everyone was clearly opposed to empire or that Christians all came from one particular social class, even though this latter issue is still being hotly debated.[56] Our question is whether there is a surplus that points us beyond empire.

Lord of the Empire

The title *Lord* is one of the oldest titles of Christ in the New Testament and one of the central notions in Paul's Christology.[57] It can be found in all of the introductions of Paul's letters. But why is it the favorite title for so many Christians even today? One reason might have to do with a widespread emphasis on personal relationships with Christ and the related confession that declares that Jesus is Lord over one's personal life. But what does that mean and how does that use of the title relate to the strong political connotations of the title? One of the central questions for ordination candidates in the United Methodist tradition is: "What does it mean to say that Jesus Christ is Lord?" A typical answer in the Bible Belt is that Jesus "saves" me and "takes care" of me. Most answers tend to stay at the personal and what we might think of as the "religious" level; few note that Jesus' lordship might have wider implications. Fewer yet realize that Jesus' lordship might somehow be related to the lords who are in charge of the empires. Such domestications of Jesus' lordship are not uncommon in the church. But what is the problem?

Native American theologians have been most acutely aware of problems with the confession of Christ's lordship. Clara Sue Kidwell, Homer Noley, and George Tinker have argued that the statement "Jesus is Lord" is "the one scriptural metaphor used for the Christ event that is ultimately unacceptable and even hurtful to American Indian peoples."[58] Because Native American cultures had egalitarian characteristics, they point out, even a chief had limited authority. From this perspective, the term *lord* is closely tied to the history of colonization and the resulting hierarchies of power; these hierarchies are reflected even in ecclesial structures and in their "bishops and missionaries (both male and female) to whom Indians have learned as conquered peoples to pay lordly deference."[59] The contemporary lack of awareness of the relation of Jesus' lordship to structures of power does not do away with this problem. Even if Jesus' lordship is seen in narrowly religious terms, common imperialistic assumptions about lords return through the back door and shape Christology by default. Any reference to Christ as Lord that does not reflect these unconscious political and economic connotations of the term that are a central part of our history shores up the powers that be. Empire theology does not have to be a conscious enterprise; many of its oppressive tendencies are produced by default.

These reflections need to be seen in light of the fact that Paul has often been used for the purposes of empire. Examples include justifications of slavery, of the subordination of women, of the Holocaust in retribution for the belief that Jews killed Jesus, and even of low-intensity warfare in Central America. In the words of Neil Elliott, "the usefulness of the Pauline letters to systems of domination and oppression is . . . clear and palpable." He is right when he concludes that "this observation must be our starting point."[60]

It is striking that New Testament references to Jesus as Lord are often read as if the title *lord* would need no special consideration or interpretation. Evangelical Christians who commonly emphasize the lordship of Christ, for instance, have debated whether or not Christ should be worshiped as lord, but there is hardly any discussion of the meaning of this title. This lack of a sustained theological debate of the meaning of *lord* is true, strangely enough, even for expositions of the title itself. When the title *lord* is described, the fact of Christ's lordship is noted but little consideration is given to its particular shape. Things are hardly different for the representatives of liberal Christianity. Liberal theologians, too, may debate the lordship of Christ (for instance, in terms of the question whether Christ is necessary for salvation[61]), but once again there is not much debate about what the term *lord* means once it is applied to Jesus.[62] The one exception seem to be some debates concerning the masculinity of the term in liturgical studies, resulting in its omission in certain hymns.[63] Only very recently has the nature of Jesus' lordship been considered in different terms. The scholars involved in the debate represent a spectrum of different opinions, including Richard Horsley, John Dominic Crossan, and N. T. Wright, the latter two well known for their opposing positions on questions of the historical Jesus.

Under the conditions of the Roman Empire the identification of Christ and emperor is a constant temptation, and the title *lord* symbolizes it. Christ and emperor have been identified at various stages throughout history. The church under Constantine is, of course, the prime example; another example is the medieval church under the emperors of the "Holy Roman Empire of the German Nation." In more recent history, the theologians who wrote and signed the Barmen Declaration in Germany in the 1930s suspected that the church was in fact putting Hitler and Christ on equal footing. Even today, many Christians identify the presidency of George W. Bush with a divine purpose—in the 2004 election two-thirds of all Christians in the United States voted for him. Nevertheless, in none of these settings has the parallel between Christ and empire ever been made as blatantly explicit as one might expect. In most cases it takes a closer look and a way of reading between the lines before the connections can be identified.

Sometimes theologians draw distinctions between how Christ's lordship is manifested in the world and in the church. Evangelical theologian Donald Bloesch, for instance, suggests that Christ rules through "suffering love" in the church and "in the overthrow of the powers of the world by the sword." In his thinking, Christ's power in the world has to do with power that "is imposed," while Christ's power in the church has do to with "grace offered"; the two images of Christ never meet since they are divided into two separate realms, and Christ as emperor goes unchallenged by Christ as love.[64] As a result, the lordship of the emperor goes unchallenged as well.

Nevertheless, there is another way of proclaiming Christ as the lord of the empire that is often more dangerous because it is less visible. Often Christ and emperor are seen as completely unrelated and thus there appears to be no need to bother with distinctions. Christ is seen as a religious figure and the emperor as a political one.[65] This is a contemporary temptation that was not an option in the ancient world where religion and politics were not seen as separate realms. No doubt, Paul himself could affirm a dual perspective of Jesus as judge ("putting all under his feet") and Jesus as loving. But it is hard to see how these roles could be bifurcated or split up according to "religion" and "politics" or "church" and "world."

If only by default, this bifurcation of the lordship of Christ and the lordship of the emperor eventually leads to the same problem as a position that explicitly takes over the commonly accepted definitions of lordship and applies them to Christ, because the lordship of Christ is not allowed to reconstruct the lordship of the emperor that ultimately determines our understanding of what a lord is. If a lord is defined as what is commonly understood by the term—namely a ruler, whether a monarch, an oligarch, or a democratically elected leader of a modern country; in short, anybody who has "power over"—the theological consequences are significant. An early example of the adaptation of Christ's lordship to "power over"—the power of the empire—can be found in the Deutero-Pauline letters, which proclaim spiritual transcendence while copying the social patterns of empire in the church. Here, as Horsley puts it, "Paul's representation of the exalted and reigning Jesus Christ as Lord and Savior would be used to consolidate the imperial order."[66] In addition, there are ambivalences and rough edges in the argument of Paul's own letters. In 1 Corinthians 11:3 Paul endorses subordination with a rather odd argument: "But I want you to understand that Christ is the head of every man, and the husband is the head of his wife, and God is the head of Christ." The idea of the subordination of Christ under God should be as troublesome to trinitarian theologians as the idea of the subordination of women under men is for progressive Christians. What does Paul have in mind? Is he promoting a problematic trinitarian theology coupled with problematic social advice? Likewise, in the famous passage of Romans 13:1-7, Paul argues that Christians "be subject to the governing authorities" (13:1). Is he asking the Roman Christians to support the Roman Empire, as this passage has often been interpreted? What about the difference of Christ and Nero—the emperor who came to power in the year before this passage was written? Has Nero, too, been "instituted by God" (Rom. 13:1)? It has been noted that there is no specific reference to Christ in this passage, and we may have to keep in mind that the context of these passages is persecution and martyrdom.[67]

Nevertheless, in this light Paul's own references to Jesus as Lord might be read in support of the Roman Empire. In 1 Corinthians 15:24-25 Paul talks about Christ's handing over "the kingdom to God the Father, after he has destroyed every ruler and every authority and every power. For he must reign until he has put all his enemies under his feet." Horsley argues that such language could easily be used to reinforce subordination within the Christian community itself.[68] Elisabeth Schüssler Fiorenza goes further, wondering whether Paul himself is reproducing structures of empire. She finds that Paul engages in practices of "othering," that is, creating polar opposites.[69] This leads to a particular distortion of lordship: the problem of "kyriarchy," that is, "the governing dominance or supremacy of elite propertied men."[70] The other side of the coin is obedience, which is the "essence of patriarchy," meaning "dependence on and control by men in power."[71] Schüssler Fiorenza is right when she identifies parallels between the hegemonic discourses of the empire and Paul's discourse—but the question is whether we are dealing with exactly the same dynamic when approached "from below." While we do need to wonder whether Paul completely overcomes the structures of empire in his own communities—here Schüssler Fiorenza's point is well taken[72]—the strategy of "othering" may not exclusively be the strategy of empire. Could it not also be a mechanism of resistance for minority groups struggling to resist empire?[73] This matter throws new light also on the egalitarianism that is often claimed for these early Christian communities.[74] Is it not the case that egalitarianism in the midst of a situation of oppression and empire can only emerge out of a determined and consistent struggle against inequality—to the point of condemning empire and its representatives and thus "othering" them?

With this in mind we need to take a closer look at the background of the term *lord*. Four possible sources have been identified: First, in Palestinian-Jewish culture, "lord" was a secular formal address, like the contemporary "sir." Second, also in Palestinian-Jewish culture, "lord" could be used in a religious sense. Both Palestinian Jews and Palestinian Jewish Christians called God "*Lord*" (based on *adonai*, one of the Hebrew pronunciations for the tetragrammaton YHWH). Third, Hellenistic Jews called God "*Lord*" as well since the Septuagint translates the tetragrammaton as *Lord*. Finally, in Hellenistic-pagan culture gods and emperors were called "*lord*."[75] In the eastern Mediterranean world the term *lord* was applied to Roman emperors from Augustus on, the first verifiable inscription of the title dating to Nero's time.[76] Representing a different perspective, evangelical scholar Larry Hurtado claims three contexts for *kyrios* in Paul, all having to do with "religious" phenomena; one is in regard to the practical life of Christians, another is in regard to the future return of Jesus, and the final one is in regard to the worship setting.[77] Hurtado makes no reference at all to political or other connotations.

Unfortunately, nowhere in this debate about sources and contexts is the actual meaning of the title and its function reflected. What particular resonances does this title produce in the setting in which this term is used? It seems that each of the researchers gets hung up on their own presuppositions. Joseph Fitzmyer, for instance, does not want to endorse the fourth source of the title (Hellenistic-pagan culture) as the only influence, because he feels that *kyrios* could not have been "just" a political term; consequently, he shows that there were "also" religious applications for the title.[78] But this strict separation of a political and a religious sphere can no longer be maintained. As we have seen, the emperor cult was not only political but also religious, and what has been considered as the religious use of the title *lord* is also political. In search for a more "religious" option, Fitzmyer dismisses the Hellenistic Jewish background in order to emphasize the second option, rooted in Palestinian Jewish culture.[79] Theologically important, he argues, is the respect of the Palestinian Jews for the name of God; applied to Jesus, the title *lord* is said to stress "a transcendence," due to the implied parallel between Jesus and God.[80] Unfortunately, Fitzmyer does not reflect on the meaning of "lord" in the Aramaic original; neither does he ask what the early church wanted to express with the term besides the religious emphasis on transcendence. In the end, Fitzmyer's approach does not even mention the Roman emperors' claim to lordship and thus imperial lordship is not challenged at all. As a result, Jesus as Lord has nothing to say to the emperor as lord. If Fitzmyer would give up his modern presupposition of a strict separation of religion and politics, he might be able to recapture the deeper implications of his own reference to transcendence: What if Jesus as Lord did not represent abstract religious notions of transcendence but had to do with "transcending," and thus challenging, the politico-religious claim that Caesar is lord?

More recent research has begun to point out the political connotations of the Palestinian references to lord, implied, for instance, in the Aramaic phrase *maranatha*. In the Nabataean culture, which is contemporary with the events of the New Testament and in close geographical, linguistic, and cultural proximity to Palestine, the term relates directly to the king.[81] Once again, however, the political implications of Paul's use of the term are left open. Only N. T. Wright is clearer about the challenge of the term *lord* when he points out that it needs to be seen in light of "its Jewish roots on the one hand and its pagan challenge on the other."[82] But the undertone is still religious: there seems to be a (pure) Jewish religious origin that somehow challenges the pagan misuse of the term. But why would the challenge be only for the pagans? Did not Paul, in his own way, wrestle with Jewish political support of empire, thus posing a challenge to the Jewish side as well?

As we have seen, in the world of the earliest Christians who began to apply the title *kyrios* to Jesus, the term itself had clear political connotations, and it is hardly conceivable that it was used in a "purely religious" way—particularly since an understanding that makes clear-cut distinctions between religion and other expressions of life (including politics) is a modern one.[83] The use of the title *lord* for the emperor is no doubt complex. While not all Roman emperors in the times of Jesus and Paul preferred to call themselves lord, the term becomes more and more popular, designating an ever-stronger monarchy and pointing to an emperor who is in control of the world.[84] Parallel to this process, the title *lord* increasingly acquires divine connotations. The growing popularity of the title indicates a shift in the empire: under the cover of a republican constitution, the monarchy grows stronger and more absolute. The occasional rejection of the title by an emperor could well have to do with the desire to maintain the cover of the republic. In the Eastern traditions, however, where Christianity first took root, the situation was clearer: there the title *lord* was typically attributed to the absolute monarch.[85] If Paul decided to use the title *lord* in this context, he was either naïve and completely aloof to the political developments in the empire (unlikely for someone who lived in constant conflict with the law), or he had a particular purpose for using it, either in support of or in resistance to the Roman Empire.

Gerd Theissen adds an important clue when he argues that the title *kyrios* can be seen as "the most far-reaching innovation after Easter." The Jesus portrayed in the Gospels did not want to be venerated. Thus, in order to remain true to Jesus, the title *lord* would need to be used in a particular way. The title *lord*, as Theissen points out, is "bound to the Galilean and Judean Jesus, to the friend of toll collectors and sinners, the critic of the self-righteous, the one who proclaimed the grace of God, the victim of priestly hostility and state power."[86] Unless this is kept in mind, Jesus is easily identified with absolute and top-down power.

In the Old Testament, as Gottfried Quell has pointed out, the name of God and the divine title *Lord* are "terms of experience" (*Erfahrungsbegriffe*); that is, what is understood as "Lord" is defined by the experience of God's history with Israel.[87] The same is true in the New Testament. In the letters of the New Testament and in the book of Acts, "Lord" refers sometimes to the "historical" Jesus (cf. 1 Cor. 7:10).[88] "Lord" is a term of experience because it reflects the early church's growing understanding of who Jesus was. During his earthly ministry Jesus was not usually called Lord, but somehow the early church experienced him as Lord. While most scholars agree on this issue, it is commonly assumed that this is a "purely religious" development, unrelated to the Roman Empire.[89]

With a few exceptions, most biblical scholars have not given much thought to the fact that Jesus' being Lord might be qualitatively different from Caesar's being lord. The work of Werner Foerster, providing one of the most influential contributions, is only one example. Evangelical scholarship once again deserves special mention because there is such strong emphasis on Jesus as Lord. Evangelical scholar Stephen G. Hatfield provides statistics for the use of the term. While he tells us that the term *lord* appears 717 times in the New Testament and 275 times in the Pauline corpus, that "his kingdom and authority are ever present," and that it takes an "intentional act of will" to respond to Jesus' lordship, there is no mention of the type of lordship that Jesus exercises.[90] The question of whether Jesus' lordship is similar to or qualitatively different from the lordship of the Roman emperors is not even in view. Likewise, in the numerous evangelical debates around "lordship theology," there is little reflection about the character of Christ's lordship. The question is whether belief in Jesus as Savior is enough or whether commitment to Jesus as Lord is also required for "salvation" (a term that invariably seems to mean "going to heaven"). The only definition that can be gleaned from the debate is that the title *lord* implies the divinity of Christ and "must mean sovereign master."[91] As a result, "Christ, being the Lord, comes into the heart of the believer as Lord and

Master."[92] But what kind of mastery is implied here? If that question had been left open in Paul's own mind, the mastery of the Roman lords and emperors would have provided the model for the mastery of Christ by default. Unfortunately, today the problem is no different. If the mastery of Christ is left undefined, the mastery as defined by the prevailing empires will provide the model. Christ is thus most certainly the lord of empire unless explicitly defined otherwise.

Another issue that is frequently brought up in this context is the exclusive nature of the lordship of Christ. Once again, the debate shows some influences of the totalitarian logic of empire. This issue, too, could be addressed differently if we were clearer about the actual nature of Christ's lordship. Is the power of Christ the Lord a zero-sum game—like in the Roman Empire where any power not accountable to the emperor had to be seen as contradicting the empire—or are there other forms of power that might be shared and that would not diminish when shared? We need to ask ourselves how much our theological perspectives and terms are indeed shaped by the logic of empire.

While mainline theology, whether evangelical or liberal, rarely draws out the lines from Christ to empire, other theologies have done so more explicitly. Vice President Dick Cheney, for instance, has brought out into the open the connection of empire and God that is usually present only in hidden form. In a 2003 Christmas card to his supporters he quoted Benjamin Franklin: "And if a sparrow cannot fall to the ground without His notice, is it probable that an empire can rise without His aid?"[93] Even the work of those theologians who would disagree with this statement is easily co-opted unless there is a clear indication of how Jesus as Lord is different from the forms of lordship promoted by empire.

A few decades earlier, statements about Jesus' lordship had a similar ring. In 1935, two years after Adolf Hitler came to power in Germany, German theologian Karl Heim talks about the *Führervollmacht* of Jesus—Jesus' authority/power to be the leader.[94] The German title *Führer*—that is, "leader"—was of course claimed by Hitler himself. Leadership can only emerge from one place, Heim argues, since no one can serve two masters (Matt. 6:24). What this means, he says, is clear to the Christians in Nazi Germany: there is an experience of a strong leader who demonstrates what leadership means and that we are not able to lead ourselves. Heim sees his position as superior to German Idealism and the Enlightenment since progress is no longer driven by ideas but by a person; true leadership is rooted in the personality of the leader. Heim's argument builds on a basic assumption of evangelical Christianity: the personal relationship with Christ. Leadership, he argues, is built on an I-thou relationship. Moreover, the authority of this *Führer* is unlimited: "If we live our life under the leadership of another, we have put in his hand even our knowledge of ultimate things."[95] In sum, Heim finds that Paul uses the ancient emperor cult to create a bridge between Christianity and empire. The difference between Christ and the *Führer* is quantitative, not qualitative: the style of leadership is the same, although Christ as *Führer* transcends the limitations of being human. Paul, affirming the lordship of Christ, is thus seen as an explicit supporter of the Roman Empire. Ellen Meiksins Wood, not a theologian, sees a straight line from this kind of Paul to Augustine, in whose hands "Christianity became not a politically rebellious sect of a tribal religion but a 'universal' spiritual doctrine that sought salvation in another realm and 'rendered unto Caesar' his unchallenged temporal authority."[96]

One of the oldest traditions of the New Testament that invokes Jesus as Lord may help to test these presuppositions. In Philippians 2:5-11, Paul refers to an even older Christian tradition, which makes this one of the very oldest passages in the New Testament. Once again, the typical modern interpretations of this passage focus on the "religious" implications, emphasizing the equality of Jesus and God and the image of religious power reflected in the statement that "every knee should bend."[97] It should be clear by now that these seemingly religious interpretations are tied up with the political; not only do they fail to identify the latent presence of the Roman Empire and thus support empire by default, they mirror the moves of the power of empire.

Even when the potential political challenge of Jesus' lordship is realized, however, is it still often unclear what kind of lord Jesus is. John White points to the imperial character of the use of the term *lord* in Philippians 2:5-11: "the image of universal prostration required of subjects underscores his role as imperial ruler."[98] White's interpretation is typical, as he sees no further need to explore the differences between Christ's lordship and the Roman emperors' lordship. Even where the challenge to empire is clearer, however, a certain romantic notion of Jesus' lordship remains. German New Testament scholar Georg Eichholz emphasizes the real power of Jesus as Lord in the passage of Philippians 2. He realizes that Jesus' power has implications for other powers: "As the powers acclaim [Jesus] as *kyrios*, they attribute all power to him, they give up their own power to him, they agree to their *disempowerment*."[99] What is still not clear, though, is what kind of power we are talking about. Furthermore, that the powers give up their power voluntarily, without a struggle, does not correspond to any real experience, whether inside or outside the church.[100]

The tension between the humiliation and exaltation of Jesus in Philippians 2 might give us a hint of the different sort of power promoted by Jesus: a power that is in diametrical opposition to the power of the emperor. Yet many scholars resolutely reject the idea that this passage refers to anything other than a mysterious transaction within Godself. Gerhard Friedrich finds in Philippians 2 merely a description of God's mysterious way of salvation.[101] Ernst Käsemann (following Barth) rejects the idea that Christ is an example for the ethical life, which could only be "ethical idealism." This pre-Pauline hymn needs to be seen "in isolation from its immediate parenetic context."[102] Others find that Christ can indeed be an ethical example, but they miss the political challenge.[103]

Other interpreters, less inhibited by German Lutheran theological categories, realize the potential challenge. Antoinette Clark Wire sees in Philippians 2:5-11 "the voluntary downward plunge of the divine" in which Paul himself participates—through his own loss of status.[104] Robert Hamerton-Kelly finds "the antidote to sacred violence" in the "identification with the victim."[105] The task of the apostles is to imitate the self-emptying process. Stanley P. Saunders points out that "the hymn clearly models the denial of self-interest, as well as the divestment of divine (and human) status and privilege." In Philippians 2:8 Paul does not simply praise humility; the word that he uses "signifies the act of placing oneself in solidarity with the humiliated, that is, complete identification of oneself with those who huddle together on the broken, bottom rungs of the human ladder."[106] Paul is here talking about life-and-death issues; after all, his own life is hanging in the balance as a prisoner.

Crossan and Reed raise the key question in regard to Philippians 2. How this question is answered decides whether Christ is the lord of empire or not: "Did that downward kenosis forever change the upward exaltation in its type, its mode, and its practice?"[107] If the downward movement does indeed make a difference, the result is a very different kind of "high Christology" than the one that is commonly proclaimed by the church,[108] decisively resisting the top-down hierarchies of the empire.

The proclamation of Christ as Lord is thus constantly appropriated by the empire, even though this does not always happen on purpose. Keep in mind, too, that empire does not always have to be seen in a morally negative light; some scholars explicitly emphasize the benevolent nature of empire. John White, for example, finds Paul's use of the title *lord* for Christ to be parallel to the understanding of the rule of Augustus, as "political leader, beneficial head of the communal family, and priestly Lord." White follows Suetonius's idealized description of Augustus as a benevolent and pious ruler who "desired public welfare rather than self-glory or personal popularity."[109] What is missing in this account, however, is a sense that empire can be problematic even when it appears to be morally correct and benevolent. What is wrong with the following picture? Augustus did much to revive traditional piety and ancient rites, and he reinstated priestly offices. He put great emphasis on what we might call "family values." Marriage was promoted to such an extent that men between twenty-six and sixty had to be married or remarry; divorced or widowed women between twenty and fifty had to find another husband within six months. Those with multiple children were granted special benefits. Belief in the moral basis of the empire is not a new phenomenon.[110] What is wrong with this picture can, however, be seen in the tensions of empire. In a fictional conversation Crossan and Reed have Pilate wonder why the Judean people oppose the Roman Empire. "We have brought them law and order. We have brought them peace and prosperity. We have brought them culture and civilization. We have brought them free trade and international commerce. Why do they hate us so?"[111] Similar questions continue to be asked by benevolent promoters of other empires as well, most recently in the United States in the aftermath of September 11, 2001. The answers are not hard to find if one considers that large groups of people do not benefit from empire and that even the most benevolent efforts are often directly geared not to the needs of the people and their self-expression, but to the expansion of top-down powers and economic interests.

One of the odd things about empire in our own time is that many people have no sense for the pressures produced by empire and do not perceive empire at work. As a result, there is no context for observing the difference between Christ as Lord and the emperor as lord. This may explain the otherwise strange attraction to "purely religious" and depoliticized language. Yet when Christians in a context of empire are unaware of the political implications of their faith, their Christ is likely to be co-opted by empire by default.

Empire is thus the proverbial "elephant in the room" when it comes to the lordship of Christ. Nevertheless, even some who are aware of this elephant have made efforts to play it down. New Testament scholar Wayne Meeks explains that "like any immigrant group, the Christians wanted to be seen as leading a 'quiet life,' causing no trouble and needing nothing, in short, 'behaving decently toward the outsiders' (1 Thess. 4:11-12)." Meeks does not stop there: "True, a prophet of the lowest social class might receive in a trance a 'revelation of the Lord' and with it the right to speak and give direction to the household assembly—but everyone still knew to whom the house belonged."[112] In other words, there is no need to worry about challenges that might come from calling Christ "*Lord*," since there was no way in which Christians would or could step outside the boundaries of their ecclesial isolation and thus step up against the powers that be. Any christological surplus is thus immediately domesticated. Likewise, British church historian Henry Chadwick is eager to explain that the mission to the pagans was not at all concerned to resist the government. In this perspective, the book of Acts justifies the idea that the Roman Empire could be a useful tool in spreading the gospel—but what about the fact, also mentioned in Acts, that Paul spent quite a bit of time in its prisons? The only thing that Christians did not like about the empire, according to Chadwick, was its "old paganism." Chadwick sees no reason for a conflict of Paul with empire: he was a dual citizen and considered the Romans as servants of divine justice who resisted evil deeds. The first conflict with the Roman Empire was, therefore, merely a matter of coincidence, as Emperor Nero needed a scapegoat and happened to pick on the Christians.[113] According to this logic, there is little need to make a distinction between Christ as Lord and the lords of the Roman or other empires.

The Resisting Lord

The purpose of interpreting Paul's Christology in light of the politics of empire is not to politicize Paul but to save him from being depoliticized.[114] As we have seen, the depoliticized Paul is the one that is—paradoxically—more political in more dangerous ways because he ends up on the side of empire by default and without our being aware of it. One of the biggest mistakes in reading Paul is, therefore, to read him in a political vacuum. Paul needs to be understood as a man of his own time, engaging the powers of his time. Daniel Boyarin, a Jewish scholar, has read Paul as an internal critic of Jewish culture, rather than as the founder of another religion who initiated a clean break.[115] On the backdrop of our growing awareness of empire, we need to ask whether Paul can also be understood as an "internal critic of the Roman Empire," rather than as someone who sought to escape into an otherworldly religious ether.

It has been argued that in Romans Paul's emphasis on God's justice (usually translated as "righteousness," a more religious-sounding term) is a challenge to the justice of the Roman Empire. In response, those who argue for a nonpolitical reading of Paul can point out that one of the first things he addresses in the beginning of the letter to the Romans is sexual perversion—usually seen as a moral rather than a political issue. Throughout much of its history, the church has picked up this concern and focused on morality instead of politics. Everything changes, however, if we realize that we are presented here with a false dichotomy, now as then. In Paul's world, it would have been understood that sexuality was tied up with power since one of the prerogatives of the powerful was sexual penetration. Certain homosexual activities in Paul's time could thus be considered displays of the inequality of power. Equally important, the sexual escapades of the emperors were well known to the people. In Romans 1:31 Paul reproaches rebelliousness against parents; most of his readers would have been aware of Emperor Nero's incestuous relations with his mother.[116] Not even sexuality and politics can easily be separated in Paul's thinking.

Another false dichotomy of religion and politics has often been introduced into the interpretation of Paul's take on the crucifixion. In the world of Paul it was highly unlikely that anyone would fail to recognize the political meaning of the cross. The cross was a common form of Roman punishment for the lower classes, particularly for political rebels in unruly provinces such as Judea, where tens of thousands of people were crucified; in the year 4 BCE, two thousand rebels were crucified together at one time. The cross was a well-known political tool for breaking the will of the people. Broad popular awareness of the cross and the atrocious agony it imposed was key to large-scale social control and, as such, was a very distasteful thing for the upper classes.[117] Making the message of "Christ crucified" central, as Paul did, could not have failed to raise some political eyebrows; here is a christological surplus that most theologians throughout the long history of the church would not have expected. The crucified Christ is indeed a strange lord. N. T. Wright is correct: "Perhaps Paul should be taught just as much in the politics departments of our universities as in the religion departments."[118]

The reasons for Jesus' crucifixion are, of course, still hotly debated. Theologians have often settled the debate by assuming that the crucifixion was God's will and that it does not really matter therefore who killed Jesus. But this theological shortcut is misleading; it shortchanges not only the historical search for evidence but the theological debate as well. We know that crucifixion was a Roman method of capital punishment, and Roman interests were well established in Palestine. But why would the Roman Governor Pontius Pilate have bothered to crucify Jesus? Certainly not just because of a "religious" quarrel or because he was a wisdom teacher.[119] In the Gospel reports, the political logic of Jesus' death seems obscured: Pilate is portrayed as giving in to the Jewish high priests and people, who pressure him to put Jesus to death. Thus, the Gospels can indeed be read as blaming the Jews for Jesus' death and thus as depoliticizing the cross, that is, letting the real political players off the hook. Religious differences seem to be at stake when attention is directed toward this other group involved in Jesus' death, often referred to with the general term "the Jews." Yet, when seen in the light of the all-encompassing nature of the Roman Empire, it becomes clear that the lines of division are not between "Romans" in general and "Jews" in general, but between those who benefit from empire and those who do not; those who clearly benefited were the Romans in power, the Herodians, and the priestly class.[120] Not all Jews, the majority of whom were peasants, would have been equally interested in getting rid of Jesus; the Gospel of Mark reports that some agitation was required and that the "chief priests stirred up the crowd" (Mark 15:11). In Mark 3:1-5, the Pharisees and Herodians are the ones who plot to destroy Jesus early in his ministry. The Gospel of Luke, on the other hand, seeks to exonerate both Herod and Pilate (Luke 23:15). Nevertheless, Luke also reports that Herod treated Jesus "with contempt and mocked him" (Luke 23:11) and that somehow Herod and Pilate became friends over this matter (23:12). There is no doubt that Herod and the Herodians would have had a political interest in the matter, but it must not be overlooked that the religious leaders, especially the higher priests, were also political players. The Jewish high priests were integrated into the Roman Empire in their own ways; they collected the tribute to Rome, and they were selected by Herod, the vassal of Rome. The Roman governors also could appoint their own nominees to the office of the high priest. Accordingly, Caiaphas, the high priest when Jesus was crucified, must have had a good working relationship with both Herod and the Romans.[121] Considering who was involved, the crucifixion of Jesus and the empire cannot easily be separated.

Keep in mind also how already the beginning of Jesus' life is framed by empire: Augustus is the emperor, Herod is his vassal, and the registration mentioned in Luke 1 was not for statistical purposes but for the sake of taxation. While the Roman Empire was secured through cultural strategies in the more central parts of the empire, in Palestine the Romans governed through economic control backed up by military terror, often through warlords such as Herod (who was instituted by the Roman Senate) and Antipas. Crucifixion of thousands, enslavement of tens of thousands, and mass slaughter were quite common; even child slaughter was not unheard of, as narrated in the childhood stories in Matthew.[122] In this context, even Jesus' "religious" actions—for instance, the challenge to the Temple, cleansing it and threatening to tear it down (Mark 11:15-19; 13:1-8)—had political connotations: from its origins under the Persians to its eventual destruction by the Romans in 70 CE, the Temple itself was part of the imperial order.[123] Jesus presented a threat to the Roman Empire and to those who benefited from it, and so it is no wonder that the empire's methods for getting rid of such threats were used against him. At the same time, this does not mean that the crucifixion was merely a political plot; images of God were at stake in all of this, but, as we now see more clearly, religion and politics cannot easily be separated.

Even seemingly apolitical theological reflections on Jesus' death can be seen against a broader backdrop. N. T. Wright points out, for instance, that the statement "Jesus died for our sins" (1 Cor. 15:3) initially referred to God's bringing Israel out of its long exile, dealing with the sins that had kept Israel enslaved, and initiating the return from exile.[124] This process cannot possibly be interpreted as purely religious. Likewise, the expiatory theology of the cross, part of Christian thinking since before Paul and referred to in Romans 3:21-31 (justification by grace through Christ "put forward as a sacrifice of atonement"), needs to be seen in a broader context of affirming God's justice over against the justice of empire.[125]

In 1 Corinthians 2:8 Paul is even more openly political when he asserts that "the rulers of this age" crucified "the Lord of glory." The good news in this context is that this is no ultimate victory because, according to 1 Corinthians 2:6, those rulers are doomed to perish; later, things are put more strongly yet when it is announced that the rulers will be destroyed—by Christ (1 Cor. 15:24). According to Neil Elliott, Paul's indictment of the rulers for the crucifixion is not limited to Pilate but includes all powers hostile to God.[126] Of course, Paul's own challenge to the empire has repercussions, expressed in 1 Corinthians 15:30-31, another passage that will be misunderstood if seen only in terms of a religious struggle: "And why are we putting ourselves in danger every hour? I die every day!"

In the midst of this struggle in which Christ's crucifixion is real enough to become the potential fate of his followers as well, hope is found in the resurrection. Christ's resurrection from the dead poses yet another challenge to empire in that it confirms the overthrow of the rulers and promises life beyond the empire (1 Cor. 15:20-25; 32).[127] In Romans 14:9, crucifixion and resurrection are seen together as the basis of Christ's rule as Lord. Jon Sobrino draws out the practical consequences of this view of cross and resurrection in relation to the lordship of Christ: "Christ's lordship is exercised by his followers in the repetition in history of God's deed in the raising of Jesus; it is exercised in giving life to history's crucified, in giving life to those whose lives are threatened. This transformation of the world and history in conformity with God's will is what gives actual form to Jesus' lordship—and incidentally, what renders it verifiable."[128] In other words, Christ's lordship has to do with a real transformation of the world in ways that go against the grain of the empire and that the empire cannot envision.

Some of the roots of Paul's resistance to the Roman Empire can be traced back to Judean apocalypticism; since the Babylonian conquest of Judea, the people have been dominated by one empire after another, and so the apocalyptic tradition is decidedly antiempire.[129] Its focus is on God's intervention by which oppressive rulers are judged or destroyed, the people delivered, and the martyrs vindicated. These motifs can also be found in Paul's letters, although, for the most part, he does not use the same terms. Paul, however, develops these concerns further, arguing that God has already intervened in the crucifixion and resurrection of Jesus Christ and that God's deliverance is for all people.[130] Jesus as Lord overcomes all other lords that build their empires on the backs of the people. In this context, a dualistic worldview may not be as wrongheaded as some current interpreters claim;[131] after all, the struggle with empire is a struggle of life and death, and it needs to be clear who is on which side. Of course, there are different kinds of dualism, a dualism of the powerful, who build themselves up on the back of other people, and a dualism of those who make up the resistance, who need to stand firm in order to survive. When, in the history of the United States, the African American slaves affirmed their faith in Christ as Lord and King, they affirmed that their masters were not lord and that Christ would set them free.[132]

Read in this mode, the title *lord* undergoes a dramatic shift. Jesus is a Lord unlike other lords, including the emperor. "Jesus is Lord and Caesar is not"; this is how N. T. Wright reads Philippians 3:20: "Our citizenship is in heaven, it is from there that we are expecting a Savior, the Lord Jesus Christ."[133] "Savior" and "lord" are Caesar's titles, and the association of those titles with Jesus introduces a fundamental ambivalence that destabilizes the commonly accepted meaning. In another passage, Romans 1:3-4, Paul once again uses key terms of the Roman Empire, like *gospel, son of God*, and *lord*, and applies them to Jesus: "The gospel concerning his Son, who was descended from David according to the flesh and was declared to be Son of God with power according to the spirit of holiness by resurrection from the dead, Jesus Christ our Lord." This passage was written for use in Rome in the year after Nero became emperor, and so it is not hard to imagine that something more is at stake here than purely religious terminology.[134] Under Nero, who was no friend of the Christians, the title *lord* must have received new urgency; the Roman Christians would have been painfully aware that Nero as lord could not easily be reconciled with Christ as Lord. But even before Nero, there are indications in Paul's writings that Christ the Lord challenges other lords.

In various passages of Paul's First Letter to the Corinthians God is portrayed as the one who defeats the rulers (1 Cor. 1:18—2:5 and 2:6—3:4; 15:24-28). Even Werner Foerster, under no suspicion of seeking to challenge empire, points out that the powers of those defeated rulers are real political powers.[135] In 1 Corinthians 8:5-6 the direct confrontation is hard to miss: "Indeed, even though there may be so-called gods in heaven or on earth—as in fact there are many gods and many lords—yet for us there is one God, the Father, from whom are all things and for whom we exist, and one Lord, Jesus Christ, through whom are all things and through whom we exist." Even the famous passage dealing with the Lord's Supper in 1 Corinthians 10:14-22 reflects a similar confrontation. While the church has always remembered Paul's language about "the cup of blessing" as a "sharing in the blood of Christ" and about "the bread that we break" as a "sharing in the body of Christ," there is little memory of Paul's challenge of the emperor cult in this same passage: "You cannot drink the cup of the Lord and the cup of demons. You cannot partake of the table of the Lord and the table of demons." Paul does not mince words here, and in his context the message would have been clear. Horsley emphasizes the strong "political realism" of this passage.[136] After a long history of spiritualizing readings of this passage—as if Paul was merely talking about some ethereal supernatural entities—the passage must now be seen in its full political implications. What is rejected here seems to be the "demonic" emperor cult. This political realism does not need to be played off against the so-called sacramental realism that is often identified with this passage; we simply need to keep in mind that these two realisms are connected.

Paul's "high Christology" and his "high and strong ecclesiology" (N. T. Wright) are tied together in the challenge of the Roman Empire. As Wright has argued, recycling the language of empire, this ecclesiology is substantial enough to envision the church as forming "colonial outposts of the empire that is to be,"[137] that is, God's coming kingdom as a completely different kind of empire and as an alternative to all other kingdoms. Paul's mission, according to Wright, is therefore not primarily that of a religious evangelist, promoting religious experience, but that "of an ambassador for a king-in-waiting, establishing cells of people loyal to this new king, and ordering their lives according to his story, his symbols, and his praxis, and their minds according to his truth."[138] This sort of "high ecclesiology" is, of course, very different from the way the term is usually understood, but it parallels a kind of "high Christology" according to which Christ's lordship is second to none. The crucial difference is that in these cases the adjective *high* does not correspond to the top-down flow of power of the Roman Empire but runs counter to it. Paul's image of the church as Christ's body says as much: when he discusses the "weaker" and "less honorable" members of the body, he points out that "God has so arranged the body, giving the greater honor to the inferior member" (1 Cor. 12:24). This amounts to nothing less than a revolution. "High" is "low," and, as the Jesus of the Gospels used to proclaim, "many who are first will be last, and the last will be first" (Mark 10:31).

With this in mind, we can now go back to Philippians 2:5-11. Crossan and Reed emphasize the difference between "the normalcy of *imperial,* or self-glorifying, divinity and the challenge of *kenotic,* or self-emptying, divinity." Divinity, along the lines of commonsense theism, is generally defined as being "in charge, in control, above, dominant, and on top. But, as Paul learned under capital charges in prison and hymned in Philippians 2:6-11, Christ received exaltation by crucifixion."[139] This *kenosis* (that is, self-emptying) is part of Paul's own story. Paul's own life modeled authority and power in stark contrast to the authority and power of the Roman Empire. He became a fool, weak, poor, victim of torture, and homeless (2 Cor. 11:21-27). If Paul came from the upper strata of society, he did not remain there; likewise, Paul may have had some political protection derived from his status as a Jew (the Roman Empire recognized the right of Jews to honor Caesar through prayers to their own God) but he gave that up as well (Phil. 3:4-11).[140] Paul's comments in 2 Corinthians 8:9-15, challenging those who have more to share with those who have less in order to achieve a "fair balance" (8:13), can now be seen as advice to practice *kenosis* in the community. This attitude is foreshadowed in the verse that precedes Philippians 2:5-11, namely, verse 4: "Let each of you look not to your own interests, but to the interests of others." This is not a typical empire move. Christ as Lord models a kind of power that is diametrically opposed to the power of the empire. No wonder that it takes a special spirit to confess that Jesus is Lord (1 Cor. 12:3): "no one can say 'Jesus is Lord' except by the Holy Spirit," and no wonder that confessing this particular Jesus as Lord is the key to salvation (Rom. 10:9).

Recently, Erik Heen has shown that the notion of Christ's equality with God in Philippians 2:6a (Christ is pronounced *isa theō*, "equal to God") also challenges the Roman emperor and his elites. If the Roman emperors claimed "divine honors" (*isotheoi timai*), attributing equality with God to Christ was no harmless move in a city like Philippi where the emperor cult was particularly well developed.[141] Yet the challenge is not only at the level of who gets to claim God, the challenge is also at the level of the meaning of lordship. Jesus' lordship is tied to a life of submission, rather than to a life of dominance over others. How can this not be a critique of top-down powers?[142] Of course, submission may not be the right word in this context, because Jesus does not model yet another form of subordination or defeat but a new form of power that moves from the bottom up.

Related to this reversal of power, Paul can even be said to have developed his own preferential option for the margins. In Romans 12:16 he advises the Roman Christians, "do not be haughty, but associate with the lowly." In 1 Corinthians 1:28 he states that "God chose what is low and despised in the world, things that are not to reduce to nothing things that are." His famous concern to "remember the poor" (Gal. 2:10) is, of course, geared to the church in Jerusalem but expresses nevertheless a similar spirit.[143] Unfortunately, those statements are often seen merely as ethical admonitions, and thus the basic theological issue at stake is overlooked. But the deeper theological issue should now be clear: God in Christ is a different kind of lord who is not in solidarity with the powerful but in solidarity with the lowly. To be more precise, Christ's way of being in solidarity with the powerful is by being in solidarity with the lowly; the powerful are not outside of the reach of Christ's lordship, but their notions of what it means to be lord are radically reversed. This position—at the heart of the new world proclaimed by Paul—directly contradicts the logic of the Roman Empire. In Roman law, there was an "inbuilt disposition" to "respect and favour the propertied classes."[144] This is not unlike contemporary logic today, where a CEO's primary responsibility is to the stockholders rather than to the workers. The inbuilt connection of authority and power needs to be noted here as well: Christ the Lord's power, which does not flow from the top down, is built on a different kind of authority.[145]

Not surprisingly, Paul himself was persecuted and most likely eventually executed by the Roman Empire, not because of a refusal to sacrifice to the emperor (as many of the later Christians) but because he was suspected of political aggression. Dieter Georgi identifies this as one possible reason for the silence of Luke about Paul's death in the book of Acts. If Paul was indeed accused of treason, this would have been too troublesome for the early church and perhaps also too dangerous.[146] Yet even in the book of Acts there remains some memory of the tensions when the following accusation is pronounced against the early Christians: "They are all acting contrary to the decrees of the emperor [*tōn dogmatōn Kaisaros*], saying that there is another king named Jesus" (Acts 17:7).

And even in the Gospels, despite their more cautious stance in matters of empire, Jesus the Lord is different from all other lords. The Lord is the servant: "You know that among the Gentiles those whom they recognize as their rulers lord it over them, and their great ones are tyrants over them. But it is not so among you; but whoever wishes to become great among you must be your servant, and whoever wishes to be first among you must be slave of all" (Mark 10:42-54). What is more, this reversal is not optional or something that could be attached as an afterthought to other more basic understandings of power; this reversal clearly excludes certain kinds of power and wealth. Jesus appears judgmental precisely at one of the few places where the churches usually refrain from judgment: "It is easier for a camel to go through the eye of a needle than for someone who is rich to enter the kingdom of God" (Mark 10:25). Even Mary, the mother of Jesus, rarely seen as a revolutionary, praises God because "he has scattered the proud in the thoughts of their hearts. He has brought down the powerful from their thrones, and lifted up the lowly; he has filled the hungry with good things, and sent the rich away empty" (Luke 1:51-53). There is a messianic trait in Jesus' lordship that refuses to legitimize the status quo; Jesus the Lord can only relativize the status quo of lordship and replace it.[147]

In subsequent histories, this spirit of the resistant Lord was never completely forgotten. In the year 180 CE seven men and five women died as martyrs at Scillium in North Africa because they upheld Christ as "king of kings." This confession clearly meant, both to the martyrs and their persecutors, an opposition to the Roman emperor's claim to be the highest king. Such confessions were dangerous enough that some of the apologists (among them Irenaeus) felt they had to tone things down and to maintain that the confession of Christ as king did not make Christians disloyal to the emperor.[148]

In sum, Christ the Lord differs dramatically from the Roman emperor as lord. We find here the old theological principle of *via negativa* rather than the *via eminentiae*. The lordship of Christ is not to be understood as a higher form of (but similar to) the lordship of the Emperor (*via eminentiae*). The lordship of Christ is the contradiction of the lordship of the Emperor (*via negativa*). Crossan and Reed try to capture this contradiction in the following statement: "What better deserves the title of a new creation than the abnormality of a share-world replacing the normalcy of a greed-world."[149] While this statement expresses the challenge to a certain degree, it reduces the matter to a moral issue that does not do justice to the real difference, which goes much deeper. Greed may be one symptom of empire, but what we are up against are not moral failures (like greed) but a logic according to which the structures of empire are endorsed as the ones that are ontologically superior and will bring happiness and peace to the world. The fundamental problem with empires, including the Roman one, is not that they happen to endorse morally reprehensible behavior but that they pursue their own logic of top-down power and thus are built on the back of the weakest; what Crossan and Reed reject as "greed," the empire would endorse as economic common sense that leads to improvements for everyone. If this is clear, Crossan and Reed's image of a "share-world" pushes us to a deeper reality and helps us expose contemporary efforts to promote top-down power and to build empires on the back of the weak; even seemingly democratic and nonhierarchical models of lordship, exercised by elected officials that appear to reflect the will of the majority such as bishops, presidents, and CEOs, need to be seen in the new light of Christ's own lordship.

The challenge is now clear: Christ the Lord does not fit easily within the categories of empire. It took a long process of assimilation to come to a point where the title *lord* could be used for Christ and the emperor in the same breath and without ambivalence, and where invoking the power of Christ would no longer be in tension with invoking the power of empire. Christian religion had to undergo a radical transformation, as Meiksins Wood notes: "It had to be transformed from a radical Jewish sect, which opposed the temporal authority of the Empire, into a doctrine amenable to, and even encouraging, imperial obedience."[150] But as Jesus himself reminds us, "no one can serve two masters" (Matt. 6:24). The christological surplus of Jesus' lordship needs to be reckoned with.

Notes

1. This can even be seen in the translations. In English, the Greek word *dikaiosyne* has for instance been translated as "righteousness" and not as "justice." The former term was often read in a modern "religious" sense, which separates religion from other spheres of life and relegates it to the private sphere.

2. This problem has been pointed out, for instance, by Wayne A. Meeks and Dale Martin in

Troles Engberg-Pedersen, ed., *Paul Beyond the Judaism/Hellenism Divide* (Louisville: Westminster John Knox, 2001).

3. See the history in Richard A. Horsley, "Introduction," in *Paul and the Roman Imperial Order*, ed. Richard A. Horsley (Harrisburg: Trinity Press International, 2004), 3–6.

4. Richard A. Horsley, *Jesus and Empire: The Kingdom of God and the New World Disorder* (Minneapolis: Fortress Press, 2003), 13. In the United States it is hard to imagine that in Germany the spirituals of the African American slaves are sometimes used without much knowledge of the context of slavery, mainly because people like their style.

5. As Neil Elliott has pointed out, the search for the historical Paul has suffered from similar problems as the search for the historical Jesus: people tend to recreate Jesus or Paul in their own image. *Liberating Paul: The Justice of God and the Politics of the Apostle* (Maryknoll, N.Y.: Orbis, 1994), 84–86.

6. In this context, the findings of the Jesus Seminar and other modern historical critical scholarship provide some help, even though they are not embraced uncritically. One of the basic differences to the older failed quests for the historical Jesus can be perceived in the advice of *The Five Gospels: The Search for the Authentic Words of Jesus* (New York: Maxwell Macmillan International, 1993), 5: "Beware of finding a Jesus entirely congenial to you." In his attack on the Jesus Seminar, Luke Timothy Johnson fails to grasp the significance of this: "What this seems to mean in effect is that a Jesus conformable to the perceptions of Christian faith must be disallowed in favor of a Jesus who is a cultural critic." *The Real Jesus: The Misguided Quest for the Historical Jesus and the Truth of the Traditional Gospel* (San Francisco: HarperSanFrancisco, 1996), 24. Johnson seems to understand his own work in terms of "disinterested scholarship" (ibid., 6). Yet the following comment, pronounced only three pages later, dispels the myth of disinterested scholarship: The "natural tendency [of religion] is to celebrate the created order more than to subvert the social order"; ibid., 9.

7. Even N. T. Wright declares that the most exciting developments in the contemporary study of Paul are not about Paul's theology (to which he himself has contributed) but about the exploration of the juxtaposition of Paul's gospel and Caesar's empire. "Paul's Gospel and Caesar's Empire," in Richard A. Horsley, ed., *Paul and Politics: Ekklesia, Israel, Imperium, Interpretation* (Harrisburg, Pa.: Trinity Press International, 2000), 160.

8. Catherine Keller, *God and Power: Counter-Apocalyptic Journeys* (Minneapolis: Fortress Press, 2005), 115.

9. Ibid.

10. Horsley points out the close relation of rhetoric and politics in the Roman Empire. "Rhetoric and Empire," in Horsley, ed., *Paul and Politics*, 75.

11. Paul Petit, *Pax Romana* (Berkeley: University of California Press, 1976), 157–58: "The imperial regime, as a personal monarchy, no longer puts facts before the public: there was no more public politics, no electioneering, no interventions by tribunes." In this situation, the people find their outlet in the streets and in the arena.

12. The concept of "religion" as it is used today has its roots in modern European thought. Talal Asad notes that in the nineteenth century religion was seen as an early human condition from which politics and other areas emerged and then became detached. *Genealogies of Religion: Discipline and Reasons of Power in Christianity and Islam* (Baltimore: Johns Hopkins University Press, 1993), 27. While twentieth-century anthropology, with Clifford Geertz and others, does not emphasize this detachment anymore, there is still an assumption that religion is conceptually separate from power (ibid., 29). Asad's own project seeks to bring these realms back together again.

13. See Günther Hansen, "Herrscherkult und Friedensidee," in *Umwelt des Urchristentums*, vol. 1, ed. Johannes Leipoldt and Walter Grundmann (Berlin: Evangelische Verlagsanstalt, 1967), 139; and John Dominic Crossan and Jonathan L. Reed, *In Search of Paul: How Jesus's Apostle Opposed Rome's Empire with God's Kingdom* (San Francisco: HarperSanFrancisco, 2004), 11. *Divus* is a deified human, *deus* is a god like Jupiter.

14. See Hansen, "Herrscherkult und Friedensidee," 139; there is some disagreement among scholars on this matter.

15. See Crossan and Reed, *In Search of Paul*, 148–52. It is interesting to note, as an aside, that those Roman emperors of the first and second century who became "drunk with power" were, in the words of Paul Petit, not "the veterans of long public careers, but princes brought up in the purple." *Pax Romana*, 155.

16. Hansen points out the parallels in the history of religion that make the Hellenistic parts of the empire more susceptible to the emperor cult. "Herrscherkult und Friedensidee," 138. But we might also wonder about how their nature as colonies contributed to this issue.

17. Hansen assumes that "rational politicians" like Caesar and Augustus made use of these religious sensitivities in order to support their political aims and claims that living cults were (mis)used for the "*Loyalitätsreligion*" (ibid., 140). While Hansen admits "genuine religious yearnings and feelings of gratitude" (ibid.), he doubts that "real religious feelings" were at the basis of this cult (ibid., 141).

18. This is an important qualification. See ibid., 141.

19. Paul Zanker has explored the impact of the images of the emperor cult on the distribution of power during a particular period of the Roman Empire. In his view, these images contributed to making the emperor cult a main vehicle of the expression of the

power of local aristocracies. *The Power of Images in the Age of Augustus* (Ann Arbor: University of Michigan Press, 1988).

20. The title *soter*, also used of Jesus, was commonly used of the emperor. See the "Inschrift aus Halikarnassos," in *Umwelt des Urchristentums*, ed. Johannes Leipoldt and Walter Grundmann, vol. 2 (Berlin: Evangelische Verlagsanstalt, 1967), 107; this document is from the time of Emperor Augustus.

21. See, for instance, Petit, *Pax Romana*, 104. Petit, listing areas that deserve more research, also mentions that the Julio-Claudian emperors were trained in "literary culture without (surprisingly enough) any political training" (ibid., 154). This cannot be a mere accident—the more effective politics appear to have been located in the realms of what we today might consider the esoteric.

22. See S. R. F. Price, "Rituals and Power," in Richard A. Horsley, ed., *Paul and Empire: Religion and Power in Roman Imperial Society* (Harrisburg, Pa.: Trinity Press International, 1997), 61.

23. Ibid., 71.

24. Crossan and Reed, *In Search of Paul*, 142.

25. See ibid.

26. See ibid., 20, 47.

27. P. A. Brunt, "*Laus Imperii*," in Horsley, ed., *Paul and Empire,* 25.

28. Cicero, *De re publica* 3:37, quoted by Neil Elliott, "Paul and the Politics of Empire," in Horsley, ed., *Paul and Politics*, 30.

30. Werner Foerster emphasizes the "Hellenistic" background of this idea, which plays off against each other the affirmation by the gods and the affirmation by the people. "Kyrios," *Theologisches Wörterbuch zum Neuen Testament*, ed. Gerhard Kittel, vol. 3 (Stuttgart: Kohlhammer, 1938), 1047.

30. Elliott, "Paul and the Politics of Empire," in Horsley, ed., *Paul and Politics*, 31.

31. Elliott exposes the false presuppositions that led to mistaking Paul for a conservative (*Liberating Paul*, 31–54). One example is the translation of 1 Cor. 7:21 and the implications for slavery. Most English Bible translations, except the NRSV, read something like: "Even if you have the opportunity to become free, make use of your slavery instead." The same passage can also be read as "if you have the opportunity to become free, by all means take it." This alternative translation corresponds to German translations based on Luther.

32. These connections are obscured even in some of the earliest reflections on Paul's ministry. The New Testament book of Acts, for instance, emphasizes the greed of the pagans and the jealousy of the Jews as reasons for the persecution of Paul, but it plays down the

interests of the Roman Empire. In Acts as well as in the Gospels, the Roman authorities generally find Paul innocent. See Crossan and Reed, *In Search of Paul*, 30–34.

33. See Price, "Rituals and Power," in Horsley, ed., *Paul and Empire*, 48.

34. See also Horsley, "Rhetoric and Empire," in Horsley, ed., *Paul and Politics*, 75–78.

35. Paul encountered this problem particularly in Corinth; see Crossan and Reed, *In Search of Paul*, 308–11. As they have noted: "Patronal relations were the ethical mainspring and moral bedrock of the Roman world"; ibid., 297.

36. The Roman strategy was to organize the empire by placing private property in the hands of wealthy landowners. Creating landed aristocracies became an important instrument of empire and extended Roman citizenship beyond Rome itself. As a result, the empire could present itself as geographically and ethnically inclusive. See Ellen Meiksins Wood, *The Empire of Capital* (New York: Verso, 2003), 28.

37. Elliott points out that Paul may not have expected much from the political forum dominated by the powerful; what matters instead is "what contours he expected their life together to assume as they lived in anticipation of God's coming triumph" (*Liberating Paul*, 184). This limitation of political action also applies to Jesus' ministry under empire. As Ched Myers has pointed out, the Gospel of Mark's narrative about Jesus "concentrates more upon subversivity than constructive politics." *Binding the Strong Man: A Political Reading of Mark's Story of Jesus* (Maryknoll, N.Y.: Orbis, 1988), 435–36. Jesus is presented as a "rival authority, challenging the hegemony of the powers who hold sway over the dominant political order."

38. Horsley, "Introduction," in Horsley, ed., *Paul and the Roman Imperial Order*, 3.

39. Horsley, "The Gospel of Imperial Salvation: Introduction," in Horsley, ed., *Paul and Empire*, 13.

40. See ibid., 16. See also Dieter Georgi, "God Turned Upside Down," in ibid., 149.

41. Cf. Paul's use of those terms in 1 Thess. 5:3, in resistance to the empire. While Helmut Koester finds a possible parallel ("Imperial Ideology and Paul's Eschatology in 1 Thessalonians," in Horsley, ed., *Paul and Empire*, 162), Traugott Holtz denies any relationship of Paul and empire. *Der Erste Brief an die Thessalonicher*, Evangelisch-Katholischer Kommentar zum Neuen Testatment, vol. 13 (Zürich, Neukirchen-Vluyn: Benziger Verlag, Neukirchener Verlag, 1986), 215 n.363. For no clear reason, Holtz feels that Paul could not possibly have had in mind a situation outside of the church or a political subtext.

42. Horsley points out the naïveté of the Corinthian *pneumatikoi* in this matter. "Rhetoric and Empire," in Horsley, ed., *Paul and Politics*, 89–101.

43. See Horsley, "Patronage, Priesthoods, and Power: Introduction," in Horsley, ed., *Paul*

and Empire, 90. Elliott puts it this way: "Much like 'trickle-down' economics in our own day, the patronage system effected a massive evaporation of wealth toward the upper strata while masquerading as the generous 'benefaction' of the rich for the poor." *Liberating Paul*, 188.

44. Horsley, "Patronage, Priesthoods, and Power," 95.

45. See Crossan and Reed, *In Search of Paul*, 250. Nevertheless, those gods all had to be approved by the state.

46. See ibid., 25, 68.

47. Johan Christiaan Beker, *Paul the Apostle: The Triumph of God in Life and Thought* (Philadelphia: Fortress Press, 1984), 320; Beker also states that "early Christian self-description provides little evidence for describing early Christianity as a 'cult'" (ibid.). On this matter see also Horsley, "Building an Alternative Society: Introduction," in Horsley, ed., *Paul and Empire*, 208.

48. Wayne Meeks, *The Origins of Christian Morality: The First Two Centuries* (New Haven: Yale University Press, 1993), 102.

49. Crossan and Reed, *In Search of Paul*, 11.

50. See also N. T. Wright in reference to Paul's statement in Phil. 3:1: "To write the same things to you is not troublesome to me, and for you it is a safeguard." "Paul's Gospel and Caesar's Empire," in Horsley, ed., *Paul and Politics*, 175.

51. Crossan and Reed, *In Search of Paul*, x–xi.

52. Horsley argues that "in claiming universal applicability, Western biblical studies unreflectively disguised its own distinctive identity." "Krister Stendahl's Challenge to Pauline Studies: Introduction," in Horsley, ed., *Paul and Politics*, 11. Claiming a universal position, Pauline scholarship has overlooked its own connections to empire. As a result, the interests of the elites have gone unchecked and have infiltrated the debates at the level of the unconscious.

53. Tyron L. Inbody states that "Luke wanted to demonstrate to Theophilus that the development of Christianity under Domitian should not be seen as a threat to the Empire." *The Many Faces of Christology* (Nashville: Abingdon, 2002), 174. See also Crossan, *Who Killed Jesus? Exposing the Roots of Anti-Semitism in the Gospel Story of the Death of Jesus* (San Francisco: HarperSanFrancisco, 1995), 159.

54. This is the famous notion of Ernst Troeltsch, taken up by Gerd Theissen in *The Social Setting of Pauline Christianity: Essays on Corinth*, trans. John Schütz (Philadelphia: Fortress Press, 1983). This position affirms love and equality, according to Troeltsch, which are seen as inner religious qualities but not in regard to the secular world. Ernst Troeltsch, *The Social Teaching of the Churches*, vol. 1, trans. Olive Wyon

(Louisville: Westminster John Knox Press, 1992), 69–79. Theissen thinks this position accepts social differences, ameliorates them through an obligation of love and respect, and imposes those obligations on those who are stronger; the weaker are expected to be subordinate, and display fidelity and esteem (*The Social Setting of Pauline Christianity*, chap. 3). The underlying assumption is that Paul seeks to protect the status of his congregations, which were seen as socially privileged.

55. Other passages in Paul's own letters that display a similar spirit—for instance, the call for the subordination of women in 1 Cor. 14:34-36 and the pronouncement of God's judgment on the Jews for killing Jesus in 1 Thess. 2:14-16—might be later interpolations into Paul's letters by others. Elliott points out that these writings are intentional corrections, emerging from rival interpretations of Paul (*Liberating Paul*, 29–30). These Deutero-Pauline moves include Christianity's increasingly negative attitudes against women and slaves. Crossan and Reed discuss an early Christian picture of St. Thecla, preaching together with the Apostle Paul, noting that her eyes and outstretched hand have been obliterated by later generations. *In Search of Paul*, xiii.

56. As Averil Cameron has pointed out, "it is clear even in the very imperfect state of our knowledge that from immediately after the death of Jesus, if not in his own lifetime, Christian groups included people from a wide social spectrum. The myth of early Christianity as the resort of the poor and underprivileged is precisely that." *Christianity and the Rhetoric of Empire* (Berkeley: University of California Press, 1991), 37. Horsley disagrees, stating that "claims that the participants of Pauline churches represent a cross-section of various classes do not match with our knowledge of sharp class divides in Roman society." Horsley, "Unearthing a People's History: Introduction," in Richard A. Horsley, ed., *A People's History of Christianity: Christian Origins*, vol. 1 (Minneapolis: Fortress Press, 2005), 10.

57. See Aloys Grillmeier, S.J., *Christ in Christian Tradition: From the Apostolic Age to Chalcedon (451)*, vol. 1, trans. John Bowden, 2d rev. ed., (Atlanta: John Knox, 1975), 15.

58. Clara Sue Kidwell, Homer Noley, George E. "Tink" Tinker, *A Native American Theology* (Maryknoll, N.Y.: Orbis, 2001), 6. For an example of ongoing problems with the term, see also ibid., 68.

59. Ibid., 68.

60. Elliott, *Liberating Paul*, 9. Elliott presents the background of the misuses of Paul, ibid., 3–19.

61. See, for instance, Gerald H. Anderson and Thomas F. Stransky, *Christ's Lordship and Religious Pluralism* (Maryknoll, N.Y.: Orbis, 1981).

62. Ibid. This debate about the lordship of Christ would change dramatically if the nature of Christ's lordship were to be considered!

63. The United Church of Christ's *New Century Hymnal* (Cleveland: Pilgrim, 1995) eliminated the term "Lord" in many of the hymns, in particular those translated from other languages, rejecting especially the emphasis on male gender. Also removed were male pronouns for Christ. While the power and authority expressed by the term seem to be an issue, gender is seen as more problematic, indicated for instance by the instruction in the context of "Orders for Worship" that "the word 'Sovereign' may be said instead of the word 'Lord'" (on an unnumbered page before p. 1). The male connotations of the term "Lord" are also at the heart of Brian Wren's critique. *What Language Shall I Borrow? God-Talk in Worship: A Male Response to Feminist Theology* (New York: Crossroad, 1993), 55.

64. Donald G. Bloesch, *Jesus Christ, Savior and Lord* (Downers Grove, Ill.: InterVarsity, 1997), 224–26.

65. See Grillmeier, who interprets worship of Christ as *kyrios* as a purely religious matter: *kyrios* exclusively opposes other Hellenistic cult-deities. *Christ in Christian Tradition*, 16.

66. Horsley, "Rhetoric and Empire," in Horsley, ed., *Paul and Politics*, 101–02.

67. Crossan and Reed argue that Paul picks up a standard advice of the Jewish synagogue for survival as there is no specific reference to Christ (*In Search of Paul*, 394). Elliott notes that this represents not a suggestion for the powerful but a word of caution for those who have to lose everything. *Liberating Paul*, 226.

68. Horsley, "Rhetoric and Empire," in Horsley, ed., *Paul and Politics*, 93.

69. Elisabeth Schüssler Fiorenza, "Paul and the Politics of Interpretation," in ibid., 45.

70. Ibid., 46. This term, parallel to the German term *Herrschaft*, includes but also transcends the term *patriarchy* by emphasizing the multidimensional aspects of power and domination.

71. Elisabeth Schüssler Fiorenza, *Discipleship of Equals: A Critical Feminist Ekklesia-logy of Liberation* (New York: Crossroad, 1993), 213.

72. In this connection, the feminist efforts to discern the voices of the Pauline communities in tension with Paul are very helpful. See the work of Schüssler Fiorenza and Antoinette Clark Wire (below).

73. See Joerg Rieger, "Dualism," in *Encyclopedia of Religion and Nature*, ed. Bron Taylor (New York: Continuum, 2005), 510–12.

74. See Schüssler Fiorenza, "Paul and the Politics of Interpretation," in Horsley, ed., *Paul and Politics*, 54–55.

75. See Joseph A. Fitzmyer, "Der semitische Hintergrund des neutestamentlichen Kyriostitels," in Georg Strecker, ed. *Jesus Christus in Historie und Theologie* (Tübingen: Mohr, 1975), 271; Fitzmyer prefers the second option. Most of the prominent European scholars fit in this scheme. Ferdinand Hahn prefers the first source; Oscar Cullmann, Eduard Schweizer, and Werner Foerster emphasize sources two and three; Wilhelm Bousset, Rudolf Bultmann, and Hans Conzelmann argue for source four. See also N. T. Wright, who emphasizes the parallels to the Septuagint, where *kyrios* stands for the Tetragrammaton, *YHWH*; as a result, the term is seen as emphasizing the unity of Jesus and God. "Paul's Gospel and Caesar's Empire," in Horsley, ed., *Paul and Politics*, 169.

76. In reference to Adolf Deissmann, see Karl Donfried, "The Imperial Cults and Political Conflict in 1 Thessalonians," in Horsley, ed., *Paul and Empire*, 217.

77. See Larry W. Hurtado, *Lord Jesus Christ: Devotion to Jesus in Earliest Christianity* (Grand Rapids, Mich.: Wm. B. Eerdmans, 2003), 115–17.

78. Fitzmyer, "Der semitische Hintergrund," 276.

79. Hellenistic Jews, Fitzmyer argues, are not a likely source, as pre-Christian versions maintain the Tetragrammaton, although in Greek letters; ibid., 282–83.

80. Ibid., 297. For an example, see 1 Cor. 16:22.

81. Helmut Merklein points out that there seems to be a strong royal connotation. "*Maranā* ['*unser Herr*'] als Bezeichnung des nabatäischen Königs," in Rudolf Hoppe and Ulrich Busse, eds., *Von Jesus zum Christus* (Berlin: Walter de Gruyter, 1998), 38.

82. N. T. Wright, "Paul's Gospel and Caesar's Empire," in Horsley, ed., *Paul and Politics*, 168.

83. Note that in rabbinical Judaism at the time of Jesus, *kyrios* designates God both as ruler of the whole world and of the individual. Foerster, "Kyrios," 1084.

84. This is what Foerster means when he calls this "an oriental kind of monarchy" (ibid., 1049). The orientalist undercurrent of this wording should be clear.

85. Foerster points out an interesting discrepancy: "What is unique about the situation of the time of the Roman emperors is that, under the cover-up of a constitutional blanket, the kind of absolute Monarchy was established for whose representatives the Orient always used the title 'lord.'" "Kyrios," 1054. Foerster tries to distinguish between political and religious uses of the term, but it is doubtful that this was much of an issue in the Roman Empire.

86. Gerd Theissen and Annette Merz, *The Historical Jesus: A Comprehensive Guide* (London/Minneapolis: SCM/Fortress Press, 1998), 557–63. Note that there are two different terms for lord in the New Testament Greek: *Kyrios* and *despotēs* are used in parallel fashion in the environment of the New Testament. *Kyrios* is the one who has power

over something; *despotēs* is the one who owns something or someone; the power of the *Kyrios* appears to be less arbitrary. See Foerster, "Kyrios," 1043–44.

87. Gottfried Quell, "Kyrios," *Theologisches Wörterbuch zum Neuen Testament*, vol. 3, 1060.

88. See Foerster, "Kyrios," 1092.

89. This assumption can also be found in ibid., 1093–94.

90. Stephen G. Hatfield, "The Lordship of Christ: A Biblical Analysis," *Southwestern Journal of Theology* 33, no. 2 (Spring 1991): 16–25. The two quotations are from pp. 23 and 25.

91. Millard J. Erickson, "Lordship Theology: The Current Controversy," *Southwestern Journal of Theology* 33, no. 2 (Spring 1991): 10. A similar argument is made by Kenneth L. Gentry Jr., *Lord of the Saved: Getting to the Heart of the Lordship Debate* (Phillipsburg, N.J.: P&R, 1992), 51–65. *Kyrios* "denotes sovereign rulership" (ibid., 65). The same is true, he says, when *kyrios* is applied to God.

92. Gentry, *Lord of the Saved*, 65.

93. Quoted by Timothy Noah, "The Imperial Vice Presidency: Dick Cheney Says the 'E'-Word," in the *Slate* magazine feature *Chatterbox: Gossip, Speculation, and Scuttlebutt about Politics*, Dec. 17, 2003; http://slate.msn.com/id/2092800 (accessed 10/30/06)

94. Karl Heim, *Jesus der Herr: Die Führervollmacht Jesu und die Gottesoffenbarung in Christus* (Berlin: Furche Verlag, 1935), 5; see also ibid., 63, 65, 69, 71.

95. Ibid., 77.

96. Meiksins Wood, *Empire of Capital*, 35–36.

97. See Foerster, "Kyrios," 1087. Foerster adds that *lord* here is the "name" of Jesus.

98. John L. White, *The Apostle of God: Paul and the Promise of Abraham* (Peabody, Mass.: Hendrickson, 1999), 189. See also 1 Thess. 4:16.

99. Georg Eichholz, *Die Theologie des Paulus im Umriss* (Neukirchen-Vluyn: Neukirchener Verlag, 1977), 146. Emphasis in original.

100. Eichholz claims that Paul usually thinks about the implications of the *kyrios* for the community—but these implications remain limited to the community of the church (Rom 14:7-8); in Philippians 2 the horizon is clearly broader, a fact that Eichholz attributes to the pre-Pauline origins of the passage; ibid., 147.

101. Gerhard Friedrich, "Der Brief an die Philipper," in *Das Neue Testament Deutsch: Die Briefe an die Galater, Epheser, Philipper, Kolosser, Thessalonicher und Philemon*, vol. 8 (Göttingen: Vandenhoeck and Ruprecht, 1981), 151. In terms of the paradigm of the strict separation of "indicative" and "imperative" under which these theologians operate, this passage is simply "indicative." Christ, Friedrich emphasizes, is not the "ideal," which no one can ever achieve.

102. Quoted in David Way, *The Lordship of Christ: Ernst Käsemann's Interpretation of Paul's Theology* (New York: Oxford University Press, 1991), 88–89. Gnosticism is seen as the background, not empire (see ibid., 90–91). In his later commentary on Romans, Ernst Käsemann seems to revise this strict rejection of Christ's example, but prefers the notion *conformitas*—"conformity" with Christ—to the notion of the imitation of Christ (see Käsemann, *An die Römer*, Handbuch zum Neuen Testament, vol. 8, 4th exp. ed. [Tübingen: J.C.B. Mohr, 1980], 369, on Rom, 15:1-6, which he reads in parallel to Phil 2:5ff.). Christ is "example and archetype of our behavior, according to which the strong have to be in solidarity with the powerless and those who are in need of help, having to endure together their humiliation and in this act they are exposed to the blasphemies of the world." In his earlier interpretation of Philippians 2, Käsemann rejected the idea of Christ as "example" (*Vorbild*); see Way, *The Lordship of Christ*, 93–94.

103. Meeks states that "Christ's self-humbling obedience is both basis and model for the practice of 'humility' and other-regarding love in the church"; *The Origins of Christian Morality*, 98. He also notes that early Christian hymns, such as Phil. 2:5-11, not only shape the communities' Christology but also the communities themselves. Of course, it could be argued that all texts do that. What is glaringly absent is any reference to the challenge provided by the notion of lordship.

104. See Elliott, *Liberating Paul*, 63; and Antoinette Clark Wire, *The Corinthian Woman Prophets: A Reconstruction through Paul's Rhetoric* (Minneapolis: Fortress Press, 1990), 69–70.

105. Quoted in Elliott, *Liberating Paul*, 198.

106. Stanley P. Saunders, *Philippians and Galatians* (Louisville: Geneva, 2001), 18, commenting on Phil. 5:1-11. Saunders also makes the helpful observation that "solidarity with the humiliated is not the same as solidarity with the humble" (ibid.). See also Klaus Wengst, *Humility: Solidarity of the Humiliated: The Transformation of an Attitude and its Social Relevance in Graeco-Roman, Old Testament-Jewish, and Early Christian Tradition*, trans. John Bowden (Philadelphia: Fortress Press, 1988).

107. Crossan and Reed, *In Search of Paul*, 290. 1 Corinthians 1–4 can be read as a commentary on that transformation that begins with the downward movement. See also Paul's statement in 2 Cor. 12:9-10: "Whenever I am weak, then I am strong."

108. N. T. Wright has pointed out that Paul's high Christology has Jewish flavor; "Paul's Gospel and Caesar's Empire," in Horsley, ed., *Paul and Politics*, 181–82. See also Wright's comments on Phil. 2:5-11: "As you look at the incarnate son of God dying on the cross the most powerful thought you should think is: this is the true meaning of who God is. He is the God of self-giving love." *Paul for Everyone: The Prison Letters: Ephesians, Philippians, Colossians and Philemon* (Louisville: Westminster John Knox, 2004), 103.

109. White, *The Apostle of God*, 191, 196.

110. See Crossan and Reed, *In Search of Paul*, 83–99.

111. Ibid., xiv.

112. Meeks, *The Origins of Christian Morality*, 49.

113. Henry Chadwick, *Die Kirche in der antiken Welt* (Berlin: Walter de Gruyter, 1972), 14–15, 19, 21. Chadwick sees Paul as a successful missionary due to his ability to translate the Palestinian gospel into a Hellenistic world.

114. Elliott tells the story of the depoliticization and mystification of Paul. *Liberating Paul*, 55–90.

115. Daniel Boyarin interprets Paul as "a Jewish cultural critic." *A Radical Jew: Paul and the Politics of Identity* (Berkeley: University of California Press, 1994), 2.

116. For this connection of sexuality and power see Elliott, *Liberating Paul*, 193–95.

117. See ibid., 94–99.

118. Wright, "Paul's Gospel and Caesar's Empire," in Horsley, ed., *Paul and Politics*, 182.

119. See Marcus Borg and N. T. Wright, *The Meaning of Jesus: Two Visions* (San Francisco: HarperSanFrancisco, 1999), 91. In Borg's words, "if Jesus had been only a mystic, healer, and wisdom teacher, I doubt that he would have been executed. But he was also a God-intoxicated voice of religious social protest who had attracted a following." Moreover, "Jesus died as a martyr, not as a victim. A martyr is killed because he stands for something."

120. See Horsley, *Jesus and Empire*, 59.

121. Ibid., 32–33.

122. See ibid., 26–31.

123. See ibid., 166, n.13.

124. N. T. Wright, in Borg and Wright, *The Meaning of Jesus*, 102–04.

125. Elliott points out that in Romans 6 the "atoning significance of Jesus' death disappears" and is "supplanted by an apocalyptic scheme of fields of power." *Liberating Paul*, 129.

126. Ibid., 113; Elliott points out that this is the symbolism of the Jewish apocalypses; ibid., 110.

127. While the spirit of our passage in 1 Corinthians 15 seems clear, the subjection of all things under Christ (15:27), including the rulers of this world and the world as a whole in Col. 3:1-2, introduces a different spirit that appears to play off against each other "above" and "below," "heaven" and "earth": "So if you have been raised with Christ, seek the things that are above, where Christ is, seated at the right hand of God. Set your minds on things that are above, not on things that are on earth."

128. Jon Sobrino, *Jesus in Latin America*, trans. Robert R. Barr (Maryknoll, N.Y.: Orbis, 1987), 156.

129. See Horsley, "Rhetoric and Empire," in Horsley, ed., *Paul and Politics*, 93; the only exception from this rule is the Hasmonean dynasty.

130. See ibid., 95–97.

131. See, for instance, Horsley's interpretation (ibid., 94). Dualistic notions can certainly be found in Paul (Boyarin, *A Radical Jew*, 59), but this does not have to imply a rejection of the body or the phenomenal world. This insight can be developed politically, in the resistance against empire, an issue that is not on Boyarin's horizon.

132. If in the African American Spirituals Christ "is the conquering King and the crucified Lord," as James Cone has pointed out, this means that he is the one "who has come to bring peace and justice to the dispossessed of the land." *The Spirituals and the Blues: An Interpretation* (New York: Seabury, 1972), 49.

133. Wright, "Paul's Gospel and Caesar's Empire," in Horsley, ed., *Paul and Politics*, 173.

134. See Dieter Georgi, "God Turned Upside Down," in Horsley, ed., *Paul and Empire*, 150–51.

135. Foerster, "Kyrios," 1090.

136. Richard A. Horsley, "1 Corinthians: A Case Study of Paul's Assembly as an Alternative Society," in Horsley, ed., *Paul and Empire*, 248.

137. Wright, "Paul's Gospel and Caesar's Empire," in Horsley, ed., *Paul and Politics*, 182.

138. Ibid., 161–62; Wright emphasizes that Paul's political agenda was driven by his theological one; ibid., 164.

139. Crossan and Reed, *In Search of Paul*, 242.

140. See Elliott, *Liberating Paul*, 61, 197. See also Wire, *The Corinthian Women Prophets*, 69-70; she calls this the "voluntary downward plunge of the divine."

141. Erik M. Heen, "Phil 2:6-11 and Resistance to Local Timocratic Rule: *Isa theō* and the Cult of the Emperor in the East," in Horsley, ed., *Paul and the Roman Imperial Order*, 125–26, 134.

142. See ibid., 150.

143. Elliott also emphasizes this option for the poor in *Liberating Paul*, 87–89: "Why not assume that Paul's vision will be clearest when seen from the standpoint of the oppressed today, and of those who work for liberation—and suffer arrest, imprisonment, and torture for their trouble?" (ibid., 88).

144. G. E. M. de Ste. Croix, quoted in ibid., 186.

145. For a discussion of the relationship of authority and power see Joerg Rieger, *Remember the Poor: The Challenge to Theology in the Twenty-First Century* (Harrisburg, Pa.: Trinity Press International, 1998).

146. See Georgi, "God Turned Upside Down," in Horsley, ed., *Paul and Empire*, 157. Paul's death most likely happened under Nero in 64 CE; in the midst of the troubles of the persecution, there was no time to pay much attention to particular stories and events. See Crossan and Reed, *In Search of Paul*, 401.

147. See Jacob Taubes, *Die Politische Theologie des Paulus*, ed. Aleida Assmann and Jan Assmann (Munich: Wilhem Fink Verlag, 1993), 178–80.

148. Jaroslav Pelikan, *Jesus Through the Centuries: His Place in the History of Culture* (New Haven: Yale University Press, 1985), 48.

149. Crossan and Reed, *In Search of Paul*, 176.

150. Meiksins Wood, *Empire of Capital*, 35.

2

Resisting and Reframing Coequality

Christology and the Creeds

THE ANCIENT ECUMENICAL COUNCILS of Nicaea and of Chalcedon marked important turning points in early Christian thinking about Christ. The Council of Nicaea in 325 CE affirmed the coequality of God and Jesus, that is, the first and second persons of the Trinity. The Council of Chalcedon in 451 CE once again affirmed Jesus' coequality with God in terms of his divinity, but it added the notion of Jesus' coequality with us in terms of his humanity. This notion of coequality, *homoousia* in Greek, is among the most famous terms in the history of Christian doctrine and is at the heart of the development of early Christian theology.[1] Nevertheless, these notions of coequality are ambivalent in the context of the later Roman Empire out of which they developed. "Coequality" can provide resistance to empire; yet it also might need to be resisted and reframed in the struggle against empire.

It must be remembered that the notion of coequality was first introduced by the Emperor Constantine. Does Constantine's influence on the Council of Nicaea, promoting Christ's coequality with God, draw Christ into the support of empire? Could it be that Christ as coequal with God is somehow identified with the emperor? Is the Christ who is coequal with God somehow removed from the messiness of life that is experienced more severely by the common people? Constantine notwithstanding, even the official Christology of the Roman Empire could not be controlled completely by the interests of empire; ambivalence remained. The Council of Chalcedon over a century later—another council convened under pressure from an emperor—affirmed Christ's humanity and coequality with us and thus, to a certain degree, his sharing in the messiness of human life. But how was this move related to the Roman Empire—did it provide challenge or support? The answer depends, in part, on how Christ's humanity is envisioned. Is Christ's humanity narrowly conceived in terms of the upper strata of the empire or does it connect with the common people? The tensions and ambivalences in the notion of coequality in both the councils of Nicaea and Chalcedon suggest that there is no easy harmony with the interests of empire and call for another look at the matter.

The history of effects of these early councils is long. While some modern theologians have assumed that these councils are antiquated and outdated, in recent theology there is a renewed interest in the creeds. Although some of this interest might have initially had to do with the culture wars between liberals and conservatives, the current interest is much broader. The Christian tradition is no longer the domain of conservatives. The most interesting approaches are now pointing out the complexity of these ancient traditions and the challenges that they hold, both for their own times and for ours. While so-called Radical Orthodoxy has sought to monopolize attention in this regard, other approaches by theologians inspired by liberation interests have developed new energies around traditional sources in their own ways.[2] Still, what is missing in many contemporary efforts is a critical investigation as to how the orthodox movements themselves are part of the powers that be. Unless these ties to the status quo are identified, we will not be able to see the truly radical elements that push beyond them.

At a time when the currency of early church theology is once again on the rise, constructive theology and Christology can afford less than ever to ignore these ancient perspectives. Identifying the ways these theologies push beyond empire, tied to an unexpected christological surplus, might help identify dynamics that exist in our age as well and that push us all further beyond empire and closer toward God.

The Creeds of the Empire

The peculiarly Christian identity of the Roman Empire was established simultaneously with the ecumenical councils of the church. The coincidence is noteworthy, especially since in the ancient world questions of religion and politics and questions of theology and power cannot easily be separated. Applying modern conceptions—such as, for instance, the "separation of church and state"—to these ancient theologies can only lead to anachronistic misunderstandings. If one were to judge the theology of these councils in terms of the separation of church and

70

state, the verdict would have to be that all of them were capital failures. Still, many theologians and a few historians have tried to disentangle church and state to find pure theology at the core of the decisions of the councils. These efforts mean to rescue the councils from being labeled as sheer political maneuvering, but they are nonetheless misleading.[3] The positive theological surplus cannot be identified through such artificial abstractions. Neither church and state nor religion and politics can be separated in the Roman Empire; at times they cannot even be distinguished clearly. Rather than trying to secure theology by playing down the impact of the empire on it, we pursue a different path in this chapter. The search is on for the ways in which Christian theology in the Roman Empire unfolds in ways that have been shaped, but cannot ultimately be explained entirely, by the dynamics of empire. Is there a theological surplus that is distinct from the interests of empire and thus might have the potential to resist empire?[4]

Emperor Constantine's conversion to Christianity (in 312 CE; Constantine ruled from 305 to 337), as narrated by his contemporary, the early church historian Eusebius, has always puzzled those who think of conversions as "purely religious" events. Constantine's conversion, in the words of Eusebius, was based on his realization that "he would need more powerful aid than an army can supply," and that "those who had confided in a multitude of gods had run into multiple destruction." Constantine came to the conclusion that the one god "who transcends the universe" was the most powerful source of that aid. After a prayer to this one god, asking him to show "who he was," Constantine saw a sign over the midday sun, consisting of a "cross-shaped trophy formed from light" and a text that said, "By this conquer."[5] Thus, it became clear that the one god was the Christian God. That the Christian God was the most powerful god was subsequently confirmed when Constantine triumphed over his enemies. Religious and political concerns cannot be separated in this account; they cannot even be clearly distinguished. Consequently, those who see religion and politics as separate realms have to doubt the sincerity of Constantine's conversion.

Yet Constantine follows a different theological logic that is not as foreign to Christian theology as it may appear to modern theologians: if God rules over everything, religion and politics cannot be strictly separated, and neither can there be a clean distinction between spiritual and worldly power; both powers have their origin in the one power of God. Following this line of thought, it does not make much sense to try to assess the sincerity of Constantine's conversion according to whether he combined political and theological interests or not. Nor does it make sense to judge the value of ancient theological positions according to whether the bishops or the emperor held them. The emperor did not see his realm as limited to politics and the bishops did not see their realm as limited to theology and religion.[6] The Orthodox Church rejects such bifurcations when it recognizes Constantine as a saint, "equal to the Apostles."[7] Even if the emperor cult is no longer practiced in the Christianized Roman Empire at the time of Constantine, we need to remember the earlier role of the emperor as *pontifex maximus* (the high priest) of the empire. Constantine talked about himself as being "a bishop appointed by God over those outside [the church]," just like the bishops were appointed over those inside.[8] If an analysis of problems with these theological positions cannot be built on pointing out the obvious lack of separation between religion, theology, and politics, a more useful question for evaluating these theologies and searching for alternatives is what respective theological and political strategies are endorsed and how to evaluate them.

In the fourth century a new and closer relationship between the Roman Empire and the churches develops. To note this close relationship does not imply that the creeds of the fourth and fifth century are mere manifestations of the empire. A certain ambivalence remains in these creeds, a surplus, that cannot be fully controlled by the powers that be. But in order to gain access to this surplus, we first need to understand the interconnectedness of the Roman Empire, the church, and the creeds. We cannot continue our theological reflections without dealing with this history.[9]

Commonly accepted critiques of the "Constantinianization" of the church, the process through which the church became an established part of the Roman Empire under the Emperor Constantine, usually imply that from that time on the otherwise pure (and mostly spiritual) heritage of the church has been misused for political purposes. These interpretations overlook, however, that the connections of church and empire go much deeper and have their beginnings long before Constantine.[10] Historian Peter Brown notes that already in the third and early fourth centuries "the Great Persecution showed that the Christian Church had changed as much as had the empire." The church had gained power and unity. "It had become a universal Church, claiming the loyalty of all believers, at just the same time as the Roman empire had become a true empire, with ideological claims on all its subjects."[11] The heritage of the church—in all its orthodox and heterodox forms—has been shaped by the intersections of empire and church since the early days. Even the theology of the Apostle Paul needs to be read in this light, as the previous chapter demonstrates.

Nevertheless, as time went on a change occurred in the culture of the empire itself: in the second century, the cities in the eastern part of the Roman Empire still enjoyed certain levels of autonomy and had their own localized religious and cultural identities. In the fourth century, more centralized structures began to produce more centralized religious and cultural identities. The new form of government in the Roman Empire of the fourth century centered on the emperor who exercised strong influence in all areas of life, including religion. In the Byzantine East after Constantine, where the most significant theological disputes took place and the most important early ecumenical councils took place (Nicaea and Chalcedon were no exception), the emperor was considered to be crowned directly by the Christian God. The emperor, in turn, consecrated the head of the Eastern Church, declaring: "By the grace of God and by our imperial power, which proceeds from the grace of God, this man is appointed patriarch of Constantinople."[12] In the West, the reverse was true: the emperor was crowned by the pope.[13]

Signs of this centralization—an early form of what we now call globalization—were all around and must have affected the churches' understanding of Christ. At the geographical center was Constantinople, now the prime city of the Roman Empire. Local traditions were under attack, and many of the local temples and cults were shut down, a process that began with Constantine and was virtually completed under Theodosius before the end of the fourth century. The Christian churches, which had their own distinct local traditions, were pulled into the more centralized outlook of the Roman Empire as well. As Peter Brown has observed, Christianity supported "a new, empire-wide patriotism. This was centered on the person and mission of a God-given, universal ruler."[14] In this process, dissenting churches were disciplined according to the guidelines set by the empire. Those declared "heretics" under Constantine, for instance, were prevented from gathering and had their church buildings confiscated.[15]

At the same time, however, the Christian religion also made its claims on the empire, and the understanding of Christ played a major role: "As a result of the events of the fourth century, it was necessary, for the next thousand years and more, to accept Christ as the eternal King if one wanted to be a temporal King."[16] Thus, Jaroslav Pelikan describes the particular character of the entwining of church and state from the perspective of the state. The Emperor Constantine required those who held political office to subscribe to the Nicene Creed (despite his own personal conversion to Arian sympathies later). This publicly mandated subscription to the Nicene Creed was still in effect twelve centuries later during the

Protestant Reformation and was one of the reasons why the Reformers emphasized their own loyalty to the creeds. The influence of the Christian churches on the Roman Empire must not be underestimated. In the words of Peter Brown: "In the last decades of the fourth century, bishops and monks showed that they could sway the will of the powerful as effectively as had any philosopher."[17] Nevertheless, that it was the will of the emperor that needed to be swayed suggests where power ultimately resided.

That bishops and other religious leaders should be compared to philosophers is no accident. What Peter Brown calls the "power of persuasion" was first brought to bear upon the Roman Empire by Greek culture, and he observes that "the more the Roman government invaded local society, the more effectively it was colonized by representatives of Greek culture."[18] This Greek culture would come to serve as the glue of people in power who often had little else in common.[19] Classic Greek education created a common space and language for the powerful elites in which they could network and carry out the tasks of government; the regulation of power in the empire followed these models.

Early Christianity supplanted this formative role of Greek culture by introducing what might be called a "Christian populism"[20] that, in contradistinction to the more elitist character of Greek influence, created space for the cultural production of common people, including lower-class monks. This populism was often promoted by the bishops, most of whom were, paradoxically, from the upper class and highly educated, such as Augustine (354–430), Ambrose (340–397), and Jerome (347–419).[21] Those men, as Brown describes the process, benefited from this shift toward popular culture as they "backed into the limelight that they had brought to bear on the illiterate monks, apostles, and martyrs."[22] They often used their ties to the people to accuse their rivals of elitism.[23] In this way, the popular movements and the interests of some of the highly educated converged in the church even before Constantine.

The bishops and other leaders of the church were able to put their connections to the masses to good use as they positioned themselves in relation to the empire. No wonder their theological struggles—in particular their views of God and Christ—would be of interest to the empire as well. The claim of the Christian bishops, for instance, to be "lovers of the poor" was an unmistakable signal to the powerful that these bishops had connections to the masses and thus had to be reckoned with.[24] At a time of growing unrest and crisis in the cities, the bishops' connections with the common people and the lower classes—who were not otherwise served and addressed and whose numbers increased in the fourth century[25]—added to their influence. The bishops' support for the poor—acts that usually required far less money than the traditional charitable contributions of the wealthy to society upon which the welfare of the civic communities depended[26]— resulted in the same kind of respect and deference that was paid to the civic leaders by their middle-class clients.[27]

But the newly gained influence came at a cost. The Emperor Constantine, promoting the expansion of funded support for the poor in the cities, put the administration of these funds exclusively in the hands of the bishops;[28] as a result both the bishops and the poor were brought under a certain control. The bishops who were instructed to take care of the poor were reminded that their place was closer to the poor than to the top of society; this may have been necessary, as Bishop Athanasius stood for others when he was accused of selling grain on the private market that Constantine had given to the church for the poor.[29] Canon 17 of the Council of Nicaea prohibits clergy to receive usury from loans of money, noting that "many enrolled among the Clergy, following covetousness and lust of gain, have forgotten the divine Scripture."[30] The general concern for the poor that began to permeate the society of the Roman Empire in the fourth century was firmly established in the fifth. The poor were brought under the control of the church: being taken care of by a particular church and its bishop meant that they could not move to other places and that they were listed on that church's poor rolls; even begging required a permit with the bishop's signature, as Canon 11 of the Council of Chalcedon would later stipulate.[31] At the time of the Council of Chalcedon in 451, the emperors of the eastern and western parts of the Roman Empire, Valentinian III and Marcian, declared that "it is a feature of our humane rule to look after the interests of the destitute and to ensure that the poor do not go without food."[32] Gradually, the bishop became "controller of the crowds."[33] This was important especially in light of the constant threat of violence in the two decades before the Council of Chalcedon. In the eastern parts of the Roman Empire—the world of the councils of Nicaea and Chalcedon—the bishops became responsible for the defense of law and order.[34]

At the beginning of the fifth century, the laws included bishops' participation at the highest strata of the governance of the empire; often they came from those strata themselves.[35] This does not mean, however, that the influence of the bishops was always secure. The transformation of the Roman Empire into a Christian empire involved struggles and turnabouts. Constantine himself underwent changes; as mentioned earlier, after intervening in Nicaea and helping to define orthodoxy, he gradually returned to heterodox Arian beliefs. A few decades later, Emperor Julian the "Apostate" even tried to restore paganism (361–363). Theodosius I in the east (378–395) was the first emperor to be baptized at a young age. He participated in the liturgy and subjected himself to penitential discipline; he strongly sided with Christianity when he approved the destruction of pagan temples and issued decrees banning pagan cults.[36] In this mutable situation, constant negotiations were necessary. The bishops played an important role in the negotiation of the role of the church, as historian H. A. Drake puts it, as "a collection of leaders with local power bases who over the course of three centuries had developed mechanisms for working with, and against, one another, to promote mutual concerns and to present a collective authority that usually was capable of controlling the peculiarly volatile and anarchistic potential of their movement."[37] In a situation that could and would change quickly with the next emperor and sometimes within the rule of one emperor, the bishops' "power of persuasion" was critically important. The bishops' position depended on their ability to assert their role as mediators of favors: between the emperor and the church or city, and between God and the emperor.[38]

There were other ways of maintaining the influence of the church within the empire as well. Cyril of Alexandria, elected bishop in 412, closed the churches of the rival Novatians and appropriated their wealth. Moreover, his Christian mobs were "set" to plunder the Jewish quarters (which spelled the end of the Jewish community) and to stone to death the politically influential non-Christian philosopher Hypatia. The fear generated by this murder could still be felt in Alexandria two hundred years later.[39] Cyril's actions came at a time of increased power of the church. In the period of Theodosius II, from 408 to 450, bishops and clergy gained more prominence than ever before.[40] Even though pagan culture had not been completely eradicated, the fifth century was characterized by an "ideology of silence"[41] as pagan worship and customs were pushed underground.

Economics helped to solidify these growing bonds between church and empire. In the words of Orthodox scholar John Meyendorff: "The new power of the Church was, first of all, economic."[42] Beginning with Constantine, large endowments and other privileges were given to the church and the christological developments need to be seen in this light as well. While this entailed indebtedness to the empire—Theodosius II, for instance, would make it known that he might check the outstanding taxes of anyone who opposed his theological views[43]—the church would also be able to use its wealth to influence the empire. A secret memo of Bishop Cyril of Alexandria reveals his efforts to ensure that Emperor Theodosius II would approve the results of the Council of Ephesus in 431. Not able to travel to Constantinople himself, Cyril mobilized influential people in the city through connections and enormous amounts of money; 1,080 pounds of gold were distributed, enough to provide the annual stipend of thirty-eight bishops or food and clothing for a year for nineteen thousand poor people.[44] The bishops had gained the oversight of enormous wealth. No emperor could afford to ignore the bishops and Christianity anymore.[45] Once they began collaborating with the emperor, the wealth of the bishops soon exceeded the wealth of the secular holders of office.[46]

A closer look at the two ecumenical councils that resonate most strongly in the history of theology, Nicaea in 325 (the first) and Chalcedon in 451 (the fourth), helps us draw some conclusions and points us toward the relevant christological connections that are the focus of this book. The councils followed the style of imperial government in that they produced decrees and pronouncements declared binding for all. Theological debates before Constantine had not produced such creedal expressions; and even as late as the Council of Chalcedon, the production of a formula still had to be enforced by the commissioners of the emperor against the wishes of the bishops and the legates of Pope Leo.[47] In this context historian Averil Cameron's statement gains force, that "if ever there was a case of the construction of reality through text, such a case is provided by early Christianity."[48] The councils present us with examples of significant texts and we will see how they contributed to the construction of reality.

The Council of Nicaea was planned right after Constantine's victory over his coemperor Licinius in 324, which made him the sole emperor of the Roman Empire (recall that Constantine first came to power in his occupation of Rome in 312). The war against Licinius was waged in terms of the liberation of Christianity, and the purpose of the council was a celebration of the unity of the empire and an effort to reaffirm it. When seen from this perspective, Arianism was not the only reason and perhaps not even the main reason for the council—rather, Arianism was perceived more as something that could endanger the council.[49]

The speech of the emperor, in the version of Eusebius, recalls the victory over Licinius, praises the resulting unity of the empire, and addresses the theological tensions that threaten this unity: "For me," Eusebius has Constantine say, "internal division in the Church of God is graver than any war or fierce battle, and these things appear to cause more pain than secular affairs."[50] Christians of all ages can testify to the painful nature of theological battles, but a political concern was certainly not lacking. Keep in mind that these theological tensions created significant political unrest: "One bishop of one city was attacking the bishop of another, populations were rising up against one another."[51] There are no historical records of the council, but Eusebius credits the emperor with overcoming the considerable tensions among the bishops and judges the result of the council as a "second victory" over the enemies of the church, following the military victory over Licinius.[52]

Constantine's basic concern thus had to do with the unification of the Roman Empire. Constantine not only called the council but also funded the travel and expenses of the bishops, determined the agenda, and chaired the meetings. In Eusebius's assessment, the major achievement of Constantine was that he brought together one God, one church, and one empire: "He brought under his control one Roman Empire united as of old, the first to proclaim to all the monarchy of God, and by monarchy himself directing the whole of life under Roman rule."[53] The monarchy of the empire mirrors God's own monarchy. Another example of Constantine's concern for unification—Eusebius names this as a key reason for calling together the Council of Nicea, in addition to quarrels on doctrinal issues—was his effort to institute a common date for Easter in order to create further cultural cohesion.[54] Concern for unification is further expressed in Eusebius's (idealizing) report of the banquet after the Council of Nicaea, in celebration of the twentieth year of Constantine's rule, in which he sees an image of the "kingdom of Christ" with the emperor in the middle and some bishops on the same pillows, with other bishops on the pillows to both sides.[55] The political efforts of unification that undergirded the Council of Nicaea can be seen more clearly in the canons attached to the creed.[56] Geographically corresponding to the provinces of the empire, provinces of the church were established, with the bishop in the capital of the province being the superior over the other bishops within the province.[57]

At the council it was the emperor who proposed the term *homoousios* in order to establish the equality of the first and second persons of the Trinity. Nevertheless, since it represented none of the theological parties involved, the Council of Nicaea dropped out of the theological discussion for some time to come. Over a century later, the importance of the Council of Nicaea is evident when the Council of Chalcedon reaffirmed it in 451 (in the form given to it by the Council of Constantinople in 381).[58] Like Nicaea, the Council of Chalcedon was also called by a Roman emperor. After Emperor Theodosius II (who favored monophysitism) died in 450, the new Emperor Marcian called the council, even though Pope Leo the Great was not able to be present. In order to monitor this council, the emperor named nineteen lay commissioners who were supposed to oversee the proceedings and to report back to him. These men also participated in the debates and made suggestions and demands. In the meetings of the council, they were symbolically seated in the middle, with each of the two parties to their sides.[59] Emperor Marcian and his wife Pulcheria were present at the important sixth session of Chalcedon, at which 454 bishops signed the doctrinal statement of Chalcedon.[60] This council brought immediate benefits for Marcian, as he was considered a new Constantine. Nevertheless, in the long run the council was able to produce unity neither in church nor empire, and in some regards made things worse.[61]

In terms of its theological achievements, Chalcedon is generally seen as a "middle road" between two competing theological camps, and can indeed be understood as proposing a consensus that seeks to bring together Pope Leo's emphasis on the two natures of Christ in his Tome with the monistic tendencies of Cyril of Alexandria.[62] This assessment applies also to the political efforts: the political middle road was supposed to provide the needed political stability for the empire by reducing unnecessary strife and diversity. In the case of the Council of Chalcedon, however, both theological and political efforts at creating a middle road ultimately backfired—it was not until Emperor Justinian's rule in the sixth century that Chalcedon was secured as the official confession of the empire.[63] Some of the council's more immediate accomplishments that helped create imperial unity can be observed in the canons added after the creedal statement. The Emperor Marcian was worried about the anarchical spirit of monasticism, and so the Canons of Chalcedon strengthen the position of the hierarchy of the church and put the monasteries, great sources of energy and creativity in those times, under the control of the bishops. Spiritual authority was becoming fused ever more explicitly with the authority of the empire.[64] Signs of this ecclesial and political integration can also be seen in the geopolitical nature of Chalcedon's proclamations and prohibitions. Those whom the church declared heretics were physically banned from the empire.[65] Canon 28 established the position of Constantinople as the New Rome, based on a political rationale: given that the "older Rome" was granted privileges by the "Fathers" because it was the imperial city (no reference is made to Peter), so, too, the New Rome has similar privileges.[66] John Meyendorff concludes: "By its location in a suburb of the capital, by the direction given to it by the imperial commissioners throughout the proceedings, by the role played by Anatolius, the bishop of Constantinople, in drafting the final statement, and even by the recognition granted to the pope's primacy . . . , the council of Chalcedon was an 'imperial' council."[67]

Averil Cameron's judgment sums up the situation for the moment: "The spread of Christianity follows the general history of the empire."[68] What are the implications of this judgment for theological interpretation?

The Emperor's Coequality

Historical theology often deals with theological ideas in isolation. In so doing, every theological statement is taken at face value, as if theological statements are uniquely unaffected by other levels of meaning. In dealing with theological ideas on their own grounds, theologians have failed to give an account of how these ideas affect and are affected by the messiness of life. Due to the close relations between empire and church, when we deal with these ancient theologies it is not possible to determine their purely "religious" or "theological" content. This insight can be applied to other theological periods as well; discovering the connections of theology and life in the Roman Empire should prepare us to see the connections elsewhere. No theology exists outside of this connection. For our interpretation of the creeds this means that creeds cannot be reduced to purely theological statements, but neither can they be reduced to purely political statements. Reading between the lines of theological statements, we need to identify the connection of theology and life and of theology and empire. Where do we find ambivalence? Is there a surplus? Which theological claims refuse to be dictated by the demands of empire?

The kind of theology that moves mostly in the realm of ideas has often made strong statements about these ancient theologies. In contemporary theology it has become fashionable to claim, for instance, that the doctrine of the Trinity as developed in Nicaea has an antihierarchical bent. At the same time, others have claimed exactly the opposite.[69] Indeed, the egalitarian implications of the relationship of the first and second persons of the Trinity, the Father and the Son as the Nicene Creed calls them, are striking. If the first and the second person are truly *homoousios*,[70] "of the same substance," as Nicaea claims, there can be no hierarchy between "first" and "second." "We believe in one God . . . and in one Lord Jesus Christ, the Son of God, the Only-begotten from the Father, that is from the substance of the Father, God from God, light from light, true God from true God, begotten not made, consubstantial [*homoousios*] with the Father," proclaims the Nicene Creed.[71] The unity of the Father and the Son implies indeed a challenge of hierarchical relations in the Godhead, particularly as it is affirmed against those who locate the Son on a lower level.[72] Nicaea might thus present a certain challenge to the monarchical structure of the empire, but what is left open is how this challenge manifests itself in the context of the Roman Empire. At the level of ideas, this formula resists the position of the Arian party, who claimed that there was indeed a qualitative distinction between the first and the second persons, with the Son taking a lower place than the Father. This qualitative distinction was expressed both temporally ("there was once when he was not") and ontologically (the second person was "an immutable and unchangeable perfect creature of God," higher than creation, but lower than the Creator).[73] In order to protect the monotheistic faith and the absolute holiness of God, Arius and his followers claimed a hierarchy where Nicaea claimed equality. At this point we might suspect that this hierarchy had both theological and political aspects. This suspicion is confirmed, for instance, by the Arian theologian Eunomius, who made it clear that he wanted to preserve both the superiority of God and the monarchy.[74] Putting the second person at the same level as the first would introduce significant disorder and messiness not only into the Godhead but also into the monarchy.

The Council of Chalcedon goes one step further when it applies the term *homoousios* not only to the relationship of the first and the second persons of the Trinity but also to the relationship of Jesus' humanity and our humanity. Over against a school of theologians located in Alexandria, represented in different ways and different generations by Apollinaris of Laodicea and Eutyches, Chalcedon affirms the full humanity of Christ. Where Apollinaris and Eutyches construed a unity of the human and the divine in Christ that left out parts of Jesus' humanity (his soul in particular) and thus seemed to devalue the humanity of Jesus, Chalcedon claims Jesus' coequality to humanity in every aspect.[75] Likewise, against the other dominant theological school of the day, located in Antioch and represented by Theodore of Mopsuestia and his student Nestorius (most of the latter's writings were burned by Emperor Theodosius II, who had initially appointed him as patriarch of Constantinople), Chalcedon claims the inextricable relation of the human and the divine in Christ, not allowing any separation of humanity and divinity.[76] In the Chalcedonian "Definition of Faith," Christ is described as "truly God and truly man, of a rational soul and a body; consubstantial [*homoousios*] with the Father as regards his divinity, and the same consubstantial [*homoousios*] with us as regards his humanity"; this Christ is "one and the same Christ, Son, Lord, Only-begotten, acknowledged in two natures which undergo no confusion, no change, no division, no separation."[77]

Nestorius's attempt to keep Christ's divinity and humanity separate, related only in a common will, has been interpreted as supporting the empire; just as the emperor is separate from the people, so the divine is separate from the human.[78] Nevertheless, the opposite camp, represented by Apollinarian and later monophysite traditions that stressed the unity of the divine and the human in Jesus at the expense of the human, can also be accused of supporting the empire and lacking in solidarity with the common people.[79] Like Nicaea, the Chalcedonian position seems to promote some sort of equality, if not egalitarian tendencies— a surprising concept then as now, particularly when it comes to the relation of humanity and divinity.

What all these arguments miss, however, is the question of how these theological assertions operated in the context of the Roman Empire and in the church of the fourth and fifth centuries. Even though egalitarian ideas are fashionable in the twenty-first century, neither the Roman Empire nor the ancient church supported an egalitarian system. Why would the emperor and the mainline bishops want to agree with positions that promoted equality?

Peter Brown, a historian who does not claim to be a theologian, makes a key observation: "It is, perhaps, no coincidence that the first generations in which the inhabitants of the imperial capital had to face the permanent and overwhelming presence among them of a godlike autocrat were marked, in Constantinople and elsewhere, by vehement Christological debates (associated with the councils of Ephesus and Chalcedon, in 431 and 451) on the precise manner in which and, above all, on the precise extent to which God had *condescended* to join himself to human beings in the person of Christ."[80] This observation mentions the Council of Chalcedon in particular, but it leads us back to the Council of Nicaea as well and informs our theological reflections. In these ancient theologies the relation of God and humanity is characterized by condescension, whatever ideas they present regarding humanity's equal participation in the nature of Christ. All of the theologians involved in the debates around Chalcedon, whether their position is ultimately affirmed as orthodox or condemned as heretical, assume not only an infinite qualitative distinction between God and humanity but an inherent opposition and hierarchy. In terms of Christ's suffering, for instance, all affirm that only Christ's human nature suffered since the divine nature— *qua definitionem*—cannot suffer.[81] Everyone—including Arius, Athanasius, the Antiochenes, and the Alexandrians, whether pronounced heretic or orthodox—is concerned to preserve God's impassibility, God's unity, and God's integrity[82]; divine omnipotence is also part of these assumptions. One might wonder whether in this unexamined presupposition there is a parallel to preserving the equally unexamined presupposition of the integrity and power of the empire as represented by the emperor.

Brown pushes the issue further with the following provocative statement: "The central issue of the Christology of the period was how to combine fellow feeling with the exercise of absolute power."[83] In the words of Pope Leo, Christians must think of the joining of the divine and human in the person of Christ in such a way that "stooping down in compassion" does not imply a "failure of power."[84] The Acts of Chalcedon report that after Leo's Tome was read at the Council of Chalcedon the bishops cried out, "This is the faith of the fathers, this is the faith of the Apostles. So we all believe, thus the orthodox believe."[85] As historical theologians have pointed out over and over again, Chalcedon and Pope Leo sought to establish a middle ground between the warring Antiochene and Alexandrian theologians, yet the character of this middle ground becomes clearer now. There is indeed an affirmation of the equal importance of the two natures of Christ, and thus a middle ground between the two extremes—between those who played down one of the natures and those who tried to pull them apart; but the roles of the two natures remain neatly separate and are defined according to commonly accepted philosophical distinctions that reflect the hierarchical social images of the time. The divine nature of Christ is upheld in all its power and glory, and Leo is careful to safeguard its absolute power. Even the intricate theological definitions that distinguish between Christ "in two natures" (this is Leo's position and the formula adopted by the Council of Chalcedon) and Christ "from two natures" (the Alexandrian position)—which the "orthodox" Cyril of Alexandria and much of the so-called Oriental Orthodox Church ultimately rejected— do nothing to question this hierarchical understanding of the roles of humanity and divinity.

This hierarchical and oppositional understanding of humanity and divinity has implications for how political power is structured in the empire: The emperor "yielded to his bishops and to holy men because even Christ himself had yielded, to become a man like those he ruled."[86] No doubt, there is a qualitative difference between the emperor and everyone else. On the other hand, there is also a common bond in human nature that includes the emperor: "A mystical solidarity was supposed to bind the emperor, despite his godlike majesty, to all his subjects. He shared with them the common frailty of the human flesh." Still: "before the emperor, as before God, all subjects were poor."[87] In the end, the type of "yielding" in the case of the emperor is really a matter of condescension, and the flow of power from the top down is not questioned.

One of the basic theological problems that we encounter here has to do with *a priori* notions of divinity and humanity. There are particular sets of *a priori* assumptions that all parties involved share, including the extremes represented by Apollinaris on the one hand and Nestorius on the other; both seek to safeguard a set of common assumptions about God. The claim that God cannot suffer, for example, belongs to the bedrock of theological presuppositions.[88] The general philosophical underpinnings of these notions have often been observed in broad strokes—Aloys Grillmeier stands for much of mainline theology when he identifies these common assumptions as the legacy of "Hellenizing" philosophical thought.[89] Nevertheless, as we are beginning to realize, philosophical concerns may not be at the core of it all.[90] A more complex assessment that understands the concepts of the human and the divine in the context of the logic of the Roman Empire leads us to a deeper insight into the problem. Keep in mind that what has been called "Hellenization" was never a strictly philosophical process either. In Alexandria, for instance, "Hellenization"—the adaptation to Greek culture and intellect—was a matter of class, that is, a way to distinguish the upper classes from the lower Coptic culture. In this context, Clement of Alexandria and Origen did away with an earlier Christian appreciation for the knowledge lower classes produced in matters of faith as they were trying to perfect Christianity through higher cognition. The audiences for "Hellenistic" ideas are the upper classes.[91] The definitions of divinity and humanity that the Council of Chalcedon presupposes are shaped in this context. In other words, both Jesus' divinity and his humanity are modeled according to the ideals of the ruling classes. As generic as these terms may appear in the Council of Chalcedon, there is a subtext.

With this in mind, we can now go back to the Council of Nicaea. Averil Cameron's statement that "the history of Christianity could literally depend on one word, as happened at the first ecumenical council at Nicaea in AD 325," needs to be seen in this light.[92] The emphasis on the coequality (*homoousios* is this one word) of the first and the second persons of the Trinity implies a strict separation of divinity and the rest of creation—rather than the more gradual differentiation that would have been customary in Roman religions and certain pre-Nicene Christian theologies that pursued subordinationist understandings of Christ. The problem does not necessarily lie in this separation of divinity and creation but in its consequences. Virginia Burrus gives an example of one such consequence when she observes how the separation of divinity and humanity plays itself out in terms of the dualism of culture and nature. Culture is put at the level of the divine while nature is put at the level of the merely human: "With the assertion of the absolute difference of deity and the accompanying suppression of the subordinationist Logos Christologies that had prevailed in the pre-Nicene era, divine Sonship became the site for the articulation of culture's triumphant subsuming of nature. Henceforth, men were 'begotten, not made,' and the observable arts of male self-fashioning . . . came to be read as signs encoding the mysteries of a purely transcendent procreation."[93]

What is the sociopolitical context of this particular distinction between God and the rest of the world? Between the second and the fifth centuries, at a time when social differentiations between those in power and the powerless were becoming more aggravated, divine power came to be identified ever more clearly in opposition to all other forms of power. This power was located in a realm that was removed, as Brown has argued, "to a quite exceptional degree—ideally, removed totally—from the ambiguity, the criticism, the envy, and the resentment that were observed to attend the impingement on fellow human beings of mere human skill, human force, and human powers of persuasion."[94] Nevertheless, this divine power was not removed altogether but represented on earth by a small elite, headed by the emperor.[95] Brown sees this elite and the accompanying shift in the "locus of the supernatural" as closely related to the church. Church leaders and bishops played an important role in this regard; along with the emperor they mediated the supernatural. These people were expected to ameliorate the tensions of the world through the stability of the changeless divine.[96] Brown does not make any explicit connections to the Council of Nicaea, but if these dynamics are seen to be at work there as well, some of the results of the council become clearer.

While Nicaea is the product of a collaborative effort of people with differing points of view, the theology and praxis of an individual theologian helps us take a closer look at what is at stake. Athanasius develops a keen interest in the Council of Nicaea fifteen years after the council had met, at a time when it did not seem to have had much of an impact on anything.[97] Arius, whose theology had been one of the targets of the council, had already died in 335 or 336. The much younger Athanasius only begins making strong references to Arius and Nicaea in 338, after Gregory (who was to replace him as bishop) came to Alexandria. In 339 Athanasius calls Gregory an "Arian," reclaiming the usefulness of the old debate and effectively redescribing Arianism;[98] perhaps this question of usefulness should also be posed to those who emphasize the importance of the Nicene Creed today. It takes yet another decade until the term *homoousios* becomes prominent (after 350).[99] While the Council of Nicaea itself can thus not be considered as the great turning point in the history of the church, its aftermath is significant. Athanasius is the one who constructs the idea of Nicaea as ecumenical and authoritative—and he only gets to this after 350 in his *On the Council of Nicaea*. Burrus reports that Athanasius comes up with the novel idea of identifying the Nicene Creed with apostolic tradition, and he is the first to call the bishops "Fathers."[100]

Athanasius's theological interests in *theosis* or "divinization" are well known and are related to his basic concern for the full divinity of Christ, which is emphasized in Nicaea's identification of Christ as *homoousios* with the Father. Based on the assertion of Christ's divinity, Athanasius sums up the key point of divinization: the divine Christ was made man so that we can be made God.[101] This approach has certain theological advantages: the doctrine of salvation, for instance, can break free of a narrow preoccupation with original sin which has come to dominate the West after Augustine; divinization creates a real change in humanity and in the world (although not to the extent that humans actually become identical with God).[102] Nevertheless, Athanasius's approach also carries with it a strictly hierarchical understanding—like Nicaea, Athanasius draws a strict line between Creator and creation[103]—that ultimately leads to a certain devaluation of humanity. This problem is also manifest in other aspects of Athanasius's Christology, which in some instances come close to the work of the later Apollinaris, who was declared a heretic.[104] R. P. C. Hanson dubs Athanasius's Christology "Space-suit Christology"; Burrus goes one step further and describes Athanasius's Christ as an extraterrestrial alien.[105] Burrus's quote from Athanasius, *On the Incarnation*, affirms these judgments: "For . . . the Logos disguised himself by appearing in a body, that he might, as a Man, transfer men to Himself and center their senses on Himself." No doubt, there is something docetic about this statement. Not only is humanity devalued here, Christ's humanity is merely seen as a disguise. The underlying assumption about divinity is once again that it is changeless and not to be infected by material things. Athanasius shares a strong suspicion of matter and its mutability.[106]

Athanasius pays little attention to the particulars of the humanity of Christ or to Christ's life. When he talks about the human body of Christ, his main argument is that Christ assumed a human body so that we can be liberated from it.[107] Christ's divine nature, his *homoousia* with the Father, is what really matters, including his impassibility and omniscience. This particular unity of Son and Father might be interpreted in terms of a homogeneous relationship between the persons of the Trinity, especially if the human nature of Christ is not allowed to make any difference. Could this tendency toward homogeneity be a parallel to Athanasius's efforts to create unity in terms of producing an (imagined) unity of the "Fathers" at the Council of Nicaea?[108] Jaroslav Pelikan, no radical in matters of doctrinal critique, puts it bluntly: "The consensus suggested by such an exposition of 'the Nicene faith' is an illusion."[109]

Two questions need to be raised: Who benefits from this illusory unity? And, what is the christological problem? Athanasius's Christology, building on Nicaea and the *homoousios*, seems to lead to an anthropological vacuum and a realm of abstractions. Burrus raises the important question: "What can a blanket denial of human attributes possibly mean?"[110] If humanity is left undefined, something will fill in the void. The same is true for divinity, the more important concern of Athanasius. Could it be that his image of divinity is defined unconsciously by some model empire and model emperor—perhaps the Emperor Constantine himself as described by Eusebius, who also strives for unity and for the homogeneity of the empire?[111] Does the *homoousia* of Jesus and God aim at this kind of divinity? And would not this definition of divinity ultimately have to swallow up the definition of humanity as well?

During Athanasius's long career—from his election as bishop in 328 until his death in 373—the political world took many turns. Several different emperors came to power (Constantius, the successor of Constantine, was an Arian, and his successor, Julian, was a polytheist) and Athanasius's political fate shifted back and forth, being exiled several times to places as far away as Trier in what is now Germany and often for several years at a time. Burrus frames these metamorphoses by noting a reoccurring dialectic between "dirty politician" and "orthodox theologian." The "dirty politician" must not be overlooked, especially by those who would much rather discuss Athanasius's orthodox theology. After all, Athanasius was not afraid to resort to violence, and he even maintained his election by force.[112] In 335, for instance, supporters of Athanasius tried to seize the Melitian Bishop of Alexandria, Heraiscus, by force. Since they were not able to accomplish that, they beat and almost killed four Melitian monks. During this incident, Athanasius also "shut one bishop in the meat-market, a priest in the prison of the camp, and a deacon in the main prison of the city."[113] Similar descriptions can be given of some of the other leading theologians as well. Frances Young wonders in regard to Cyril, one of the later successors of Athanasius as bishop in Alexandria, "How can a man apparently be both saint and sinner—or in his case perhaps we should say, great theologian and moral blackguard?"[114] As noted above, Cyril did not prevent the Christian mobs, which were led by his guards, from exerting violence. These problems were not isolated misdemeanors, but the deliberate ways in which bishops of Alexandria maintained their power,[115] and should not be reduced to issues of personality. The question is not whether theologians like Athanasius and Cyril meant well.[116] Neither should these matters simply be seen as a cultural handicap. Even opposing and culturally differing parties like the Antiochenes and the Alexandrians were not much different from each other at this point.[117]

There are underlying theological issues here that point us back to the theological separation of divinity and humanity. Burrus comments, from a feminist perspective: "This sustained dichotomy helps structure a subjectivity that paradoxically both inscribes a sharp cosmological opposition between the human and the divine and reassigns 'divine' status to men—disowning the messes made on the earthly plane, which are swallowed up by the 'great maw' of the salvific Word."[118] Put more broadly, a quasi "divine" status is being assigned to all those who are in positions of power. By the same token, whatever happens on the "human" plane is excused as "merely human" and "fallible" and thus it can be neglected theologically. When seen from this perspective, the empire and its pressures do not need to be taken seriously and can even be embraced and used for "divine" purposes. There are very close theological parallels between Athanasius and Cyril in this regard—even the latter's critique of "Arianism" restates the arguments of the former.[119] But Young points out another, often-overlooked factor when she comments about Cyril that "like many other figures of history, he identified his standpoint with Truth, and was prepared to stop at nothing to ensure its triumph."[120] This problem is not first of all personal or cultural; it is indeed theological.

These reflections bring us back to the Council of Chalcedon. Although Cyril died before Chalcedon, his theological views shape the position of the Alexandrians at the council. There, the struggle is about the full divinity and full humanity of Jesus and, as we have seen, one of the problems with the Alexandrian theological tradition was that it did not give enough room to Jesus' humanity. Apollinaris had argued for the full divinity but had limited Jesus' humanity in such a way as to exclude his human soul; Eutyches went further along this path. While Cyril does not go to the extremes of either Apollinaris or Eutyches, both of whom were to be condemned as heretics, he has considerable sympathies with a position that tones down the human nature of Christ in favor of his divinity. We are no longer surprised to hear that the struggle around these issues was waged like a political campaign.[121]

Cyril escaped the label of heresy, in part because his christological maneuvering can be shown to be in accord with the mainline (both in terms of church and in terms of empire). In contemporary theology, Grillmeier has come to Cyril's theological rescue. He admits that Cyril sounds Apollinarian but assures us that Cyril meant well and maintained his emphasis on the "one nature" of Christ because he thought that "this was a formula sanctioned by the church." He was simply deceived by "Apollinarian forgers."[122] The ultimate problem, according to Grillmeier, has to do with the fact that his position appeared to some as "one-sidedness"; everything appears to be safe when Grillmeier can show that "Cyril occupies a position midway between Apollinaris and Nestorius."[123] This is the way most theologians now interpret the Council of Chalcedon: it all ushers into a middle road, somewhere between the heresies of Apollinaris and Nestorius and somewhere in the middle between the orthodox positions of Cyril and Pope Leo. In Grillmeier's words: Chalcedon demonstrates the "right mean between monism and dualism, the two extremes between which the history of Christology also swings."[124]

Here we must note another signature trait of empire: the middle road. Grillmeier, who has provided the standard account of these early developments, emphasizes over and over how Chalcedon comes down in the middle between the different parties. In the end, he concludes, "all the important centres of church life and all the trends of contemporary theology, Rome, Alexandria, Constantinople and Antioch have contributed towards the framing of a common expression of faith."[125] There is an interesting connection between the centers of the empire and the centers of theology: apparently the position that comes down in the middle— that covers the interest of all the smaller centers in the name of the ultimate center—is the most powerful one. Orthodoxy is, therefore, part of the mainline in the truest sense of the word. This brings to mind the famous definition of Vincent of Lérins, who described orthodoxy in just this way, as that faith which is believed "everywhere, always, by all [*ubique, semper, ab omnibus*]."[126] In Vincent's context, this argument was used against Augustine and his understanding of predestination, declared to be an innovation and deviation from the tradition. Then as now, the argument is often used in sync with the powers that be. In the aftermath of the Council of Nicaea, Athanasius followed a similar logic when he justified his position by pointing to "so many bishops in unanimity" with him who could not possibly be wrong.[127] The problem with the heretics, according to this position, was that they were too extreme, unable to find a "middle road," somehow not in touch with what the majority considered tradition and in opposition to the so-called "Fathers." Of course, there is a problem with this middle road because it is ultimately determined by the powers that be. The middle is not the most balanced place, as is commonly assumed, but the place most attuned with the status quo. As Pelikan points out: "Not everyone had equal weight in the determination of what was believed by all; priests counted for more than laymen, bishops for more than priests, synods and councils for more than individual bishops."[128]

In sum, the logic of the empire is mirrored by the logic of certain theological moves of the Councils of Nicaea and Chalcedon and the theologians who pursued the insights of those councils. Not only the content, however, but also the form matters. The push for unity and homogeneity, one of the strategies of empire, has been considered providential by many Christians, together with Roman universalism. It has often been assumed—both in the ancient world and today—that this is what made possible the transmission of the gospel. Already Origen argued that Jesus was born during the reign of Augustus for a reason; with Augustus the many kingdoms on earth were reduced to a single empire. "It would have hindered Jesus's teaching from being spread through the whole world if there had been many kingdoms."[129] Eusebius is Origen's intellectual heir, arguing that God used the empire in order to prepare the way of the gospel; what God began with Augustus he completed with Constantine.[130] From this point of view, the *Pax Romana* was created not by the Romans but by Christ, and therefore it was to be promoted by the Christian churches. A divided church meant a divided empire, and unity in faith was to be achieved through the methods of the empire, through "clear creedal formulas, understood not only by Christian theologians, but also by the Roman officials in charge of organization, procedures and financial disbursements."[131] In a context that still had pluralistic traits, homogeneity did not come naturally but had to be produced. One strategy to achieve more theological homogeneity, demonstrated by Athanasius's construction of Arianism, was to produce the illusion of a homogeneous heresy.[132]

While our focus has been mostly on the eastern parts of the Roman Empire, we should note that the church helped preserve Roman ideals and Roman universalism in the west as well, even after Rome was permanently occupied by the Goths in 476. Meyendorff concludes: "Thus, between a Roman Empire, culturally diverse, but united administratively, and a universal Christian Church, equally tolerant of cultural pluralism, but committed to territorial unity, there was a structural affinity which made their alliance even more natural."[133] But what happens to diversity as the empire continues to unite? The kinds of unity and universalism that crowd out difference are often connected to a position of power that leaves no room for those without power.

A final note: the Christian theological struggles that developed at Nicaea and Chalcedon were not obscure theological or metaphysical debates restricted to the ivory towers. These debates aroused strong public interest, as Gregory of Nyssa reports in regard to the doctrine of the Trinity.[134] This can mean various things— among others, that these debates were for some reason much more influential in shaping the public arena than modern theologians can imagine. But it can also mean that Christian theological struggles such as the Arian controversy provided the inhabitants of otherwise struggling cities where unemployment was high and poverty rampant with welcome diversions and alternative outlets for tensions. The reverse, however, has also been argued—different theological positions and alliances, in turn, could contribute to such social tensions as well. However this issue might be decided, we need to note that doctrines such as the matter of coequality were closely related to everyday concerns and real-life issues.

The Resistance Factor of Coequality

The Roman Empire had a significant impact on the formation of Christology. The theological centers of Alexandria, Antioch, Constantinople, and Rome were located in the largest cities of the Roman Empire, and what happened in the urban centers set the tone for what happened in smaller cities.[135] The crucial question now is in what sense the creeds exceed the perspective of the empire. Is there some ambivalence in how they talk about Christ that escapes being homogenized by the empire, some christological surplus that pushes in a different direction, providing different theological and political impulses? There is something about Christianity that challenges the status quo of the empire. After all, already the second-century philosopher Celsus perceived Christianity as a threat to the Roman Empire and a voice of rebellion; Christian monotheism, he claimed, would lead to the rejection of the values and gods of the wider community.[136]

Once again, the main problem is not that bishops and emperors were "political" when they developed the creeds. Being "nonpolitical" was and still is simply not an option. The question has to do with whose politics are played out and whose politics are repressed as the creeds are formulated. As we have seen, early Christianity was a socially (and theologically) diverse group that included not only the powerful but also large groups of lower-class people. While these lower classes received more attention and care from Christianity than from anyone else in the Roman Empire—the development of Christian charity set new standards—it is not clear how much influence and how much of a voice they ultimately had. Their influence might be envisioned in various ways—and here is where we need to begin our search for the christological surplus of the creeds.

Brown formulates one of the basic paradoxes: "In the name of a religion that claimed to challenge the values of the elite, upper-class Christians gained control of the lower classes of the cities."[137] This means, first of all, that the lives of upper-class Christians and the lives of the lower classes were intertwined in a special way. In early Christianity there was not as strict a separation between the classes as was customary elsewhere in the Roman Empire. This connection between the classes might have been beneficial for all but it had particular benefits for the rich because it supported their claim to power and justified their wealth.[138] The churches themselves were major landowners and employers; the Great Church at Constantinople, for instance, had separate departments that would oversee land in different regional holdings.[139] Some of this might remind the contemporary interpreter of certain strategies of what is now called "compassionate conservatism" and the faith-based welfare programs of the Bush administration, where providing charity to the poor appears to be somehow connected with efforts to link the providers of charity with the political agenda of funding sources. Once again, charity provides particular benefits for those who are better off. Nevertheless, these interconnections of rich and poor might also have had unexpected impacts on the formation of doctrine in the councils. As Peter Brown has shown, the sense of solidarity with the poor that distinguished Christianity in the third, fourth, and fifth centuries from a more general Roman sense for the civic community "challenged the rich and powerful to be aware of the sufferings of their fellow humans, as God himself had shared in human suffering." At the core is the "early

Christian sense of the joining of God and humanity in the person of Christ, and by mysterious extension, in the persons of the poor."[140] This joining of God and humanity had practical consequences that seem radical even today: the Council of Orange in 441, for instance, stated that "whoever seeks refuge in a church may not be surrendered, but must be defended out of reverence of the [holy] place." The Theodosian Code includes five laws (from 392 to 432) that support church asylum and endorses it as an existing ecclesial practice. Asylum seekers included not only people unable to pay their debts but also people accused of criminal charges.[141] At a time when we still remember the controversies around the Christian Sanctuary Movement of the 1980s and 1990s, we might be surprised to find that granting asylum in churches is an ancient practice.[142]

One of the problems of Nicaea, as we have seen, is that the unity Athanasius constructed after the fact produces a kind of homogeneity that was not realized at the council itself. The notion of *homoousios*, for instance, is not a homogeneous concept and it is commonly noted that this term, suggested by the Emperor Constantine, does not have much precision.[143] But this imprecision and the ambivalence that goes with it might turn out to be a good thing. Even a historical theologian like Grillmeier, who does not problematize Nicaean homogeneity, praises the open-endedness of the *homoousios*.[144] To him, this open-endedness signifies the faithfulness of the Nicene "Fathers" who did not take control by devising their own narrow concepts; instead, they took up an earlier baptismal creed "and inserted into it their clauses directed against Arius."[145] In the indeterminacy of the *homoousios* and the fact that the council relied on older theological resources Grillmeier even notes a certain independence from the empire. We might add to these older theological resources the rarely noted parallel to Philippians 2:6a, where Jesus is pronounced equal to God. Going beyond Grillmeier's still fairly idealistic portrayal, we might find in this indeterminacy a mark of the multitude of people who cannot easily be pressed into one form.[146]

If the *lex credendi* is indeed the *lex orandi*—that is, if what is believed is rooted in common worship[147]—we need to allow for the possibility that some aspects of the indeterminacy and ambivalence of the term *homoousios* have to do with popular worship. In this case, the piety connected to the lives and struggles of the people cannot easily be pressed into Athanasius's efforts to create homogeneity. Ambivalence and open-endedness might therefore be closely tied to the fact that the empire can never completely control the people. This ambivalence might also remind us of the diversity of the bishops, who most of the time were not in agreement either, an important fact that is suppressed in Athanasius's later accounts. Orthodoxy itself, we must note, contains tensions and ambivalences. The mistaken assumption that orthodoxy is changeless (or at least that it develops in linear and controlled fashion) and that only heresy undergoes dramatic development has prevented closer investigations of orthodoxy and its own metamorphoses.[148] Once this belief in the homogeneity of orthodoxy is challenged, the homogeneity of empire can be challenged as well and orthodoxy itself can be seen in a new and constructive light.

Here we need to rethink the ways in which we usually judge theological concepts. In regard to the *homoousios*, for instance, we tend to assume that if the term is conceptually vague and indeterminate, it must be because it is politically rather than theologically motivated. But what if the opposite is true? In the Roman Empire, the desire to give precise and unequivocal definitions seems to be pushed by those who seek control and who pursue the politics of top-down power.[149] There may be good theological reasons to keep things open and indeterminate. Even Lewis Ayres, who has produced the most recent account of the theology of Nicaea, talks about "the pluralistic nature of this original Nicene theology," which was "a fluid and diverse phenomenon, and one that kept evolving."[150] This does not necessarily mean that everything is relative. As Ayres, who is no relativist, has pointed out, while no one may have been able to say what the term *homoousios* included, the key point of the council was that everyone would have known what it excluded—in other words, the Arian position that somehow subordinated the Son to the Father: "The promulgation of *homoousios* involved a conscious *lack* of positive definition of the term."[151] In the end, Athanasius's own understanding may have been more open than is commonly realized; he later broadens his own horizons and accepts the theology of the *homoiousios* camp.[152] As we have seen, the efforts to homogenize heresy can support empire.[153] Nevertheless, a position that develops limits rather than positive guidelines also leaves some space for surplus and resistance. If orthodoxy itself is seen as a complex phenomenon that contains tensions and disagreements, it cannot be unilaterally claimed by the powers that be.

The diversity that was a fact of life in the Roman Empire and particularly in the early church might therefore be seen as a place where resistance could ferment, even though, of course, not without ambivalence.[154] Contrary to a common assumption, the history of the church is not that of initial unity that branched out into diversity later, but of a diverse and complex reality that did not easily conform to an empire seeking to inspire and enforce uniformity.[155] This diversity comprises both theological and social positions, and the open-endedness of such positions can help resist the grab for power by the few over the many. Expressed in terms of social diversity, Burrus and Lyman's reminder sums up the challenge to empire: "Perhaps the most notable characteristic of ancient Christian communities . . . is the instability and flexibility of social hierarchies, rather than their absence."[156] This is especially true in the fifth century, after the Council of Chalcedon: Chalcedonians in the later "Byzantine Commonwealth" lived next to many other Christian groups, especially Monophysites.[157] In addition, what otherwise might look like "seemingly irrational zigzags" can at times be marks of the resistance of the people to the homogeneity and universality of empire.[158]

Another way in which the Council of Nicaea's affirmation of Jesus' coequality with God challenges the Roman Empire has to do with what most likely was one of the worries of Arius. Arius's resistance to the coequality of God and Jesus appears to have had less to do with a "low Christology" (as liberal theologians have tried to understand him) than with a very high view of the unity and the holiness of God. Claiming divine coequality and putting Jesus on the same level as God would challenge both the unity and the holiness of God. Such a God would no longer be absolutely separate from and above the messiness of the world. In addition, putting Jesus on the same level as God introduces the latent threat of challenging God's impassibility and immutability and an erosion of unilateral top-down power. In this sense, Nicaea's efforts to put Jesus and God on the same level opens the door to another understanding of God—although this was probably not yet recognized by most of the Nicene "Fathers" or by the Emperor Constantine: the Arians might have been clearer about this and were thus rightly worried. This move has long-term consequences, both theological and political. The Nicene connection of Jesus and God introduces not only equality but also a messiness into the divine itself that challenges homogeneity and deconstructs conformity and notions of sameness. Once again, a homogeneous understanding of unity is questioned and with it a homogeneous understanding of power. By introducing another person into the Godhead, difference becomes part of the divine heart of reality and unilateral control is challenged.

Church historian Justo González has formulated another possible consequence, based on Jesus' life and ministry: "If a carpenter condemned to death as an outlaw, someone who had nowhere to lay his head, was declared to be 'very God of very God,' such a declaration would put in doubt the very view of God and of hierarchy on which imperial power rested." González argues that this challenge to the empire was the reason why Constantine had second thoughts and why he ordered Arius readmitted into the church.[159] In an older contribution that appears to struggle against the empire politics of the German Third Reich, a somewhat similar argument is made. Erik Peterson argues that while the empire is supported by monotheism—assuming that monotheism and monarchy are closely related—the orthodox doctrine of the Trinity poses a threat to empire. The doctrine of the Trinity, as Gregory of Nazianzus pointed out already in the fourth century, establishes a peculiar sort of monarchy that is not governed by one ruler but by a triune ruler. Since this model cannot have a parallel in nature, Peterson concludes, it cannot be claimed and therefore misused by the powers that be.[160] But there might be more to this position than Peterson realizes.

Following a similar logic as González, theologian Rowan Williams (now the Archbishop of Canterbury) claims that Nicaea pushes toward the recognition that "God is not an individual"; this means that "God's will cannot be adequately understood in the terms of self-assertion or contest for control in which so much of our usual discourse is cast."[161] Seeing God in this way—as a nonindividualistic, nonhierarchical, and differentiated community of equals—would be a significant step beyond the logic of empire, although Williams does not address this issue.

By introducing Jesus into the Godhead, Nicaea also opens the way for future questions about the immutability and impassibility of Godself—although virtually everyone at the time, whether heretic or orthodox, from Arius to Athanasius, agreed that God is impassible.[162] If Jesus did indeed suffer and die on the cross, God's own immutability and impassibility would eventually need to be reassessed.[163] Moreover, including Jesus into the Godhead as coequal (*homoousios*) challenges a kind of metaphysics that regards being, *ousia*, as static and predetermined. God's being now needs to be seen in connection with the work of Jesus Christ—Christ's life in all its complexity, divine and human, including his resistance to the powers that be, which cannot be controlled by the homogeneity of empire (and its "myths of origin"[164]). It is hardly an accident that the life of Christ is not mentioned in the creeds; such "accidents," like Freudian slips of the tongue, always point to deeper repressions (and the surpluses that spring from them). The challenge to empire posed by the life of Christ would have just been too great. Yet the subversive potential of the creeds is located precisely where they are connected to the deeper realities of Christ's particular life (in solidarity with the outcasts of his time and challenging the religious and political establishment), even if only at the levels of the unconscious. Where the creeds without particular attention to the life of

Christ are considered sufficient, on the other hand, this challenge is lost, which makes the "orthodox" position so convenient for the empire.

While the Council of Nicaea—via Athanasius—is often read as a homogenizing moment in the life of the church, the Council of Chalcedon can hardly be considered such a success. In fact, the declaration of the council led to deep divisions almost immediately after the council was over: The Alexandrians felt that the council had ceded too much ground to the Antiochenes, and later they moved further away from Chalcedon and pursued Monophysite directions, thus abandoning the two natures of Christ. The Antiochenes felt that their ideas were represented in the creed, but they were alienated by the fact that Chalcedon upheld the condemnation of Nestorius and exiled those who considered themselves Nestorian. Emperor Marcian and his successor had to use military force to keep pro-Chalcedonian bishops in office both in Alexandria and Jerusalem. After Marcian's death, resistance to Chalcedon grew so strong that the pro-Chalcedonian bishop of Alexandria was lynched.[165] Nevertheless, these theological differences and ambivalences might have a silver lining. Emperor Justinian, for instance, who like any other Christian emperor "expected to govern the church in his domain," found his match and ended up "frustrated by the religious passions of the easterns and by the inflexibility of Rome."[166] Keep in mind also that these theological differences are dynamic and not set in stone: the churches at the heart of the conflict, the Eastern Orthodox and the Oriental Orthodox churches, continue to work out their relationships to this day.[167] The current interpretations that see Chalcedon as "the height of Christian unity during the period of the early church"[168] are therefore quite misleading and may not be entirely unrelated to another power-grab in the church today.

One of the advantages of the Alexandrian position that made it into Chalcedon was that it promoted a closer relation between God and humanity than the Antiochenes' position allowed. Cyril challenged the Antiochene position, pointing out that Nestorius had made God as remote from humanity as a "Persian monarch";[169] in this case popular stereotypes of the rival powers in Iran came in handy. Such a statement would ultimately imply a critique of developments in the Roman Empire as well: the emperor should not model himself after the autocratic rule of the Persian emperors. Nestorius's approach, on the other hand, seems to have lacked that sort of a critique of the empire. According to Brown, many people of the day were yearning for a less distant emperor and a kind of closeness to the powerful "that was based on a mystique of cohesion and on a sense of solidarity."[170] Thus, the relation of divinity and humanity in Christ—including the Alexandrian view of Mary as *Theotokos*, the bearer of Godself through whom God became human—helped create a new sense of solidarity that resisted some of the most grossly hierarchical trends of the empire. There is, no doubt, a surplus to be mined here. At the same time, however, the relationship established here does not necessarily do away with all power differentials. If God in his relation to humanity is seen as "condescending" to humanity in Christ, "condescension" also becomes the model of relation between the rich and the poor.[171] This approach not only fails to explore the fuller potential of the coequality of divinity and humanity, it also keeps in place the basic relations of power on which the empire is built.

The twofold notion of coequality promoted by the Council of Chalcedon (Jesus as coequal with God and coequal with us) has its own potential for providing resistance to empire. Peter Brown notes a basic solidarity promoted by the church that appears to be connected with a certain understanding of *homoousia*: "The poor were nourished not because they were the fellow citizens of a specific city, but because they shared with great men the common bond of human flesh."[172] Jerome puts it even more strongly: "He whom we look down upon, whom we cannot bear to see, the very sight of whom causes us to vomit, is the same as we, formed with us from the self-same clay, compacted of the same elements. Whatever he suffers, we also can suffer."[173] This *homoousia* of human beings, the coequality in which Christ shares as well, is the first step to understanding a more basic equality and introduces a hybridity that reminds us of the complexities of equality. Human beings are hybrid because we do not exist in isolation, and by sharing in each other we acquire our distinctness. Of course, equality was not always the direct result of the notion of *homoousia* and the poor were often still viewed from "a great height," so that to care for the poor meant to "bow down."[174] Here, much remains to be done even today.

If we follow Chalcedon's logic that Christ was indeed both human and divine, the coequality of Christ's humanity and our humanity introduces a whole new perspective in matters of the divine. Not that the participants at Chalcedon, whether bishop or imperial lay commissioner, would have seen a need to pursue this aspect—for them humanity and divinity were given concepts that did not need to be questioned or rethought. But there is some surplus here that, if explored, pushes against the status quo, provided that the humanity in question is similar to that of Christ as reported in the Gospels—a humanity under pressure, suffering, struggling against the powers of empire.[175] This particular humanity will, no doubt, reshape commonly held notions of divinity as well. Ultimately, both humanity and divinity need to be rethought in relation to each other without absolute, *a priori* terms.[176] Can God still be thought of as impassible, for instance, if divinity is truly related to humanity? Even Pope Leo shows some affinity to what has been called "theopaschism," the suffering of the divine: "One can say that the Son of God was crucified and buried, because one understands that there is a unity of person in both natures."[177]

The coequality of humanity and divinity in Christ might also be rethought in a slightly different way, making use of categories of postcolonial theory. Virginia Burrus suggests an understanding of the two natures of Christ as hybrid.[178] This hybridity is modeled on the fragmented existence of colonialized people who combine in themselves the tensions between different identities. This hybridity is not defeatist but results in new energy and in the potential of resistance. It is in "feeling for the fracture lines, the sites of reversal, the effects of ambivalence that expose the partiality of the God-Man (and thus also of both Manhood and Godhead) and uncover not only the perverse desire for violence that sustains essential difference as difference-in-power but also the violence of desire that may productively pervert such ontologized hierarchies."[179] In other words, Jesus as fully divine and fully human "hybrid" might pose the ultimate challenge to the empire's aspiration to clear-cut definitions and essences on which its power rests.

In our own time, however, we face yet another challenge. Unlike in the early church, Chalcedon's affirmation of the coequality of our humanity with Christ's humanity does not seem to be such a big deal anymore and may therefore not do much to challenge empire. In fact, we are often led to believe that every person bears something good within and is therefore in possession of a part of the divine. On this basis is built the American Dream—and the whole notion of the "self-made man" who pulls himself up by his very own bootstraps, which supports the logic of empire. This brings to light two key problems: First of all, what is defined as "divine"? Is the divine somehow likened with the success of those in power (or other preconceived notions from the top down), or is the divine linked to the Christ who cannot easily be defined and whose power moves from the bottom up instead of from the top down? Second, how do we understand humanity and its relationship with divinity? If we understand humanity or divinity according to the private-property model (as if humans would "own" some part of God), we will not get much beyond an identity politics that closes the doors to deeper encounters with Christ and the complexity of his full humanity and full divinity. Only if we do not own the divine can divinity in Christ yet surprise us by being other than we imagine.[180]

One of the most important similarities between Nicaea and Chalcedon, particularly in terms of potential resistance against empire, is in what those councils do not do. Neither gives a precise definition of the coequality of God and Christ, and of Christ and humanity, that would resolve paradox and tension.[181] In this way, they promote some open-endedness where we might least expect it.[182] As a result, they allow those who are not served well by the status quo of empire to perceive that things are not set in stone. There is thus some room for hope that God might break in, surprise us, and change things. Nicaea and Chalcedon also display some potential for resisting empire when they set limits. As we have seen, they limit hierarchical and subordinationist frameworks of divinity that tend to mirror the structures of top-down power. This does not mean that the councils themselves flesh out and develop the alternatives, but they create space for them and thus leave room for the production of a surplus that can never be quite captured by empire.

A final note: at a time when traditional and classical Christology is often identified in terms of theories that deal with Christ's "sacrifice," reflected by the phenomenal success at the box office of the Mel Gibson movie *The Passion of Christ*, the Christologies developed by the councils of Nicaea and Chalcedon offer some relief. Whatever their shortcomings and however much they support empire, neither council canonizes theories of sacrifice and substitution.[183] Their stubborn focus on the incarnation of Christ might push us in new directions that emphasize what is life giving rather than death dealing.

Notes

1. Lewis Ayres argues that it is not certain whether the term was intended as the technical focus of the creed. *Nicaea and its Legacy: An Approach to Fourth-Century Trinitarian Theology* (New York: Oxford University Press, 2004), 93. Athanasius, in his letter "On the Decrees of Nicaea," seems to have identified the core of Nicaea in the phrase "from the *ousia* of the Father," implying *homoousios* as "necessary supplement" (ibid., 142). This is also the strategy of Athanasius's later piece "On the Councils of Ariminum and Seleucia"; ibid., 171. Nevertheless, Athanasius consciously emphasized the *homoousios* and in this case the history of effects speaks for itself.

2. See, for instance, the spirit of *Radical Christian Writings: A Reader*, ed. Andrew Bradstock and Christopher Rowland (Oxford: Blackwell, 2002), a collection of texts from

the Christian tradition that are not mainstream and have too often been ignored. The new theological effort presented by the Workgroup on Constructive Theology, *Constructive Theology: A Contemporary Approach to Classical Themes*, ed. Serene Jones and Paul Lakeland (Minneapolis: Fortress Press, 2005), also deserves mention, as it deals with traditional theological resources and themes in light of contemporary conflicts.

3. This position is represented for instance by Aloys Grillmeier, S.J., *Christ in Christian Tradition: Vol. 1, From the Apostolic Age to Chalcedon (451)*, trans. John Bowden (Atlanta: John Knox, 1975). Grillmeier puts strong weight on how Constantine understood his own role; he states that this question is "of the utmost importance for conciliar history and the history of Christian belief" (ibid., 256) . . . "in his own documents he does not claim to have directed the synod" (ibid., 260). Nevertheless, the emperor sees the need to intervene when the bishops "fail" (ibid., 259). It is Eusebius who portrays things as if Constantine were in charge. See Eusebius, *Life of Constantine*, introduction, translation, and commentary by Averil Cameron and Stuart G. Hall (Oxford: Clarendon, 1999), III.4–22, 122–31. Constantine is reported to have given the final speech and "delighted at his success" (ibid., III.22). Even some historians have tried to show that the influence of Constantine at Nicaea was not as strong as some have argued. See, for instance, Timothy Barnes, *Early Christianity and the Roman Empire* (London: Variorum, 1984). Barnes points out that Constantine did not preside at the Council of Nicaea and was technically not even a member; Ossius, his personal theological advisor, presided instead (ibid., 57). But this argument does nothing to defuse the political character of Nicaea's theology and the fact that the emperor's interests are maintained. For the empire and its theology to function smoothly, there is no need for the emperor to be physically present at all times.

4. Reductionistic accounts, whether they reduce the evidence to the sociological or to the theological, are of little help here. Nevertheless, simply leaving open room for "supplementation from other styles of investigation in the field," as Ayres proposes, will no longer do either; *Nicaea and its Legacy*, 5. While there is much to be learned from the close theological readings of Ayres (who is aware that no theology begins in the abstract [ibid., 300], but applies this insight mainly to internal issues of theology) one wonders how much deeper things would go if theology were seen as inextricably related to the dominant developments of the time.

5. Eusebius, *Life of Constantine*, I.27–28, 79–81. Eusebius also reports that Constantine observed this devotion to "the God who transcends the universe" from his father, and that this God had bestowed on his father "manifest and numerous tokens of his power" (ibid.).

6. Grillmeier proceeds assuming such limits, for instance, when he considers the interference of the emperor in the Council of Nicaea as "dangerous." *Christ in Christian Tradition*, 255. H. A. Drake discusses the classical misunderstanding of Jacob Burckhardt, who charged Constantine with "merely" being interested in politics, thus failing to discern the difference between Constantine's world and his own. *Constantine and the Bishops: The Politics of Intolerance* (Baltimore: Johns Hopkins University Press, 2000), 12–19.

7. John Meyendorff, *Imperial Unity and Christian Divisions: The Church 450–680 A.D.* (Crestwood, N.Y.: St. Vladimir's Seminary, 1989), 7.

8. Eusebius, *Life of Constantine*, IV.24, 161.

9. Virginia Burrus points out that many secular scholars of late Roman religion and culture are careful not to venture too far into "territory jealously guarded by historians of Christian doctrine." *"Begotten Not Made": Conceiving Manhood in Late Antiquity* (Stanford: Stanford University Press, 2000), 10. The theological task is what interests me.

10. Drake also exposes the common misunderstanding that the alignment of church and state was simply a result of Constantine's personal initiative, as if no other dynamics were at stake; *Constantine and the Bishops*, 24. An interesting parallel to the Indian empire of that time is drawn by Garth Fawden without claiming a direct connection; the Indian emperors were able to use their relationship to Buddhism for their own purposes; Constantine was in diplomatic contact with them. *Empire to Commonwealth: Consequences of Monotheism in Late Antiquity* (Princeton: Princeton University Press, 1993), 82–85.

11. Peter Brown, *The Rise of Western Christendom* (Malden, Mass.: Blackwell, 2003), 62. This church had developed a hierarchy with powerful and prominent leaders. Those were the people targeted in the three great persecutions of 250, 257, and 303. Christians were more and more among the influential people of the empire.

12. Jaroslav Pelikan, *Jesus Through the Centuries: His Place in the History of Culture* (New Haven: Yale University Press, 1985), 54.

13. We will encounter the struggle around the issue of investiture in the next chapter. Pelikan points out that the Western structure was falsely attributed to the emperor Constantine in a forged document of the eight century, *The Donation of Constantine;* ibid., 56.

14. Brown, *Power and Persuasion in Late Antiquity: Towards a Christian Empire* (Madison: University of Wisconsin Press, 1992), 17–19.

15. Observed by Pelikan, *Jesus*, 53.

16. Ibid.

17. Brown, *Power and Persuasion*, 4. The emphasis of Brown's book on the eastern parts of the Roman Empire is particularly appropriate for our subject. The role of the philosopher in earlier times was that of a person who had developed a certain freedom from society and who therefore could challenge the powers that be. See ibid., 62–70.

18. Ibid., 38.

19. Ibid., 45–46, explains the power of Basil of Caesarea in this way.

20. Ibid., 74.

21. Christian clergy were primarily recruited from the middle class; the major bishops were mostly upper class (Ambrose, for instance, was provincial governor but unbaptized when he was chosen as bishop of Milan); the *coloni* or slaves could not become clergy. See Meyendorff, *Imperial Unity*, 18. "The growing prestige of the church, along with political upheavals that brought the collapse of imperial structures in certain parts of the empire, contributed to making ecclesiastical office attractive to aristocrats" (Michele Renee Salzman, *The Making of a Christian Aristocracy: Social and Religious Change in the Western Roman Empire* [Cambridge, Mass.: Harvard University Press, 2002], 205). See also Claudia Rapp, *Holy Bishops in Late Antiquity: The Nature of Christian Leadership in an Age of Transition* (Berkeley: University of California Press, 2005), 199–203, 211–15.

22. Brown, *Power and Persuasion*, 74. Note also that many philosophers of the elite became bishops; ibid., 136.

23. See Virginia Burrus and Rebecca Lyman, "Shifting the Focus of History: Introduction," in Virginia Burrus, ed. *A People's History of Christianity: Vol. 2, Late Ancient Christianity* (Minneapolis: Fortress Press, 2005), 3, 4.

24. See Brown, *Power and Persuasion*, 77–78. Brown points out that before the fourth century, "love of the poor" was a fairly restricted phenomenon, not much more than care for Christians who were worse off. See also Peter Brown, *Poverty and Leadership* (Hanover, Vt.: University Press of New England, 2002).

25. See Brown, *Power and Persuasion*, 93; the numbers of the poor also increased through growing numbers of immigrants who were not only needy but also in search of groups to which to belong.

26. Claudia Rapp points out that the public donations of the classical world were mostly directed at their peers. *Holy Bishops*, 223.

27. See Brown, *Power and Persuasion*, 97. In general, the poor were seen as existing for the sake of the rich, "to offer them opportunities for beneficence or to test them," Salzman, quoting Augustine, says that God makes "the rich to come to the aid of the poor, and the poor to test the rich." *The Making of a Christian Aristocracy*, 209.

28. See Brown, *Power and Persuasion*, 98, for reference to Athanasius, *Apologia contra Arianos*, 18.30. It is noteworthy that Christian charity was extended to all, even to non-Christians. Rapp, *Holy Bishops*, 223.
29. See Brown, *Poverty and Leadership*, 30–32. Brown also notes the need to impress the emperor; ibid., 39. Athanasius himself denies the accusation; see Timothy D. Barnes, *Athanasius and Constantius: Theology and Politics in the Constantinian Empire* (Cambridge, Mass: Harvard University Press, 1993), 178.
30. "The Canons of the 318 Holy Fathers Assembled in the City of Nice, in Bithynia," in Philip Schaff and Henry Wace, eds. *Nicene and Post-Nicene Fathers of the Christian Church,* Second Series, Vol. XIV (Grand Rapids, Mich.: Wm. B. Eerdmans, 1986–89), 36.
31. "The XXX Canons of the Holy and Fourth Synods, of Chalcedon," in *Nicene and Post-Nicene Fathers*, Vol. XIV, 276.
32. Quoted in Brown, *Poverty and Leadership*, 1.
33. Brown, *Power and Persuasion*, 148; the bishops' power was limited only in matters of taxation.
34. Ibid., 125.
35. See Rapp, *Holy Bishops*, 288. One primary source describing the making of a bishop in the early fifth century can be found in Ralph W. Mathisen, *People, Personal Expression, and Social Relations in Late Antiquity*, vol. 1 (Ann Arbor: The University of Michigan Press, 2003), 164–66. What is telling is his noble birth, elite upbringing, and his prominent role in civil authority before he became a bishop; in the process, his wife becomes his sister, and his wealth is dispensed to the poor.
36. See Meyendorff, *Imperial Unity*, 7–8.
37. Drake, *Constantine and the Bishops*, 30.
38. See Rapp, *Holy Bishops*, 269.
39. There is agreement that Cyril was somehow connected to the killing of Hypatia in 415, three years after his election as bishop. Hypatia was a powerful woman and a Neoplatonist philosopher who had a strong influence over the governor. She was seized by a Christian mob, led by a lay reader of the church, which stoned her to death in front of a major church, cut her body to pieces, and burnt her. See Frances Young, *From Nicaea to Chalcedon* (Philadelphia: Fortress Press, 1983), 243–44. See also Brown, *Power and Persuasion*, 115–17. In 415 Cyril "set a Christian mob to plunder the Jewish quarter."
40. See Brown, *Power and Persuasion*, 119.
41. Ibid., 128.

42. Meyendorff, *Imperial Unity*, 13. The building of huge basilicas is one example. It should be noted that Meyendorff, no theological or historical radical, was one of "the most distinguished representatives and exponents of the Orthodox tradition in theology and historiography." Henry Chadwick, foreword, *New Perspectives on Historical Theology: Essays in Memory of John Meyendorff*, ed. Bradley Nassif (Grand Rapids, Mich.: Wm. B. Eerdmans, 1996), ix. Jaroslav Pelikan strongly endorsed Meyendorff's book *Imperial Unity*.

43. See Brown, *Power and Persuasion*, 29. Coincidentally, Theodosius's theological views were shaped by Eutyches.

44. The list also includes "24 carpets, 25 woolen tapestries, 14 hanging carpets, 24 silken veils, 18 curtains, 28 cushions, 60 stools (8 of ivory), 14 ivory high-backed thrones, 36 throne covers, 12 door hangings, and 22 tablecloths." Brown, *Power and Persuasion*, 16.

45. Karl Kautsky's comment that the property owned by the community of the church increasingly became "the property of their administrators, though not their personal property, but that of the bureaucracy as a corporation," helps to put things into perspective. See Karl Kautsky, *Foundations of Christianity* (New York: S. A. Russell, 1953), 387. Kautsky states that "the bishops were now the lords who along with the emperors ruled the Empire"; ibid., 388.

46. See Perry Anderson, *Passages from Antiquity to Feudalism* (London: NLB, 1974), 91.

47. In the words of Meyendorff, "the absence of a clear and universally accepted method for solving doctrinal controversies by the Christian Church made it inevitable that the emperors would try to devise and impose such methods, using their own approach and initiative." *Imperial Unity*, 16; see also 171.

48. Averil Cameron, *Christianity and the Rhetoric of Empire: The Development of Christian Discourse* (Berkeley: University of California Press, 1991), 21. Cameron, following perhaps too closely the theories of Michel Foucault, seems to overlook the official character and function of these particular texts. These are not generic texts.

49. Grillmeier reports that the ecclesiastical disputes between Alexander and Arius caused Constantine "sleepless nights." *Christ in Christian Tradition*, 257.

50. The speech is reported in Eusebius, *Life of Constantine*, III.12, 125–26.

51. Ibid., III.4, 123. In these attacks, says Eusebius, the quarreling parties "were all but coming to physical blows with each other."

52. Ibid., III.14, 127.

53. Ibid., II.19, 102.

54. Ibid., III.5, 123. This matter is addressed in great detail in a letter by Constantine to the churches, reproduced in ibid., III.17-20, 127–130 ("Our Saviour has passed on

the day of our liberation as one . . . and it is his purpose that his universal Church be one" [III.18]). Nevertheless, Alexandria and Rome could not agree on this. The significance of holidays for the unity of the empire can also be seen in the fact that in 321 Constantine declared Sundays to be holidays.

55. Ibid., III.15, 127. See also Hans Christof Brenneke, "Nicäa I," in *Theologische Realenzyklopädie*, ed., Gerhard Müller, vol. 24 (Berlin: Walter de Gruyter, 1994), 436.

56. Due to the later importance of the council, more canons were added over time, particularly in the east.

57. See Brenneke, "Nicäa I," 435.

58. Our knowledge of the Council of Constantinople is very fragmented; none of its acts have been preserved, not even the theological definition that followed the creed. The creed itself is only preserved in the Council of Chalcedon; see Ayres, *Nicaea and its Legacy*, 253.

59. Lionel R. Wickham, "Chalkedon," in *Theologische Realenzyklopädie*, ed. Gerhard Krause and Gerhard Müller, vol. 7 (Berlin: Walter de Gruyter, 1981), 668–69; Meyendorff credits those commissioners for ordering the procedures, which included the presentation and discussion of draft resolutions. *Imperial Unity*, 168.

60. See Meyendorff, *Imperial Unity*, 168, 178.

61. See Averil Cameron, ed., *Cambridge Ancient History, Vol. XIV: Late Antiquity, Empire and Successors, 425–600* (Cambridge, U.K.: Cambridge University Press, 2000), 44.

62. This is proposed, for instance, by Wickham, "Chalkedon," 674. See also Grillmeier, who emphasizes the middle position over and over again. *Christ in Christian Tradition*, 534–35.

63. Resistance to Chalcedon can be found in various places. In Egypt Chalcedon is mostly rejected; in Palestine and Constantinople there are substantial tensions over it. Emperor Zeno nullified the dogmatic regulations of Chalcedon in 482. Wickham, "Chalkedon," 674.

64. See Meyendorff, *Imperial Unity*, 185. See also Wickham, "Chalkedon," 673.

65. After the Nestorian community was condemned in 431, two decades before the Council of Chalcedon, the Nestorians were exiled to Persia where they worked with the local Syriac-speaking community. See Meyendorff, *Imperial Unity*, 17.

66. "The XXX Canons of the Holy and Fourth Synods, of Chalcedon," 287. See also Meyendorff, *Imperial Unity*, 183.

67. Meyendorff, *Imperial Unity*, 179. Jaroslav Pelikan points out that "more often, however, the geographical identification of a creed or confession is its political identification as well." Jaroslav Pelikan and Valerie Hotchkiss, *Creeds and Confessions of Faith*

in the Christian Tradition, Vol. 1 (New Haven: Yale University Press, 2003), 219. Nicaea and Chalcedon are in close geographical proximity to Constantinople.

68. Cameron, *Christianity and the Rhetoric of Empire*, 13.

69. For an overview of both tendencies see Rowan Williams, *Arius: Heresy and Tradition* (Grand Rapids, Mich.: Wm. B. Eerdmans, 2001), 14–15, 237. See also Meyendorff, *Imperial Unity*, 28.

70. For the history of the term, which may have initially been coined by the Gnostics, see Grillmeier, *Christ in Christian Tradition*, 269.

71. Pelikan and Hotchkiss, *Creeds*, 159. The exact phrase in Greek is *homoousion tō patri*.

72. Ayres summarizes the main thrust of Nicene theology, which includes later developments on the basis of the Nicene Creed, in terms of unity. *Nicaea and its Legacy*, 301. The common concern of pro-Nicene Trinitarian theology is "shaping our attention to the union of the irreducible persons in the simple and unitary Godhead."

73. Arius, as quoted by Athanasius, *Orations against the Arians*, Book I.5, in *The Trinitarian Controversy*, trans. William G. Rusch (Philadelphia: Fortress Press, 1980), 67. Since most of Arius's texts have been destroyed, we have to go by the references given by Athanasius and others. The second phrase, talking about the "perfect creature," is from a letter by Arius to Alexander of Alexandria; ibid., 31. The phrase "there was once when he was not" is explicitly condemned in the anathema of the Nicene Creed.

74. See Erik Peterson, *Der Monotheismus als Politisches Problem: Ein Beitrag zur Geschichte der Politischen Theologie im Imperium Romanum* (Leipzig: Jakob Hegner, 1935), 94.

75. Maurice Wiles shows that Apollinaris was the first to talk about Christ's human nature as *homoousios* with human nature. In this, he repudiates claims that Christ's human nature is *homoousios* with God but he fails to teach Christ's full human nature. He only talks about Christ's flesh, excluding his human soul. "*Homoousios Hemin*," *Journal of Theological Studies* 16 (1965): 456.

76. The translations of texts by Apollinaris, Theodore, Nestorius, and Cyril in the anthology of Christopher Norris, *The Christological Controversy* (Philadelphia: Fortress Press, 1980), give a firsthand overview of the debate. The summary given here is based on those texts.

77. Pelikan and Hotchkiss, *Creeds*, 181. The exact phrases in Greek are *homoousion tō patri* and *homoousion hēmin*.

78. See Brown, *Poverty and Leadership*, 100–01. While the emperor was expected to relate and "fraternize" with his soldiers, for instance, he did not "become" a soldier.

79. This is pointed out by ibid., 108.

80. Ibid., 155; emphasis mine.

81. See the various texts by Irenaeus, Tertullian, Origen, Athanasius, Apollinaris, and Theodore of Mopsuestia, translated in Norris, *The Christological Controversy*. This assumption is made in various ways by each of the authors on the following pages of this volume: 56, 63, 76, 90–94, 107, 122.

82. Athanasius, *Orations against the Arians*, Book I.18, may serve as an example, when he applies these principles to the Trinity as a whole: "The Christian faith knows an unmoved, perfect, constant, blessed Triad." Rusch, *The Trinitarian Controversy*, 81.

83. Brown, *Power and Persuasion*, 155.

84. Pope Leo, "The Tome of St. Leo," in *Nicene and Post-Nicene Fathers,* Vol. XIV, 255. See also Brown, *Power and Persuasion*, 155.

85. "Acts of Chalcedon, Session II," in *Nicene and Post-Nicene Fathers*, Vol. XIV, 259.

86. Brown, *Power and Persuasion*, 157.

87. Ibid., 154. Deacon Agapetus writes to the emperor Justinian: "The Emperor is honored by bearing the image of God, but the image of the [mortal] clay has been worked into this, so that he might learn that he is equal in nature to all other persons."

88. Both make sure that the divinity is kept safe: in Apollinaris Christ's humanity takes the backseat because it does not have a human mind; in Nestorius, Christ's humanity is more fully developed, but kept in neat separation. Apollinaris, "On the Union in Christ of the Body with the Godhead," argues that Christ's "body lives by the sanctification of the Godhead and not by the provision of a human soul"; Norris, *The Christological Controversy*, 106. Nestorius, in "First Sermon against the Theotokos," points out that "I divide the natures, but I unite in worship"; ibid., 130.

89. Interestingly enough, Grillmeier wants to defend Nicaea against this challenge: "Christian monotheism is preserved from Arian Hellenization." *Christ in Christian Tradition*, 267.

90. Even Rowan Williams, in his extensive reflections on Arius and his philosophical influences, admits that although Arius "belongs firmly in a post-Plotinian and post-Porphyrian world," he is "not a philosopher, and it would be a mistake to accuse him of distorting theology to serve the ends of philosophical tidiness. On the contrary: the strictly philosophical issues are of small concern." *Arius*, 230.

91. See Eduardo Hoornaert, *The Memory of the Christian People* (Maryknoll, N.Y.: Orbis, 1988), 122–23. Hoornaert argues that Irenaeus, Justin, and Tertullian had an appreciation for the knowledge of the poor.

92. Cameron, *Christianity and the Rhetoric of Empire*, 21.

93. Burrus, *Begotten Not Made*, 34.

94. Peter Brown, *The Making of Late Antiquity* (Cambridge, Mass: Harvard University Press, 1978), 12.

95. In the pagan Roman Empire, the emperor was thought to be divine; this did not change abruptly but "was integrated into a new Christian understanding of Roman society." See Meyendorff, *Imperial Unity*, 29. While pagan worship of the emperor did not continue, his person was considered "sacred in character," as among those who had direct personal access to God. On earth the emperor is the "image and agent of Christ." As Pelikan points out, it was assumed that "Christ the King had elected to exercise his sovereignty over the world through the emperor." *Jesus through the Centuries*, 54.

96. See Brown, *The Making of Late Antiquity*, 17. Brown notes that this model is older than Constantine, who appropriated it for himself. For this reason, the monks of Egypt, who were among the first to model this authority, played a more enduring role in the making of Late Antiquity than even Constantine. At any rate, "the power that came from contact with the supernatural was not for everyone to use"; ibid, 98.

97. See Burrus, *Begotten Not Made*, 15.

98. See ibid., 60–61. Athanasius was reinstated as bishop in 346. Ayres talks about Athanasius redescribing the controversies of Nicaea, beginning with his first *Orations Against the Arians*. *Nicaea and its Legacy*, 107.

99. See Barnes, *Athanasius and Constantius*, 112.

100. Burrus, *Begotten Not Made*, 63.

101. In his *Orations against the Arians*, Book I.39, Athanasius puts it like this: "Thus, not[:] being man, he later became God; but being God, he later became man, that instead he might deify us." Norris, *The Christological Controversy*, 102. See also Young, *From Nicaea to Chalcedon*, 72.

102. While theology in the West hardly dealt with this concept, in the eighteenth century John Wesley appropriated it for the Methodist movement in his reflections on sanctification.

103. "Athanasius' fundamental ideas all derive from his radical distinction between the Creator and everything created out of nothing." Young, *From Nicaea to Chalcedon*, 75.

104. Even Young admits this, although she quickly defends Athanasius in Platonist terms; ibid., 74.

105. R. P. C. Hanson, *The Search for the Christian Doctrine of God: The Arian Controversy, 318–381* (Edinburgh: T&T Clark, 1988), 448. Burrus, *Begotten Not Made*, 40–41.

106. Burrus draws out the parallels between this suppression of materiality and what, from a feminist perspective, can be interpreted as the "masculinization" of the self. *Begotten Not Made*, 45, 57.

107. Athanasius, in *Orations against the Arians*, Book III.33, argues that "if the properties of the flesh had not been reckoned to the Logos, humanity would not have been completely liberated from them." Norris, *The Christological Controversy*, 91. Young points out that references to Christ's life appear only to prove that he had taken on a human body. *From Nicaea to Chalcedon*, 74.

108. Unfortunately, there are no "acta" of the Council of Nicaea; it is fairly clear, however, that there is a high level of dissension, which is later changed to a reputation for unity, claimed by Athanasius. See Burrus, *Begotten Not Made*, 59.

109. Jaroslav Pelikan, *The Emergence of the Catholic Tradition* (Chicago: University of Chicago Press, 1971), 207.

110. Burrus, *Begotten Not Made*, 55.

111. Eusebius reports the pattern of a typical public speech by Constantine. *Life of Constantine*, IV.29. Beginning with a critique of polytheism, he would emphasize the sovereignty of the one God (and after that talk about Christ and divine judgment). Grillmeier tellingly describes Eusebius's emphasis on the unifying force of the empire: polytheism is overcome by monotheism just as polyarchy is overcome by monarchy. *Christ in Christian Tradition*, 251. In this context, the Roman monarchy represents the heavenly monarchy; Grillmeier notes that Eusebius was "obsessed with the idea of unity"; ibid., 261 n.49.

112. This is reported by Young, who is hardly a severe critic of the "Fathers." *From Nicaea to Chalcedon*, 67. She puts it like this: "He was a bit of a tyrant, and violent acts were committed in his name"; ibid., 82.

113. Barnes points out that "despite his protestations of innocence, Athanasius exercised power and protected his position in Alexandria by the systematic use of violence and intimidation." *Athanasius and Constantius*, 32.

114. Young adds that "it is clear that he gave more than tacit support to any who acted for Christianity against its two powerful religious rivals." *From Nicaea to Chalcedon*, 242, 244.

115. See Barnes, *Athanasius and Constantius*, 32–33. "If the violence of Athanasius leaves fewer traces in the surviving sources than similar behavior by later bishops of Alexandria like Theophilus, Cyril, and Dioscurus, the reason is not that he exercised power in a different way, but that he exercised it more efficiently and that he was successful in presenting himself to posterity as an innocent in power, as an honest,

sincere, and straightforward 'man of God'" (ibid., 33).

116. Young talks about the "sincerity of [Athanasius's] belief that he was safeguarding the truth of scripture"; ibid., 68.

117. Young reports that Nestorius was nicknamed "Firebrand" after burning an Arian chapel and for his persecution of heretics. After his consecration, he asked for support from the authorities: "Give me, my prince, the earth purged of heretics, and I will give you heaven as a recompense"; ibid., 234.

118. Burrus, *Begotten Not Made*, 39.

119. See Young, *From Nicaea to Chalcedon*, 245.

120. Ibid., 242.

121. Grillmeier reports that Eutyches spreads propaganda and puts up posters "to interest the people in his case." *Christ in Christian Tradition*, 527.

122. Ibid., 473–78.

123. Ibid., 480. But Grillmeier says the same thing about Chalcedon, too.

124. Ibid., 553; Grillmeier is happy to report that the actual formula of Chalcedon was worked out by a committee of twenty-three bishops, assembled with the nineteen imperial commissioners, "formed at the Emperor's pleasure"; ibid., 543.

125. Ibid., 544.

126. Vincent of Lérins, "A Commonitory," in *Nicene and Post-Nicene Fathers of the Christian Church*, ed. Philip Schaff and Henry Wace, Second Series, Vol. XI (Grand Rapids, Mich.: Wm. B. Eerdmans, 1986), II.6, 132. Vincent is concerned about "universality, antiquity, and consent"; yet he seems to understand some of the limits: consent is to "the consentient definitions and determinations of all, or at least of almost all priests and doctors."

127. See Pelikan, *The Emergence of the Catholic Tradition*, 334.

128. Ibid., 338.

129. Origen, *Contra Celsum* II.30; quoted in Garth Fowden, *Empire to Commonwealth: Consequences of Monotheism in Late Antiquity* (Princeton: Princeton University Press, 1993), 89.

130. Eusebius does not mention Augustus but summarizes the great deeds of Constantine; Constantine himself participated in the spread of the gospel when he testified "with a loud voice for all to hear, that they should know the God who is, and turn from the error of those who do not exist at all." *Life of Constantine*, I.4-6, 69. Peterson points out that this idea of Eusebius had an enormous effect historically; it can be found almost everywhere in patristic writing (for instance, in Chrysostom, Diodor, Theodoret). *Der Monotheismus*, 82. Meyendorff mentions the agreement on this

issue of Eusebius, John Chrysostom, Gregory of Nazianzus, Prudentius, Ambrose, Jerome, and Orosius. *Imperial Unity*, 30.

131. Meyendorff, *Imperial Unity*, 33. Meyendorff quotes Gregory of Nazianzus (Note 75a, *Oratio IV Contra Julianum*): "the state of the Christians and that of the Romans grew up simultaneously and Roman supremacy arose with Christ's sojourn upon earth, previous to which it had not reached monarchial perfection"; ibid., 30.

132. Lewis Ayres mentions that one of the goals of Athanasius's *Orations against the Arians* was to produce a unified heresiology that draws together a complex and wide-ranging controversy that contained many tensions under the specter of "Arianism." *Nicaea and its Legacy*, 117. Ultimately, this view was adopted, but an indication of the fabricated nature of this position was that it was not immediately ratified. Even in the 340s, few theologians shared Athanasius's presentation; see ibid., 126.

133. Meyendorff, *Imperial Unity*, 21.

134. See Gregory of Nyssa's famous remark that even shopkeepers, bakers, and bath attendants would discuss the doctrine of the Trinity in their daily conversations, referenced in Brown, *Power and Persuasion*, 89–90.

135. See ibid., 81.

136. Reference in Peterson, *Der Monotheismus*, 60-61.

137. Brown, *Power and Persuasion*, 78.

138. "Love of the poor also provided an acceptable *raison d'être* for the growing wealth of the church"; ibid., 94.

139. See *Cambridge Ancient History*, 337. Transitions in the empire create a new class, the "*colonus*," the dependent peasant tenant who is not a slave but completely dependent on the large estates. See Anderson, *Passages from Antiquity to Feudalism*, 94. Ninety percent of the rents of the church were drawn from agricultural production (ibid., 96). This is a clear sign of social polarization that is, however, less visible in the east than in the west.

140. This is the summary of his book *Poverty and Leadership*, 111–12. This sensibility is, as Brown points out, "distant music" for most of us now. Nevertheless, Brown steps out of his role as historian when he identifies the challenge of solidarity with the poor as a challenge that is still valid for us today.

141. See Rapp, *Holy Bishops*, 254, 257.

142. The Sanctuary movement supported Central American refugees by sheltering them in their churches from United States Immigration and Naturalization Service authorities. Approximately five hundred churches participated.

143. See, for instance, Wiles, "*Homoousios Hemin*," 454. Grillmeier points out Constantine's

confusions in his understanding of the first and second persons of the Trinity, and questions how much sense his *homoousios* would have made. *Christ in Christian Tradition*, 261–64. For the prehistory of the term see Ayres, *Nicaea and its Legacy*, 92–96.

144. Grillmeier, *Christ in Christian Tradition*, 270.

145. Ibid., 266.

146. For the notion of multitude as resisting empire see Michael Hardt and Antonio Negri, *Multitude: War and Democracy in the Age of Empire* (New York: Penguin, 2004).

147. This is Prosper of Aquitane's principle: "the rule of prayer should lay down the rule of faith." Pelikan makes a point that theological differences are tied to differences in worship and, we might add, to differences in popular piety as well. *Emergence of the Catholic Tradition*, 339. Pelikan's example is the notion of Mary as *Theotokos*. See also the interesting observation in Pelikan, *Creed*, 347: "the title may be said to have moved upward rather than downward."

148. Jaroslav Pelikan states: "This widely held view, that in a basic sense it is heresy rather than a changeless orthodoxy that has experienced development by a movement through time, has led to at least one lamentable by-product. As a result of it, we are in some sense far better informed by the documents of the church about the history of heresy during the first three centuries of the church than we are about the history of orthodoxy and its creeds during that same period." *Credo: Historical and Theological Guide to Creeds and Confessions of Faith in the Christian Tradition* (New Haven: Yale University Press, 2003), 21.

149. A somewhat related argument is made by Drake, who questions whether religious sincerity can be measured in terms of religious intolerance: that seems to be indeed the default assumption. See Drake, *Constantine and the Bishops*, 20–34. Drake states that "Christian use of coercion to enforce belief in the latter part of the fourth century was not the inevitable product of inherent Christian intolerance"; ibid., 27.

150. Ayres, *Nicaea and its Legacy*, 99.

151. Ibid., 90–91, emphasis in original. The two main concerns of Nicaea, according to Ayres, were that the creed could be approved by the majority, "however grudging," and to reject certain perceived errors of Arius and his supporters. See ibid., 99.

152. What matters to him is that there is a common opposition to those who see Christ as a creature. See Pelikan, *Emergence of the Catholic Tradition*, 210.

153. Burrus and Lyman note how this position can also be useful for empire: "If heresy was now made a matter of public security for the imperial church, orthodoxy thrived

less by the articulation of clarity at the center than by the proscription of error at the edges." "Shifting the Focus of History: Introduction," 21.

154. There existed a certain amount of pluralism in the empire—more so in the east, but keep in mind that "the imperial government was tolerant of cultural diversity, as long as its political authority was not challenged," Meyendorff, *Imperial Unity*, 25.

155. If it is a misunderstanding that the church was unified at first, and then branched out into diversity later, the image of the "hourglass" is more appropriate—the narrow part signifies the efforts of the Councils to create unity. See Gregory J. Riley, *One Jesus, Many Christs: How Jesus Inspired Not One True Christianity, But Many* (San Francisco: HarperSanFrancisco, 1997), 101.

156. Burrus says that ancient Christianity "may thus be seen as a broadly popular and democratizing movement." *A People's History of Christianity*, 2:22.

157. Of course, the empire did not disappear; Chalcedon's canon 28, for instance, authorized Constantinople to consecrate even bishops "as are among the barbarians." "The Canons of the 318 Holy Fathers Assembled in the City of Nice, in Bithynia," in *Nicene and Post-Nicene Fathers*, 287.

158. Fowden quotes Immanuel Wallerstein: "Universalism is a 'gift' of the powerful to the weak which confronts the latter with a double bind: to refuse the gift is to lose; to accept the gift is to lose. The only plausible reaction of the weak is neither to refuse nor to accept, or both to refuse and to accept," a course of "seemingly irrational zigzags." The reference is to nineteenth- and twentieth-century history. *Empire to Commonwealth*, 133–34.

159. Justo González, *Mañana: Christian Theology from a Hispanic Perspective* (Nashville: Abingdon, 1990), 108.

160. See Gregory of Nazianzen, "The Third Theological Oration. On the Son," *Nicene and Post-Nicene Fathers*, ed. Philip Schaff and Henry Wace, Second Series, Vol. VII (Edinburgh, Scotland: T&T Clark/Grand Rapids, Mich.: Wm. B. Eerdmans, 1989), 301. The same text can be found translated by Rusch, *The Trinitarian Controversy*, 131–32. Peterson's argument is not without problems, however. He makes use of Gregory's argument that lists three opinions of God: anarchy, polyarchy, and monarchy. According to Gregory, Christians support the idea of monarchy, yet a monarchy of a triune God, which has no parallel in nature. This lack of a parallel means that a trinitarian rule exists only in God and not in God's creatures, which makes it politically useless. As a result, the connection of Christian proclamation and the Roman Empire is severed. Peterson's argument does not seek to reclaim the political implications of trinitarian theology. There

is also a somewhat anti-Semitic strain in Peterson's argument, when he claims that the Fathers begin to realize that monotheism arose from the Hellenistic transformation of Judaism and thus is not genuinely Christian. Peterson argues against "political theology," which, he argues, can only exist in pagan or Jewish religions. See *Der Monotheismus*, 96–100.

161. Williams identifies parallels to the German church struggle in the 1930s, drawing a parallel between Barth and Athanasius; both rejected theological efforts to split up the existence of God and thus to control God. *Arius*, 267, 237–38. Of course, he also notes that such theologies are "capable of as much ideological distortion as [their] opposites" (ibid., 239). Athanasius's faith can be both a resource of resistance and the justification of "unscrupulous tactics." Ayres points out that modern notions of personhood introduce too much division into the Trinity and distort the Nicene sense of "the mysterious and incomprehensible union of the Godhead." *Nicaea and its Legacy*, 412.

162. See also González, *Mañana*, 106: "Even though perhaps unwittingly, the Council refused to accept uncritically the supposed immutability and impassibility of God, and the doctrine that it promulgated would forever remind the church of the difference between the active, living God of Scripture and the fixed 'first cause' or 'Supreme Being' of the philosophers and of much of Christian theology."

163. This has been the project of Jürgen Moltmann, *The Crucified God: The Cross of Christ as the Foundation and Criticism of Christian Theology*, trans. R. A. Wilson and John Bowden (New York: Harper and Row, 1974).

164. Arius seems to have perpetuated one of these myths in his famous claim about Christ that "there was a time when he was not" (see the reference in the previous section).

165. See *The Cambridge Ancient History*, 44.

166. Ibid., 735.

167. See Paulos Gregorios, William H. Lazareth, Nikos A. Nissiotis, eds., *Does Chalcedon Divide or Unite? Towards Convergence in Orthodox Christology* (Geneva: World Council of Churches, 1981), viii; this common statement of Orthodox churches after four unofficial consultations between 1964 and 1971 pronounces that the churches are able to "recognize in each other the one orthodox faith of the Church."

168. Mark S. G. Nestlehutt, "Chalcedonian Christology: Modern Criticism and Contemporary Ecumenism," *Journal of Ecumenical Studies* 35, no. 2 (Spring 1998): 176.

169. Brown, *Poverty and Leadership*, 103. Constantine's efforts to take over Iran—an unsuccessful venture on which he brought along a tent shaped like a church—is discussed by Fowden, *Empire to Commonwealth*, 95–96.

170. Brown, *Poverty and Leadership*, 102; Brown continues: "A sense of essential separateness of the emperor, relaxed by carefully chosen moments of accessibility, was the daily norm in Constantinople."

171. See ibid., 92; 105–06; Brown does not give his own judgment on these new kinds of relationship, yet the theologian cannot shy away from this task. Brown cautions that he does not aim at a social explanation of the christological controversies that does not respect a certain level of independence of theological thought; ibid., 107. Yet we need to push further for a relation of the social and the theological.

172. Brown, *Power and Persuasion*, 152.

173. Jerome, quoted in ibid., 153.

174. Ibid., 153.

175. As Colin Gunton has pointed out, if the heavenly Christ is separated from the earthly Christ, "who renounced the use of legions of angels," it is possible to use Christ for the purposes of empire; Gunton follows this line of argument and emphasizes Chalcedon's stance that Christ is of one substance with us as well; unfortunately, the only thing that makes Christ's humanity distinct in Gunton's account is that in it God is involved in the world in a "gracious and non-coercive way." Colin Gunton, "The Political Christ: Some Reflections on Mr. Cupitt's Thesis," *Scottish Journal of Theology* 32, no. 6 (1979): 534–36, reference to Werner Elert. This vague grasp of Christ's humanity is conveniently used by Gunton against more radical tendencies, including liberation theology.

176. Wiles's comment that no Platonic argument is necessary is helpful. If Christ is *homoousios* with us, this does not require identity or the claim that there is one essence of humanity. "*Homoousios Hemin*," 461.

177. Quoted in Meyendorff, *Imperial Unity*, 173.

178. Virginia Burrus, "Radical Orthodoxy and the Heresiological Habit: Engaging Graham Ward's Christology," in *Interpreting the Postmodern: Responses to "Radical Orthodoxy,"* ed. Rosemary Radford Ruether and Marion Grau (New York: T&T Clark, 2006), 41.

179. Ibid., 52–53. Rather than arguing for a liberal multiculturalism/multigenderism, Burrus proposes to stick with Jesus' complex masculinity.

180. In this connection a more relational model of grace might help.

181. "Both affirmations support the paradox of the God-human that preserves a tension that is difficult to maintain." Nestlehutt, *Chalcedonian Christology*, 177 (drawing on John Macquarrie's idea of a "dialectical tension"). But then he also states that "both seek to protect and preserve the divinity and the humanity of Christ." What exactly is preserved here?

182. As with Nicaea, Grillmeier points out once again that the Chalcedon formula is "in agreement with tradition." *Christ in Christian Tradition*, 544. He emphasizes the nonphilosophical character, "the formulas are carefully developed, but only in connection with an already formed tradition"; "none of them could even have given a definition of the concepts with which they had no expressed christological dogma"; ibid., 545. Grillmeier appreciates the openness. But what comes in through the back door? Not philosophy but politics.

183. When the Nicene Creed talks about salvation, it says that "for us humans and for our salvation [Christ] came down and became incarnate, became human, suffered and rose up on the third day, went up into the heavens, is coming to judge the living and the dead." Pelikan, *Creeds*, 159.

3

Resisting and Reframing the God-Human

Christology and Empire in the Middle Ages

Anselm of Canterbury's investigation of the God-human (*deus homo*) or God-become-human has become a classic. This model for thinking about Christ is among the most influential of all time. Nevertheless, already in its own medieval times did Anselm's thought prove to be ambivalent. His conception of God-become-human has often been seen as repressive and in need of being resisted and reframed in the struggle against empire. At the same time, as we will see, it can also provide resistance to empire.

The claim of Anselm of Canterbury (1033–1109) that only a God-human can restore the violated honor of God and thus effect salvation was developed in the context of medieval empire formation—the Norman conquest of England, the first Crusade, the expansion of the lands of "Latin Europe," and the extension of the power of the pope. It is commonly overlooked that all of these factors left their mark on Anselm's approach, as they left their mark on other intellectual developments. Those factors lead one to wonder whether Anselm presents us with anything but empire theology par excellence.

The history of effects points in this direction as well. Anselm's Christology has more often than not been used to shore up the status quo. This is true even for some of its popular forms today that are often deployed against "liberal" Christianity and against efforts at transforming the church. Anselm's approach has often been deployed as if any faithful Christian would need to embrace it—hiding the fact that there are various different Christologies even in the Bible itself and overlooking that Anselm himself opposed some of the classical orthodox positions, such as the "ransom theory."[1] Keep in mind, however, that those who reject Anselm do not necessarily oppose empire by default; sometimes Anselm was rejected in favor of empire. Nineteenth- and twentieth-century critics often opposed Anselm's Christology because it did not conform to the dominant assumptions of their times, as we shall see below.

This chapter will argue that, despite the entanglements with empire, the empire and its structures cannot contain the God-human. There is a christological surplus in Anselm's approach that can be located if we analyze the context of empire historically and theologically. Ultimately, God-become-human in Christ may prepare the ground for resistance. Anselm's approach might be reinterpreted, for instance, in a way that emphasizes God's powerful act of overcoming virtually insurmountable structural sin and thus produces an inspiration pushing us beyond what seems to have been Anselm's immediate goal: the restoration of the status quo.

This fresh perspective is significant not only for a deeper and clearer understanding of Anselm and the potential of his approach for his own time but also for the construction of contemporary forms of resistance against empire. Constructive theology and Christology in the twenty-first century will find some unexpected lessons in the Middle Ages.

Another Empire Theology

Some analyses of medieval theology continue to be heavily influenced by the critiques of the Protestant Reformation that saw the Middle Ages as a fall from true Christianity. Reasons for this verdict range from suspicion of scholastic rationalism and its overemphasis on human achievement to a rejection of mysticism.[2] Yet the Middle Ages, and particularly the times of Anselm of Canterbury, were times of great energy and creativity in all areas of life, and other theological orientations have long appreciated this. Anselm's currency continues to run high, even among those otherwise suspicious of medieval theology, and his christological argument has become so popular in Christian circles that it is often equated with Christology *per se* and has displaced other models.

Despite all these theological concerns for and about the Middle Ages, and despite the popularity of Anselm, there is virtually no theological reflection on the fact that the Middle Ages were once again the stage for empire. To be sure, the Christian empire was perhaps not quite as far-reaching and powerful as the Muslim empire of those times, but it was an empire nonetheless, and it expanded substantially during the time of Anselm's work—particularly during the years in which the foundations of his understanding of Christ were developed in his book *Cur Deus Homo* ("Why God [Became] Human"; hereafter referred to as *CDH*[3]). Anselm's time was a time of progress and of technological advancement; the beginnings of the use of the iron plough, of improved harnesses for horses, and of the water mill fall into this period. Other advancements include increased agricultural production, expansion of land use (for instance, through retrieval of wastelands), and a series of expansions of power and territory. For these and other reasons this period at the beginning of the second millennium is often seen as qualitatively different from the previous age. The beginnings of the economic system of feudalism can be located here.[4] This new age can further be seen in the fledgling organization of markets and credit and in the fact that the population of England, for instance, tripled between the tenth and the fourteenth century. Life expectancy rose from twenty-five years in the Roman Empire to thirty-five years in thirteenth-century England.[5] Some of this growth is reflected also in significant building projects, including the substantial expansions of the Canterbury Cathedral under Anselm.

This growth had its effects also on intellectual life, and we need to see Anselm's thinking about Christ in this perspective as well. The so-called twelfth-century renaissance, commonly dated from 1050 to 1250, produced strong intellectual and cultural activity.[6] Historians have long noted the "growing sophistication and a powerful impulse toward reason and system" expressed in administration, diplomacy, law, theology, and religious practice of the time.[7] These intellectual developments were, for the most part, in the hands of the clergy and the church since even many of the rulers were functionally illiterate. At the end of the eleventh century, the clergy had a virtual monopoly of academic training, and Anselm was at the forefront of it all.[8] Not surprisingly, the church has been considered one of the key mentors of the development of empire.[9] By the time of Anselm's death, Pope Paschal II oversaw an empire that, in the words of R. W. Southern, was "more powerful and more rapidly expanding, more loyal to its ruler and richer in resources for future development, than that which any western ruler including the ancient Roman emperors had ever commanded."[10] Southern sums up the overall spirit of the age by stating that during the time of Anselm and for the next two centuries "the West was in the grip of an urge for power and mastery to which there appeared no obvious limit."[11]

These insights urge us to reconsider the relationship of theology and empire. What does this context mean for medieval theology and for Anselm's thinking about Christ in particular? There can be no doubt that Anselm's Christology belongs among the most influential theological treatises ever written; countless interpretations of it have been produced and published through the centuries. These interpretations usually focus on Anselm's stellar philosophical achievements, his intellectual sources, his method, and the beauty and cogency of his ideas. Judging from the interpretations of Anselm, one might conclude that he was mainly a philosophical theologian who developed his thought in the protection and isolation of the proverbial ivory towers. Is it possible, however, that this seemingly free-floating approach was intertwined somehow with the structures of empire? And could this connection with empire be among the reasons for the enduring utility and extraordinary success of his model?[12]

Empire in Anselm's time was, at first sight, not a monolithic entity. Charlemagne's Franco-German Empire, dating back to the ninth century, sought to recreate the Roman Empire and called itself the Holy Roman Empire of the German Nation (*das Heilige Römische Reich deutscher Nation*).[13] This empire, in the heart of Europe, developed its own trajectories that led to subsequent clashes with the popes in Rome about whose authority was to have primacy. German Emperor Heinrich IV's famous pilgrimage to Canossa in Northern Italy in 1077, where the emperor stood barefoot for three days outside the palace of Pope Gregory VII to plead for a reversal of his excommunication, tells one part of this story. The other part is that a few years later, in 1081, the same Heinrich invaded Italy and with his army surrounded the pope at his Castel Sant'Angelo. The Germans occupied northern Italy for several years thereafter.[14] Nevertheless, despite this interruption, the popes would claim more and more authority and power in Europe and would become increasingly autonomous.

One important aspect of the history of the medieval empire, however, the so-called investiture struggle between emperor and pope about who would have the authority to institute bishops and clergy, shaped up differently in Anselm's world than in the rest of Europe. This constellation had an impact on Anselm's thinking about Christ, as we shall see. England had become part of the Norman Empire in 1066, less than three decades before Anselm was named Archbishop of Canterbury in 1093; he was only the second archbishop instituted by the Normans. After the initial conquest, Norman control over the Anglo-Saxon population encountered resistance, and its success depended on the Normans' ability to produce unity. The Norman conquerors, acutely aware that they were a small minority in England, sought to achieve unity through centralization. This was a direct attack on the

Anglo-Saxon custom of local independence; Anglo-Saxon social cohesion was produced not by centralized institutions but by common culture, language, and religious practice.[15] Immediately following the conquest, William the Conqueror distributed five thousand fiefs in order to occupy and control the country. These fiefs, contrary to practices on the continent but in line with the Norman goal of centralization, had to swear allegiance not only to their immediate lords but also to the king. In the process, the Anglo-Norman Empire became the most unified and solid domain of its time in western Europe.[16] This unification and solidification was also supported by violent acts. William the Conqueror's efforts to centralize Anglo-Saxon England reflect a strong politics of violence. In one case, he stormed a town that had offended him and ordered the right hand and right foot of every adult male inhabitant cut off. William's son, William Rufus, also applied strict discipline. He would severely punish even the smallest failings of his vassals by turning their properties over to those with more subservient minds.[17] Is there a connection of this culture of centralization and violence to Anselm's thinking about Christ, particularly to the theory of satisfaction?

In their efforts to centralize their new empire, the Norman conquerors were aware of the importance of the church. The fact that they endowed the church with lands, annuities, and other privileges shows their appreciation and reminds us of older connections of church and empire in the later Roman Empire. Anselm's income as Archbishop of Canterbury put him in the very highest class of barons, head of a "very large-scale business,"[18] as R. W. Southern has put it. Overall, one-fifth of all land in England was given to the church. In return, William expected the services of the church, primarily in terms of the production of social cohesion. In order to maintain the support of the church, William and his successors tried to keep as much control of ecclesial appointments as possible. For this reason, he sought to limit the power of the pope.[19] His son William Rufus (or William II), who was king when Anselm was archbishop, followed the course set by his father, and thus a struggle about investiture was unavoidable. In other words, although the relations of church and empire were not without tensions, the story of Anselm's investiture as Archbishop of Canterbury signals a relation of church and state that was different from the situation in the rest of Europe.

According to Anselm's own reports and the reports of his biographer Eadmer, Anselm tried to resist his institution as Archbishop of Canterbury in 1093. He only gave in after repeated efforts by King William Rufus (who was believed to be on his deathbed at the time but recovered) to press the pastoral staff in his hand, and after the bishops forced open his fist and put the staff in his hands. The reports of Anselm and Eadmer on the situation are the only ones in existence, and there are some inconsistencies in their stories. Was Anselm really as opposed to becoming archbishop as he says? Even after this event, Anselm could have backed out of the office, but he did not do so. Why did the majority of the monks at Bec not support Anselm's move to Canterbury? Why did they seem to have a different sense about his ambitions? Southern asserts that "our interpretation of [Anselm's] motives and the trustworthiness of his explanations must depend on our judgment of his character and aims as a whole."[20] But this argument misses the point. The primary question is not whether Anselm did or did not want to become archbishop and how he felt about the position. What is of interest is whether or not Anselm accepted the call, and on what terms. As we know, Anselm did accept, but the terms of his acceptance are noteworthy. He was instituted not by the required election of an ecclesiastical body but by the personal wishes of the Norman king William Rufus. There is no record that Anselm ever questioned the unusual process of his investiture. In addition, Anselm failed to challenge his investiture by the king, even though the Lateran Council of 1078 had clearly condemned such practice. According to Southern, Anselm did not take any steps to become acquainted with this ruling, and Southern claims that he had not been aware of it during his fifteen years as abbot at Bec (1078–1093).[21] These compounded irregularities are surprising and should not be explained away by arguments about Anselm's personal character. Something more is at stake here.

While Anselm's response to the king's call is indeed an expression of his ideas of freedom and obedience, which include his monastic renunciation of self-will,[22] the question is, Whose call did Anselm think he had to follow? Whatever call Anselm ended up following, he would have seen it ultimately as the call of God. Even if we give him the benefit of a doubt that he indeed failed to realize that the pope in Rome had some sort of call on him and that he simply forgot about the requirement of an election by the church, why would Anselm see the king's call as God's call and reject the call of his community at Bec, which wanted to have him back? This deeper problem raises the question of Anselm's fundamental allegiance, which is closely related to Anselm's interpretation of Christ.

Sally Vaughn puts things in a somewhat different light and thus helps us understand better those allegiances. She notes that Anselm's reported humility regarding his vocation as bishop followed centuries-old customs: even late Roman emperors "routinely protested their accessions on the grounds of humility."[23]

Anselm's emphasis on his resistance to the office has also to do with the public image that he wanted to project—specifically, that he was not after the riches of Canterbury, which happened to be the wealthiest and most powerful bishopric in the Anglo-Norman world.[24] The argument that Anselm was unaware of the problem of lay investiture by the king is difficult to maintain. Already at his investiture as abbot of Bec in 1079, Anselm must have noted some problems with lay investiture.[25] Vaughn affirms the suspicion that "Anselm's personal inclinations are quite beside the point." What matters, even in his own mind, is obedience to God and—we must add from a theological perspective—how he perceives the character of God. In his reply to the monks of Bec Anselm writes that he could not refuse to accept God's call. "Thus," Vaughn concludes, "if one asks if Anselm sought the archbishopric as an act of submission to God's plan, the answer is clearly yes."[26] Ultimately, Anselm interprets the various elements of his calling as proof of God's will. The physical coercion by the bishops and the order of the Norman authorities embodied by the king are important signs to him. He even seems to interpret the unanimous acclamation of clergy and people present as some sort of election.[27] The crucial point to be noted here is that in all this Anselm makes a clear and unmistakable choice as to where he finds God: God is most clearly manifest at the top of society, with the highest powers that be. Thus, he follows the call of the king rather than the call of his monastery. As a result, God is seen in Anselm's theology from the top down, as ruler par excellence in a hierarchy in which Anselm takes his place. His thinking about Christ will no doubt have to engage this fundamental presupposition.

Even as Anselm accepts the divine call from the top levels of society, however, it should be noted that Anselm's relationship with the English kings, first with William Rufus and later with Henry I, was by no means always smooth and without tensions. Anselm even went into exile twice (to Rome, in 1098 and again 1103), protesting these kings. But none of these tensions call into question his basic allegiance to the Norman Empire. Anselm did put up a fight when the kings encroached on the status and property of the church, and he could indeed be critical of them. Yet some of the quarrels between king and archbishop are not unusual for the time and do not imply a fundamental critique of the feudal order; rather, they presuppose it: the king needed revenues and wanted to preserve the status quo, and the archbishop needed to protect and expand his own influence, often by ensuring that the economic foundation of the church would not be eroded.[28]

At first, the relationship of Anselm and King William Rufus was characterized by struggles. From 1095 to 1097, however, the time when he began writing *Cur Deus Homo*, Anselm worked in support of the king and was able to establish his primacy over all of Britain.[29] Anselm saw his own position in geographically expansive terms, as "Archbishop of Canterbury and Primate of All England, Scotland, Ireland and the Adjacent Isles" or, in the words of his student Eadmer, as "pope of another world." Apparently Pope Urban II had welcomed Anselm upon his arrival in Rome in 1098 with just these words, as "equal" and "the apostle and patriarch of another world."[30] Anselm did not fail to make use of the expansions of the Norman Empire, expanding his ecclesial jurisdiction into Scotland, Wales, and even Ireland. In this context, the empire and the church went hand in hand, as "the way for ecclesiastical expansion was prepared by conquest or marriage."[31] What Anselm resisted was the king's interference with this expansion, and the king's claim of the church's land and its other prerogatives. In these situations Anselm held recourse to the "law of God."[32]

The relationship between Anselm and King Henry I, who followed William Rufus in 1100, was closer and more congenial after some initial quarrels. Henry and Anselm collaborated substantially. Henry granted more room to Anselm, including the freedom to call a church council. Nevertheless, a three-sided struggle emerged. The pope rejected lay investiture and homage, the king defended his ancestral rights, and the archbishop sought to strengthen Canterbury.[33] The centralizing moves of the Norman rulers were matched by centralizing moves in Rome that were most forcefully expressed by Gregory VII (pope from 1073 to 1085). Gregory's "Dictates" state, among other things, that the pope alone can instate and depose bishops, has the power to depose emperors, is judged by nobody, and may use the imperial insignia.[34] This strong position of the pope initiated the investiture struggles in Europe.

The English church under Anselm never pushed things to the same degree. In fact, Anselm's position on investiture is somewhat unclear and has been interpreted in opposite ways. Some interpreters see him as fighting for the independence from the crown.[35] Southern, on the other hand, argues that Anselm was not worried much about his own investiture by King William Rufus. Only later, after he had attended the Roman synod of 1099 where clerical homage and lay investiture were condemned, did he reject King Henry's request to be invested by him and to pay homage. In the resulting quarrel, Pope Paschal II dropped the issue of clerical homage, and King Henry, pressured by a Norman war, agreed to abandon lay investiture in 1105. Anselm eventually did pay homage to the king.[36] According to C. Warren Hollister, "Anselm, who never expressed any personal concern about lay investiture, was caught in the middle" between king and pope.[37] Eventually, Anselm related to Rome in a way that can be characterized by "respectful but strictly limited subordination—obedience from a distance."[38]

Anselm is often mistaken for an otherworldly churchman who did not care much about politics and public images, an interpretation with serious consequences for the interpretation of his Christology. This image can no longer be maintained. Sally Vaughn points out the political savvy of Anselm and his talent for creating a public image.[39] Already as abbot of Bec in France, Anselm was responsible for large land-holdings that extended all the way to England and showed his ability to relate to wealthy benefactors[40]—many of whom had become wealthy through the conquest and settlement of England—and to others in power, and his influence led to the expansion of Bec's property, fame, and number of monks. Under Anselm, Bec produced numerous influential leaders of the church.[41] As archbishop, his responsibilities were even larger. Anselm's networks throughout Europe, constantly expanding during his rule as archbishop, must not be overlooked. Vaughn summarizes Anselm's influence thus: "He advised many of the crowned heads of Europe and the Crusader states, lay and ecclesiastical, in person and in letters, as well as their lay and clerical magnates and aristocracies."[42]

Politically, Anselm saw king and archbishop as "corulers of the Christian realm" and pointed out how in England the "plow is drawn by two oxen outstanding above the rest."[43] Interestingly enough, there was a sense of equality, if only at the highest level of the empire, and this can be seen as a critique of the traditional claim of the Norman kings to be corulers with God.[44] Anselm had to defend his position in England against the kings' expectation of "divinely sanctioned kingship responsible for ruling over the church."[45] In Anselm's perspective, the king was not lord of the church; rather, the king was the protector, the advocate of the church.[46] Since the time of Charlemagne, European kings considered themselves divinely instituted. In this context, Anselm did in fact limit the reach of the empire: "Despite the prevailing opinion around him, Anselm maintained that kings were merely mortal beings."[47] Nevertheless, Anselm's perspective is also different from the two-swords theory, where the spiritual sword is higher, as expressed by Pope Gregory VII. Perhaps this would not have been possible in the Norman Empire to begin with, since the king did not even appreciate Anselm's notion of equality of king and archbishop.[48] Thus, Anselm's struggle can be seen as a struggle for the freedom of the church within the limits of his own context, and as thus furthering the "sacerdotal element in society," which became more important and powerful around 1100.[49]

Despite Anselm's emphasis on equality of archbishop and king, we must not overlook the growing power of the church in the Middle Ages. Anselm was at the beginning of the development described by Southern in the following words: "From the papal summit down to the holders of parochial benefices, the clergy became a force capable of laying down and imposing on the world at large the fundamental rules, not only of ecclesiastical discipline, but also of lay behaviour," all the way to the "provision of armed force to combat external or internal enemies of the faith."[50] Anselm did indeed command and camp out with his troops in defense of England against invasion and rebellion in 1095 and 1101 as part of his feudal dues to the king. Yet while the archbishop would on occasion assume a military role in the king's defense, the king would also participate in church councils.[51] In Anselm's times the secular and the sacred cannot easily be separated. While the secular is represented by the king and the sacred by the archbishop, there is considerable overlap. As in the earlier periods discussed in previous chapters, our modern conceptual distinctions of religion and politics do not apply here. Ultimately, both king and archbishop would have understood these collaborations as furthering the divine will.

From the perspective of the empire, the role of the church needs to be seen first of all in its ability to provide stability—another clue for reconsidering Anselm's thinking about Christ. Southern sums it up: "Despite all its violence and the rapidity of its changing face it was reasonable to think of society as stable, for the growth of wealth on the whole increased the well-being of the traditional rulers of society." The church played perhaps the most significant role in producing this stability: "The intellectual predominance of the clergy and the success of their scholastic procedure in solving practical and theoretical problems gave unity to the creations of the age."[52] In other words, the church holds the empire together and produces cohesion and unity. And this unity is seen in terms of discipline, obedience, and uniformity. While this has been considered to be one of the main contributions of the Middle Ages, we have noted earlier efforts at producing this sort of unity already in the context of the earliest ecumenical creeds. Southern, leaving his usual role of objective historian for one brief moment, realizes a problem, which we will need to address in the next part: "Perhaps it was a great mistake."[53]

128

In conclusion, let me repeat that any problems that we might identify here must not be judged at the level of Anselm's personality or as moral failures. Anselm led, according to most historians, an exemplary life above reproach. He could not be manipulated easily on the personal level. Vaughn mentions "Anselm's total immunity to the attractions of personal wealth and power."[54] This made him indeed dangerous to the king, but the question pursued in this book is a different one and goes deeper: How do Anselm's theology, his thinking about Christ, and his most fundamental allegiance relate to empire?

The God-Man of the Empire

This broader context of empire in which *Cur Deus Homo* was written continues to be overlooked by interpreters addressing Anselm's theological thinking.[55] A closer look at *CDH* in terms of its context thus charts new ground and will help us realize the broader interconnections of theology and empire, in Anselm's time and beyond. The purpose, as before, is not to reduce theology to context but to grasp where theology is beholden by it and to find out where its constructive potential pushes beyond it. *CDH*, begun between 1094 and 1097 and finished in 1098, was written during Anselm's tenure as Archbishop of Canterbury. This setting proved to be very different from the monastic setting in which he wrote his earlier works, the *Monologion* and the *Proslogion*. In the words of Southern: "After thirty years of peaceful monastic development, when all his problems arose within himself and the religious community, he was to have another twenty in which nearly all his problems came from sources outside the main stream of monastic life."[56] While Anselm's years as an abbot cannot have been as peaceful and inwardly focused as Southern describes it, *CDH* was indeed written during one of the most politically active times of Anselm's life. How does this intensified political involvement relate to the project?

The basic question at the beginning of *CDH* is posed by people whom Anselm calls "unbelievers," no doubt located somewhere at the other end of the spectrum of the questions the monastic community raised. These people have a clear agenda, here formulated by Boso, one of Anselm's students and his dialogue partner in *CDH*: "Unbelievers, deriding us for our simplicity, object that we are inflicting injury and insult on God when we assert that he descended into a woman's womb; was born of a woman; grew up nurtured on milk and human food and—to say nothing of other things which do not seem suitable for God—was subject to weariness, hunger, thirst, scourging, crucifixion between thieves, and death"

(*CDH* I, 3, 268). It seems as if the traditional Christian images of the incarnation, life, suffering, and death of Christ endanger the established classical notions of the immutability, impassibility, and omnipotence of God. Do those images point to weaknesses of the Christian God, and perhaps even to the weakness of the Christian empire? No wonder that Boso, speaking for the "unbelievers," demands "a cogent reason which proves that God ought to have, or could have, humbled himself for the purposes which we proclaim" (*CDH* I, 4, 269). Anselm's response quickly provides this reason, arguing that God had a plan for humanity and that this plan cannot be voided: "The human race, clearly his most precious piece of workmanship, had been completely ruined; it was not fitting that what God had planned for mankind should be utterly nullified, and the plan in question could not be brought into effect unless the human race were set free by its Creator in person" (*CDH* I, 4, 269). With this response, Anselm puts control firmly back into the hands of God. At the heart of *CDH* is, therefore, the defense of God as omnipotent ruler, an image of God that is assumed by Christians and non-Christians alike. After all, neither God's existence nor the general attributes of theism are called into question by these mysterious "unbelievers." The key challenge posed by the non-Christians is that a God who has no alternative ways of acting seems powerless (*CDH* I, 6, 271). In response, Anselm goes on to defend the power of the Christian God, emphasizing that God is in charge and that there are good and valid reasons for doing what God does in Christ.

The problem is, according to the non-Christian critics, that the "beautiful notions" of the Christian tradition that talk about the incarnation and the death of Christ are "like pictures," and are not proof in and of themselves. "If there is nothing solid underlying them," worries Boso, Christianity will be a failure in the eyes of those challengers (*CDH* I, 4, 269). In addition, the challenge is raised that a God who goes through such an ordeal could not be considered wise or just if there were an easier way (*CDH* I, 6, 271; *CDH* I, 8, 275). Responding to those concerns, Anselm tries to show that there is nothing "more logical" or more rational (*nihil rationabilius*)[57] than the Christian faith and that God's response to the problem is "fitting."[58] Without ever straying too far from the Christian tradition, Anselm's argument proceeds by "unavoidable logical steps" even "supposing Christ were left out of the case" (*remoto Christo*) in order to address the concern of the non-Christian critics that the Christian faith "militates against reason" (*CDH*, preface, 261).

Unfortunately, even the most prominent interpreters of Anselm see the ensuing challenge mainly on the level of ideas. Anselm is reacting, it is assumed, to the ideas of certain Jewish rabbis from Germany who had newly arrived in London and to the fact that some Christians were being converted to Judaism. The theological challenge emanating in this context is considered to be straightforward and has to do with a defense of the Christian God's stability and unchangeability, ultimately forcing Christian theologians to prove the necessity of the incarnation, not merely the possibility.[59] But how does that challenge relate to the situation of the Jews in the emerging Norman Empire, and what, if anything, does this situation have to do with the substance of the argument in *CDH*?

The argument thus far raises at least two noteworthy questions that have a bearing on Anselm's Christology. Who are those non-Christians?[60] And what is the role of Anselm's claim to prove matters by reason and fittingness? At the end of the argument, Boso concludes that Anselm was able to show that "it is a matter of necessity for God to become man," that it is "logical and incontrovertible," and that it would "satisfy not only Jews, but even pagans" (*CDH* II, 22, 355). At this point, the seemingly purely theoretical realm of theological discourse begins to reveal some of its underlying motivations, mostly repressed from later discussions of *CDH*. "Jews" and "pagans" occupy an important place and might be seen at the heart of Anselm's argument. This comes as a surprise because Jews in Europe have mostly been repressed, not only by society but also by theological discourse. The reference to "pagans" that inhabit the theological unconscious of Anselm's mind points to another entity that poses a more visible threat but is repressed as well: the Muslim Empire. That Anselm would be so concerned by their questions as to compose a response is noteworthy and cannot be explained entirely by the arrival of a few foreign Jewish theologians. Is there a more sublime problem here, given the fact that these questions are so powerful and that the central question of *CDH* is raised by these "unbelievers"?

The theological problem faced by Anselm is inextricably tied to the political and economic fluctuations of empire; the situation of the Jews is ultimately produced by it. Economic developments of the times resulted in Jewish migrations to various urban areas of the Norman Empire, even though within the empire the situation of the Jews was often marked by ghettoization and persecution. Some of the more systematic persecutions of Jews had their beginnings at this time.[61] Eventually the Jews were expelled from England in 1290, but until that time they "served all sorts of theological, political, social, and economic purposes, being alternately commended or condemned according to the interests of their observers," as Sylvia Tomasch has argued. Tomasch also points out that while the Jews had to be removed for security reasons, they were needed "for the sake of self-definition." Indeed, even after the expulsion, images of Jews played a significant role in British culture.[62] In this context, Anselm's concerns cannot be limited to the questions of a few individual Jewish theologians. These Jewish developments are also related to the European encounters with Muslims during the Crusades, resulting in a new perception of alliances between Jews and Muslims against Christianity. These "others" are therefore an important factor in the development of the identity of the Norman Empire and its theology. The flip side of these observations is that even in the Middle Ages Christian identity is not as monolithic or as secure in itself as is commonly assumed, especially by those who would like to project a Christian Golden Age in the past, before the disruptions of the Reformation and the Enlightenment. Christian identity in the Middle Ages is, like any other imperial identity, constructed in relation to others and often on their backs.[63]

Anselm, it seems, develops his own way of dealing with a perceived Jewish threat in Europe. He does not encourage the persecution of Jewish people; he engages them in a philosophical argument instead. It is noteworthy that he appears to win his case—thus defusing the threat—simply by means of logic, reason, and the reference to what is "fitting." The form of "interreligious dialogue" in which Anselm engages appears to be peaceful for the most part and even resembles certain recent forms of dialogue: on the basis of some common assumptions about God, the conversation can proceed by way of logic and reason. Nevertheless, by taking for granted that one side has the superior logical arguments—an assumption confirmed by the fact that there does not seem to be a need to double-check what happens when these arguments reach their target—a clear asymmetry of power is expressed; the outcome of the dialogue is far from uncertain. Despite appearances, and despite the initial impression that Anselm is facing a tough challenge and a set of difficult questions, this is not really a *dia*logue, that is, an exchange between two equal partners.

The Muslim question has its own dynamics. Two major points of connection with the Muslim world exist at the time of the writing of *CDH*, both having to do in their own ways with the substantial power and authority of the Muslim Empire, the first one being political and the second intellectual. The first point of connection is related to the first Crusade in the year 1095, and it is probably no accident that many of the persecutions of the Jews began with the Crusades as well.[64] Among the reasons given for the Crusade were tensions in the Muslim nations, expressed in popular hostilities toward Christians, even though those incidents were likely not as severe as those who supported the Crusades made them look.[65] Nonetheless, the Christian Empire responded to the perceived threats from both Jews and Muslims with violence. Other motives for the Crusade, openly expressed by Pope Urban II, had to do with the expansion of the Christian Empire. Europe felt a lack of space and sought relief by reclaiming Jerusalem—seen as the center of the world and the place "flowing with milk and honey." As a result, the two empires of the day—one Muslim, the other Christian—clashed in a power struggle. To those who went on the Crusade, salvation was promised, thus placing in close proximity the notions of spiritual salvation and the salvation of empire.[66] The first Crusade took place from 1095 to 1099. Thirty thousand knights plus another thirty thousand participants were mobilized. In 1099 they marched into Jerusalem and spared few people, not even women and children; it has been estimated that sixty to seventy thousand people were killed.[67] Nevertheless, unlike the Pope, Anselm did not support the Crusades.[68] Anselm seems to have no particular use for the violence promoted by the Crusades, even though he would later advise some of the leaders of the states the Crusaders established.

In light of these observations we begin to suspect that there are deeper reasons for Anselm's approach in *CDH*. Perhaps Anselm does not really need the Crusades because he has developed a better and perhaps more effective way of dealing with those whom he calls "pagans" and with the Muslim threat to the Christian Empire. Anselm's intellectual work in *CDH*, using the concepts of logic, reason, and fittingness, convinced of their superiority and universality, helps to solve not only the Jewish but also the Muslim problem. Keeping in mind the underlying power struggles between the Muslim and the Christian world, it should be clear that Anselm is not engaging in harmless apologetics or "interreligious dialogue" at the level of ideas alone. He achieves by intellectual means what the Crusades achieve only through fire and sword, a victory over the Muslims and the Jews.

This observation is supported by Anselm's response to the second point of connection with the Muslim world, which is a cultural and philosophical one. The Christians were sorely aware that they had only recently discovered Aristotle, while the Muslims and the Jews had known him much longer. In this awkward situation, the Christians needed to prove themselves philosophically superior and victorious, and Anselm seeks to achieve just that. Georg Plasger is right that Anselm's concern here is not primarily the conversion of unbelievers but amounts to a demonstration of the reasonableness of the Christian faith.[69] But there are broader implications. This demonstration of reason is located not just at the level of ideas.

Anselm's argument, as far as Muslims and Jews are concerned, is a demonstration of power *qua* logic and reason—thus his concern with "fittingness."[70] The "fitting" or commonsense arguments that he proposes are in fact based on the common sense of the Christian Empire and work best in the shadows of its power. While the Crusades may not be directly necessary for the theologian and philosopher, they too help make his point about the power of God that seems to be challenged by God-become-human. Anselm makes it clear beyond a doubt that Christians do not proclaim a God who is weak or powerless, even though things might look that way on the surface. While the frame of the argument is thus set, the argument can proceed in a seemingly autonomous conceptual space. If it seems that in the process of the argument the unbelievers are somehow "repressed," we need to keep in mind that what is repressed is precisely what calls the shots and provides the basic direction, as Sigmund Freud has argued for the psyche and Jacques Lacan has shown for interhuman and sociopolitical relations.

Keeping in mind these encounters with Jews and Muslims, we can now go back to the main concern of *CDH*. Ultimately, the theological question is how Christology shapes up in light of God's power. How can ideas like the immutability and omnipotence of God—taken for granted in both the Christian and the Muslim Empires—be related to the lowliness of Jesus Christ in his incarnation and death? Anselm's goal is to defend the power and omnipotence of God in light of those who ask astute questions about Christ's lowliness and suffering and who wonder with good reason what light this would throw on Godself. Once this defense is achieved, the message can be projected thus: the Christian God is not powerless and mutable after all. Moreover, the Christian God is in control, and everything works according to God's superior intent and plan. In view of the Christian Empire, it seems to be tacitly assumed that if the Christian God is in control, so are we. In the process, theological and philosophical reason combine to shore up the Christian Empire. This becomes even clearer when one realizes that Anselm never uses reason to challenge empire. The Christian Empire of his day is not questioned by the faculty of reason but rather is presupposed by it. Unlike the logic of the God-human, the logic of the empire—like the logic of God as immutable, impassible, and omnipotent—does not have to be argued or proven. Reason (if only unconsciously) presupposes the superiority and power of the empire, just as it presupposes the superiority and power of God, and can rest secure on this basis.

Anselm's use of logic and reason is thus based on the assumption of the similarity of God's power and the power of the empire. The development of his argument shows these assumptions and points us toward the connection of God and empire. In order to illustrate the necessity of God's work in Christ, Anselm introduces the term of God's honor (Lat.: *honor*). God had to become human in Christ and die on the cross, Anselm argues, because God's honor has been violated by human sin.[71] Only through Christ's death on the cross can this honor be restored. Theologians have often overlooked the fact that this argument makes very little sense apart from the logic of empire. Without an understanding of the logic of the Norman Empire and the importance of the notion of honor in this particular context, God appears either as a sadist or masochist as God either takes pleasure in killing another or in killing part of Godself. Without taking into account the logic of empire, the question must be raised (as it has been, seemingly innumerable times), Why could God not simply swallow God's pride and forget the whole thing? God's power appears to be arbitrary and that of a tyrant.[72]

The usual defense of theology seeking to make sense of the question of God's honor is to point to certain philosophical commitments of Anselm, and possibly some legal ones, too. But Anselm does not seem to be heavily concerned about legal issues; he was not even concerned much about canon law when he was Archbishop of Canterbury.[73] Neither does the notion of God's honor seem to be shaped by general philosophical questions. Going beyond legal and philosophical matters, cultural issues have been introduced into the discussion of the background of Anselm's use of the term *honor*.[74] Only if we rethink the question of power, however, will we get to a deeper understanding of what is at stake. The role of empire is not accidental to *CDH*; the empire provides the context for Anselm's Christology like water provides the context for fish.

Hermann Cremer in the nineteenth century was the first to claim that Anselm's interpretation is shaped by Germanic conceptions of law.[75] This insight gives us a first clue about the relation of Anselm's logic to empire. Others, like Adolf von Harnack and Albrecht Ritschl rejected this theory and promptly hit an impasse: Anselm's theory simply makes no sense if God is portrayed as a powerful individual or "private person" (*Privatmann*) who gets angry simply because of an insult.[76] A recent interpreter, David Brown, seriously misunderstands the matter when he assumes that Harnack set the course that must be followed if one wants to understand Anselm in terms of his feudal context.[77] In Harnack's reading there is a serious problem with God because God appears to be arbitrary or at least narrow-minded. Cremer, therefore, realized something of importance: we need to understand Anselm's image of God in relation to his broader world. Going beyond Cremer, however, we need to address the fact that these assumptions are specifically Norman rather than generically "Germanic."[78] As we have seen earlier, in the Norman Empire the issue of homage to the king was a central matter in Anselm's political existence as archbishop.[79] This is where the matter of honor is located: honor is based on the interpersonal relation between lord and vassal, and everything else in the empire finds its place in relation to this order (*ordo*). Honor is about this relationship, and if it is violated, the order of the universe breaks down. This relationship and order is, therefore, what is at stake, for it is impossible that God's personal honor should be taken away, says Anselm.[80] The term *order* occurs frequently in *CDH*, and sometimes it is translated by different terms in English, including "station in life," an expression that shows the relational but also hierarchical qualities of the term.[81] This order, based on the relation of ruler and ruled, guarantees stability and welfare. Peace, justice, and the unity of the empire rest on the maintaining of this order.

The whole system is thus based on the recognition of the honor and status of each member. At stake is not personal honor or outward appearances but one's place in society—what we might call the "ontology of the empire."[82] Nothing is worse in matters of universal order than "that a creature should take away from the Creator the honour due to him," Anselm states (*CDH* I, 13, 286). Honor is what orders society and makes possible relationship in general.[83] If the honor of a king is violated, this means the breakdown of order as a whole and the result is total chaos everywhere. Sin, interpreted by Anselm as the violation of God's honor, is therefore not primarily an insult of God but the destruction of the order of the world.[84] Vice versa, restitution of the king's honor amounts to a restitution of this order. In this system, both the violation and the restoration of order depend on the mutual relationship of ruler and ruled. The offended ruler cannot simply overlook the offense—the solution to the problem is not up to him alone since the problem is located at the level of a relationship. In other words, God is no tyrant who is able to make decisions arbitrarily, independently, and absolutely—this image of God applies only in later developments of empire at the time of Thomas Aquinas.[85] For Anselm's God, who is not an independent ruler, there are only two ways in which honor can be restored. Order can be restored either through punishment (*poena*) or by satisfaction (*satisfactio*).[86] Satisfaction, in this context, is preferable because it allows for the restitution of order through interpersonal arrangements that overcome the distortion of the relationship.[87] Since punishment often means deadly revenge and war, satisfaction provides a better alternative because it allows

136

for a peaceful way to restore honor. In a context where only two options are available, punishment or satisfaction, the latter is preferable because it is the only way to preserve order in a peaceful way.[88] No doubt, Anselm's theological argument proceeds on the basis of the logic of the empire of his day.

Southern is obviously correct that Anselm did not approve of every facet of the empire, but it is not necessary to claim such wholesale approval in order to make my point. What is important is that Anselm uses these feudal images because, as Southern has to admit, he "valued hierarchy as an expression of the rule of reason."[89] The feudal order stands for rationality and against chaos, and this argument extends to feudal arrangements of power, with the king and the archbishop at the top of the hierarchical pyramid. Anselm's argument depends on the rationality of the order of the Norman Empire and, for this reason, he lends his support to this order. This is where John McIntyre goes wrong when he argues that, from a theological perspective, Anselm's argument works even without the feudal imagery.[90] Even Southern, who gives McIntyre the benefit of a doubt in matters of theology, disagrees as historian: *CDH* "bears the marks of this rigorous and—if the word can be used without blame—repressive regime. Anselm's favourite image of the relations between God and Man was that of a lord and his vassals."[91] In view of this evidence, we can no longer do our theological work in splendid isolation but need to accept the historical challenge and come to grips with Anselm's empire theology, not in order to assign blame but in order to find out how to transcend its logic and to harvest any theological surplus that we would not be able to identify otherwise.

If honor and order are among the basic principles of Anselm's thought, the restoration of honor and order through Christ can be seen as a positive event of cosmic dimensions. If sin has destroyed the order of the world by violating God's honor (Anselm's famous comment to Boso toward the end of Book I of *CDH* is that he had not yet considered the weight of sin [*nondum considerasti, quanti ponderis sit peccatum*] [92]), the only way to restore the order of the world is through an act of satisfaction that restores God's honor, which is, as we have seen, not God's personal honor but the relationship of God and God's creation. Yet satisfaction demands a "proportional recompense" that humanity in and of itself cannot make (*CDH* I, 20, 303). Because humanity needs to make satisfaction, but only God can accomplish it, already at the end of Book I of *CDH* the necessity of a God-human is implicitly proved.[93] Moreover, satisfaction is ultimately achieved through the voluntary death of the God-human: The God-human, like any other creature, owes God obedience, but because he is without sin, he does not have to die; only his voluntary death can accomplish satisfaction. Through this death Christ earns a reward that he passes on to humanity, which can thus be saved.[94] The important thing here is that Christ's death on the cross is not the appeasement of an angry God who could conceivably be asked to swallow God's pride but the restoration of the order of the world and the source of true life. Through Christ's satisfaction God's order of creation is restored that was destroyed when God's honor was violated.

Nevertheless, this order not only implies social stratification; this order is built on it and depends on it. Anselm sees nothing wrong with order expressed as hierarchy. Society, in his mind, can be described as a pyramid, with the emperor and pope at the very top, followed by king and archbishop.[95] The pyramid is comprised of three orders—*oratores, bellatores,* and *laboratores* (those who pray, those who fight, and those who work); those who work make up the largest part of the population: more than three-fourths were *laboratores* or "serfs."[96] Anselm comes from a family located at the top of the pyramid; like high-standing clerics in general, he belongs to nobility by birth. The perspective of the three orders is commonly held in Anselm's day and breaking out of it would demand incredible efforts, as the example of St. Francis illustrates, who broke out in order to move downward.[97] Moving up would be even harder if not altogether impossible. No one would be surprised, either, that in Anselm's view, "monks are the most important group in society" as "vanguard on the pilgrimage toward the celestial home in search of the beatific vision of God."[98] Anselm is a man of the church, and within the institution of the church he sees the monasteries as closest to the divine life. This makes one wonder, of course, why in *CDH* he does not use an example of God where God is not king but pope or bishop.[99] Perhaps he felt his portrayal of God as king or emperor was more "logical" and more "impressive" (in the literal sense of the word as providing the necessary pressure provided by empire) to those so-called "unbelievers" that are the specter of *CDH.*

Nevertheless, even in this rigid order there exists some flexibility,[100] and here lies the problem with Anselm's Christology. By not simply accepting order but elevating it to the highest realms of logic and reason and connecting it with Christology, he manages to set the system in stone. Keep in mind that he is not merely using the order of empire as an "example" or a "hermeneutic tool," as some of his interpreters have argued.[101] Anselm's empire theology assumes that this is the way things are—universally, even for Jews and Muslims, to the end of the earth—and it seems to assume that empire is "here to stay" (as another prominent figure from the British Isles, Prime Minister Margaret Thatcher, used to claim for capitalism). The firm ground that Boso demands is provided here—by empire. When Southern points out that as archbishop Anselm argued from "first principles" rather than from case studies and collections of canon law,[102] we can now see the wider horizon of the matter, since these "first principles" are ultimately not based in abstract metaphysical orders but in the orders of the Norman Empire. And this—for the most part unconscious—import of first principles based on the order of empire secures the status of empire in a whole new intensity. Now the empire has managed to shape the theologians' christological unconscious and their imagination of "the world in general." In this light, the following statement by Southern takes on a much fuller and more threatening meaning than he intended: "Anselm carried into politics his search for an eternal order of truth and justice, unshakeable and subject to no alteration," built on "the eternal order which expressed the unchanging nature of God."[103] Anselm's image of God is static. There is no deficiency or imbalance in God, despite the somewhat messy details of the incarnation—one of the basic issues that *CDH* sets out to resolve.[104] It is not by accident that Anselm shows no interest in the life of Christ or in the life of the people. He simply does not need to: his fascination with "order" fills in the gaps.

In the history of effects, Anselm's empire theology may have created a problem more severe than Anselm's link with empire in his own time. Once the feudal framework was gone, Anselm's presuppositions about God as omnipotent and immutable, built on hierarchical order, needed to remain (at least between the lines) for the model to be effective. Now the model functions to shore up the hierarchies of another age and of other empires. Could this have been part of the interest in the recent celebration of satisfaction theory portrayed by Mel Gibson's movie, *The Passion of the Christ*? The question needs to be raised: What are the interests of theological positions that draw on these ancient theological approaches? In the debates around Gibson's movie, for instance, the "classical" approach was often juxtaposed with some "liberal humanist" approach, and the implication was that people either accept the "classic view" or they believe nothing at all.[105] Anselm may have felt the same way: those who reject the perspective of "order" of his own "classic" view are worse than the Jews and Muslims who at least accept the order of empire. Thus, in contemporary embraces of Anselm's model, empire and hierarchy can easily come in through the back door as the foundation of the world. It is this order that many references to Anselm through the centuries seemed to be only too happy to uphold. Southern's comment about the feudal images in Anselm, that "it is unlikely that many now will find this aspect of his thought attractive," is only half true.[106] While few people would vote for the reintroduction of feudalism, there is some strange attraction to hierarchy that does not seem to go away even in a more egalitarian postcolonial empire.[107] The organization of late capitalism itself shows some feudal tendencies, for instance, in the extremely high salaries and other financial benefits of its leaders, and in a hierarchical order where those on the lower ranks of transnational corporations are subjected in more and more severe ways to the commands from above. In addition, the U.S. government's efforts to support big business and give tax cuts to the rich at the expense of support for the rest of the population through public support of schools, welfare, and health care point in similar directions.

The Resisting God-Human

Having shown how Anselm's approach is intertwined with empire, we can now move on to the question that is the focal point of our investigation: Is there a surplus? Is there a sense in which Anselm's approach does not conform to the demands of the Norman Empire and thus pushes beyond it in a way that enables resistance? Given all the critiques of Anselm's approach, finding the resistance factor of his christological argument is not easy; nevertheless, there are traces. The paradox that is at the basis of our project keeps building: openly addressing matters of power and empire leads us not only deeper into the problems but also deeper into the alternative potential of particular theological approaches. The theological surplus can only be identified by taking into account the distortions.

Anselm's approach creates a place for human action. Even though the power of God is affirmed, God does not work in absolute fashion, without limits (as we have seen) and without the collaboration of humanity. This is what happens in Christ: divinity and humanity collaborate in constructive fashion in order to restore the world so that it becomes more livable. Human freedom is acknowledged and modeled according to Christ's own freedom: "The Father did not coerce Christ to face death against his will,"[108] says Anselm. This collaboration has the potential to resist the world of a feudal empire if it encourages human agency and initiative at precisely those points where the empire insists mostly on subservience and obedience. The problem looks different in a modern and postmodern situation, where human agency is taken for granted and people assume that they are able to pull themselves up by their own bootstraps.[109] Contemporary interpreters should take note that Anselm's approach does not demand impossible actions of humanity—causing hopelessness especially in those who are less powerful—because it claims a human-divine collaboration.[110]

Despite the social stratification of Anselm's time, there are some fundamental, even though mostly hidden, connections to and endorsements of the struggles of the common people. Southern puts it this way: "From one point of view all the religious movements of the later Middle Ages were an attempt to harness, guide, and express some elements in popular religion which drew their strength, not from the organized teaching and worship of the church, but from pressures in ordinary life which were beyond all control. The chief sources of mass religious movements were disease and despair."[111] It is not immediately obvious how these popular struggles affect Anselm's thinking, even though he seems to have had some sympathies with the people pressured by the politics of the Norman Empire. While the Normans tried to repress local Anglo-Saxon celebrations and festivals in the effort to centralize their empire, Anselm as archbishop gave permission to the monks at Canterbury to reclaim some of those celebrations. In two of his sermons he argues for the recognition of the feast of the Ordination of St. Gregory, considered to be an Anglo-Saxon saint. Perhaps Anselm's interpretation of God's incarnation in Christ could be understood along those lines too, if only Christ's humanity would not stay completely abstract but would be identified with some of the traits of the common people who also suffer and die every day. This position, too, would move counter to the Norman politics of centralization and open up new possibilities. Resistance to empire, as in Christ's own time, is closely tied to recognizing the subversive potential of those who suffer and those who are trampled underfoot. The christological surplus is tied up with this perspective. Nevertheless, in Anselm's *CDH* these possibilities exist only below the surface at best: there is no explicit recognition by Anselm of any of this and the vacuum left by the abstract humanity of Anselm's Christ tends to get filled in terms more convenient to the empire. As for Anselm's appreciation of the local customs of the people, the ambivalence of the situation must not be overlooked. His nod to popular religion was not just a noble gesture but also helped to strengthen his position in the Norman Empire, as Archbishop of Canterbury.[112] In fact, there were many roadblocks since Anselm himself did not even speak the language of the people, English; until the thirteenth century no English king spoke English either.[113]

Yet there are other, more radical moves in Anselm's Christology that are often overlooked by those who see only his "conservative" affiliation with the status quo. One of the most radical theological proposals of Anselm's *CDH* is his complete rejection of the classical theological position according to which the devil had a just claim on humanity.[114] This "ransom theory," widely popular in patristic theology and no doubt widely accepted as orthodox at the time of Anselm and even today, states that the devil had acquired some right to humanity and that through Christ God strikes a deal with the devil or at least deceives him in order to accomplish the redemption of humanity. Anselm, who "had never before disagreed with a traditional doctrine,"[115] refuses to accept any claim that would give power to the devil and according to which there would be any potentially shady transactions between God and another power of significance, such as the devil. For Anselm, power stays in the hands of God. While an empire motive might be detected in this affirmation of the unilateral power of God, potential for resistance mounts as well through Anselm's reconstruction. If God is in control like a king and the devil has no power at all, the doors of salvation might indeed be open wider than previously imagined.[116] As a powerful ruler, God can and does make a difference in the world, and not only the elites will benefit from his kingship. How much those who are not elite benefit depends, of course, on how God is envisioned, and here we might have to develop our own perspectives that go beyond Anselm.

There are, however, also potential problems with removing the devil from the system. J. Denny Weaver has pointed out that this move involuntarily makes God the "bad guy" who is in charge of punishment,[117] and Darby Ray has recently argued for the continuing usefulness of the patristic images of the deception of the devil by Christ: "While the idea of divine deceit may appear immoral to some, it points to the reality that any struggle against oppression and injustice that seeks to avoid violent means or that emerges from a context of relative powerlessness must rely on cunning and ingenuity rather than ascribed authority or power. The centrality of the trickster theme in African and African American narrative traditions reflects this realization."[118] While Weaver's critique does not apply directly to Anselm because God does not punish, Ray points out an important alternative to centralized power that could have been helpful in resisting the strategies of the Norman Empire. Still, Anselm's emphasis on the power of God could be quite pungent if it would be understood that God's particular kingship cannot necessarily be modeled after the kings of this world and their empires but that it constitutes an alternative. Rethinking the character of God's kingship along different lines that follow the kind of kingship manifested in the life and ministry of Jesus Christ would liberate us from the perennial call for the "strong man" and help us to envision a different world. Once again, however, this alternative exists only between the lines of Anselm's theology, as potential surplus buried in the deep recesses of the empire. Anselm does not quite go there, with the exception of certain restrictions that he imposes on God's omnipotence (see below). What backfires here is his method to consider the God-human, "supposing Christ were left out of the case, as if there had never existed anything to do with him," a phrase that excludes, in particular, scriptural references concerning the work and ministry of Christ (*CDH*, preface, 261).

Another aspect of Anselm's refusal to give credit to the devil is his strong emphasis on sin. The ultimate theological problem to be redressed by his Christology is not the devil but human sin. The problem is enormous, for sin has done nothing less than destroy the whole order of creation (*CDH* I, 21, 305). While Anselm sees no need to scare people by invoking the devil, he does not allow for shallow optimism, as if sin would not be a serious concern and perhaps might even go away by itself. What comes as a surprise at this point are the potential family resemblances of Anselm's approach to perspectives of contemporary liberation theologies that, in clear opposition to liberal theologies, emphasize sin as a most serious and structural problem. Such an emphasis on sin might indeed function as a critique of empire and its claims to omnipotence or, in contemporary terms, its notoriously optimistic fix-it and winner-takes-all mentality. Neglect of the gravity of sin (including its structural nature) fails to take seriously the grave offenses against humanity that are taking place under the conditions of empire and that are mostly perpetrated by the powers of empire. Unfortunately, Anselm does not give us much of an idea about where to look for sin in the empire of his own day. We find out little about what happens to those who do not benefit from empire in his time. In the contemporary United States, the many reports of torture by U.S. soldiers in military prisons in Iraq and Guantanamo Bay illustrate the problem; Anselm's emphasis on sin helps question the usual response that these problems are only due to a "few bad apples" and represent only the transgressions of individual soldiers who act on their own free will. Anselm could have told us that "free will" does not seem to be much of an option either for soldiers or sinners, thus initiating an investigation into the deeper issues at the heart of the problem.

Furthermore, since sin is actually overcome by Christ, Anselm might have a hopeful message for those who want to resist empire: despite the utter gravity of sin, we do not need to be paralyzed by it. Moreover, guilty feelings are beside the point because sin is a transpersonal, structural reality. This could present a powerful message to those middle-class Christians in the United States who are confronted by an even more overbearing empire today and who often internalize their frustrations in feelings of guilt. The ultimate test of the usefulness of a strong notion of sin in the resistance against empire is, however, the way sin is defined. Here, Anselm tells us very little. Sin, for him, is simply the resistance to the God-given order of the world, and this definition can deliver us right back into the hands of empire. More complex notions of sin are needed. Examples can be found in various liberation approaches that further develop Anselm's sense that sin is structural by addressing the problem of structural violence (where sin is perpetuated not just by individuals but by institutions embedded in systems).[119]

The notion of satisfaction is the element of Anselm's approach most likely to be offensive to modern readers. For this reason alone, we would suspect to find the logic of empire here. There is, however, another way to read Anselm, which leads us to one more potential surplus in his model. The theory of satisfaction holds, if read from the side of the one of whom satisfaction is required, that justice must not be unreasonable. In other words, the demand for satisfaction cannot make outrageous and limitless claims on those who owe satisfaction. Here is a parallel to the world of the book of Exodus in the Hebrew Bible, where the famous rule "eye for eye, tooth for tooth" (Exod. 21:23), sets limits to otherwise limitless struggles for revenge. If there is to be revenge, this rule appears to say, one must *not* demand *more* than a hand for a hand. Satisfaction theory, in this light, can be understood as an effort at damage control; perhaps, as has been argued, it is even a precursor to modern modes of arbitration. The reign of William Rufus during Anselm's time illustrates the problem, since the king's revenge could end up mutilating large numbers of people for seemingly small offenses. As a recent interpreter has pointed out in regard to the question of satisfaction, "the medieval conduct of conflicts consisted in large part of demonstrative, ritualized acts"; "those involved were familiar with and practiced a diverse range of threatening and yielding behavior that ended the feud in an amicable manner before it could escalate into something worse—in other words, before an armed conflict began in the first place."[120] Satisfaction is thus a relational concept, just like the notions of honor and order. This goes against our common sensitivities, as we usually do not think of any of these concepts in terms of relationship. Yet in Anselm's paradigm, humanity and God are seen in terms of a relationship and God cannot be conceived outside of this relation. The most surprising thing with Anselm, and perhaps one of the strongest impulses for resistance against empire, is that not even Godself is above this relationship. Thus, God cannot be a tyrant who arbitrarily does as "he" pleases. Moreover, even God's omnipotence is somehow restricted. In hindsight, this might have been a good lesson for the United States as it modeled itself in terms of the omnipotence of a "hyperpower" in its responses to the terrorist attacks of September 11, 2001;[121] this lesson might be even more important to keep in mind for the future.

Anselm can also help us avoid some of the features of modern theology that are failing us in the resistance to empire. In response to images of a judgmental God and a judgmental empire, liberal theology has at times played down notions of judgment and justice and emphasized the notion of love. Yet Anselm makes it clear that justice and love belong together. God's love is not sentimental and, more importantly, God's love is not soft on injustice. In Anselm's words: "it is not fitting for God to do anything in an unjust and unregulated manner, it does not belong to his freedom or benevolence or will to release unpunished a sinner who has not repaid to God what he has taken from him" (*CDH* I, 12, 286). Even God's benevolence and God's mercy are not above the demands of justice, as the somewhat terrified Boso notes.[122] Feminist theologians Joanne Carlson Brown and Rebecca Parker, who are quite clear about the problems of an abusive God, have expressed appreciation for Anselm's claim that love and justice cannot be separated. Nevertheless, they have also claimed that "his view of justice is not that wrong should be righted but that wrongs should be punished."[123] This is not quite correct. As we have seen, Anselm rejects punishment as the alternative that God does not pursue. Instead of punishment, God in Christ provides for satisfaction of the demands of justice in a way that is ultimately restorative.[124] As a result of Christ's death on the cross, which was not forced by God but willed by Christ as a result of his resolve to speak truth and justice(!),[125] justice and the order of creation are restored. With this insight Anselm might indeed help to resist empire. Christ restores justice; and what Christians need to imitate is not Christ's death but his resolve to speak truth and justice—knowing that this might have consequences.[126] Keep in mind, however, that the roots of this justice cannot be played off against God's mercy. Anselm finds God's mercy "so great, and so consonant with justice, that a greater and juster mercy cannot be imagined" (*CDH* II, 23, 354). At the level of the human being, justice and love go together as well. God created us for love, "but loving the highest good is something which rational nature cannot do unless it is [just]."[127]

Of course, the kind of justice/love that Anselm envisions has to do with order and the restoration of relationships—and this leads us back to the order and the hierarchical relationships that structure the empire. Anselm seems hardly able to overcome the frames of empire—although there is another surplus that might be mined. When Anselm talks about justice, at one point he notes that "supreme justice (*summa iustitia*) . . . is none other than God himself" (*CDH* I, 13, 286). Here, Anselm's argument might be brought together with biblical notions of justice in the resistance against empire. Biblical notions of justice emphasize the relationship of God and humanity (a covenant) that is rooted in God. More precisely, this relationship is expressed in terms of God's faithfulness, which implies God's special concern for those pushed to the margins of the covenant and who are excluded.[128] God's justice has to do, therefore, with a particular concern for the restoration of relationship with those who are being pushed to the margins of the covenant, such as the proverbial widows, orphans, and strangers of the Old Testament, and the fishermen, prostitutes, and tax collectors of the New Testament. Justice as preference for those who experience injustice and who are excluded from the covenant by those who feel closer to God (whether due to their success, their power, or their religious privilege) provides resistance to the empire.[129]

In sum, the key concepts of Anselm's approach, including justice, love, order, honor, and satisfaction, emphasize relationship. But the question is what kind of relationship we envision and whether the hierarchical kinds of relation of empire can give way to the kinds of relationship in God's kingdom where, according to Jesus' repeated reminder, "many who are first will be last, and the last will be first" (Mark 10:31).

In his preface to *CDH*, Anselm apologizes for not being able to clear up all the tensions of the system, due to pressures of time. But this may turn out to be a good thing. Resistance to empire is often like a blade of grass growing through concrete; it happens precisely where ambivalence is acknowledged, tensions are not resolved, and where the pressure is greatest. The goal of Anselm's *CDH* is to argue that through God-become-human in Christ the order of all of creation is restored through the restitution of the honor of God. If this system is perpetuated without awareness of the tensions, we end up reinscribing the social hierarchies of Anselm's times, including his anti-Semitic and anti-Muslim sensitivities. In our search for a surplus, perhaps Anselm's perspective, which extends to the restoration of creation, allows for some unexpected spaces that have not yet been claimed by the powers that be. We might go back to where we started in Anselm's theology, to his fledgling optimism about human reason, which the Reformers found so troublesome. This emphasis, if put in the service of empire, is indeed problematic because reason is always shaped by outside factors, whether this is acknowledged or not. But philosophy, unlike for modern thinkers, is not yet an autonomous discipline for Anselm; philosophy and reason are still decentered by theological frameworks, and here lies some hope for further inspiration and challenge, especially if ambivalence persists; ambivalence that filters into the relation of divinity and empire, for instance, can make a tremendous difference.[130]

Paul Tillich has argued that in twelfth-century Europe there were some forms of theonomy that were quite positive, not because people were better then but because "the entire life was concentrated in the great cathedrals; the whole of daily life was consecrated in the cathedral."[131] This observation is significant, and theonomy might provide indeed some resistance to empire—but only if the divine is seen in alternative terms. For this purpose, however, the focus cannot be primarily on the cathedrals that are also products of empire, built on the backs of the people (recall that Anselm expanded his own cathedral at Canterbury significantly during his rule). The focus needs to be on something else that deserves greater attention than Anselm affords it: Christ's life, his solidarity with those under pressure, and his untiring resistance to empire and the powers that be. This solidarity was probably better expressed in some of the popular religious movements of the Middle Ages than in the cathedrals, but if read in this light, Anselm's God-human takes on a new shape.

Notes

1. Even the current Pope Benedict XVI went on record against Anselm, arguing that the God of Anselm promotes a form of justice and anger that goes against the message of love. See Joseph Ratzinger, *Einführung in das Christentum: Vorlesungen über das Apostolische Glaubensbekenntnis* (Munich: Kösel, 1968), 231.

2. One example is the Lutheran theologian Gustaf Aulén's *Christus Victor: An Historical Study of the Three Main Types of the Idea of the Atonement*, trans. A. G. Herbert (New York: Macmillan, 1969), whose Christology will be discussed in chapter 6 of this book.

3. Anselm of Canterbury, *Cur Deus Homo*, trans. Janet Fairweather, in *Anselm of Canterbury: The Major Works,* ed. Brian Davies and G. R. Evans (Oxford: Oxford University Press, 1998).

4. See Perry Anderson, *Passage from Antiquity to Feudalism* (London: NLB, 1974), 182–86. Anderson notes a "silent social struggle for land which gave its economic vitality

to the age"; ibid., 189. Territorial expansions happened in the Baltic, the Iberian peninsula, and the Levant. Anderson provides a list: "Brandenburg, Prussia and Finland were conquered and colonized by German and Swedish knights. The Moors were driven from the Tagus to the Sierra Granada; Portugal was cleared *in toto* and a new kingdom founded there. Palestine and Cyprus were seized from their Muslim rulers"; ibid., 196. In addition, Constantinople was conquered.

5. See R. W. Southern, *Western Society and the Church in the Middle Ages* (Grand Rapids, Mich.: Wm. B. Eerdmans, 1970), 35. An emphasis on trade takes off after the early twelfth century: the canon lawyers, realizing the growing needs of society, "modified some principles and interpreted others until a large field was cleared for commercial enterprise"; see ibid., 40. Anderson reports that the population in Western Europe increased from 20 million to 54 million between 950 and 1348; less growth in Italy and Spain pulled down the higher averages in Britain, France, Germany, and Scandinavia. Anderson, *Passage from Antiquity to Feudalism,* 190, and n. 19.

6. See Clifford R. Backman, *The Worlds of Medieval Europe* (New York: Oxford University Press, 2003), 231.

7. Sally N. Vaughn, *Anselm of Bec and Robert of Meulan: The Innocence of the Dove and the Wisdom of the Serpent* (Berkeley and Los Angeles: University of California Press, 1987), 364.

8. Southern explains, "this gave the clergy a monopoly of all those disciplines which not only determined the theoretical structure of society but provided the instruments of government." *Western Society,* 38. Southern points out that "there is no side of the great change in the mind and imagination of Europe that began in his lifetime which he did not in some way touch or stimulate." *Saint Anselm: A Portrait in a Landscape* (Cambridge: Cambridge University Press, 1990), 5.

9. See Anderson, *Passage from Antiquity to Feudalism,* 137; and Southern, *Western Society,* 34. Southern also mentions that this trend comes to an end by 1300, when canon law became a closed system and Thomas Aquinas completed the theological system.

10. Southern, *Saint Anselm,* 4.

11. Southern, *Western Society,* 35. Southern gives a starting date of 1100, which is roughly the time in which Anselm wrote his *Cur Deus Homo.*

12. Sally N. Vaughn states that "most authors . . . intrigued by Anselm's philosophy and piety, have ignored his political career or minimized its importance." *Anselm of Bec and Robert of Meulan,* 3. Vaughn makes an important contribution to understanding Anselm's political moves, but she does not pay much attention to the question of power within empire and she certainly does not venture to give a theological interpretation.

13. "With the Carolingian State, the history of feudalism proper begins. For this massive ideological and administrative effort to 'recreate' the Imperial System of the old world, in fact by a typical inversion, contained and dissembled the involuntary laying of the foundations of the new." Anderson, *Passage from Antiquity to Feudalism*, 137. According to Anderson the church was the "official mentor" of those processes.

14. See Backman, *The Worlds of Medieval Europe*, 217–19. Anselm considered Heinrich as one of the bad kings like Julius Caesar, Nero, and Julian the Apostate, since he refused to submit to the pope; see Walter Fröhlich, "Anselm's *Weltbild* as Conveyed in His Letters," in *Anselm Studies: An Occasional Journal*, ed. Joseph C. Schnaubelt, OSA, Thomas A. Losoncy, Frederick Van Fleteren, and Jill A. Frederick, vol. 2 (White Plains, N.Y.: Kraus, 1988), 514. Fröhlich overlooks, however, Anselm's own adaptation to the English kings and sometime resistance of the pope—the problem might be that by simply following the letters of Anselm, Fröhlich is unable to transcend the self-image conveyed by Anselm.

15. See Backman, *The Worlds of Medieval Europe*, 194.

16. See Anderson, *Passage from Antiquity to Feudalism*, 160. Backman reports a kingdom-wide inventory of all land in 1089 that "symbolized the ruthless efficiency of Norman centralism." *The Worlds of Medieval Europe*, 194.

17. See Backman, *The Worlds of Medieval Europe*, 193, 195.

18. Southern, *Saint Anselm*, 239.

19. See Backman, *The Worlds of Medieval Europe*, 194.

20. Southern, *Saint Anselm*, 193. For a different suggestion, namely that Anselm "had quietly but actively sought the archbishopric, while publicly refusing the office," see Sally N. Vaughn, *St. Anselm and the Handmaidens of God: A Study of Anselm's Correspondence with Women* (Turnhout, Belgium: Brepols, 2002), 23.

21. Southern, *Saint Anselm*, 190–91.

22. See ibid., 193–94.

23. Vaughn, *Anselm of Bec and Robert of Meulan*, 116–18. The list of famous bishops who reportedly resisted becoming bishop is long and includes Cyprian, Martin of Tours, Ambrose, and even Augustine.

24. See ibid., 129.

25. See ibid., 53.

26. Vaughn also points out that Anselm's visit to England immediately before his calling as archbishop must be seen in light of his expectation to be installed in this office. Ibid., 121, 123–35.

27. See ibid., 130.

28. "With Anselm needing a pallium and Rufus refusing to recognize either pope (Urban II, with France, or Clement III, with Germany), trouble was inevitable—but it had nothing to do with lay investiture or clerical homage." C. Warren Hollister, *Henry I* (New Haven and London: Yale University Press, 2001), 375.

29. See Vaughn, *Anselm of Bec and Robert of Meulan*, 191–96. Anselm asked the king to permit a journey to Rome so that he could receive the pallium, to work with him toward reform of the church by calling a council, and to protect the lands of his see; ibid., 176. The problem was that the king had not yet acknowledged the pope and that the king wanted greater control, and monetary support for his war against Normandy (five hundred pounds, offered by Anselm, was not enough), and so permission was not granted. Only in 1095 did Anselm receive the pallium from a papal legate—rather than from the king—and William Rufus acknowledged the pope. In 1097, Anselm asked again for permission to travel to Rome, requesting help against the king who infringed once more on the lands of Canterbury and refused to give permission to hold a council. Anselm then hoped to shame the pope into action by asking him to be released of his duties in Canterbury; ibid., 205. Nevertheless, the pope did not deliver a strong show of support.

30. See Vaughn, *St. Anselm and the Handmaidens of God*, 253, and n. 4.

31. Southern, *Saint Anselm*, 337.

32. In a letter of 1098 to Pope Urban II, Anselm repeats his resistance to being Archbishop of Canterbury, his "weakness and ignorance," and his desire to "flee from all worldly activities"; he also reports his struggles with King William Rufus, who wanted to maintain control over the abbeys and who was expropriating land that belonged to the archbishop. In Anselm's own words: "I saw the law of God, the canons and the Apostolic authorities overrun by arbitrary usages." *The Letters of St. Anselm*, vol. 2, trans. Walter Fröhlich (Kalamazoo, Mich.: Cistercian, 1993), 147. In a letter of 1099 or 1100 to Pope Paschal II, Anselm mentions again "things contrary to the will and law of God," and it sounds as if the situation got worse. He asks the pope not to send him back to England unless "I be allowed to place the law and will of God and the Apostolic decrees above the will of man, and unless the King restores to me the church lands and whatever he took from the archbishopric because I appealed to the Apostolic See. . . . Otherwise I would make it appear that I put man before God." Ibid., 158.

33. See Vaughn, *Anselm of Bec and Robert of Meulan*, 214.

34. See Backman, *The Worlds of Medieval Europe*, 217–18.

35. See Ludwig Hödl, "Anselm von Canterbury," *Theologische Realenzyklopädie*, ed.

Gerhard Krause and Gerhard Müller, vol. 2 (Berlin: Walter de Gruyter, 1978), 761; and the long essay by Walter Mohr, "Anselm von Canterbury als Reformer und seine Auswirkung auf die Entwicklung der Gewaltenfrage in England," in *Analecta Anselmiana: Untersuchungen über Person und Werk Anselms von Canterbury,* ed. Helmut Kohlenberger (Frankfurt am Main: Minerva, 1975), 223–312.

36. Southern explains that homage was not concerned with spiritual functions; it was only about the tenure of land. *Saint Anselm,* 283.

37. Hollister, *Henry I,* 376.

38. Vaughn, *Anselm of Bec and Robert of Meulan,* 153.

39. Vaughn notes that Anselm was concerned about creating a public image with the very carefully edited collection of his letters: "In essence, the collection of the correspondence was part of Anselm's concern with politics and political issues." See Vaughn, *St. Anselm and the Handmaidens of God,* 2, 20–35, against Southern. Vaughn's case is argued also by other prominent Anselm scholars, including Walter Fröhlich.

40. Southern explains that Anselm's social background suited him well in offering counsel and aid to benefactors; even members of the military aristocracy tended to see him as one of themselves. *Saint Anselm,* 183, 184.

41. Southern points out that "as England became more settled, Bec felt the benefit of a new flow of endowments, and these led to a remarkable change in its position in the world." *Saint Anselm,* 185.

42. Vaughn, *St. Anselm and the Handmaidens of God,* 8.

43. Reference in Vaughn, *Anselm of Bec and Robert of Meulan,* 150–51.

44. Mohr argues that there is a tradition of kings understanding their rule as "*conregnare*" with God. "Anselm von Canterbury als Reformer," 267.

45. Vaughn, *Anselm of Bec and Robert of Meulan,* 18, as expressed by Robert of Meulan, chief adviser to William Rufus and Henry I.

46. See Fröhlich, "Anselm's *Weltbild*," 513.

47. Ibid., 512.

48. See Vaughn, *Anselm of Bec and Robert of Meulan,* 211.

49. Southern mentions the "sacerdotal element." *Western Society,* 37. Hödl emphasizes Anselm's struggle for the freedom of the church. "Anselm von Canterbury," *Theologische Realenzyklopädie,* vol. 2, 763–64.

50. Southern, *Saint Anselm,* 233.

51. During Anselm's rule as archbishop, "there emerged in the Anglo-Norman world a new conception of the English church, the English kingdom, and even political

conduct," explains Vaughn, *Anselm of Bec and Robert of Meulan*, 2. Vaughn also notes that "the lay and ecclesiastical spheres were not . . . clearly divided." Ibid., 150 n.5.

52. Southern, *Western Society*, 43.

53. Southern notes that this demand for unity became divisive; ibid., 72. Southern also reports that the three main methods of pursuing unity were military conquest, political negotiation, and religious reconciliation and adds that the third emerged only in light of the failure of the first two; ibid., 73. But from what we have seen, there may not be such a clear priority since the church was involved from the very beginning.

54. Vaughn, *Anselm of Bec and Robert of Meulan*, 176.

55. As recently as 2003 another book on *Cur Deus Homo* was published that makes no mention at all of these outside issues: Dániel Deme, *The Christology of Anselm of Canterbury* (Hampshire, Eng.: Ashgate, 2003). Usually, there is a split between the historians and the theologians. Scott Matthews, nevertheless, claims to pay more attention to Anselm's embeddedness in his world. He points out, for instance, that Anselm was a monk when he composed the *Proslogion*; but he limits Anselm's environment to his religious community. *Reason, Community and Religious Tradition: Anselm's Argument and the Friars* (Hampshire, Eng.: Ashgate, 2001), 15. Anselm's thought originates "within the private, devotional context of an eleventh-century monastery" and is then received "within the public and adversarial atmosphere of the universities of the thirteenth century"; ibid., vi–vii.

56. Southern, *Saint Anselm*, 175.

57. *CDH* I, 14, 287; II, 19, 353; both times this is asserted by Boso.

58. *CDH* I, 3, 268; Anselm is interested in showing how "fitting" the whole issue is; the notion of fittingness appears over and over again in the text. Southern notes that this search for fittingness is "one of the hall-marks of the Anselmian school." *Saint Anselm*, 181.

59. See Southern, *Saint Anselm*, 200. Southern further points out that these Jews were "semi-outlawed and wholly despised." Ibid., 198.

60. For a history of interpretation on this issue, see Georg Plasger, *Die Not-Wendigkeit der Gerechtigkeit* (Münster: Aschendorffsche Verlagsbuchhandlung, 1993), 51–57. It is striking that some interpreters choose to ignore these questions altogether. Even Plasger concludes that the identity of those unbelievers makes no difference in the understanding of Anselm's argument in *CDH*. Southern notes the role of the Jews in the formulation of *CDH*; but this role is mostly limited to an intellectual debate, and due to the fact that Anselm had some time to write at that moment. *Saint*

Anselm, 197–202. We are told that the Jews raised theological questions and "were the only learned, the only uncompromising opponents of Christianity in Europe"; ibid., 198. Still, Southern maintains that "the Jewish controversy was one of the incentives for writing the *Cur Deus Homo*"; ibid., 201.

61. Persecutions of Jews were not uncommon. In 1010, the bishop of Limoges arranged for a four-week-long proof of Jesus as Messiah from the Old Testament to the Jewish population. When most of them refused to convert, they would be exiled or killed; see Karlheinz Deschner, *Abermals krähte der Hahn* (Düsseldorf: Econ Verlag, 1962), 453. See also Robert Chazan, *European Jewry and the First Crusade* (Berkeley and Los Angeles: University of California Press, 1987), who shows the complexity of the situation, "complicated by longstanding tensions between the Jews and their urban neighbors"; ibid., 84.

62. See Sylvia Tomasch, "Postcolonial Chaucer and the Virtual Jew," in *The Postcolonial Middle Ages*, ed. Jeffrey Jerome Cohen (New York: St. Martin's, 2000), 245.

63. See also Jeffrey Jerome Cohen's introduction to his edited volume *The Postcolonial Middle Ages*, which calls for new reflections on the domination of Christianity in relation to religious others; ibid., 7.

64. See Deschner, *Abermals krähte der Hahn*, 454.

65. Pope Urban II, in a speech at the Council of Clermont in France in 1095, gives all kinds of reasons for the Crusades and emphasizes the evil deeds of the Muslims, calling for revenge: "To whom, then, has the duty of avenging these evils and recovering this land fallen, if not to you? You, upon whom God has bestowed more outstanding glory in arms, more greatness in courage, more vitality and strength than anyone else." Quoted in Backman, *The Worlds of Medieval Europe*, 220.

66. Once again Pope Urban II: "This land that you inhabit, enclosed as it is on all sides by the seas and surrounded by the mountain peaks, is too small for your vast population; neither does it abound in wealth; and it produces barely enough food for those who live here." Jerusalem is the center of the world and the land flowing with milk and honey; it needs to be liberated and taken back by the Christians. Those who go receive remission of their sins and the assurance of glory in heaven. Reference in ibid., 219–21.

67. See Backman, *The Worlds of Medieval Europe*, 222.

68. See Southern, *Saint Anselm*, 169. Perhaps there is a parallel with Anselm's different priorities from the Pope in matters of lay investiture.

69. Plasger, *Die Not-Wendigkeit der Gerechtigkeit*, 54.

70. G.R. Evans notes that the concern with "fittingness" is not unusual for the period but that it is particularly pronounced in Anselm. "Anselm's life, works, and immediate

influence," in *The Cambridge Companion to Anselm*, ed. Brian Davies and Brian Leftow (Cambridge: Cambridge University Press, 2004), 21. Matthews understands the philosophical challenge but he neglects the issue of power: "In the context of the Crusades and the expansion of medieval Europe, the Christian response to Aristotle had to be acceptable not just within the Christian community, but also beyond it." *Reason, Community and Religious Tradition*, 34.

71. *CDH* I, 11, 283. To sin, says Anselm, is "nothing other than not to give God what is owed to him." What we owe God is that we submit to God's will, and "this is the sole honour, the complete honour, which we owe to God and which God demands from us." "Someone who does not render to God this honour due to him is taking away from God what is his, and dishonouring God, and this is what it is to sin." Ibid.

72. This concern is also at the heart of many contemporary feminist critiques. See, for instance, Joanne Carlson Brown and Rebecca Ann Parker, "For God So Loved the World?" in *Christianity, Patriarchy, and Abuse: A Feminist Critique* (New York: Pilgrim, 1989), 8.

73. See R. W. Southern, *Scholastic Humanism and the Unification of Europe* (Oxford: Blackwell, 1995), 261–63.

74. Plasger explores the cultural and legal background, referring, for instance, to Anselm's personal cultural background and to the basic question of the reach of Roman law. Plasger also shows that the older emphasis on Anselm's grounding in Germanic law resonates with a certain nationalism of the German scholars who emphasize this argument. *Die Not-Wendigkeit der Gerechtigkeit*, 90–98.

75. Hermann Cremer, "Die Wurzeln des Anselm'schen Satisfactionsbegriffes," *Theologische Studien und Kritiken* 53 (1880): 7–24; and idem, "Der germanische Satisfactionsbegriff in der Versöhnungslehre," *Theologische Studien und Kritiken* 66 (1893): 316–45; see the reference in Gunther Wenz, *Geschichte der Versöhnungslehre in der evangelischen Theologie der Neuzeit*, vol. 1 (Munich: Chr. Kaiser Verlag, 1984), 44 n.9.

76. See Adolf von Harnack, *Lehrbuch der Dogmengeschichte*, vol. 3 (Darmstadt: Wissenschaftliche Buchgesellschaft, 1964), 408; see also Albrecht Ritschl, *Die christliche Lehre von der Rechtfertigung und Versöhnung*, vol. 1 (Bonn: A. Marcus, 1870), 32.

77. David Brown, "Anselm on Atonement," in *The Cambridge Companion to Anselm*, 291. In this essay, Brown's attempt to read Anselm's terms in *CDH* independently from Anselm's feudal context fails because he is unaware of the specifics of the Norman Empire and of Anselm's fundamental commitment to this world, which has nothing to do with the particular tensions between Anselm and some of the kings or with his position on investiture (as Brown wants to argue, ibid., 294).

78. Another aspect is introduced by Anderson in terms of feudal rule—England was never very deeply subject to the Roman Empire. Anderson notes that in England, a centralized feudalism was imposed by the Normans; the Anglo-Saxon society, built on Germanic culture, succumbed to the Norman invasion. *Passage from Antiquity to Feudalism*, 158.

79. Gisbert Greshake argues that in Anselm's time the Germanic understanding of homage was at the pinnacle of its importance and systematization; see also the arguments of Southern. "Erlösung und Freiheit: Zur Neuinterpretation der Erlösungslehre Anselms von Canterbury," *Theologische Quartalschrift* 153 (1973): 331 n.34.

80. *CDH* I, 15, 288: "But when a rational being does not wish for what is right, he dishonours God, with regard to himself, since he is not willingly subordinating himself to God's governance, and is disturbing, as far as he is able, the order and beauty of the universe. In spite of this, he does not harm or besmirch the honour of God to the slightest extent." Anselm defends God's immutability. *CDH* I, 15, 288.

81. In *CDH* I, 15, 288–89; in this paragraph, *ordo* is translated into English both as "order" and "station in life."

82. This is stronger than Greshake's suggestion to talk about Anselm's interpretation of God's honor sociologically. "Erlösung und Freiheit," 329.

83. That Anselm may have been aware of the biblical roots of the term honor, as David Brown in his effort to refute the idea that Anselm uses categories of feudalism notes ("Anselm on Atonement," 294), does not mean that it cannot therefore also be connected to empire. Southern explains that "'Honour' was essentially a social bond which held all ranks of society in their due place." *Saint Anselm*, 226. Plasger notes that the term *honor* emphasizes the relationship of two parties. *Die Not-Wendigkeit der Gerechtigkeit*, 97.

84. See, once again, *CDH* I, 11, 283. See also Greshake, "Erlösung und Freiheit," 333; and John McIntyre, *St. Anselm and His Critics: A Re-Interpretation of the* Cur Deus Homo (Edinburgh: Oliver and Boyd, 1954), 92ff.

85. Greshake argues that once Roman law replaces Germanic law in the decades following *CDH*, Anselm's argument loses its power. "Erlösung und Freiheit," 335. In Thomas Aquinas, who operates under the Roman understanding of law, God is the one who is absolutely sovereign, who can forgive sin out of his own free will. In order to give a fuller account of this change, and following the trajectory of this chapter, we would need to examine more closely the corresponding transformations in empire.

86. *CDH* I, 12, 284: "If no satisfaction is given, the way to regulate sin correctly is none other than to punish it." *CDH* I, 13, 287: "Either the honour which has been taken away should be repaid, or punishment should follow."

87. Greshake, "Erlösung und Freiheit," 332 n.39. In this context notions like honor, law (*Recht*), peace, and order are virtually synonymous. See ibid., 331.

88. See also ibid., 332.

89. Southern, *Saint Anselm*, 226–27.

90. McIntyre, *St. Anselm and His Critics*, 221. This position has been asserted lately by J. Denny Weaver, who argues that Anselm's theory is about "punishment" in general. *The Nonviolent Atonement* (Grand Rapids, Mich.: Wm. B. Eerdmans, 2001), 201.

91. Southern, *Saint Anselm*, 221–22.

92. *CDH* I, 21, 305.

93. *CDH* I, 25, 313. In *CDH* II, 6, 319–20 and II, 7, 320–21, Anselm explicitly confirms this point.

94. *CDH* II, 10-11, 325–32; *CDH* II, 14, 335; *CDH* II, 19, 353.

95. See Vaughn, *Anselm of Bec and Robert of Meulan*, 151–52.

96. Backman, *The Worlds of Medieval Europe*, 194; see also Anderson, *Passage from Antiquity to Feudalism*, 161. See the parallel with Hildegard von Bingen.

97. St. Francis notes that "nobody showed me what to do," quoted in Bernard Jussen, ed., *Ordering Medieval Society: Perspectives on Intellectual and Practical Modes of Shaping Social Relations*, trans. Pamela Selwyn (Philadelphia: University of Pennsylvania Press, 2001), 121.

98. Fröhlich, "Anselm's *Weltbild*," 504.

99. Anselm is certainly not shy about claiming the authority of the bishop. In a letter, he states: "Bishops maintain their authority as long as they are in agreement with Christ"; "every bishop who has Christ's voice is Christ." "Letter to Waleran, Cantor of the Church of Paris," *The Letters of St. Anselm*, vol. 2, 52.

100. Note the layered system of homage—the peasant to his lord, that lord to another lord, various links all the way to the king. Anderson, *Passage from Antiquity to Feudalism*, 148). Anderson notes a "world of overlapping claims and powers, the very plurality of whose 'instances' of exploitation created latent interstices and discrepancies impossible in a more unified juridical and economic system"; ibid., 149.

101. This is one of the shortcomings of the otherwise very instructive article by Greshake, "Erlösung und Freiheit," 340. For a more accurate assessment see G.R. Evans, who states that Anselm "treated the feudal framework . . . as something more than a convenient image. Its structures appealed profoundly to his sense of 'right order.'" "Anselm's life, works, and immediate influence," 18. The contrasting judgment by David Brown ("Anselm on Atonement," 294; in the same book as Evans!) that "Anselm does not seem to have committed himself deeply to the formal structures of his own time," is simply untenable.

102. Southern, *Saint Anselm*, 254–59.

103. Ibid., 346.

104. Some of his students became the earliest proponents of the Immaculate Conception of the Virgin Mary. See ibid., 181.

105. Susan Hogan-Albach, "The Purpose of the Passion," *Dallas Morning News*, Feb. 21, 2004, 4G. The basic argument is that people either believe the "classic view" or they believe nothing, even rejecting "original sin." This assumption overlooks that there are various "classic" models that contradict each other, like Anselm's "satisfaction theory" and the older "ransom theory." The most popular atonement theologies combined aspects of the ransom theory (Jesus' death freed humanity from Satan's hold), the satisfaction theory (Jesus' death makes amends for humanity's sin), and sacrificial theory (Jesus' death is the ultimate sin offering to God).

106. Southern, *Saint Anselm*, 223.

107. For the term *postcolonial empire*, see chapter 7.

108. *CDH* I, 8, 275. See also Greshake, who goes too far, however, when he argues that this move endorses the freedom and autonomy of the human being. "Erlösung und Freiheit," 337.

109. Gustav Aulén's critique of Anselm in his book *Christus Victor*, which is concerned about human agency, makes more sense in modern times than it does in Anselm's situation. See note 2, above.

110. This point is also emphasized by Greshake, "Erlösung und Freiheit," 344–45.

111. Southern, *Western Society*, 305.

112. See Southern, *Saint Anselm*, 323; 387–88.

113. Like the Norman kings Anselm spoke Norman French and, of course, Latin. See Backman, *The Worlds of Medieval Europe*, 194.

114 Anselm makes it clear that "the devil had no jurisdiction over man." *CDH* I, 7, 272–74.

115. Southern, *Saint Anselm*, 205. Here is a parallel to Abelard, whose school of thought was the only one to agree with Anselm on this point.

116. Anselm likens God to a king; *CDH* II, 16, 338–39. For support of the claim that this position opens wider the doors of salvation, see also Southern, *Saint Anselm*, 215.

117. Weaver, *The Nonviolent Atonement*, 201–02.

118. Darby Ray, *Deceiving the Devil: Atonement, Abuse, and Ransom* (Cleveland: Pilgrim, 1998), 138–39.

119. See also Flora A. Keshgegian, who appreciates Anselm's emphasis on relationship, which connects him to feminist approaches, but points out the difference in terms of sin as that which destroys this relationship; in Anselm, there is no concept of

victimization. "The Scandal of the Cross: Revisiting Anselm and His Feminist Critics," *Anglican Theological Review* 82, no. 3 (Summer 2000): 489.

120. Jussen, *Ordering Medieval Society*, 271.

121. See also the critique by Catherine Keller in *God and Power: Counter-Apocalyptic Journeys* (Minneapolis: Fortress Press, 2005), chap. 2.

122. See, for instance, *CDH* I, 25, 313.

123. Joanne Carlson Brown and Rebecca Parker, "For God So Loved the World?" 7.

124. Greshake is right that satisfaction is no punishment but goes too far when he says that, as the restoration of God's honor, it is something "purely positive." "Erlösung und Freiheit," 334.

125. *CDH* I, 8, 275; *CDH* I, 9, 277: "God . . . did not force Christ to die, there being no sin in him. Rather, he underwent death of his own accord, not out of an obedience consisting in the abandonment of his life, but out of an obedience consisting in his upholding of righteousness [justice] so bravely and pertinaciously that as a result he incurred death."

126. Anselm briefly speaks about the imitation of Christ in *CDH* II, 19, 353.

127. *CDH* II, 1, 316. The Latin term *iustus* can be translated as "just" or as "righteous." I have replaced "righteous" with "just" here in order to emphasize the parallel to the term *justice* (*iustitia*).

128. Most interpreters are now agreed on the centrality of the covenant and of relationship in the understanding of the biblical notions of justice. See, e.g., Christopher D. Marshall, *Beyond Retribution: A New Testament Vision for Justice, Crime, and Punishment* (Grand Rapids, Mich.: Wm. B. Eerdmans, 2001); and Walter Kerber, Claus Westermann, and Bernhard Spörlein, "Gerechtigkeit," in *Christlicher Glaube in moderner Gessellschaft*, Teilband 17 (Freiburg: Herder, 1981).

129. For a more detailed account see Joerg Rieger, "That's Not Fair: Upside-Down Justice in the Midst of Empire," in *Interpreting the Postmodern: Responses to "Radical Orthodoxy,"* ed. Marion Grau and Rosemary Radford Ruether (New York: T.&T. Clark, 2006), 100–05.

130. Perhaps this is the reason why Southern considers Anselm "pre-scholastic" in his "depreciation of human powers." *Scholastic Humanism*, 42.

131. Paul Tillich, *Perspectives on 19th and 20th Century Protestant Theology* (New York, Harper & Row, 1967), 239.

4

Resisting and Reframing
the Way of Christ

Christology and Early Colonialism

I N THE MIDST OF THE SPANISH CONQUEST OF THE AMERICAS, Bartolomé de Las Casas's (1484–1566) reference to the "way of Christ" as "the only way" for the New World has often been seen as an expression of christological resistance to empire. Emphasizing compassion and peace, Christ's way resists the way of fire and sword, promoted by the Spanish conquistadors. Yet even Las Casas's way of Christ harbors ambivalence and needs to be examined in terms of its potential support of empire. Questions about Las Casas are raised, for instance, from the perspective of the Native American populations both in the South and in the North of the Americas and the slaves imported from Africa, wondering whether he contributed to the colonial system despite his good intentions.[1]

While Las Casas did more to resist the worst manifestations of empire than most theologians, his christological approach nevertheless displays certain affinities with the presuppositions of empire. To be sure, these affinities are, for the most part, not at a conscious level. There is no doubt that Las Casas resisted the atrocities of the conquest and saw his role as protector of the Native peoples against the more notorious forms of the Spanish Empire and its colonialism. Nevertheless, there is an undercurrent that flows in a different direction and needs to be noted—not for the sake of diminishing Las Casas's achievements but for the sake of uncovering the reach of empire, which does not stop even at our best intentions to overcome it. Realizing this reach can strengthen our resistance and help us to identify with greater clarity those christological aspects of his approach that cannot be controlled by the powers that be.

In this chapter we proceed in slightly different fashion—examining an approach to Christology that is not often identified with support of empire and colonialism, and which has at times even been seen as one of the precursors of contemporary Latin American liberation theology. Rather than dwelling on the conquest of Latin America, we will take a look at softer forms of colonialism that emerged simultaneously and that prefigure more modern forms of empire.

Las Casas's influence is significant and remains so even in later centuries. His book *The Only Way*, initially drafted in 1534, introduces a new spirit.[2] This book is his major theological work and was being studied in the great universities in Spain already during his lifetime. It influenced many of Las Casas's contemporaries and circulated widely in the New World after his death. While this book posed challenges to certain forms of colonialization, it was not the work of an outsider to colonialism. Las Casas was very well connected; he had known Columbus and his family, his own possessions were given to him by Columbus, and he met with popes and kings. His thought found many followers in his own time and would influence even the pope and the Spanish king. The Third Mexican Provincial Council of 1585, accepted as a code of canon law until 1918, was shaped in part by his influence.[3] At this council, the bishops argued in favor of Las Casas's method of "peaceful penetration and colonization," and this was the system that the Spanish monarchy eventually adopted.[4]

Las Casas's posthumous influence reached beyond the Americas, all the way to the Philippines.[5] In later centuries, missionaries often found a positive model in Las Casas's struggle for the Amerindians, and the colonial enterprises of other countries, such as the Dutch and the British, found ammunition against the Spanish Empire in Las Casas's work. When compared to the atrocities committed by the Spanish conquest, both the Dutch and the British enterprises appeared in a favorable light. No wonder that the work of Las Casas was rejected in seventeenth-century Spain.[6] Las Casas found admiration once again in the age of the American, French, and Spanish American revolutions. Yet, in the process, he was also critiqued for his paternalism, which kept the inhabitants of South America from "developing a capitalist spirit of development and enterprise."[7] In the twentieth century, Las Casas was seen in a positive light due to what progressive groups in Latin America and Europe, including the governments of Cuba and former socialist East Germany, perceived as his resistance against imperialism.[8] Las Casas's ideas can also be found in documents of the United Nations and the Indian Claims Act of the United States of 1948, which provides for financial restitution for land taken from the Native Americans in cases of litigation. The Latin American Bishops' Conferences of Medellín (1968) and Puebla (1979) also witness to his influence. Keeping in mind this history of effects, the question to be pursued in the following is what difference these early colonial struggles make in our thinking about Christ and in our contemporary resistance to empire.

The Theology of Early Colonialism: Stronger and Softer Versions

The history of empire cannot be written without reference to the sixteenth-century conquest of the Americas. As is well known, sword and cross went hand in hand as the Spanish and the Portuguese moved across the Americas. In these events, theology played a crucial role, not so much by directly fighting the battles—this was the role of the sword—but by endorsing and justifying them. Moreover, while theology did not wield the sword, at times it did help guide it. It may come as a surprise that even in this situation a christological surplus can be identified.

Spanish expansion, according to Enrique Dussel, roughly followed the pattern of the Roman Empire, also embraced by the Medieval Crusades and the Arab Empire: military occupation was followed by the formation of a government; conversion to the religion of the invaders was the last step.[9] Even in this scenario where empire is blazed by the sword, the gain in power and wealth is not everything; while modern empires may be somewhat more flexible on the religious questions, the Spanish conquest is not conceivable apart from its religious stance. What we need to explore, therefore, is how the gains of the economic and political powers are related to the gains of the religious (ecclesial) powers. Reversing the trajectory of the conquest, Las Casas put his emphasis on religious powers first, arguing that economic and political success would come as a result of religious work. Thus, he argues for a different road map for empire without necessarily rejecting the idea of empire altogether.

Among the most prominent Spanish theologians of the early conquest were the Spanish theologians Juan Ginés de Sepúlveda and Francisco de Vitoria; the work of the latter would become instrumental in laying the foundations for modern law. The arguments of both converged, nevertheless, in their defense of the war against the Amerindians, and it is not hard to imagine the implications of this attitude for the understanding of Christ, although the debate was not conducted in strictly christological terms. In 1544, Sepúlveda wrote a manuscript justifying the wars against the Amerindians, based largely on what he saw as their inferiority. In it, his thinking is strictly hierarchical;[10] he considers the Spanish Empire, like the Roman Empire, to be entitled to subjugate barbarians in order to civilize them. He regards the Amerindians as inferior to the Spanish, and, following Aristotelian concepts, declares them barbarians, incompetent to govern themselves, and destined to serve. War is necessary to Christianize them.[11] Nevertheless, Sepúlveda does not argue that people be converted directly by war, but that war is necessary to suppress obstacles and resistance to conversion. This includes the possibility, however, that people may be compelled by force to listen to preaching. Sepúlveda's distinction of the different uses of war, meant to limit war, is thus rather weak.[12] Victory in war, while not leading directly to conversion, plays an important role, Sepúlveda argues: the losers tend to be attracted to the customs of the victors.[13] Closer attention to the position of power presupposed by this argument might have raised a red flag for Las Casas, whose position also picks up the argument of attraction, as we shall see.

Vitoria agrees that war cannot be a means of conversion. On the whole, he is more supportive of the Amerindians than Sepúlveda when he acknowledges, for instance, their right to self-determination.[14] Nevertheless, he identifies different ways for establishing and maintaining Spanish rule. Horrified by the cruelty of the conquest, Vitoria supports war only under certain well-defined conditions. War is not permissible, for instance, because of a difference of religion or for the "enlargement of empire."[15] War is permissible only when the safety of the Spaniards is threatened or when "the barbarians . . . obstruct the Spaniards in their free propagation of the Gospel."[16] Furthermore, war is legitimate when it is a matter of love of neighbor; for instance, when it helps prevent human sacrifice and when it helps to prevent idolatry.[17] In sum, war and other actions against the Amerindians (including "plunder, enslavement, deposition of their . . . masters") are legitimate once the Spaniards "have demonstrated diligently . . . that they have every intention of letting the barbarians carry on in peaceful and undisturbed enjoyment of their property"; whatever action is taken, however, "must be done with moderation, in proportion to the actual offence."[18]

Las Casas, too, considers war in general to be justifiable. Yet he imposes further restrictions on what might be considered a just war. While the conquistadors compared their own activities to the Christian heroes of the reconquest of Spain from the Arabs, Las Casas finds significant differences between that war, which he considers a just war, and the war against the Amerindians. After all, the Arabs had seized Spain and tried to destroy the Christian faith—the Indians had done nothing of the kind.[19]

Las Casas, Sepúlveda, and Vitoria all agree on one point: the purpose of war in relation to the Christian message is not to convert by force but to remove obstacles to the faith. Nevertheless, in his debate against Sepúlveda in Valladolid between 1550 and 1551 (during which at one point Las Casas talked for five straight days), Las Casas charges Sepúlveda's agreement with the restriction of war to the removal of obstacles as a "willful deception" (*The Only Way*, 147; hereafter *OW*). Although Las Casas seems to have won the debate—Sepúlveda's book *About the Just War Against the Indians* fell victim to the Inquisition—things do not easily change in Latin America.[20]

In this same debate Las Casas imagines, for the sake of argument, a case in which "conquest" would submit "pagans" to "Christian political power" and thus would remove people's "political defenses"; this would, in turn, open them to Christianity. Las Casas notes that the logic of this case is flawed since no "pagan in his right mind" would submit to such power and therefore "there would have to be war."[21] Of course, the Amerindians were frequently subjected to force, and Las Casas elsewhere describes "the brutal missionary" who submits people to bodily torture (*OW* 151). During the conquest war was a constant reality, and in one of his most influential writings Las Casas reports that the Spanish "have commanded notice to be given the Indians to accept the holy faith and render obedience to the kings of Castile; otherwise war would be made on them with fire and blood, and they would be killed and made slaves."[22] In all of this, church and state collaborated closely: the Spanish emperors, bearing the title "Holy Roman Emperor," understood the Americas to be a donation by Pope Alexander VI, in reverse analogy to the donation of Emperor Constantine.[23]

In the context of the Spanish conquest, the work of Las Casas brought some relief, and his thinking about Christ is an important factor, as we shall see below. Although Las Casas is not a pacifist and allows for the possibility of just war, he opposes the war against the Amerindians as "mindless, wrong, evil, [and] tyrannical."[24] Moreover, those who engage in this war commit a mortal sin (*OW* 164ff.). In challenging war, Las Casas challenges one of the key methods of the conquest. War often amounts to tyranny because it is "violent, ruthlessly cruel, reckless." He increasingly opposes this form of colonialism because "the [Spanish] militants prefer their own particular worldly profit to the common good of all— to the honor due to God, to the salvation, the spiritual and temporal well-being of countless groups and individuals" (*OW* 164). Such rule is not only contrary to the laws of nature and of God but inherently unstable: "it can in no way endure."[25]

Nevertheless, colonial rule is not altogether rejected by Las Casas. Making his case with reference to Aristotle and St. Thomas Aquinas, he envisions a world in which people may freely choose it: "The rule which people grant to someone as a gift, grant it freely, with no force or fear or coercion involved, so someone rules willing subjects—that rule is a noble rule, natural, just, virtuous, and judged to be the best."[26] While this might sound almost like a democracy, Las Casas does not give up the idea of monarchy and continues to support the Spanish Crown; neither does he give up a sense that the monarchy's reach of power might rightfully be extended in the Americas: "A rule at its best is a rule constituted for the common good of the subject, not for the profit and glory of the prince, though profit and glory may come as a consequence."[27] "So the more the subjects enjoy a liberty which does not ruin peace and tranquility, nor do damage to the common good, the better the rule is, the more noble, the more lasting" (*OW* 101). In other words, an empire that is benevolent is the most stable.

In this spirit, Las Casas exposes the shortsightedness of empire, particularly of those who want to get rich quick, and he is able to secure the support of both kings and popes for his position at various times. Over and over again he points out that the main problem for the destructiveness of the conquest is greed. Colonialism as such does not seem inherently problematic; problems arise from its distortion.[28] Early in his life, he understood that the *encomienda* system—based on forced labor in plantations and mines—was deeply problematic because it impeded what he saw as the main purpose of the Spanish Empire: the establishment of the Christian faith.[29] As an *encomendero* Las Casas had owned slaves. Even though he seems to have treated his slaves well and without violence, he realized that the problem was with the system that enslaves Amerindians, and so he gave up his own *encomienda*. Nevertheless, while he rejects the *encomienda* system, Las Casas does not encourage the Spanish to withdraw from the New World altogether; neither does he advocate for a position that would let the Amerindians freely determine their own lives. He continues in various ways to develop more constructive models for living together. In this context, he promotes a new level of respect for the other, without a doubt one of his major achievements and legacy for later generations.[30]

In the 1540s, the New Laws of King Charles V restricted the *encomienda* system by declaring that *encomiendas* could not be inherited and that the Amerindians should all be set free within a generation, although these laws never went fully into effect.[31] Employing Amerindians in forced relations of labor and without reward for their labor had led to a severe loss of life. On the island of Hispaniola, the Indigenous communities had been completely wiped out, and in all the colonized areas together more than twelve million people died during forty years, due to the hardships imposed on them.[32] In this context, the early Las Casas feels that African slave labor is more productive than Indian slave labor and he endorses it—a position of which he later repents.[33] Nevertheless, this endorsement of slave labor is not only problematic in itself, as some critics of Las Casas have argued; it points to a deeper problem. While Las Casas's view of Amerindians is more enlightened than his view of Africans, he continues to promote a hierarchical view of humanity; not all human beings are seen as being on the same level. Colonization is thus still an option. Tsvetan Todorov notes the greater effectiveness of the colonization theory over against the enslavement theory: if the other is considered to be more subject than object, he will be more productive, a lesson that might still be employed successfully in empires today. In fact, the colonized other can be allowed to rise to become an "intermediary subject" in the production of objects, while he or she is never quite recognized on the same level as the self.[34]

Las Casas's defense of the Amerindians is grounded in a positive evaluation of their human qualities and of their religious efforts. He even commends them for not giving up their positions lightly—"they would be fickle and worthy of reproach and punishment" if they put aside their own traditions right away "and believe these soldiers . . . without being convinced by more probable reasons."[35] Therefore, Las Casas adds, it is necessary to learn their language and religion, and many later missionaries would follow his advice. He examines and describes Indigenous habits—developing early prototypes of anthropological and sociological study. This approach is particularly important in understanding differing practices of the Indigenous communities that were often used as justifications for the conquest, such as human sacrifice, cannibalism, and even homosexuality.[36] In this vein, Las Casas develops some basic appreciation for what others would classify as idolatry: he observes that they do not adore rocks but the divine power who makes them and in this way "reach out for the one true God."[37] Still, in Las Casas's investigations his own presuppositions loom large; this "one true God" looks a lot like the God whom Christians already know.

Although contemporary scholars who question the depth of Las Casas's descriptions have a point,[38] the better question would be, What accounts for this lack of depth? Is it simply a matter of lack of the right tools, or does Las Casas somehow develop blinders that keep him from developing a clearer view? Is he romanticizing the situation, similarly to what Walter Mignolo has called

"Occidentalism,"[39] albeit with a more decidedly positive spin? The following passage from Las Casas's writings is reminiscent of the romanticizing myth of the noble savage, long before Jean-Jacques Rousseau coined the term: "God has created all these numberless people to be quite the simplest, without malice or duplicity, most obedient, most faithful to their natural lords, and to the Christians, whom they serve." Since they are simple people with few possessions, they are "neither proud, nor ambitious, nor avaricious."[40] While the goal is to affirm that the Amerindians are fully human, there was little exploration of the question what kind of human beings they were until the end of the sixteenth century.[41] In all this it needs to be kept in mind, of course, that Las Casas is not interested in giving descriptions for the sake of description. His main goal is to refute theories that portray the Indians as not fully human.

In his seminal work *The Only Way,* Las Casas makes a strong case that the Amerindians "are all human beings." There is no doubt that "their minds are very quick, alive, capable, clear."[42] Furthermore, "there exist extraordinary kingdoms among our Indians" that are "properly set up" with "kings, judges, laws, all within civilizations where commerce occurs, buying and selling and lending and all the other dealings proper to the law of nations." In fact, they have "laws that are often superior to our own" (*OW* 64). These people are even teachable in the Western arts of grammar and logic (*OW* 65). The Indians have what we might call a "comparative edge" since they are equal to the ancient Greeks and Romans "and in a good many customs they outdo, they surpass the Greeks and Romans." Moreover, Las Casas asserts that "they surpass the English, the French, and some groups in our native Spain" (*OW* 65–66). Culturally, Las Casas asserts, "in the old days of paganism" many peoples "were much less rational in their use of mind than our Indians, peoples who had customs far more horrible, vices far more depraved" (*OW* 66). Once again, the purpose of this argument is polemical, to counter those who have "defamed our Indians" (*OW* 66). But why does he continue to talk about *our* Indians? The term, even if it were meant in an endearing sense, needs to be read on the colonial background, which transcends personal relationships and points to a relationship that signifies ownership. Not surprisingly the very first paragraph of the book talks about "our Indian nations" (*OW* 63).

Many commentators have noted Las Casas's emphasis on the equality of the Indians in terms of their general humanity. Yet this equality is determined by their potential rather than by their actual accomplishments: "All have the power and ability or capacity . . . to be instructed, persuaded, and attracted to order and reason and laws and virtue and all goodness."[43] Todorov identifies the problem with this emphasis on equality because (worse than hierarchy) it "consists in identifying the other purely and simply with one's own 'ego ideal' (or with oneself)."[44] The Spanish self sets the standard for measuring the Indigenous other. The flipside of Las Casas's emphasis on equality is a lack of awareness of the difference of the other that, ironically, leads back to a justification of colonization:[45] While Las Casas's efforts to elevate the achievements of the Amerindians leave them on a developmental scale that matches other "high cultures," they still remain below the Spanish culture at its best. Not surprisingly, Las Casas also talks about necessary improvements: despite their "good and natural intelligence" and their "ready wills," they need to be "drawn to and taught a complete and sound morality" and, of course, the Christian faith. Their intelligence and will is remarkable not in and of itself but because it makes them teachable and receptive for Christian values.[46] The perceived distances at the cultural level are expressed as distances in time: the Amerindians are simply less developed or more backward.[47] As a consequence, "when some very rustic peoples are found in the world, they are like untilled land."[48] The task is to cultivate this land.

Anthony Pagden's conclusion aptly sums up the problem: "Once he had passed through the theoretical grid of Las Casas' comparative method, the 'other' came out looking, after all, very much like 'us,' albeit now a remote, barely imaginable 'us.'"[49] While this approach is intended to help the Amerindians, it harbors harmful aspects as well, ushering in their assimilation to the Spaniards. After all, the cultured Spaniards—and with them the Spanish Empire—are the norm. In sum—and this will surely come as a surprise—insistence on equality can further colonialism; once the Amerindians are seen as equal in terms of human potential, there is now an obligation to raise them up to our levels.

When it comes to matters of religion the problems of Las Casas's notion of equality become clearer yet. He harbors no doubt that the Christian task is to evangelize the inhabitants of the Americas. In *The Only Way*, he asserts that they are "in common ignorance of divine things" (*OW* 134). This concern for evangelization is at the very core of his concern for the Amerindians, and here a Christian colonial spirit returns through the back door, as it were.[50] As a result of this need for conversion, Las Casas asserts, the colonial relationship is put in place by God. "Certain kingdoms and their peoples, solely because they are pagans and need to be converted to our holy faith, have been committed and entrusted by God and by Holy Apostolic See in his name to the sovereigns of Castile and Leon."[51] Here the colonialist element in Las Casas's theology is most obvious.

Nevertheless, the later Las Casas grows more critical of colonial structures, even to the point that he argues for the expulsion of most of the Spaniards from the Americas. This does not mean, however, that he is abandoning the colonial project altogether. Las Casas realizes that there is simply no need for the presence of so many Spaniards in order to take care of the two central concerns, to preach the gospel and "to assert and preserve there the princedom, sovereign dominion, and universal jurisdiction of the kings of Castile." In each of the Indigenous kingdoms, three or four towns of Spaniards would be enough. "Few armies are necessary to maintain peace among a naked people, clad only in skins . . . and without any weapons." The Amerindians that are thus "set free" can be expected to "serve the king with their blood, if necessary, and will give him 2 or 3 million [ducats]." This, Las Casas concludes, "is the true and prime way for the kings of Castile to be lords of the Indies and to be able to extricate them from tyranny."[52] In addition, Las Casas also calls for restitution of everything that was wrongfully taken from the Indigenous communities—in this way, he feels, the Spanish kings can recover their rightful jurisdiction over the Indies.[53]

In all of this, financial considerations are never missing. The conquest itself has, of course, often been interpreted in terms of the desire for gold. But Las Casas's alternative Christian colonial model also considers the importance of money. He is fully aware that in order to maintain their jurisdiction over the empire, the Spanish monarchy is in need of funds; after all, King Charles V financed his election through a bank in Augsburg, Germany.[54] A centralized colonial system would promise not only more control but also more revenue—now wasted on the excesses of the *conquistadors*. With this anticipation of revenue Las Casas hopes to attract the undivided attention of the empire; in his own thinking this amounts to an offer "to buy Christ back with promises of revenue for the king."[55] Would not anyone who saw Christ's sufferings, he wonders, attempt to buy him back by whatever means? Here Las Casas, although working within the confines of colonial logic, takes an unusual step that points us toward a potential surplus in his work that we need to pursue later: he identifies the sufferings of Christ and the sufferings of the Amerindians.

Las Casas thus promotes a peaceful alternative to conquest, which nevertheless amounts to a new form of colonialism. Hans Magnus Enzensberger is mistaken when he argues that "there is no peaceful colonialism. Colonial rule cannot be founded on the plough and the word but only on the sword and the fire."[56] Granted, Las Casas's efforts at peaceful settlements by Spanish farmers and priests encouraged by the king, first in Cumaná (today in Venezuela) and then in Verapaz (now Honduras), between 1520 and 1540 were not always successful.[57] After his first conversion in 1514, Las Casas proposed an alternative to the *encomienda* system—the development of new communities that nevertheless still depended on Indigenous labor. The difference in the *encomienda* system was the collective character of the enterprise; in charge was no longer one individual owner but a community of Spaniards, and the Amerindians were no longer the property of one individual. Furthermore, they were allowed to collaborate and work together; they could, in Las Casas's own words, "cultivate their fields together," and "those who gather gold should gather the gold together"[58]—the expression "gather gold" being no doubt a euphemism for "mining." In these settlements, the Spanish would live together in Spanish towns and the Indigenous communities in pueblos, where their numbers would grow, but the latter would still be working for the former.[59] In addition, Las Casas favored "peasant colonialization," which would allow peasants who struggled for survival in Spain to establish themselves in the Indies. The Spanish peasants would teach the Indigenous peasants and initiate them into the Spanish way of life and civilization. Some proponents of development continue to perpetuate this attitude today when they proclaim, "don't give people fish, teach them how to fish," as if people were lost without our way of life. This plan was actually implemented from the 1530s on.[60]

In terms of our overall assessment of empire, it is important to note significant differences between the Spanish conquest and the later colonial enterprises of the British in North America. Unlike the British, the Spanish depended on the Indigenous communities for the exploitation of the wealth of the land—particularly through farming and mining, but also in other ways—for instance, through diving for pearls. Likewise, they needed Indigenous women because the conquest was basically accomplished by Spanish males. Consequently, Spanish America became *mestizo*, while English America did not.[61] Of course, a strict hierarchy remained that continued to prefer people of direct Spanish background to Creoles (those born in the new world) and to *mestizos* (those of mixed race, at the lower rungs of the ladder).

Lewis Hanke sees things in a positive light: The conquest was "one of the greatest attempts the world has seen to make Christian precepts prevail in the relations between people." The two main principles are that all humans are equal before God and that Christians are responsible for the welfare of others, "no matter how alien or how lowly they may be."[62] Hanke concludes that no European nation "took her Christian duty toward native peoples so seriously as did Spain." The English, by contrast, merely "hoped to meet the . . . Indians in heaven, but wished to keep apart from them on earth."[63] Todorov relates this difference to a difference between Catholicism and Protestantism: the Catholics identify the Amerindians with themselves and regard them as equals; the Protestants emphasize difference and isolate their communities.[64] In both cases, as Todorov correctly notes, the identity of the Amerindians is denied. The English and Spanish approaches to colonization, however, differed not only because of the religious systems underpinning them but also because of the nations' differing economic systems. Hanke finds a middle road—which to him signifies the achievement of the Spanish but also signifies the deeper problems to us: both conquistador and missionary, he claims, "were inseparably yoked, sent together into a new world and together were responsible for the action and achievement of Spain in America."[65] Church and empire are inextricably related here.

The Christian nature of the Spanish conquest as well as the alternative type of colonialism proposed by Las Casas need to be noted. Christian influence in the creation of Latin America has been pervasive, as Hubert Herring has observed: "The last Spanish flag has long since been hauled down, but the Cross is still silhouetted against the sky from Mexico to Argentina."[66] According to Dussel, "in the organization of the Hispanic empire, the Church became the primary organism responsible for and committed to the perpetuation of the Hispanic world view."[67] Schools and the printing and distribution of literature were controlled by the church; the intellectual elites were the priests. Emphasizing the ambivalence of this process in which Las Casas himself is caught, however, Dussel also maintains that most of the positive things that were done for the Indigenous communities were done by the missionaries.

The Colonial Way of Christ

The Spanish Empire harbored few doubts that it was following the way of Christ in the conquest of the Americas. The often-voiced assumption that in these events of conquest church and empire simply followed greed and crude expansionism fails to take into account the broader picture. No doubt, violence and greed were rampant; Las Casas denounces both with good reason. But the general course of the conquest was endorsed and sometimes even guided by theology. Empire and Christianity were connected in intimate ways. As we have seen in earlier chapters, the history of this connection predates the conquest.

Early in his life, Las Casas himself was part of the majority that saw nothing wrong with a Christianity whose Christ supported the conquest and the *encomienda* system. His initial conversion was not a conversion from "the world" to Christ but—and this is often the more difficult kind of transition—from one understanding of the way of Christ to another. As Roberto Goizueta has pointed out, for Las Casas "*metanoia* [conversion] implied not only a different way of living but, in so doing, it also implied belief in and worship of a radically different God from the 'god' to whom he had previously been offering the mass."[68] Las Casas's new understanding of Christ posed challenges for both the practices and the beliefs of the church in the midst of the colonial situation. Christ opposed the ways of the conquest and modeled a different way of relating to the Amerindians—Las Casas presented it as "the only way," thus the title of his book. As Helen Rand Parish notes, these ideas presented as the only way "have influenced mission theory and practice for centuries throughout the world" (*OW* 3). In this context, the widespread assumption that Las Casas is thoroughly anticolonialist has created problems; not only has it led people to an uncritical reading of his work, but it has also covered up the sort of colonial structures that are less blatant than the *conquistas'* method of fire and sword.

In a first step, I will explore how Las Casas's Christology maintains certain colonial traditions and attitudes even after his conversion. The purpose of this exploration is not to put down his work (or to cover up the worse atrocities of the official Spanish conquest) but to examine more closely where Las Casas ultimately transcends the colonial spirit. Identifying the surplus of Las Casas's Christology will help us bring out the challenges of Las Casas for us today as well. In a second step, we will look at how Las Casas's "only way" of Christ works itself out in a particular colonization project of "pacification."

Las Casas's "only way" focuses on the question of evangelization. At its most basic level, evangelization has to do with the transmission of faith to non-Christians. In the context of the Spanish conquest, however, practically all other questions are worked out in relation to evangelization as well. As a result, the "way of Christ" not only models the transmission of faith but also models politics and economics. In the pursuit of the way of Christ and of evangelization, a distinction is made between heaven and earth (*OW* 144; 97). Christ's kingdom is understood, first of all, as a heavenly kingdom, "the kingdom above, the everlasting kingdom" (*OW* 94). Despite the Spaniards' fascination with the economic and political possibilities of the conquest, heaven, as the place of eternal salvation, is on everyone's mind; in the big picture, the worst thing is to cause someone else's eternal damnation (*OW* 150–51; 168). Nevertheless, this kingdom of heaven also sets the stage for what goes on in the world; Las Casas insists that the way of Christ should be the model for the rulers (*OW* 95).

The way of Christ takes a central place in Las Casas's thinking about human interaction. The model for dealing with the Amerindians is Christ, who did not send "armed soldiers to take possession" but "holy men, preachers, sent sheep among wolves" (*OW* 67). Violence is contrary to the way of Christ and can never be endorsed in the encounter between Amerindians and Spaniards (although the encounter between Muslims and Spaniards is seen as a different matter).[69] The later Las Casas goes so far as to argue that the relationship needs to be that of two parties who can choose freely. He postulates that the Amerindians should be able to choose freely whether or not they want to be subject to the Spanish crown. The same is true for the Christian faith: the Amerindians need to be completely free to choose whether or not they want to adopt this faith—but once they have adopted the faith, they are subject to the Spanish king as well.[70] This admirable openness is backed up by various insights and presuppositions, however. First, Las Casas does not seem to be terribly worried that the Amerindians would reject either the Spanish Crown or the Christian faith. In both cases he presupposes an inherent superiority (*OW* 156): Christians are to Amerindians as angels to humankind, as the spiritual to the material. This superiority makes their acceptance natural. If the material do not follow the spiritual, he states, they "feel uneasy in their presence" and "are filled with shame and confusion if they do not follow them" (*OW* 156). As Luis Rivera Pagán has pointed out, the Thomist distinction of nature and grace provides the theological paradigm: the sovereignty of the Amerindians is merely based on nature, but the sovereignty of the Spaniards is based on divine grace; nevertheless, while grace is superior, it does not destroy but perfects nature. As a result, the sovereignty of the Spaniards does not eradicate the sovereignty of the Amerindians; they are related like that of an emperor to his many kings.[71]

Earlier, Las Casas had argued that Jesus' ministry shows that faith comes easily (*OW* 84). "In the natural order of things," Las Casas explains, "lower creatures imitate higher ones insofar as they can" (*OW* 85). Such voluntary acceptance, Las Casas argues, will be beneficial to all involved. Violence and force are ultimately not effective: in regard to the Christian faith, forced conversions are inferior and can easily turn into their opposite. In regard to the Spanish Empire, a forced conquest is only of limited benefit. Of course, fear can be useful in cases of resistance,[72] but for the most part it is simply not necessary.[73] In these colonial endeavors, Las Casas can be assured of the support of both king and pope.[74] There is no need to be too anxious about the colonial order—it is not merely natural but ordained by God's grace. While there is a difference between heaven and earth, the two cannot be separated. In fact, if kings and empires seek the kingdom of God, they will be rewarded with earthly wealth and success.

The "only way" modeled by Christ for transmitting the Christian faith to others is therefore "the way that wins the mind with reasons, that wins the will with gentleness, with invitation." This way "has to fit all people on earth" (*OW* 68), and is "remarkably kind, gentle, peaceable, sensible, faultless, edifying, lovable. It is suffused with compassion, patience, forgiveness, charm, with charity abounding in benefits freely given to those who hear preached the name of Christ" (*OW* 80). Christ's way is "a gentle, coaxing, gracious way" (*OW* 68) that leads to responses that "flow easily," since there is a "leaning built into nature" according to which following the ways of God in Christ is the most appropriate thing to do. "We call something good and virtuous when it acts harmoniously with itself, and thus with the goal set for it by God, in God's own way," says Las Casas (*OW* 69; see also 100). Christ, as second person of the Trinity, is thus not only the one who teaches and preaches how to live and act, but also the one who makes it possible.[75] Grace has an important role to play in Las Casas's model.

Based on this confidence in God's grace in Christ is Las Casas's emphasis on persuasion, the key to the "only way of Christ." Las Casas talks about "gentle persuasion" (*OW* 73, 93), emphasizing that Christ "forced no one" (*OW* 102). Christ is seen as a "winner," someone who is in sync with the flow of things, rather than as one who swims against the current: "People submitted to Christ the King avidly, viscerally, once they heard His words of eternal life, once they saw His miraculous deeds"; this statement might be challenged by those Gospel accounts that report Jesus' experience of rejection and his struggles, but in Las Casas's mind "the words of our Savior were truly attractive, truly effective" (*OW* 102). Ultimately, Christ "left to each one the choice to keep the kingdom or to kill it" (*OW* 103). In these passages Las Casas reads not unlike later liberal theologians, including Schleiermacher (see next chapter). Despite a world of difference between these theological positions, they have a similar feel because they operate from positions of self-confidence and power. Such a position of power can be seen, for instance, in the way good works are thought to help the business of persuasion: "For the apostles to heal the sick at no cost, to raise the dead, to cleanse lepers, to rid tormented bodies of demons, was a winning way indeed; it gained the good will of people, it was influential on them" (*OW* 76). Quoting Theophilact, Las Casas puts it this way: "if you cure first, and preach after, your words will come easily" (*OW* 76–77). Power is tied to a virtually unfailing sense of the effectiveness of Christ and the Christians. Note that Las Casas emphasizes the fact that the apostles resisted wealth; gain is seen not primarily in terms of economics but in terms of "influence."

The problem with this gentle way of Christ, as promoted by Las Casas, is that power differentials are blended out; Las Casas's proposal operates on the basis of covert power. Clearly, there was no equal relationship between Spaniards and Amerindians. The latter in particular would have harbored few illusions about the power of the former, which allowed them to push their own interests at any point of the relationship. Whether in the conquest itself or in the softer colonial models suggested by Las Casas, the Christian Spanish Empire remained firmly in control. As Dussel notes, the Amerindians could not help but be impressed by the gods who protected the Spaniards and thus they would have been attracted by Christianity in order to align themselves with such powerful gods.[76] Christ's power, therefore, guarantees success without undue force. According to Las Casas, the effectiveness of the apostles has to do not with violence, bribes, or even their superior rhetoric. The effectiveness of the apostles comes from the fact that "they were cloaked with [this particular] Christ" (*OW* 91; quotation from Chrysostom).

It is interesting that liberation theologian Gustavo Gutiérrez does not register problems with Las Casas's emphasis on persuasion. While he understands that preaching the gospel from a perspective of power is problematic, he fails to realize that giving up violence and direct force (conquest) does not mean giving up the power of empire as such.[77] Even persuasion draws its effectiveness from the established powers. Ultimately, persuasion is not less effective than conquest; if anything, it is more effective: "There was a great gain in being gentle," Las Casas writes in reference to Jesus' own mission (*OW* 80). This greater effectiveness of persuasion can also be measured in terms of its long-term effects. As Las Casas notes: "What you choose to do, you keep doing; what you are forced to do, you drop quickly" (*OW* 96; quotation from Gratian). In all of this, Las Casas is not merely drawing up idealistic dreams. To a large degree, this is how mission actually took place in the Americas. Dussel sums it up: "At times it involved the use of arms, that is, forced conversion. But primarily it was by missionaries who pacified the Indians through preaching, persuasion, and direct involvement."[78]

Some of the powerful leaders of the church understood, consciously or unconsciously, the reliability of these power structures. Las Casas quotes Gratian's reference to Pope Leo: "Kindness does more to correct than harshness, bolstering more than lullying, charity more than force" (*OW* 113). In the context of the present-day United States, the administration of President George W. Bush might have benefited from these insights; perhaps it would have been more successful in its own declared missions of fighting terrorism and establishing democracy in Afghanistan and Iraq. Earlier embodiments of U.S. Empire—for instance, during the presidency of Bill Clinton—seemed to be much more in tune with Las Casas's insights, to the point where even the status of the United States as empire would have been questioned. The greater effectiveness of this latter approach is becoming clearer in light of the failures of the Iraq war as it has been handled by the Bush administration.

The task of those who follow the "way of Christ" can be described, in Las Casas's own words, as bringing the "whole world" "under the culture of Christ" (*OW* 93). Las Casas left no doubt that Christ's culture is different from that shaping the Spanish conquest: in its rule of peace, humility, and compassion it reaches the "pinnacle of charity which is the greatest of all the virtues" (*OW* 95). Humility and peace fit with how God created us and thus draw "people to moral life quicker and better—the way Christ intended—than force of arms" (*OW* 96). None of this would sound foreign to contemporary missionary enterprises; humility, compassion, and peace remain guiding values. But it must not be overlooked that peace is also a value of empire. The *Pax Romana* was the principle of the Roman Empire upon which the Middle Ages built. In this context, peace and (a very particular) order always go together. Las Casas quotes Augustine: "Peace is the tranquility of order" (*OW* 74). According to this logic the common good always comes before the individual good; even terms like justice, that are today often invoked to critique empire, are defined as "right order," that is, the God-given order of the empire.[79] Here, one of the bigger concerns of Las Casas becomes clear: the problem with the Spanish Empire was not that it was an empire but that it had developed certain forms that went against the divine order of things. Las Casas felt that the massacre of the innocent resulted in the destruction of the existing world order, the collapse of civilization, thus foreshadowing the ultimate catastrophe, namely, the end of the world.[80]

There is a long history of effects connected to Las Casas's approach. Later projects of mission and evangelization have often taken the form not only of preaching a specific message but also of trying to help other people through various projects of "civilization" or what sometimes was called "modernization." The problem is tied to what is presupposed by this approach. Whether they come to preach or to help, the missionaries understand themselves as somehow more advanced because they have the gospel—often this assumption is not reflected at a conscious level and the missionaries are not aware of it.[81] Whatever the form, mission and evangelization thus often lack any real notion that the others know something about God. The others are only considered to hold some limited knowledge of God if their insights match those of the missionaries. As a result, the others are not able to pose challenges. Thus, even though Las Casas identifies Christ in the Amerindians, this Christ is passive rather than active. This Christ resembles the Christ already known—there is no real surplus, and at no point does the Indigenous Christ seem to transcend or challenge the Spanish Christ. At the core is a developmental notion: the Spaniards bring the gospel because they are more advanced; or, to put matters the other way around, being more advanced has something to do with having (and being charged to spread) the gospel.

Las Casas's approach has often been interpreted as a "dialogue" between Indigenous communities and missionaries, including both give and take.[82] Gutiérrez, who has picked up that argument, nevertheless sees part of the problem when he reinforces the advice given to missionaries to China, namely, that missionaries should not persuade others "to change their rites, their habits, and their customs, unless these be plainly contrary to religion and morality."[83] But who determines what is "contrary to religion and morality," and whose religion and morality is ultimately normative? While Las Casas does not advocate the type of mission that seeks to erase the identity of Indigenous communities, the two-way street that Gutiérrez suggests does not seem to be developed very far in his approach.

If seen in contrast to Las Casas's attitude toward the Muslim Empire, however, his attitude toward Amerindians is more positive. Typical for the mood of his day, which carried over into the Latin American conquest, Las Casas rejects the Muslim Empire and shows no sympathy for it whatsoever (*OW* 144ff.). Todorov argues that Las Casas has no sympathy for the Muslims because, unlike the Amerindians, they cannot be portrayed as potential Christians.[84] The related but bigger problem is that the Muslim Empire poses a direct challenge to the Christian Empire; and since, unlike in the relation with the Amerindians, the power differential was less clear, no peaceful cooperation seemed possible. In other words, persuasion is never seen as an option in this case where the differential of power to back it up did not exist. This observation points us back to the main thing that is missing in the relation of Christians and Amerindians: there is as yet little sense that the relationship is open in both directions and that the Spanish Christians might indeed be challenged by the Christ of the Indies. Evangelization and mission operate mainly in one direction. The Amerindians can pose a challenge only where the Spaniards make obvious mistakes and act contrary to their own gospel.

This approach can be seen in Hanke's account of one of Las Casas's missionary enterprises. After writing *The Only Way*, Las Casas was invited by Bishop Marroquín of Guatemala to convert the Indigenous communities of his area who were considered dangerous. Las Casas had accomplished a similar mission, just prior to writing *The Only Way*, with the people of the guerilla chief Enriquillo: this Indigenous and African group, which had been at war with the Spaniards for fifteen years, was "pacified" by Las Casas and only one other priest.[85] Now, Las Casas's method again proved successful in establishing the territory of Verapaz (literally: "true peace"). In Hanke's account, "Las Casas selected for his demonstration the only land left unconquered in that region." To leave no doubt of the challenge, Hanke adds that the area was "filled with fierce beasts, snakes, large monkeys, and, to boot, a land without salt" and that the "natives living there were ferocious, barbarous, and impossible to subjugate." The Spaniards had tried three times to take them by force, with no success. The mission was clear: to "induce them voluntarily to become vassals of the king of Spain and pay him tribute according to their ability; to teach them and to preach the Christian faith."[86] Las Casas's demands, in return, were that the Amerindians would be subject only to the king and that no other Spaniards should enter the province for five years. As a first step, Las Casas and the other missionaries composed some ballads in the native language that told the history of Christianity. Next, Las Casas taught those ballads to some Indigenous merchants whom he sent into the region, their merchandise complemented by Las Casas with some scissors, knives, mirrors, and bells. These Indigenous merchants, trained as catechists, proclaimed that the Amerindian gods were idols and demons, and they denounced human sacrifices. Following Hanke's description, due to the "novelty of the situation" they "excited great wonder and admiration."[87] After these merchants had instructed the tribes for several days, the tribes asked for more, and they were told that they needed to invite Las Casas and his companions. At first, only one friar was sent who spoke the native languages well, and he was royally received. The chief even offered to build a church. According to Hanke's narrative the chief was so impressed by the "friar's vestments and cleanliness, for his own priests went about in filthy clothes," that he converted to Christianity together with his whole tribe. However, it did not take long for the experiment to deteriorate. Las Casas was called back to the capital in 1538 and the problem, as Hanke describes it, was that there were no "Spanish colonists as selfless in their attitude as Las Casas."[88]

In this account, Las Casas went to considerable lengths in his efforts to relate to the Indians. He even learned their language. Gutiérrez interprets this concern for the native language as an expression of Las Casas's concern and care for the Indians. It is part of what he identifies as the main achievement of Las Casas: "adopting the perspective of the natives of the Indies."[89] While Las Casas's concern and care do not have to be disputed, the question is whether his approach ultimately fed back into the structures of the Spanish Empire. Following the "only way of Christ" no doubt challenged the other way of Christ followed by the *conquistadors*. George Pendle comments on the conquest's way of Christ that the conquistadors' missionaries "recognized that baptism and religious observance did not necessarily signify true conversion, and they showed a wise tolerance."[90] Indeed, for the *conquistadors*, true conversion (in the sense of a holistic change of life) was not the point; there was a marked difference between Spaniards and Amerindians, and that difference did not need to be eliminated; indeed, it facilitated exploitation. Las Casas's "only way of Christ," on the other hand, is much more interested in true conversion and it is better at accomplishing it. Since the Amerindians are equal in terms of human potential, the missionaries have an obligation to raise them up to their level. This insistence on equality may have amounted to a different colonialism, but it resulted in colonialism nonetheless. In any case, Las Casas's plea for conversion by persuasion led to an assimilation of Indigenous communities to the Spanish-Christian world that was stronger and deeper than what the conquest would have been able to accomplish without it.

The Resistance Way of Christ

Todorov, who raises significant questions of Las Casas, nevertheless notes that he does not want to suggest that Las Casas should or could have behaved differently.[91] Las Casas was a man of his own time, faced with the impossibility of leaving behind the confines of his world. Nevertheless, there is a christological surplus in his work that must not be overlooked; as in the previous chapters, this surplus can only be recognized when the christological implications of the colonial system are accounted for. When Las Casas moves into the worlds of the Amerindians, a certain hybridity (in the sense of Homi Bhabha's use of the term) emerges that works both ways, despite the obvious power differentials.[92] While Amerindians are assimilating to the Spanish-Christian world, they also assimilate some of it for their own purposes. This hybridity can be seen in all aspects of life: the "colorful clothes," for instance, of Indigenous communities in the Andean regions of Latin America that are much admired today by tourists and other observers are hybridized versions of Spanish peasant clothing. Some of the earliest music after the conquest brings together Mary and Pachamama, hybridizes them, and thus forges a two-way street that is often overlooked.[93] Such phenomena, commonly devalued as "syncretism," open new perspectives; developing a Christology that is aware of hybridity can deepen our understanding of Christ. Our search for a christological surplus needs to take a close look at oppression related to religious images, including christological ones, and what emerges in response to it. In any case, response and even resistance did develop in the midst of the colonial situation, making use of colonial symbols, and we can learn from this dynamic.

Examining the resistance factor of the way of Christ in the work of Las Casas, we can begin with his emphasis on Christ's praxis: "What Christ did was law to us, more than what He said" (*OW* 87). Thus, Las Casas identifies the basis of the gospel in the form of a motto that also informs his approach to mission and evangelization: "deeds first, words later" (*OW* 90). The point is not to play off words and deeds but to avoid the kind of separation that he suspects in the theology of conquest (and that seems to plague a certain kind of top-down theology in general). In Christ, unlike in some Christologies, there can be no dichotomy between deeds and words. Ultimately, Las Casas argues, "Christ's deeds are his words."[94]

Christ models an alternative way of life (and also provides the grace that enables humans to follow him). The Christ who could have had control through power and might "led a lowly life, a kind, peaceful, poor, a marginal life" (*OW* 94). Furthermore, "publicans and sinners sat with Him as well as disciples. That could not have happened if He bore Himself as a king or led an upper-crust life, pompous and vain" (*OW* 96–97). This is the way of life that is most fitting for the missionaries (and ultimately for all Christians). Las Casas's rules for the "ideal missionary," modeled after the way of Christ, push for a new way of life: like Christ, the missionary should want "no power over them as a result of the preaching" (*OW* 103), should not "itch . . . after their wealth" (*OW* 103), should show respect (*OW* 104) and charity (*OW* 106), and should harm no one (*OW* 109).

This way of life, the "only way," was also followed by the apostles. In Las Casas's own words: the apostles were "poor, humble, kind—not after gold, not after silver, not after coin, not after stuff of any kind" (*OW* 75). Despite the various entanglements of theology and the colonial enterprise, we need to repeat that personal economic benefit was not the driving force behind the work of the missionaries. That the missionaries nevertheless ended up supporting the colonial system shows the difficulty of coming up with alternatives and the degree to which the colonial system had become a way of life.[95] Nevertheless, we can identify a christological surplus even here; there are some elements in Las Casas's own thought that point beyond the entanglement of theology and colonialism.

Throughout his life, Las Casas continues to learn and, in response, develops stronger and more effective forms of resistance against violent forms of exploitation. Most important is the fact that Las Casas finds a fresh encounter with Christ in the suffering Amerindians. The people are not merely the recipients of the gospel, they also participate in the reality of Christ to some degree. By finding Christ in the suffering Amerindians, Gutiérrez has argued, Christology "becomes flesh and history in the Indies and the backbone of [Las Casas's] thought."[96] Gutiérrez finds the following sequence to be the key to Las Casas's spirituality and theology: (1) Las Casas finds Christ in the suffering Amerindians; (2) the suffering of Christ is repeated in the suffering of the Amerindians; (3) as a result Las Casas feels that he has to do anything in his power to end this suffering. Here is a parallel to Matthew 25, because what is done to one of the "least of these" is done to Christ (see also *OW* 136). This move goes beyond the commonly noted emphasis on the humanity of the Amerindians and, as Gutiérrez has claimed, infuses a completely new tone into the theology of the sixteenth century, where Sepúlveda argues for the inferiority of the Amerindians and Vitoria argues for their human rights.[97] Nevertheless, the crucial step still missing in Las Casas, overlooked by Gutiérrez, is an awareness of how the Amerindians relate to Christ's active work. In Las Casas's reflections it appears as if the Amerindians relate to the imposed and (seemingly passive) sufferings of Christ, while the Spanish missionaries relate to Christ's active work. An understanding of suffering as active and as a step of resistance would open new horizons.

There is indeed a development in Las Casas's position that may ultimately point in this direction. Gutiérrez notes a gradual development toward a clearer position in favor of the Amerindians.[98] It is based on a deepening relationship, which leads to a deepening of Las Casas's Christology as well. The christological surplus becomes more pronounced in this process, as I will show. Gutiérrez, noting the snags in the development process, concludes: "Not without sluggishness, not without limitations, these persons, whose cultural distance from the Indians was so great, gradually divested themselves of their spontaneous sense of superiority and sought to move to the viewpoint of the dispossessed."[99]

Todorov interprets this development in Las Casas's position as the development of what he calls "perspectivism."[100] This perspectivism, according to Todorov, understands that there is no longer one God who is universal—like the God of Christianity. What is universal is the idea of divinity. In this interpretation Las Casas comes out looking like a religious relativist, and Todorov praises his "egalitarianism" and neutrality, which serve as a model for "today's ethnologist."[101] Unfortunately, Todorov's comments show little sense for how differentials of power operate, and that egalitarianism and neutrality might not be sufficient to put up resistance to empire. Las Casas's Christology takes us beyond Todorov when he begins taking the side of the Amerindians, thus anticipating contemporary challenges to modern scientists' claim for neutrality. In response to the Spanish king's rescinding parts of the New Laws, Las Casas and some other bishops present a document in which they state that the church has a responsibility for the poor; in fact, the Amerindians are to be put directly under the "protection and shelter" of the church.[102] The theological underpinnings must not be overlooked: Las Casas operates on the basis of God's care about the "smallest and most forgotten."[103] Nevertheless, this move in and of itself does not yet transcend colonialism since it does not reverse the flow of power. Gutiérrez makes an important point, however, when he argues for a basic difference between those who see things from the perspective of power and those who see things from the perspective of the victims.[104] Only when coming into closer connection with Amerindians are the Spanish able to realize the implications of colonial structures. In this sense we might agree with Gutiérrez that here are the "foundations of an anticolonialist position" in Las Casas.[105] In this context, Las Casas's belief that all people have a certain knowledge of God, however confused, gains depth,[106] even though it is not unproblematic, as we have seen.

Gutiérrez is right when he reminds us that "there is no innocent theology."[107] Theology, and therefore Christology, is never done from a neutral and innocent position. This is true not only for the opponents of Las Casas but also for Las Casas himself. Nevertheless, we need to name more clearly than Gutiérrez the places where theology does become guilty. In Gutiérrez's interpretation, the decision Las Casas puts before theology is whether its concern is for God or gold. But is the alternative really so clear-cut? Is this not first of all about two different understandings of the way of Christ—one according to which Christ endorses the harsher forms of colonialism represented by the Spanish conquest, and the other according to which Christ endorses the gentler ways promoted by Las Casas and others? The problem, therefore, lies at the heart of Christology itself, and it is here that Las Casas's contribution is important for us today. Using Las Casas's model, but going beyond it, we might distinguish two understandings of the way of Christ, one according to which Christ is understood as authorizing and supporting the powers that be, and the other in which Christ is essentially related to people at the margins.

The achievement of Las Casas's Christology is its clear rejection of a strict colonialist position that identifies Christ with the purposes of conquest and does not shy away from enslaving the Indigenous communities in the most cruel and deadly ways possible.[108] Las Casas's sense of a connection of Christ and the Amerindians (however rudimentary it may be) pushes toward a new horizon. Todorov's point that modern perspectivism is better than medieval colonialism captures one aspect of this new horizon. But, as we have seen, there are some limits even when there is a sense of equality and a common humanity; modernity invents its own colonialisms, as the next chapter will show. Pointing beyond those limitations is Las Casas's ability to relate to the other, to be open to a certain level of hybridity, and even to change his mind in relation to the other.

However limited Las Casas's ability to change in his encounter with the other, we need to pursue Gutiérrez's sense that "Las Casas presents a discourse upon faith that emerges with a profile of his own against the background of sixteenth-century theology."[109] One of the things that set Las Casas apart from Sepúlveda, for instance, is the relation of reflection and commitment, faith and social analysis.[110] In this regard, Las Casas's early anthropological and sociological efforts prove helpful: he corrects the exaggerated estimates of people sacrificed by Indigenous communities, often used to justify conquest and colonization, and points out that the war waged by the Spanish against these communities cost many more lives. A comparative perspective is helpful in this regard, as Las Casas points out that many "ancient peoples" had similar customs. Finally, Las Casas argues that the idea behind offering the very best—human life—to God is not in itself evil.[111] These insights are connected to Las Casas's openness to the other in which he begins, albeit in rudimentary ways, to adopt the viewpoints of the other, "as if he was an Indian."[112] Since innocent and neutral perspectives do not exist, as postcolonial and other critics have taught us, Las Casas appears to be moving in the right direction toward deeper levels of understanding.

Nevertheless, we are also aware now that Las Casas's interest in the other can be turned against the other; the knowledge of the other can reinforce and support colonizing efforts. Although Gutierrez strongly disagrees with this argument,[113] we need to take note of the problem, which is not primarily with Las Casas but with the system. This problem is a perennial one and can also be the unintended outcome of so-called "mission trips" in the contemporary church and what are called "area studies" in the academy.[114] The risk of reinscribing colonization through our attempts at relationship and deeper understanding can only be overcome if we realize the nature of the problem and actively oppose it. We need to move beyond where Las Casas left off.

In his book *The Only Way*, the progress made by Las Casas can be seen. There are substantial references to the classical traditions and sources that were revered by his contemporaries; but Las Casas uses them in a fresh way. While these resources were commonly used against the Amerindians, Las Casas reinterprets them, including the Bible, in their support. The method of Las Casas's reading is instructive, as he rereads the ancient texts in the context of the suffering of the Indigenous communities that he witnesses. Here is one of Las Casas's most original contributions to the debates about conquest and colonialism.[115] Following the structure of Roman law, Las Casas brings together fact and law (*ius et factum* [Lat.]; *hecho y derecho* [Span.]) in new ways. What matters are not legal facts in isolation but legal facts related to facts about the world. As facts and law are brought together and tensions emerge, the law (as well as theology) needs to be adjusted. This is where Las Casas's approach is most fundamentally different from the traditional approach represented, for instance, by Juan Ginés de Sepúlveda, who would disregard facts if they were not in accordance with the law. For Sepúlveda, some facts simply did not matter, while for Las Casas all facts had to be taken into account.[116] Gutiérrez sharpens the focus: Las Casas is concerned not just about facts in general but about facts seen from the perspective of the "victims of history." Once again, this is the view from the perspective of the "other"; Las Casas models the significance of putting oneself in the position of the other and, as we have seen, some of the problems connected with doing so, as well.[117]

Perhaps the radical nature of Las Casas's proposals can best be seen in light of his context. Alonso de Veracruz, a contemporary of Las Casas, also challenged certain aspects of the conquest but, unlike Las Casas, he did not condemn the conquest as a whole, seeking to reform the *encomienda* system rather than to abandon it, and believing "that international law justified in limited instance and under certain circumstances the conquest of the New World."[118] Some commentators have noted a distinct "realism" in Las Casas's position. Fernando Mires points out that Las Casas was not utopian: if Las Casas would not have geared his demands to the interests of the king and the state, they would not have listened to him. [119] Gutiérrez, too, notes that Las Casas worked from within the system: "Had Bartolomé wafted above what was happening in the Indies, he would not have made certain errors in his proposals. . . . But then perhaps he would not have left us the witness that is engraved in our memories today."[120] In this context, Las Casas chooses between the lesser evils: Mires points out that Las Casas preferred the government over the "private sector" in colonial affairs,[121] and Gutiérrez argues that Las Casas preferred the ways of the church.

What Las Casas manages to challenge from the perspective of his realism is worth noting. His christological position helps him to challenge the common support of war. Christ does not really need war, he argues, as "peaceful king, rare, strong, good, all-powerful king—a king who shows power solely by pardon and compassion" (*OW* 126). In addition, war can destroy respect for God and respect for the Christian religion (*OW* 164); a lesson that Christians in the contemporary United States are learning the hard way. The problem runs deeper than Las Casas seems to realize, because war not only destroys the victims' respect for God but also the warriors' respect for God—or at least it alters their images of God dramatically. That war is contradictory to the way of Christ (*OW* 124) does not seem to be such a radical statement and should go without saying. Nevertheless, in light of the current U.S. wars in Afghanistan and Iraq—often defended in the name of a certain Christianity—the significance of the challenge posed by Las Casas might become somewhat clearer. There is another interesting reversal in Las Casas's thoughts about war that cannot even be openly addressed in the contemporary United States: the Indigenous communities, against whom this war is waged, he says, have a right to use force against abuse of the invaders.[122]

Las Casas poses another challenge to the theology of salvation that has often been promoted in the colonial context. The argument that non-Christians will be punished and cast into eternal damnation has often been used to support evangelizationatanycost,includingbyforceandbywar.LasCasas,followingMatthew 25:31-46, turns the argument around when he claims that even non-Christians will go to heaven if they love their neighbors, while many Christians will not.[123] He is not the only one who makes this point in Latin America: his ally Domingo de Soto also believes that people who have never heard of Christ can be saved.[124] Contrary to the expectations of many contemporary supporters of "evangelism," this position does not lead Las Casas to abandon his efforts at evangelization, but there is a significant change in style.

Las Casas's understanding of love reflects this significant broadening of the horizon. His fundamental definition of love is "the love, the affection, by which God is cherished directly, and humankind indirectly on account of God" (*OW* 129). Such love has its center beyond humanity and the colonial structures. This insight poses a challenge not only to the conquest itself but, eventually, even to Las Casas's own softer version of colonialism. Las Casas also understands the biblical relation of love of God and love of other people: "Love of God cannot exist without love of neighbor," he claims, and, turning things around, "love of neighbor [cannot exist] without love of God" (*OW* 136). The challenge of the first part of the equation seems to be fairly obvious: the *conquistadors* who waged war against the Amerindians and who enslaved them did not show much love for the neighbor.[125] If the warriors have no love for other people, there must be something wrong with their love for God, too. But what about Las Casas and his friends? What about the pope (and to a certain degree even the king) who, at least in principle, is also opposed to violence and slavery? What is missing here might be grasped by another term that is contained in the notion of love but not mentioned by Las Casas: respect. At stake is not just the kind of love for others that does not kill them or that cares for them; at stake also is the kind of respect for others that is the foundation of a truly mutual relationship that has the potential to cut through the (ubiquitous) differentials of power. Las Casas seems to have some implicit sense of this respect when he talks about the connection of the other person and God. The designation *holy*, he points out, refers to "someone manifestly at home with others, peaceful, dignified, unassuming, patient, pure, honest, spiritual, someone intent on heavenly things, not on earthly good" (*OW* 144). When Las Casas turns things around in the second part and argues that there is no love of neighbor without love of God, he begins to create the foundation for a new respect of the Amerindians. Now the challenge continues: What if the missionaries truly understood that their love and respect for human beings is a manifestation of love and respect for God?

Las Casas's insights have the potential to challenge the top-down approaches that have become so characteristic of Christian missionary efforts, including the "mission trips" organized by churches in the twenty-first century. Las Casas's thought deconstructs colonial and neo-colonial one-way streets and provides a better basis for mutual relationships. There is a clear understanding that other people are human—like us. But the question might also be turned around so that it becomes: How are we like other people? Here is a blind spot in Las Casas's thought that has been pointed out by contemporary Native American thinkers in the United States.[126] Christology could help overcome this blind spot: Is the ultimate challenge of the way of Christ not that Christ is human like us but that we are human like him?

But we still need to address the implications of the power differential between the Spanish and the Indigenous communities. Some sense of this power differential might come into play when Las Casas calls the conquest a crime. Here a strange reversal takes place, for those who consent to crime are worse than the criminals themselves; their "consent is fourfold: carelessness, complicity, cooperation, cover-up—the misuse of authority" (*OW* 169). The misuse of power does play a role here. Furthermore, this misuse of power is tied to the resistance way of Christ because what is ultimately at stake is not just correct ethical behavior but salvation—the salvation of the Spanish conquistadors themselves and of their supporters (*OW* 173). No wonder Las Casas insists that nothing less than restoration is required (*OW* 171).

Las Casas's approach, informed by his understanding of Christ, therefore goes beyond what José Carlos Mariátegui identified as a real limitation of approaches based on notions of charity. Mariátegui talks about the "complete obsolescence of the humanitarian and philanthropic points of view" that seem a "prolongation of the apostolic battle of Las Casas." The problem lies in reducing the issue "to an exclusively administrative, pedagogical, ethnic, or moral problem in order to avoid at all cost recognizing its economic aspect."[127] By identifying the larger issue of salvation—ultimately a matter of life and death for Christians—Las Casas introduces a broader perspective that transcends the narrow realm of morality. And by attributing a role to the Amerindians, however small, Las Casas pushes us beyond the one-way streets of traditional mission work and charity, broadening our view for the way of Christ, who walks not first of all with the colonizers who are always on the go but with those who walk in less conspicuous ways at the margins. Nevertheless, we continue to struggle with the economic aspect noted by Mariátegui.

Why was Las Casas's work so effective? One answer is given by Helen Rand Parish: he was effective "because [he] learned that you cannot preach the first commandment unless you live the second."[128] While this is an odd judgment for a historian, it points us back to the christological surplus of Las Casas's thought; his connections with the Amerindians did indeed make a difference. Las Casas's *The Only Way* in particular needs to be seen in terms of its effects. It was the basis for a papal encyclical by Pope Paul III, *Sublimis Deus*, in 1537, which proclaimed the rationality and freedom of the Amerindians and argued for peaceful conversion. Ultimately, it became a foundation for King Charles V's New Laws of 1542–1543.[129] Even though the encyclical was sent back from the New World to Rome and the New Laws were challenged as early as 1545, Las Casas's influence did not go unrecognized. His approach did make a difference. The fact that Las Casas experienced strong opposition adds depth to the christological surplus that comes through in his work. After the New Laws, he was considered to be the "most hated man in the Indies."[130] Even in the twentieth century he was accused of being "mentally ill," "a pigheaded anarchist," "a preacher of Marxism," "a dangerous demagogue," and "possessed by the devil."[131]

Rand Parish remarks that Las Casas "saw the New World as it was."[132] This is more than most of us can hope for and there is a hint of romanticism in her judgment. But there is a sense in which Las Casas learned to see things in a new light and to read between the lines; his understanding of the way of Christ kept pushing him beyond his own comfort zones. Of course, Las Casas was not alone. There were other prominent church people such as bishops Juan de Valle and Antonio de Valdivieso. Many of these people risked everything, including their own lives, but so did Christ.[133]

Notes

1. "Even those missionary 'heroes' who are most revered in modern memory, from Las Casas in the south to [John] Eliot in the north, conspired with the political power of the colonial oppressors to deprive Indian people of their cultures, destroy native economies, and reduce culturally integruous communities to subservient dependence—all for the sake of the 'gospel' and with the best of intentions." George Tinker, *Spirit and Resistance: Political Theology and American Indian Liberation* (Minneapolis: Fortress Press, 2004), 103. See also the questions raised by José Carlos Mariátegui (below).

2. Bartolomé de Las Casas, *The Only Way*, ed. Helen Rand Parish, trans. Francis Patrick Sullivan (New York: Paulist, 1992), 56 (hereafter *OW*).

3. See C. M. Stafford Pole, "Successors to Las Casas," *Revista de historia de america* 61–62 (January-December 1966): 92.

4. See ibid., 105, 106; "the frontier was pacified," says Stafford Pole, by mission, diplomatic negotiation, and purchase.

5. See Mariando Delgado, "Las Casas' posthumer Sieg: Zur Kontroverse über die Missionsart und die Tributfrage im Zusammenhang mit Conquista und Evangelisation der Philippinen," in *Synodus: Beiträge zur Konzilien- und allgemeinen Kirchengeschichte*, ed. Remigius Bäumer et al. (Paderborn: Ferdinand Schöningh, 1997). This article shows the influence of Las Casas in the Philippines soon after his death.

6. See Benjamin Keen, "Introduction," in *Bartolomé de Las Casas in History: Toward an Understanding of the Man and His Work*, ed. Juan Friede and Benjamin Keen (DeKalb: Northern Illinois University Press, 1971), 10–12, 15, 16. Eighteenth-century British opinion of Las Casas, however, swung back to a more negative assessment, as Spain's power declined and the polemic became less important; ibid., 21.

7. Ibid., 30.

8. See ibid., 55.

9. Enrique Dussel, *The Church in Latin America, 1492–1992* (Maryknoll, N.Y.: Orbis, 1992), 43.

10. Tsvetan Todorov emphasizes that this hierarchy is also seen in terms of the opposition of good and evil. *The Conquest of America: The Question of the Other*, trans. Richard Howard (Norman: University of Oklahoma Press, 1999), 153–54.

11. See Anthony Pagden, *Lords of All the World: Ideologies of Empire in Spain, Britain and France 1500–1850* (New Haven: Yale University Press, 1995), 100; and *OW* 47. One of the significant differences between Sepúlveda and Las Casas has to do with their different opinions on the capacity of the Amerindians to govern themselves, a capacity that Sepúlveda did not want to acknowledge. See Luis Rivera Pagán, *Evangelización y violencia* (San Juan, Puerto Rico: Editorial CEMI, 1992), 125.

12. See Gustavo Gutiérrez. *Las Casas: In Search of the Poor of Jesus Christ,* trans. Robert Barr (Maryknoll, N.Y.: Orbis Books, 1993), 134.

13. Juan Gines de Sepúlveda, *Apología*, reference in ibid., 135.

14. See Pagden, *Lords of All the World*, 52.

15. Francisco de Vitoria, "On the Law of War," in Francisco de Vitoria, *Political Writings*, ed. Anthony Pagden and Jeremy Lawrance, Cambridge Texts in the History of Political Thought (Cambridge: Cambridge University Press, 1991), 302–03.

16. Francisco de Vitoria, "On the American Indians," in ibid., 285; see also Gutiérrez, *Las Casas*, 128.

17. See Vitoria, "On the American Indians" 3.5 par. 15, 288. See also Gutiérrez, *Las Casas*, 168, 171.

18. Vitoria, "On the American Indians" 3.1 par. 8, 283. Vitoria also observes that the Spanish emperor is "not master of the whole world" (ibid., 2.1 par. 25, 253) and neither is the pope (ibid., 2.2, par. 27, 260).

19. See Anthony Pagden, *European Encounters with the New World from Renaissance to Romanticism* (New Haven, Ct.: Yale University Press, 1993), 78–79.

20. See Anthony Pagden, *Peoples and Empires: A Short History of European Migration, Exploration, and Conquest from Greece to the Present* (New York: Modern Library, 2001), 69; and Hans Magnus Enzensberger's introduction to Las Casas's *The Devastation of the Indies: A Brief Account*, trans. Herma Briffault (New York: Seabury, 1974), 32.

21. *OW* 117. Las Casas's description of war on the following pages describes the evils of war in such detail that little romanticism remains; he does not leave out the effects of what today is called "blowback," that is, the consequences of imperial aggression, manifest in its victims as rage, hatred, vengefulness, depression, sorrow, fear, horror, and despair; see *OW* 120. For further description of Spanish cruelties, see George Sanderlin, ed. and trans., *Witness: Writings of Bartolomé de Las Casas* (Maryknoll, N.Y.: Orbis, 1992), 148–50 (hereafter *Witness*). "All of us know they will harbor an undying hatred and bitterness against their oppressor"; *OW* 147.

22. *Witness,* 148, A "Very Brief Account."

23. See Pagden, *Lords of All the World*, 31–32. The papal bulls, granting the Spanish monarchs to occupy "such islands and lands . . . as you have discovered or are about to discover" were issued in 1493.

24. *OW* 158–64. For Las Casas's defense of war for the sake of "saving the nation" as a defensive war or as offensive war against tyranny, see *OW* 101.

25. *OW* 164. "That rule is tyrannical, violent, and never long lasting which is acquired by force of arms, or gotten without some consent of the conquered"; *OW* 101, reference to Aristotle's *Politics*.

26. *OW* 101, reference to "all the philosophers, the Catholic theologians, and St. Thomas."

27. Ibid., reference to Aristotle's *Ethics* and *Politics*.

28. *Witness,* 146: "The reason why the Christians have killed and destroyed such infinite numbers of souls is solely because they have made gold their ultimate aim."

29. For one of his strongest attacks, see *Witness*, 151–58. Gutiérrez notes that Las Casas struggled against the *encomienda* system throughout his life. *Las Casas*, 280.

30. This is the main point of Gutiérrez's positive evaluation of the legacy of Las Casas.

31. See Dussel, *The Church in Latin America,* 51.

32. See Las Casas, *Witness*, 145. Las Casas reports that of the three million native inhabitants

of Hispaniola not even two hundred are left (ibid.). Las Casas's numbers have often been questioned, but recent historiography has confirmed the severe loss of life. Of nearly seventeen million people in Mexico in 1532, only one million remained in 1608, see Dussel, *The Church in Latin America*, 42. Cautious estimates put the population of the colonized territories at seventy million before the Spaniards arrived, and at ten million in 1625. See Gutiérrez, *Las Casas*, 461–62.

33. Robert L. Brady explains the cultural background on which Las Casas' judgment was produced, choosing the "lesser of two evils." "The Role of Las Casas in the Emergence of Negro Slavery in the New World," *Revista de historia de america* 61–62 (January-December 1966): 43–55. Brady argues that African slavery in Spain was "both humane and terminable . . . regulated by laws based on Christian principles"; ibid., 46–47.

34. Todorov, *The Conquest of America*, 175–76. Todorov's alternative, however, is not particularly convincing: he claims that the next step after colonialism is a system in which communication is key, and here the problems seem to disappear. Todorov makes a distinction between whether something is imposed or proposed: "A thing is not imposed when one can choose another thing instead, and knows one can choose"; ibid., 181. But who is ever in a position to choose freely? Even when something is merely proposed—in a modern consumer society—does this mean that there are no hidden pressures?

35. *Witness*, 167.

36. See Gutiérrez, *Las Casas*, 154, 167.

37. Reference in ibid., 166.

38. Todorov argues that Las Casas is projecting Christian ideals on them and thus his accounts of the Amerindians are not much more nuanced than those of Columbus. *The Conquest of America*, 163–64. He goes too far, however, when he claims that Las Casas's description of the Indians is poorer than even that of Sepúlveda; ibid., 165.

39. Walter Mignolo talks about Occidentalism as the approach that, having had its beginnings in the sixteenth century, had a significant impact in shaping Europe, preceding the eighteenth- and nineteenth-century developments of Orientalism. *Local Histories/Global Designs: Coloniality, Subaltern Knowledges, and Border Thinking* (Princeton: Princeton University Press, 2000), 18–21.

40. *Witness*, 144.

41. Dussel points out that there were very few descriptions of the Indian mentality or of the mythical structures of their beliefs and their systems of thought; a deeper interest can only be found in the second generation of missionaries, in the last quarter of the sixteenth century. *The Church in Latin America*, 65.

42. *OW* 63; this comes from God, says Las Casas, "who wished to make them so."

43. *Witness*, 176.

44. Todorov, *The Conquest of America*, 165.

45. Here is Todorov's extended argument: Las Casas insists that the Amerindians possess Christian traits; in fact, Las Casas professes that their "most characteristic feature is their resemblance to Christians" by using such descriptors as "humility," "obedient," and "peaceful" (quoted in Todorov, *The Conquest of America*, 163). The Amerindians evince little interest in material wealth not because they are lazy, as the Spanish claim, but rather because they possess a Christian morality; ibid., 165. Yet if the Indians are potential Christians, then they are fundamentally no different from the European Christians sent to proselytize them. While Las Casas refuses to condemn the Indians because they are different, he simultaneously refuses to admit that they are different; ibid., 167. Consequently, Las Casas is able to justify colonization on spiritual grounds, to be carried out by priests instead of soldiers; ibid., 171.

46. *OW* 66; in this context, Las Casas clarifies that some groups are not as developed as others, "some peoples in some places have not yet developed political maturity"; but even the more highly developed groups need to be developed further.

47. Even Dussel puts things in this way: "The 'cultural distance' . . . between the Spanish and the Indians," particularly the high cultures of the Mayan-Aztecs and the Incas, "was more than five thousand years. The rest of America was secondary and in an absolutely primitive state." *The Church in Latin America*, 37. He compares the Latin American high cultures to that of the Egyptians. Todorov explains how this evolutionary scheme reduces respect for difference and produces a perspective of sameness. *The Conquest of America*, 167.

48. *Witness*, 176.

49. Pagden, *European Encounters*, 81.

50. *OW* 156. Todorov wonders whether there is violence in the conviction that one possesses the truth and thus is called to evangelize others. See below for more reflections on evangelization. *The Conquest of America*, 168.

51. *Witness*, 152.

52. All quotes in this paragraph are from *Witness*, 171–72.

53. See Manuel M. Martínez, "Las Casas on the Conquest of America," in Friede and Keen, eds., *Bartolomé de Las Casas in History*, 346.

54. See Enzensberger's introduction to Las Casas's *The Devastation of the Indies*, 26.

55. Quoted in *OW* 27.

56. Enzensberger, "Introduction" to Las Casas's *The Devastation of the Indies*, 33.

57. Dussel states that the first project failed because of the "questionable selection of colonists who accompanied Las Casas," and other mishaps, and finally because of an attack by the Indians. *The Church in Latin America,* 48.

58. Marcel Bataillon, "The *Clérigo* Casas, Colonist and Colonial Reformer," in Friede and Keen, eds., *Bartolomé de Las Casas in History,* 364.

59. See ibid., 365.

60. See ibid., 372; see also *OW* 30. Lewis Hanke notes that even the older Las Casas (in 1559) hangs on to this plan, promising the king that this would give him a "great realm larger than Spain, which would make the king of France tremble; indeed by securing the New World the king of Spain would hold the whole world within the grasp of his hand." *Bartolomé de Las Casas: An Interpretation of His Life and Writings* (The Hague, Netherlands: M. Nijhoff, 1951), 23. See also *OW* 21–22, n.23, which correctly notes that this is not a utopian plan.

61. See George Pendle, *A History of Latin America* (Baltimore: Penguin, 1967), 52. This argument could be used in different ways—at the turn of the twentieth century the social Darwinist Bernard Moses would argue that mixing the races explained the slower development of Latin America; see Friede and Keen, eds., *Bartolomé de Las Casas in History,* 41.

62. Hanke, *Bartolomé de Las Casas,* 2.

63. Ibid., 91.

64. Todorov, *The Conquest of America,* 191.

65. Hanke, *Bartolomé de Las Casas,* 95.

66. Hubert Herring, quoted in Pendle, *A History of Latin America,* 56.

67. Dussel, *The Church in Latin America,* 43.

68. Roberto Goizueta, "Knowing the God of the Poor," in *Opting for the Margins: Postmodernity and Liberation in Christian Theology,* ed. Joerg Rieger (New York: Oxford University Press, 2003), 148. Goizueta emphasizes the "intrinsic connection between the option for the poor . . . and authentic Christian belief and worship"; ibid., 148.

69. *OW* 144–51. Las Casas accuses the Muslims of trying to convert people by force—just like the conquistadors; *OW* 147.

70. Gutiérrez oddly talks about this as "democratic coexistence of peoples"; *Las Casas,* 385. While there is no obligation to accept the Spanish emperors before conversion, after the Indians are converted, they are obligated to acknowledge them—this is in opposition to Sepúlveda, who argued that the Indians must first be subjected to the

emperor. It is important to note that the later Las Casas does not seem to hold to this position anymore; ibid., 387.

71. Pagán, *Evangelización y violencia*, 107, 109. Pagán points out that Las Casas never proposed that Spain should give up its rule over the New Word; with an "utopian idealism," Las Casas develops the vision of a paternal and beneficent empire; ibid., 105.

72. *OW* 156. Earlier, Las Casas points out that the punishment for rejection belongs to God, not to humans; *OW* 78–79.

73. See Todorov, *The Conquest of America*, 168. Even Hanke agrees: force is "unnecessary. Once the Indians accepted Christianity the next and inevitable step would be for them to acknowledge the king of Spain their sovereign." *Bartolomé de Las Casas*, 25.

74. *OW* 156–57; see also *OW* 114–15, referring to a 1537 decree of Pope Paul III who argues that the Indians must not be deprived of liberty, property, and self-determination, and that they must not be enslaved.

75. "So Divine Wisdom, Divine Providence are behind this way of teaching people a living faith, winning their minds, winning their wills, etc. Both the conclusion and major premise are clear because Christ, the Son of God, is the Wisdom of His Father, is true God, one God with His Father and Holy Spirit." *OW* 70.

76. Dussel, *The Church in Latin America*, 67.

77. Gutiérrez, *Las Casas*, 161–62.

78. Dussel, *The Church in Latin America*, 50.

79. *OW* 95. The notion of justice as "right order" reflects traditional philosophical sensitivities. *OW* 163.

80. See Pagden, *European Encounters*, 70.

81. See Joerg Rieger, "Theology and Mission in a Postcolonial World," in *Mission Studies: Journal of the International Association for Mission Studies* 21, no. 2 (2004): 201–27.

82. See, e.g., Gutiérrez, *Las Casas*, 188. Gutiérrez refers to Vatican II: "If evangelization is a dialogue, it will not exist without an effort to understand the positions of one's interlocutor from within." It is, therefore, necessary "to give as well as to receive"; ibid. 189.

83. Ibid., 625 n.2.

84. Todorov, *The Conquest of America*, 166.

85. See *OW* 32–34.

86. Hanke, *Bartolomé de Las Casas*, 26–27.

87. Ibid., 28.

88. Ibid., 29.

89. Gutiérrez, *Las Casas*, 90.

90. Pendle, *A History of Latin America*, 57.

91. Todorov, *The Conquest of America*, 172.

92. Homi Bhabha has developed the notion of the hybrid for postcolonial theory. Hybridity rejects the rigid separation of oppressor and oppressed and aims at "the construction of a political object that is new, *neither the one nor the other*," and which therefore "properly alienates our political expectations." *The Location of Culture* (London: Routledge, 1994), 25.

93. Some of this music has been reconstructed and is performed by SAVAE, the San Antonio Vocal Arts Ensemble; see, for instance, their CD *El Milagro de Guadalupe* (October 1999).

94. *OW* 88. Referring to Thomas Aquinas, Las Casas argues that faith is more certainly affected through the eye than through the ear; *OW* 89. This is a welcome balance to the classical Protestant emphasis on hearing the word, *fides ex auditu*.

95. George Tinker has written the history of missions to Native Americans in the United States in this light. See his book *Missionary Conquest: The Gospel and Native American Cultural Genocide* (Minneapolis: Fortress Press, 1993).

96. Gutiérrez, *Las Casas*, 11, 62–63, 456.

97. Ibid., 65.

98. Ibid., 383. Gutiérrez claims that Las Casas's support of religious freedom leads to later support of political liberty. Moreover, in his opposition to the *encomienda*, Las Casas moves from a critique of abuses to a rejection of the system as a whole.; ibid., 384.

99. Ibid., 455. Further Gutiérrez writes, "the attitude was necessary also in order to avoid evangelization becoming just another way of subjugating the Indian nations."

100. Todorov, *The Conquest of America*, 189.

101. Ibid., 192, 193, 240. Todorov's concern is to show "what can happen if we do not succeed in discovering the other"; ibid., 247. Western Europe, he notes, has tried to assimilate the other for almost three hundred and fifty years.

102. See Gutiérrez, *Las Casas*, 317–18; "only in the church can the Indian nations find support and defense." Ibid., 319.

103. Ibid., 61.

104. See, e.g., ibid., 153.

105. Ibid., 301.

106. Emphasized once more by ibid., 179.

107. Ibid., 193.

108. According to Enzensberger's introduction to Las Casas's *The Devastation of the Indies*, Las Casas's report "treats of colonialism in its earliest stage; that is, the stage of robbery pure and simple, of unconcealed plundering. . . . In its primal state colonialism could do without the fiction of partnership, of bilateral trade"; ibid., 11.

109. Gutiérrez, *Las Casas*, 6.

110. See ibid., 6–7.

111. See Gutiérrez, *Las Casas*, 177, 178, 180.

112. Ibid., 185.

113. The argument was initially made by Todorov; for Gutiérrez's disagreement see ibid., 487 n.33.

114. For a contemporary critique, see Mignolo, *Local Histories/Global Designs*.

115. Pagden agrees; *European Encounters*, 74. Pagden also hints at the problems with this approach, because the eyewitness of Las Casas, the reliance on an "I" could easily be questioned before the later modern turn to the self. Las Casas could offer compelling stories, but was not able to appeal to "objectivity"; ibid., 82–83.

116. See also my account in Joerg Rieger, *Remember the Poor: The Challenge to Theology in the Twenty-First Century* (Harrisburg, Pa.: Trinity Press International, 1998), 47-51.

117. Gutiérrez, *Las Casas*, 85. Gutiérrez does not seem to notice the problems.

118. Ernest J. Burrus, S.J., "Las Casas and Veracruz: Their Defence of the American Indians Compared," *Neue Zeitschrift für Missionswissenschaft* 22 (1966): 211–12.

119. Fernando Mires, *La colonización de las almas: misión y conquista en Hispanoamérica* (San José, Costa Rica: DEI, 1991), 85.

120. Gutiérrez, *Las Casas*, 8. The depth, Gutiérrez asserts, comes from the roots in the gospel.

121. "Un tipo de colonización más estatal que privada," Fernando Mires, *La colonización*, 85.

122. See Gutiérrez, *Las Casas*, 156.

123. See ibid., 261.

124. See ibid., 245–46.

125. *OW* 137: "warriors do not love either themselves or their neighbors with the love of charity."

126. The consistent failure had to do with a failure to acknowledge the personhood of the Amerindians. "Even as they argued liberally for the humanity of Indian people, they denied our personhood." Tinker, *Missionary Conquest*, 104.

127. As a result, José Carlos Mariátegui wants to begin "by categorically asserting [the Indio's] right to land." *Seven Interpretive Essays on Peruvian Reality*, trans. Marjory Urquidi (Austin: University of Texas Press, 1971), 31. Nevertheless, he also shows a certain admiration for Las Casas; ibid., 32.

128. *OW* 58.

129. See *OW* 4, 38.

130. *OW* 42.

131. See Enzensberger, "Introduction" to Las Casas's *The Devastation of the Indies*, 7–8.

132. *OW* 11.

133. For a longer list see Dussel, *The Church in Latin America,* 51.

5

Resisting and Reframing
Prophet, Priest, and King

⟶⟫●⟨⟵

Christology and Later Colonialism

R EFORMED THEOLOGY HAS DRAWN TOGETHER the christological titles of
prophet, priest, and king, and Friedrich Schleiermacher (1768–1834),
father of modern liberal theology, follows that tradition. Nevertheless, in
the colonial worlds of the nineteenth century, those titles prove to be ambivalent.
The titles of prophet, priest, and king can provide resistance to empire in some
cases; yet they might also need to be resisted and reframed in the struggle against
empire in others.

Schleiermacher's work serves as an example for Christology interacting with
colonial attitudes; at one point he uses the three offices of Christ to endorse the
progress of the so-called Christian nations. Nevertheless, Schleiermacher's Christ
does not stand for raw power. He redefines the power of Christ in terms of
attraction ("attractive power," *anziehende Kraft*[1]) rather than coercion. Could this
be a critique of colonialism? What is the relation of this definition of power to
the softer and more enlightened forms of northern European colonialism that no
longer proceed by fire and sword, as did the Spanish and Portuguese conquests? It
appears as if the notion of attraction reflects a shift in the strategies of empire and
a new concept of power.

In the history of effects, the titles connected to the three offices of Christ have
often fostered empire and colonial attitudes. Asserting Christ's power as king, for
instance, has led to images of Christ's kingship that resembled the political powers
in control. Here are some close parallels to the classical affirmation of Jesus as
Lord, discussed in an earlier chapter. Since Christ's power is easily adapted to

197

the various forms of empire and colonialism, it takes a conscious effort to resist this tendency. Does Schleiermacher's use of the three offices of Christ invariably usher us into particularly German forms of "culture Protestantism," a charge often leveled by his later critics? Is there still a potential christological surplus, a different vision of the work of Christ that helps us see things in a different light?[2]

Modern theology, by and large, is not aware of its colonial underpinnings. While there are now a few contemporary theologians who reflect on the matter,[3] most theologians in Europe and the United States have hardly given any room to such considerations. Nevertheless, colonial mentalities go hand in hand with the modern spirit. It is no accident that the Enlightenment, the beginnings of modern capitalism, and the projects of modern colonialism shape up simultaneously. It should not come as a surprise that even a reflective and morally astute thinker such as Schleiermacher, one of the most creative pioneers of modern theology, shared some of the common colonial mentalities of his day. These colonial mentalities are not always visible on the surface; we need to search for them in the repressed recesses of theological reflection.

Contemporary theology is beginning to acknowledge that modern theology following in Schleiermacher's mold was strongly influenced by its commitments to the emerging middle class;[4] however, a new aspect is introduced into the discussion by the fact that modern theology was also influenced by colonial mentalities. This broader horizon raises new questions for the present. If modern theology is unconsciously tied to the colonial sentiments of its time, is it possible that contemporary theology, too, is affected by colonial projects? How much is our own work influenced by the neocolonialist sentiments that shape our own time? More importantly yet, how can these unconscious influences be detected and resisted, and how might theology contribute to alternative visions and ways of life?

The general trajectory of our project continues in this chapter: as we cut through some of the colonial layers in our search for a christological surplus, new possibilities open up. There is hardly a more urgent task for constructive theology and Christology in the twenty-first century than to identify the neglected colonial character of our modern theological inheritance and to push beyond it.

The Colonial Character of Modern Theology

Modern theology has come under increasing criticism from various directions in recent years. The challenges range from postliberal and evangelical charges of an undue emphasis on human experience and a related neglect of the authority of the texts of the church, to postmodern charges of lack of appreciation for otherness and difference, and the more general impression fostered by critics informed by liberation theologies that modern theology is plagued by self-centeredness and narcissism. None of the standard critiques of modern theology, however, give much consideration to the colonial character of modern theology and its relations to empire.[5] Yet modernity, colonialism, and empire are not only simultaneous and parallel developments but also reinforce each other. What does this mean?

The old caricatures of the academic ivory tower overlook the fact that even those theologians who never move much beyond their desks are somehow embedded in real-life matters. And even if those matters are not made explicit, they still shape the concerns and thought processes of theology. Modern contextual theologies have long since acknowledged that we do not exist in a vacuum. The theology of Friedrich Schleiermacher is contextual in that it takes into account the context of his own times, both within and outside of the church. The principal concern of much of his theology, however, is not with context in general but with the context of the emerging modern middle class. This class was represented, for instance, by the members of the salons of Berlin at the turn of the eighteenth and nineteenth centuries. In these salons, a newly emerging class of wealthy citizens would open their homes to young intellectuals, prominent scholars, and other interested observers. These groups showed progressive tendencies; here diversity was appreciated, women played important roles, and other religions were tolerated, a toleration highlighted by the prominence of Jewish members. Later modern theologians have picked up Schleiermacher's budding concern for the middle class and developed it in their own ways. Ernst Troeltsch in Germany was concerned about the contribution of Christianity to society and the ruling classes of the modern state, and Paul Tillich in the United States focused on the existential pressures of the middle class in terms of their experiences of anxiety, meaninglessness, and despair.

What neither these theologians nor most of their interpreters recognize, however, is that the context of modern theology cannot be limited to the middle class. The context of modern theology relates to a number of subtexts that are rarely acknowledged. It is well known that in Schleiermacher's modern, middle-class circles there was a critical interest in philosophy, religion, culture, and the arts. We are even beginning to develop greater awareness of the fact that, while the Prussian government discouraged political critique in Schleiermacher's times, these circles were not apolitical; Schleiermacher could at times be found in opposition to dominant political moves, even though his general approach was, on the whole, supportive of the monarchy.[6] Nevertheless, the wider horizon of the context of the modern middle class and its cultural and political production is hardly noted. Key to our investigation is that this middle class takes shape not in isolation but in close relation to (and on the back of) the lower classes both at home and abroad. The context of modern theology is closely connected to political and economic processes that signal the coming to power of the middle class, including the limitation of the powers of feudalism and the old aristocracies by emerging capitalist relations, growing industrialization at home, colonial relationships abroad, and the growing exploitation of the lower classes.

In regard to this colonial impulse, it needs to be noted that while Germany was not a colonial power at the time of Schleiermacher (Germany as a nation did not even exist yet), Schleiermacher's Prussia had expanded its territory toward the east, and there was great excitement about the colonial spirit; Schleiermacher himself was drawn into this excitement. Colonial concerns were widespread in Schleiermacher's world in various ways. It is often overlooked that individual Germans participated in colonial enterprises as far back as the Spanish conquest. Trade relations with the colonial powers and some of their colonies flourished in Schleiermacher's time.[7] Las Casas, at one point during the Spanish conquest, denounced a group of German merchants whom he, playing with words, called the *animales alemanes* ("German animals") for being crueler than the Spaniards. This denouncement, as Susanne Zantop has shown, had a strong impact on later generations of Germans, at a time when Las Casas's work had become widely known. Yet, although the denouncement of violent colonialization was common in Schleiermacher's time, it was projected on the other colonial powers and thus opened the way for alternative German colonial fantasies.[8] In Germany, the colonial spirit preceded the sustained colonial action of the years 1884 to 1919.

Among the few critics of modern theology who sensed these larger connections early on are Karl Barth and, to some extent, Paul Tillich.[9] Barth shows some awareness of parallels between colonialism and conquest on the one hand, and the modern self's striving for absolute power and control on the other. But Barth does not develop this intuition much beyond the general insight that "the grandiose attempt of the eighteenth century, undertaken with a grandiose self-confidence, to treat everything given and handed down in nature and in history as the property of man, to be assimilated to him" extends also to the way theology operates.[10] Apart from this parallel in the "assimilation" of various subjects, however, Barth sees a discrepancy at the heart of modernity, a "double activity": "While Gellert was writing his *Odes* and Kant his *Critique of Pure Reason*, while Goethe was writing his letters to Frau von Stein, and even later, the two things were actually being done simultaneously by absolute man: piety was practised at home, reason was criticized, truth made into poetry and poetry into truth, while abroad slaves were being hunted and sold."[11] In other words, Barth identifies an irreconcilable tension between the stellar activities of culture and the crass activities of colonialism, which included the slave trade. What he does not yet investigate in greater detail, however, is the question of hidden connections between the developments in Christian faith and culture on the one hand and the atrocity of colonial practices on the other. Even Christian Fürchtegott Gellert's poetry was not isolated from colonialism, shown, for instance, in the fact that Gellert would at times make romanticizing references to the colonial context.[12] We need to keep in mind that the colonial mentality was not separate from the rest of modern German society; it was supported ultimately by the same people who would practice piety, criticize reason, and write poetry. In the following statement, Barth assumes that colonialism somehow has to do with a lack of faith, culture, and even morality, failing to note that colonialism might indeed grow out of faith: "Moral scruples, let alone Christian ones, were so little in evidence that it was even possible to say without contradiction of the flourishing town of Liverpool that it was built on the skulls of negroes."[13] Nevertheless, the problem with modern colonialism, as we will see, is not first of all lack of "moral scruples" but rather a particular kind of morality and faith that incorporates and further develops colonial assumptions. What if the colonial system, including the slave trade, were somehow connected with modern piety, reason, and literary production?

Schleiermacher's own interests in colonial affairs can best be seen in recently published documents that contain what little has survived of an extensive work on the British settlement of Australia, which he produced for the greatly expanding market of travel writings.[14] Part of Schleiermacher's work consists of a translation into German of a popular book published in London in 1798 by David Collins, *Account of the English Colony in New South Wales*, but Schleiermacher insisted on supplementing it with his own research. The focus of Schleiermacher's study is on New South Wales on the east coast of the Australian continent, originally called New Holland (*Neuholland*) in honor of the Dutch who had discovered the coast of Australia in the seventeenth century. Schleiermacher worked on this project, which was under contract but never published, between 1799 and 1802. It has been characterized as a major project among his literary endeavors of that time.[15] This work is characteristic of other German scholarship of the time in that it does not gather firsthand knowledge through travel and immersion, but relies on the reports of others, particularly British, French, and Dutch explorers. Nevertheless, as Edward Said has pointed out in regard to European perspectives on the Orient, "what German Orientalism had in common with Anglo-French and later American Orientalism was a kind of intellectual *authority* over the Orient within Western culture."[16] German thinkers could perceive of their interpretations of the Orient as authoritative, we might add to Said's observation, precisely because they could bring to it a more detached and objective perspective that was not tainted by the messiness of colonial power struggles.[17] To be sure, this mentality was not restricted to the Orient per se; Schleiermacher studied Australia, and Germans at the time seemed strongly attracted to Latin America.

As recent research has shown, the general German interest in these matters was driven by colonial fantasies[18]—envisioning that Germany, too, could become a colonial agent. The authors of German travelogues, which were often translations from other languages, saw themselves as objective observers, from a distance; often this amounted to sympathy for the indigenous populations who had been treated unfairly in the past. All this contributed to what might be called "intellectual colonialism" that would appropriate "hitherto undiscovered worlds into Eurocentric categories."[19] Schleiermacher himself remarks on the unusual nature of the project, which he knows is new and strange to him. He notes, however, that he has a special desire (*besondere Lust*) to do this work and that he does not know where this particular desire comes from, adding that he does not need the money—and does not have any substantial material desires.[20] Could this mysterious desire be related to unconscious colonial fantasies?

What remains of Schleiermacher's appropriation and interpretation of the descriptions of New South Wales and its original inhabitants is interesting on various levels and will eventually help us take a closer look at his thinking about Christ. The descriptions of nature that he selects from his sources have a strongly factual character but always usher into a discussion of the usefulness to the British colonizers. The climate is not only identified as "healthy" (for the colonizers) but allows for year-round agricultural use; animals such as sheep, pigs, and goats can easily be raised here.[21] The products that are named as giving the place its "greatest importance" are fir trees and flax. Both are useful primarily for further colonial exploration in other parts of the world. Flax can be used for sails and ropes, and fir trees as masts for the British fleet in East India. In this report, which recalls the first encounter with the land, there are no references to the inhabitants of the land.[22] The colonial project is consistently at the core of these descriptions. Yet rather than following the "orientalist" trajectory, Schleiermacher seems to follow more the "occidentalist" impulses of his time.[23]

Schleiermacher's descriptions of the original inhabitants of Australia are even more telling than his descriptions of the land and help us dig deeper into the underlying colonial mentality. The following notes are, unless otherwise noted, developed in his own manuscript. He describes the Aboriginals as barely human— or human at the very lowest rung of human civilization (*auf der niedrigsten Stufe der menschlichen Bildung*). The Aboriginals, he continues, are worse off than the ants that live in the same area; at least ants have their anthills and thus housing.[24] There is no trace of law or civil order to be found among them, not even of religion or superstition.[25] In an earlier section of the project, Schleiermacher notes in an excerpt of a 1789 book by Watkin Tench that the only act of submission— obviously a sign of civilization and order in his eyes—is a certain level of respect that the younger pay the older.[26] Furthermore, there is neither agriculture nor artisan capacity of any kind. The Aboriginal people are described as "completely naked"—a statement that reflects Schleiermacher's prejudice about clothes since he notes in the next passage that they wear adornments (*Schmuck*) and color their skin.[27] A country populated with such people, he concludes, was of no use to the Dutch, and thus they abandoned it.[28]

Overall, Schleiermacher's seemingly objective descriptions and comparisons that do not prescribe strong forms of colonialism display clear hierarchical tendencies. Hierarchical thinking provides the underlying structure of his comparisons of different tribes, some of whom "seem to deserve more the sparse adornments" than others. Comparing the inhabitants of Australia to the inhabitants of Africa, he notes their black skin and "wooly hair" but, in his opinion, they lack "the peculiarly repulsive facial features of the negro."[29] Schleiermacher's colonial mentality is displayed here in a way that does not compare favorably even to others who also promote softer colonialisms without violence and war, like the earlier Bartolomé de Las Casas.

The colonial attitudes that come through in Schleiermacher's descriptions differ in some fundamental ways from the more violent colonialisms of the Spanish and Portuguese in Latin America, which proceeded by fire and sword. He rejects the slave trade, which was still going on during his own time, and he praises the efforts to live in peaceful relationship with the Aboriginals—a relationship that is represented not just by the example of one particular governor in New South Wales but is grounded in the instructions of the British government.[30] Yet a closer look reveals the reasons. Peaceful coexistence was called for neither primarily because of an enlightened "feeling of original equality" (*Gefühl ursprünglicher Gleichheit*) that was displayed by the colonizers, nor because of a "more noble feeling of honor" (*edleres Ehrgefühl*) that entails a refusal to repeat the atrocities of earlier colonial histories. Peaceful coexistence is called for on the basis of a "natural rule" (*natürliche Maaßregel*), according to which there was simply nothing to be gained from exploitation or any other relationship. There was absolutely no use for the Aboriginals in the colonial system, not even as labor force. Schleiermacher also notes that they owned virtually no property and that all they possessed was the original "spark" that set in motion the progressive civilization of humanity, without, however, displaying any noticeable progress. The Aboriginals are arrested at the "lowest rung of pleasure and action," and therefore they would not pose any threats or prevent the colonizers from owning the treasures of the land.[31]

Consciously or unconsciously, Schleiermacher's interpretation is based on a position of colonial power and a sense of cultural and religious superiority. Said's summary of the attitudes of Orientalism applies to Schleiermacher's perspective as well: "Even as Europe moved itself outwards, its sense of cultural strength was fortified. From travelers' tales, and not only from great institutions like the various India companies, colonies were created and ethnocentric perspectives secured."[32] In Germany, travel writing and other literature dealing with colonial fantasies and "the other" helped generate a sense of self-identity and unification that was not available otherwise and that could not easily be examined because it was based on others who were closer but different (as in the case of Jewish neighbors)[33] or very far away (as in the case of the Australian Aboriginals). As Zantop has argued, against Said, the fact that Germany lacked colonies made German colonialist discourse not less but more powerful; this lack created a "pervasive desire for colonial possessions and a sense of entitlement to such possessions," which could develop without being challenged by colonial subjects. More than mere "intellectual authority" (Said), a "mythological authority over the collective imagination" (Zantop) evolved.[34] It is no accident that the modern concepts of race and gender emerge in the late seventeenth century, defined in terms of a natural hierarchy.[35] The modern European self affirms its own value and superiority over against the different other. In the case of Germany, this self-affirmation is connected also to a sense of moral superiority over the colonizing nations.[36] Could this be at the root of Schleiermacher's inexplicable desire to explore these matters? Does he simply go along with the sensitivities of his own time? Is there resistance?

Most important for our interpretation of Christology is the fact that Schleiermacher's colonial mind-set has parallels in his theological thought. It is increasingly recognized that European intellectual movements are tied to colonial relationships. Romanticism, for instance, the intellectual environment of Schleiermacher, is tied to newly emerging relations of Germany with the rest of the world. The writings and drawings of German explorer and scientist Alexander von Humboldt, informed by his travels in Latin America from 1799 to 1804, had a profound impact in this regard. Humboldt, unlike others interested in scientific observation before him, "did not write or travel as a humble instrument of European knowledge-making apparatuses, but as their creator." He produced, in the words of Mary Louise Pratt, "his own journeys and subject matters and spent a lifetime of energy promoting them."[37] Schleiermacher knew him from his early days in the Romantic networks of Berlin. Encounters with the colonial other had a significant impact on German intellectual life.

It has been argued that Schleiermacher's study of the Aboriginal other had an important impact in two areas of his work. If the notion of religion were to include Aboriginals, religion could not be a matter of "knowing" or "doing" but only of feeling or intuition. Likewise, hermeneutics became a necessary tool if the huge gap that separated Europeans from these Aboriginals was to be bridged. The conclusion, drawn by Stephen Prickett, is that had "Schleiermacher not begun to read of the English settlement at Sydney Cove, the history of Romanticism, and indeed of Western culture, would have been profoundly different."[38] Of course, we know now that the backdrop was a cultural climate of colonial fantasies. Along these lines, it might perhaps be argued that the awareness of the Aboriginal other and of the colonies had a positive influence on the development of modern theology and thought, but the problems in this relationship need to be taken into account as well.

A possible link between the emerging colonial mind-set and theology can also be seen in Schleiermacher's description of the work of Christ in human beings. He rejects interpretations of the work of Christ in terms of coercive action. Schleiermacher's Christ, it seems, is not at work like the Spanish colonizers with fire and sword, overwhelming people by sheer force and coercing them into his kingdom. Rather, Christ is at work through "attraction" and "pervasive influence," the kinds of actions that we might describe as love. Schleiermacher describes Christ's work as "impulses [that] flow to us from Him," that operate to pull us into "His sphere of living influence" through "attractive power" (*anziehende Kraft*) (*The Christian Faith*, 425–427; hereafter *CF*). At first sight this is a much more liberating understanding of Christ's power than a view that identifies Christ's power with the top-down coercions of crude military and political power; yet the colonial context raises questions. Is the oppressive relation between colonizers and colonized really overcome in this more enlightened colonial setting?

In *The Christian Faith*, Schleiermacher draws on the example of teacher and student when he talks about the "attractive power" of those "to whose educative intellectual influence we gladly submit ourselves," an influence that is not only "person-forming" but also "world-forming" (*CF* 427). Here this attractive power operates under the assumption of a clear hierarchy of teacher and student. This hierarchy can perhaps most clearly be seen in his taxonomy of religion. While Schleiermacher acknowledges other religions outside of Christianity—just as modern thought following Las Casas acknowledged the basic humanity of non-Europeans—he also insists on a classification that allows for "different states of development,"[39] with European Protestantism being at the highest level. Elsewhere in *The Christian Faith* he talks about a "most manifold gradation of life, from the lowest and most imperfect forms up to the highest and most perfect"; a gradation that is willed and put in place by God, "the divine good-pleasure" that is to be received in "quiet acceptance." Both human nature and the "sphere of spiritual life" are permeated by this gradation (*CF* 556–57). This same logic applies to the colonial enterprises of the British in Australia. If the colonizers are superior in relation to the colonized, and if they are representatives of the "attractive power" that is a trait of those higher up, the latter have no choice but to "gladly submit" to the former. Anything else would be irrational. Christ's attractive power models this superiority: attraction works because of a differential of power. The differential between Christ and the Christian gets translated into the differential between colonized and colonizers. Nevertheless, one might wonder which differentials are greater, the ones between Christ and the European Christians or the ones between European Christians and Native Australians who even lack religion.

Here are some interesting parallels to changes in modern colonial societies as they develop out of premodern feudalist forms. In the eighteenth-century transitions from feudalism to capitalism the notions of power and force change. Power is transferred from the hands of the noble ruler into the hands of a more democratically organized bourgeois state; even in Prussia, while the monarchy is affirmed and the kings retain their power, there are moves to distribute power and authority more broadly. In this context, notions of power and force gradually begin to change. Michel Foucault's analyses of the prison system are instructive, where power is gradually transformed from public and physical forms to a form that is hidden and internalized socially and psychologically; in a situation of surveillance in a panopticon, where prisoners can be watched at all times but never know whether they are being watched or not, no strong physical acts of coercion are necessary since power is internalized.[40] In similar fashion, the top-down powers of the feudal rulers become more dispersed and internalized in the modern world and can thus afford to be less severe without losing power. The field of Christian mission is a good illustration for these developments: here, too, power that used to be expressed through physical coercion is increasingly internalized. In the Protestant missions of Schleiermacher's time power is expressed less by force than during the heydays of the Spanish conquest; power now finds expression more and more through language.[41] Related to this use of language is the power of knowledge; as Homi Bhabha (in reference to Michel Foucault) has pointed out: "the late eighteenth century . . . could not tolerate areas of darkness and sought to exercise power through the mere fact of things being known and people seen in an immediate, collective gaze."[42] At the turn to the nineteenth century, power is increasingly expressed through phenomena that function at the level of the symbolic. Cultural developments, which take place at the level of the symbolic, thus deserve a closer look, but so do new forms of politics and economics that function at the level of the symbolic in their own ways. Modern theology needs to be seen as part of these processes. Especially in Germany the study of theology and religion becomes one of the outlets for intellectuals through which to participate in the exercise of power, since there were few opportunities yet to influence politics directly.

Prophet, Priest, and King, Colonial Style

Schleiermacher's interpretation of the Reformed doctrine of the three offices of Christ introduces us to the problems of Christology in a modern European colonial framework.[43] At the same time, Schleiermacher's work is also an example for how colonialist attitudes are not easily identified by merely scanning the surface of the material to be interpreted. In fact, he explicitly opposes various mechanisms that have supported colonialist structures in the past, including violence, wars of aggression, and forceful colonization.[44] These positions make his work particularly interesting for our purposes, since clearly identifiable statements of a colonialist nature on the surface would not prove much more than the fact that theologians have bought into the prejudices of their time in which colonialism was a commonly accepted fact of life.[45] Is it possible that theologians would resist some aspects of the public colonial sentiment but their work would still remain beholden to colonialist structures? How are colonial dynamics at work below the surface, and thus shaping theological and other assumptions in ways that may be not less but ultimately more powerful? Said's insights into Orientalism also apply to the particular colonialist framework encountered in modernity: statements that concern the other, Said observes, have less to do with their world than with our own world.[46] In this way, "European culture gained in strength and identity by setting itself off against the Orient as a sort of surrogate and even underground self."[47] Yet while Said focuses on the surface, the exteriority of the statements, we will need to deal with the less visible manifestations, the "repressed real."[48]

In Schleiermacher's Christology, the classical Reformed doctrine of the three offices of Christ is developed in relation to the other—in this case, mostly in relation to the Jewish other.[49] Like the modern colonial relationships described above, Schleiermacher does not perceive the relationship of Judaism and Christianity as antagonistic. In the *Speeches* he is "charmed" by Judaism's "beautiful childlike character,"[50] although at times he also utters harsher criticisms of what he perceives to be the limits of the Jewish religion, beginning with the statement that "by its limitation of the love of Jehovah to the race of Abraham" it "betrays a lingering affinity with Fetishism."[51] Schleiermacher's 1799 stance on the place of Jews in Germany mirrors his complex position on colonial matters. Supporting the equality of Christians and Jews in civil matters, he rejects the idea of Jewish conversions to Christianity that enforce baptism and only lead to what he calls a "judaizing Christianity." In an open letter of 1799 Schleiermacher claims that reason dictates "that all people should be citizens but knows nothing of the notion that all people should be Christians."[52] Assuming support from his Jewish friends and Reformed Judaism, he not only demands that Jews should subordinate their ritual laws to the laws of the state, but that they should give up their hope for the Holy Land.[53] There is no doubt a colonial impulse here, as Jonathan Hess has noted, expressed in Schleiermacher's strong claim that it would be "strange to be out to make conquests when we still have wastelands to reclaim and swamps to dry out within our borders."[54] Nevertheless, his goal, in keeping with the spirit of his work as a whole, is to seek "harmony"[55] and a broadening of love. How is this relationship between Christians and Jews further developed in his thinking about Christ, and what might be the underlying assumptions about colonial power?

As prophet, Christ's work is defined by teaching, prophesying, and by working miracles. These three expressions of prophecy belong together and cannot be separated. The Old Testament prophets, Schleiermacher explains, needed to perform miracles as "special proof of their authority," not least because their speech challenged society and the status quo (*CF* 441). Christ's uniqueness, no less a challenge to the status quo than that of the Old Testament prophets, is displayed in various aspects of his prophetic work: his teaching is unique, for instance, in that it cannot be limited to "a purification and a development of the ethics current among the people, springing out of universal human reason" (*CF* 443). While Christ did not intend to destroy Jewish law, his teaching transcends it and is based on "the absolutely original revelation of God in Him" (*CF* 443). Here we might spot something of a countercolonial impulse, for Schleiermacher seems to challenge the dominant Enlightenment reference to universal human reason that has often been used to claim the superiority of Europe and the Western world. Christ's teaching transcends such reason and thus becomes "the climax and the end of all prophecy" (*CF* 445). There is simply no higher stage of development and no higher form of reason, whatever its claim to universality; no teaching can ever go beyond Christ's message. Nevertheless, Schleiermacher's challenge at this point is addressed to universal Jewish reason—reason before the birth of Christ—rather than to universal reason in general.

Working miracles is perhaps the most spectacular aspect of Christ's prophetic office. The individual miracles of Christ, however, Schleiermacher argues, do not necessarily distinguish him from other miracle workers. Our advantage over the contemporaries of Christ is that we can see beyond individual miracles to the "general spiritual miracle, which begins with the person of the Redeemer and is completed with the completion of His Kingdom" (*CF* 449). Once again, Christ transcends both the Jewish limitations and the limitations of the present and is both the "climax" and the "end of miracle" (*CF* 449). Everything that might be perceived as miraculous is now simply the further development of Christ's work. This could be another instance of a countercolonial moment in Schleiermacher's work: although he claims this limitation of miracles only for the religious sphere,[56] he shuts out extreme forms of top-down religious domination that claim a special connection to the miraculous. At the same time, however, Schleiermacher's conclusion on miracles firmly reestablishes the colonial framework in another way: "Even if it cannot be strictly proved that the Church's power of working miracles has died out. . . , yet in general it is undeniable that, in view of the great advantage in power and civilization which the Christian peoples possess over the non-Christian . . . , the preachers of to-day do not need such signs" (*CF* 450). Miracles are unnecessary because of the "power and civilization" of the Christian nations compared to the non-Christians. In other words, Christianity itself appears to be the divine miracle and its colonial history is the proof. Even the Jewish-Christian relationship testifies to this. While Christ is the climax and end of teaching, prophecy, and miracle, European Christianity is closest to Christ— closer than the Jewish religion and certainly closer than the rest of world.[57] Even though Schleiermacher does not try to base his christological argument on "social psychology," Ernst Troeltsch has argued that he is in fact doing so since he emphasizes the difference between the weaknesses of the non-Christian God-consciousness and the new era of humanity beginning with the Christian God-consciousness.[58] Christ as prophet is on the side of European colonial Christianity, and Christ's challenge is only a matter of degree. In fact, Christ's challenge is mainly to those who are seen as less civilized and less powerful, and it is presented to them in the form of European Christianity.

As priest, Christ's work is defined by obedience to and intercession with the first person of the Trinity, the "Father." Christ is the one who "gives pure and full expression to the dominion of the God-consciousness in human nature" (*CF* 454). We are connected to God through him. And while the prophetic office of Christ is supposed to present certain challenges to us, the priestly office is supposed to comfort us and remind us that "we share His perfection, if not in execution, at least in impulse" (*CF* 455). In this context, Schleiermacher discusses Christ's suffering. He does not deny or play down Christ's suffering, as is often the case in other modern interpretations of Christ, but he attributes it entirely to Christ's "passive obedience." Suffering, he says, is characteristic of the "victim [who] has no independent activity" and is therefore "completely passive in everything which happens to it" (*CF* 459). The "details of His suffering" over which Christ had no control, are "not to be regarded as being for Him significant elements in experience" (*CF* 459). Christ's suffering, while showing sympathy with the victims, contributes nothing to the whole. Ultimately, Schleiermacher agrees with the early church fathers that the divine nature itself cannot suffer.[59] While Schleiermacher's embrace of Christ's suffering might create sympathy for the suffering of the colonized, it blocks any constructive understanding of their suffering. Suffering, described as the passive spirit of the victim, is devoid of an active spirit expressed, for instance, in resistance and refusal. Thus, the colonized remain victims without agency, dependent on the actions of others. The colonizers, on the other hand, can neglect suffering: "Our own experience teaches us that an ordinary ethical development and robust piety have as their reward the almost complete overcoming of physical sufferings in the presence of a glad spiritual self-consciousness" (*CF* 437). In contrast to much of humanity, the modern European self that stands above the colonized can afford to forget about suffering.

Even in his priestly office, Christ must conform to the commonly acknowledged standards of the day that, by default, are those of colonial society in the broadest sense. In the context of Christ's death, for instance, Schleiermacher argues that we need to understand it in terms of generally accepted values and norms: "For if we wish to assert the reality of human moral nature in Christ, we must not ascribe to Him, even in this connection, any other rules of conduct than such as we have to recognize as valid for us all; otherwise there would be a danger that His life would cease to be an example, and consequently that it would cease to be an ideal" (*CF* 462). In order to be an example or ideal, Christ must fit into the preconceived value system of middle-class Prussia. As an example Schleiermacher refers to the common value that "self-preservation is a duty of all." It is on these grounds that he then rejects an understanding of Christ's death as a "voluntary death." While this is a healthy warning against a martyr complex or other self-destructive tendencies and might help resist certain colonialist excesses such as slavery, the train of thought is noteworthy: Christ cannot break through commonly accepted norms and rules. By implication, if society is shaped by the norms and rules of a colonialist mind-set, so is Christ.

In relation to Judaism, Schleiermacher points out that Christ is the climax and the end of the priesthood: "He is the most perfect mediator for all time between God and every individual part of the human race" (*CF* 465). As climax and end, Christ transcends his Jewish context and becomes the universal Christ. One can only suspect what this "universality" looks like, and it would not be completely wrong to wonder whether it has some European features. This suspicion is supported when Schleiermacher goes on to emphasize that "the high-priesthood of Christ has passed over to the fellowship of the faithful" (*CF* 465). There is some emancipatory thrust here, since this move ends all qualitative distinctions between priests and laity. Nevertheless, the old distinction between priests and laity survives in the relation of Christianity with the rest of the world. Schleiermacher points out that "Christendom as a whole . . . stands to the rest of humanity in the relation in which the priests stood to the laity." Theologically, this means that "the Christian community, as inseparable from Christ, appears before God for the whole race and represents it" (*CF* 465). But what Christian community does Schleiermacher have in mind? The answer is that he is thinking mainly of his fellow Prussian Christians, primarily the Protestants.[60] Who is defined as "in" and as "out" and what kinds of power and authority over others are attributed to Christians has not only theological but also political ramifications.

Finally, we learn what kind of power Christ as king exerts. This power, Schleiermacher argues, must neither be understood as a tyranny nor as democracy. The power of a tyrant is unlimited but "not natural." More importantly, it is selfish and "might have other aims than the free development and the natural prosperity of those over whom it was exercised." The power of democratically delegated authority, on the other hand, is too limited since it is derived from others. Christ's power, by contrast, is self-initiated and "is in the interest of those over whom it is exercised"; to this power corresponds the claim that "submission . . . must always be voluntary"—a theme that resembles some of Las Casas's thinking about the relation of Indians to the Spaniards, discussed in the previous chapter. Furthermore, Christ governs in different ways than many of the powers of this world. He does not exert power via "constraint which requires superiority in material forces" nor via "enticements or threatenings" (*CF* 467). Surely, this power is different from some of the older colonial powers, but since it matches the more enlightened colonial powers, a colonial rub remains.

It might come as a surprise that Schleiermacher further limits this power of Christ when he seems to take it out of the political circuits of power of his day: "His kingly power is not immediately concerned with the disposal and arrangement of the things of this world—which means that nothing remains as the immediate sphere of His kingship but the inner life of man individually and in their relation to each other" (*CF* 467). In other words, Christ's kingship has to do with the nonpolitical sphere. This sphere is not individualistic, as is often suspected. The nonpolitical sphere emphasizes community and interdependence—virtues embodied by the Christian church. While the so-called kingdom of power, the kingship over the political sphere, belongs only to the Father, the work of the Son is effective in terms of the "kingdom of grace," which takes form "in a purely inward way," related to the "sanctification" and "edification" of the people in the church who thus move on to ever higher stages of humanity.[61] Still, Christ also maintains a claim on the world, however limited: "the kingdom of Christ can increase only as the world . . . decreases, and its members are gradually transformed into members of the Church, so that evil is overcome and the sphere of redemption enlarged" (*CF* 469). Ultimately, Schleiermacher does not fail to assert, "the extension of the influence of Christ over the human race knows no limits," and "no people is able to offer it a permanently effective opposition" (*CF* 470). This does not necessarily mean that everything rests with the church, for there is "no stage of purity and perfection which does not belong to Christ's Kingdom" (*CF* 470). Nevertheless, Christ's power as expressed in the church shows the way and we have access to him no longer directly but only through the church.[62] As with the other three offices, Christ is "climax and the end"—in this case, of "all spiritual kingship" (*CF* 472). While Schleiermacher continues to maintain a clear separation between religious and political powers,[63] these reflections are particularly interesting because they claim the irresistibility of Christ's power. While perhaps not as forceful as the Father's political power, the Son's religious power goes deeper and is more sensitive to the needs of the other.[64]

Schleiermacher's Christ cannot be called a brutal colonialist. He does not rule through coercion but through attraction and love. Coercion cannot produce civilization and undermines the expansion of the Christian faith in other parts of the world.[65] This distinction between coercion and attraction mirrors the other distinction between "hard" and "soft" imperialism, manifest in the contemporary United States in the difference between the presidencies of George W. Bush and Bill Clinton, although the harder forms now also emphasize their civilizing mission. As to the structures working below the surface, it cannot be said that Schleiermacher displays anti-Semitic sentiments as strong as some of his acquaintances, like, for instance, Achim von Arnim, the founder of the *Christlich-deutsche Tischgesellschaft*.[66] Schleiermacher does not demonize or reject the Jewish other. Nevertheless, while Schleiermacher's argument picks up and builds on Jewish traditions, there are clear assumptions of progress and superiority. The Jewish other presents a highly developed yet somewhat lower position than the Christian, a judgment that can also be found in Schleiermacher's typology of religion. In the final account, the Jewish other is different and this difference is where the problem lies; consequently, "whatever is most definitely Jewish" in the Old Testament has "least value" (*CF* 62). We need to consider the possibility that the Jewish counterimage says more about the Christian self than about the Jewish other, and here is where the colonial impulses need to be identified. Even though some appreciation for the other is maintained, Schleiermacher's version of Christianity considers itself superior.[67] Keep in mind that, as the early Schleiermacher stated in regard to Judaism, "the original intuition of Christianity is more glorious, more sublime, more worthy of adult humanity, penetrates deeper into the spirit of systematic religion and extends itself further over the whole Universe."[68]

What is the general focus of Schleiermacher's Christology? It has become a commonplace in the field of theology to argue that Schleiermacher, despite his critique of the Enlightenment, perpetuates a self-centeredness that is characteristic of the epoch. The position of Christology within the structure of *The Christian Faith* is telling. Christology is discussed in relation to the first part of the system, the human state.[69] The two other parts of the system, the constitution of the world and the divine attributes, come only later. Christology is thus geared to the concerns of humanity, which are seen as universal. When all is said and done, Schleiermacher's Christ is nothing less than the completion "of the creation of human nature" (*CF* 366). In this function, Christ's humanity, according to Schleiermacher, must be general humanity, "for otherwise he would necessarily be more of an example for some than for others." He continues that even "race" does not matter, for "such a determination in no way concerns the real principle of His life but only the organism" (*CF* 384). Here Schleiermacher follows in the tracks of the universalizing tendency of modernity, which promotes a general notion of humanity. Such universals mirror the power of the modern self and provide system and control in modern thought.[70] But what does "universal humanity," abstracted from race and other signifiers like class and gender, look like? The problem is that Schleiermacher, having previously gotten rid of specifics of Jesus' humanity like his Jewishness and social location, ends up with an empty signifier that eagerly awaits definition. The theological problem that must be observed at this point is that universal humanity is already known *before* it is attributed to Christ.

In Schleiermacher's Christology, however, as in all other modern references to the universal, universal humanity is never really universal. There is no universal humanity, except in the minds of those in power. Schleiermacher's point of reference for what is universally human is the rising middle class of his time, those who are most agile in matters intellectual and economic. Those members of the middle class are seen as closest to universal humanity and are the driving forces of colonialism and empire of the day; they are the representatives of the "great advantages in power and civilization which the Christian peoples possess over the non-Christian."[71] It is this particular humanity that is universalized—with the implicit assumption that the rest of humanity needs to adapt and will eventually evolve in this direction.

Christ's work consists, therefore, not so much in the critique or radical transformation of the basic parameters of the colonialist self, but in building up this self on grounds of its innate potential: "As certainly as Christ was a man, there must reside in human nature the possibility of taking up the divine into itself, just as did happen in Christ."[72] In this context, redemption takes on a specific form that mirrors relations between more and less developed humanity. Schleiermacher critiques Enlightenment theology for abandoning the notion of redemption, understood as removal of sin (*CF* 431ff.). The basic definition of sin for the Christian who is part of the fellowship of Christ is that sin is "simply an incapacity"[73] for what has come to be in Christ. Sin, in relation to Christ's redeeming power, is a shortcoming of humanity at the point where it is to be transformed into the new creation. Even though Schleiermacher does not fall into the trap of Enlightenment theology that neglects the reality of sin, his approach shares some of its traits. Sin is not the perversion of even the best of human intentions—a definition that might give us a clue as to the underlying trouble with modern colonialism, which rejects the old conquest model but still ends up subduing the other—but simply a human shortcoming, a "not enough."

In sum, Schleiermacher's christological "canon" consists "in the formula that in Christ the creation of man first reaches completion," signifying the fullness of God's presence. Apart from that, "Christian preachers must have the freedom granted to the poets" (*CF* 411). The list of christological adiaphora is long. Among the nonessential components of Christology are resurrection, ascension, and final judgment; all of them can be neglected since "the disciples recognized in Him the Son of God without having the faintest premonition of His resurrection and ascension, and we too may say the same of ourselves" (*CF* 418). Similarly, creation and preservation are also only indirectly ascribed to Christ (*CF* 424). Further added to that list are virgin birth, suffering, and, last but not least, the cross.

Key to the work of Christ is the connection of supernatural and natural, which in some ways mirrors the colonizers and colonized.[74] In Christ, the supernatural becomes natural. This is a very powerful image in that it appreciates "vital human receptivity in virtue of which alone that supernatural can become a natural fact of history" (*CF* 365). If we recall that the relation of Christ and Christianity models the relation of Christians and non-Christians, or colonizers and colonized (those with higher levels of God-consciousness are considered superior to those with lower levels[75]), this position ascribes some agency to the colonized "natives," at least in terms of their receptivity. A certain two-way street is required since those on the receptive end have some influence on the shape of things. But, at a deeper level, the power differential is not given up and the colonial relationship remains in place.

Schleiermacher's Christ, despite some ambivalence, fits right in with the colonial fantasy. Insofar as he is also human, Christ "stands under the law of historical development"; his supernatural powers are integrated into the historical order, which is the order of colonial modernity (*CF* 367). No radical challenge is posed and no fundamental transformation takes place. Christ helps the colonial self to get over its shortcomings. Thus, while Schleiermacher is taking a stronger stand on Christ's intervention in human nature than other modern theologians, the results are basically the same: the colonial self is affirmed and strengthened.

Resisting Prophet, Priest, and King

Despite all the connections with colonialism, Schleiermacher's approach also harbors some ambivalence, as we have seen. In this part, we will look at some of his other writings in order to explore the ambivalences discovered in the previous part further. Is there a surplus in his thinking about Christ that escapes the colonial status quo? Do Schleiermacher's encounters with Christ somehow push beyond the limits of the colonial system?

It is noteworthy that Schleiermacher does not promote the rugged individualist ideologies of other modern forms of colonialism, like the ones modeled by the emerging business interests of the early capitalism of his day or the ones that eventually found expression in the pioneer spirit so typical of the expanding United States. The reconciling activity of Christ brings about a "corporate feeling of blessedness," an experience of relatedness and community within Christianity. In this community the Christians' "former personality dies, so far as it meant a self-enclosed life of feeling within a sensuous vital unity, to which all sympathetic feeling for others and for the whole was subordinated."[76] Unfortunately, however, this community appears to be fairly homogeneous, without much use for those who are outside of it and with little sensitivity to those in its midst who do not fit in for various reasons. There is as yet no constructive place for suffering or for the outsider in this model.[77] Suffering in such a community would not be a sign that something is wrong with the community; neither would it present a challenge to the community. Suffering would merely signal that someone is not yet fully integrated and can only be overcome by pulling people more fully into the community's "corporate feeling of blessedness." By the same token, the existence of outsiders and underdogs would not be seen as a sign of a fundamental problem; it would merely be a reminder to the community of the need to be more inclusive yet. The christological surplus of Schleiermacher's emphasis on community is thus rather limited.

Yet there is hope for the broadening of this community, seen in Schleiermacher's hope for universal salvation, tied to his understanding of Christ as high priest. "Christ is still sent not only to, but also for, the human race," he points out in *The Christian Faith*. Consequently, "we should not lightly reckon anyone among the rejected." This broadens some of the narrower colonial horizons: no one can claim that salvation is mostly for the colonizers. Nevertheless, salvation is perceived strictly in Christian terms, and so "it is an essential of our faith that every nation will sooner or later become Christian." This statement introduces some ambivalence once again.[78] God does indeed care about all of humanity, not only about the Europeans and not only about the Christians, but Schleiermacher's stance is summed up in the conclusion that "God regards all men only in Christ."[79] Perhaps an explicitly anticolonial image of Christ could bring relief. Yet, the claim that the Christian church must "increasingly overpower the unorganized mass to which it is opposed," can once again be read in a colonial sense. It all depends, of course, who the "unorganized mass" is. That Schleiermacher identifies this "unorganized mass" as "the world opposed to [the church]," might leave room for a different reading of who really is in opposition to the church (*CF* 528). This could open up completely new possibilities of resistance if colonial efforts would be seen as "worldly" and opposed to the true character of the church.

It is often overlooked that even for Schleiermacher Christianity poses a distinctive challenge. In his *Speeches*, he identifies Christianity as a "higher power of religion," which seeks to expose "a widely-extended godlessness" and is therefore "through and through polemical." In this connection, even a self-critical bent emerges, since Christianity is "as sharply and strongly polemical within its own borders." Schleiermacher has a sense that not only religion but Christianity itself might be the problem. Schleiermacher's understanding of Christ is crucial here too, and he quotes a saying of Jesus that contemporary liberals would hardly find appropriate: "I am not come to bring peace, but a sword."[80] The realization that there is a "corruptibleness of all that is great and divine in human things" introduces a new note hardly struck in colonial circles that should hold out a warning even in the current context in the United States.[81]

Furthermore, there is a material quality to Schleiermacher's reflections that can lead to a different kind of appreciation of the world and history: "From all finite things we should see the Infinite," he claims. This might allow for the possibility to find God in unexpected places, including unexpected places in the colonial system, even though Schleiermacher does not emphasize this.[82] In addition to this attention to the world, there is an attention to history that once again introduces a self-critical moment: noting that "religious men are throughout historical," religion cannot be perceived apart from its particular history, although religion must not be confused with this history; not "everything found in the heroes of religion or in the sacred sources" should be considered as decisive sources of religion.[83] This insight makes us take another look at the colonial history of the Christian religion. What if we looked at history and finite things differently than Schleiermacher, waiting for a different set of what he calls "new ambassadors from God" and another kind of rebirth of Christianity in "a new and more beautiful form"?[84] What if we developed a more historically informed view of Christ, which would appreciate factors like his Jewishness and his solidarity with the "least of these"? Due to Schleiermacher's ambivalence about the colonial, we might take his cue and appropriate it in a different way. After all, the younger Schleiermacher of the *Speeches* is hopeful that "younger, and, if possible, stronger and more beautiful types of religion arise outside of this corruption," and he refrains from colonial uniformity: "as nothing is more irreligious than to demand general uniformity in mankind, so nothing is more unchristian than to seek uniformity in religion."[85] The question might be raised on the basis of these reflections: What if colonial Christianity were not the highest stage of religion?

Schleiermacher's *Christian Ethics*, published posthumously, provides additional insights in our search for glimpses that push beyond colonial Christology. Ethics, for Schleiermacher, is not simply an afterthought of theology. The two fields are inextricably related.[86] Ethics is related to Christ; it is the "exposition of the community with God, effected through the community with Christ, the redeemer, inasmuch as this is the motif of all Christian actions."[87] Theology and ethics have their common root in Christ, and this common root contains a surplus. Since Christian ethics is rooted in the statement that "Christ is the redeemer of humanity," its task is to define that statement. In accord with the self-critical bent noted above, Schleiermacher points out that if the statement is repeated without clear definition, even heretics can easily affirm it.[88] This insight is key in times when Christianity is used in order to shore up the powers that be; both in Schleiermacher's Prussia and in the contemporary United States, a self-critical examination of what is meant by basic christological statements (like "Christ is the Redeemer," or "Jesus is Lord") might well be the first step of a critique of empire theology.

One of the key tasks of Christian ethics, according to Schleiermacher, is to develop the principles for the ongoing challenges to be met by Christian action.[89] Christian ethics is not static but rooted in a growing relationship with Christ. This horizon points to a significant difference between theology and ethics in Schleiermacher's mind; while theology is based in Scripture and creed, ethics needs to give deeper accounts of history and historical change. The relation of lords and servants, one of Schleiermacher's examples, is different now from what it was in biblical times. For this reason, ethics needs to take into account, in addition to Scripture and creed, the common praxis of the church that is always in flux. In fact, recognizing this flux, according to Schleiermacher, accounts for the particularly Protestant character of his ethics.[90] Adding to this approach an analysis of modern colonialism and its hidden power differentials might result in a whole new approach to ethics; the remainders of modern self-centeredness to be found in Schleiermacher's work might give way to a focus on others that could open up a new vision of the divine Other as well.[91]

Schleiermacher identifies three kinds of actions that structure his *Christliche Sitte* (*Christian Ethics*; hereafter *CS*): purifying action, broadening action, and representational action (*reinigendes Handeln, verbreitendes Handeln, darstellendes Handeln*).[92] Each action could be seen as related to one of the offices of Christ, although Schleiermacher does not make this connection, presumably since each office also contains traits of the other actions. Purifying action has affinities with Christ as prophet in that it provides a challenge, broadening action with Christ as priest in that it brings us closer to Christ's perfection, and representational action with Christ as king in that it proclaims the extent of his rule.

Purifying action is important in the Protestant tradition, Schleiermacher claims, because, unlike in Roman Catholicism, the church is not seen as perfect (*CS* 122). "Individual members of the whole" are an important source of purifying action (*CS* 126). The model for purifying action is Christ himself: Christ, as an individual, is the basis of our redemption and growth as humans (*CS* 121). Here we might identify a christological surplus in Schleiermacher's approach that pushes beyond the powers that be: as individuals become actors, the power base is broadened along potentially democratic lines as influence is dispersed into the hands of many. In the process, the church creates an alternative space in the midst of the colonial world. From this perspective even divisions in the church can be legitimate. While Christianity is "destined to spread out to all humankind," Schleiermacher explains, "human nature" is "organized and individualized much too differently" as that "similar relations of all to each other" could exist. What is affirmed here is not individualism or fragmentation, since the individual actors remain part of communities and accountable to them; what is affirmed is unity in difference.[93] Yet Schleiermacher's approach remains ambivalent for various reasons. The presuppositions of his approach limit the emphasis on difference and individual initiative: the most likely ones to make a difference would be the most prominent and influential members of a community.[94] Furthermore, Schleiermacher sees purifying action as an inside process: it cannot be set in motion from without and it cannot be "revolutionary" in that it overturns existing organizations (*CS* 126).[95] Clearly, the actions of less prominent individuals, perhaps even from the lower classes or from the colonial world, are not yet in view; after all, it is those actions that are most likely to lead to revolutionary tendencies. Elsewhere, Schleiermacher makes things worse yet when he advocates difference primarily in order to maintain the status quo: if the upper classes of different nations were to develop too much similarity, he argues, the individual nations would be weakened, especially in countries where the relation of upper and lower classes is already weak, as in Germany.[96] Could unity in difference be a matter of shoring up the status quo already in Schleiermacher's times, long before postmodern sensitivities have had a chance to domesticate the concept? Even the softer empire remains an empire. Finally, Schleiermacher rejects a more democratic approach when it comes to the civil community, which "rests essentially in the opposition between the governing authority and its subjects."[97] The christological surplus remains limited.

Another interesting aspect of purifying action is how it engages children. While the ethical action of children is supposed to be that of obedience, Schleiermacher rejects punishment and reward as educational tools because they fail to acknowledge—and they perhaps even cover up—the stronger power of Christ's Spirit. This can be considered a progressive move even today and runs counter to colonizing efforts. Others in Schleiermacher's day who promoted colonial models of education, like Joachim Heinrich Campe in his 1779 German version of *Robinson Crusoe*, promote "paternal kindness" and provide a "model for domesticating little 'savages' in Germany"; the inevitable result of this approach being the annihilation of Native culture.[98] Since the "special mission of Germans to educate" is one of the pillars of German colonialism in the late nineteenth century, Schleiermacher's insights might be somewhat of a counterweight.[99] Unfortunately, when Schleiermacher talks about the family in the context of the state, punishment and reward are reintroduced and seen as appropriate (*CS* 235). In much of Schleiermacher's *Christliche Sitte* there is a curious submission of Christianity to the state that is justified by the idea that the state (defined as the basic form of human community) is older than Christianity and that, while Christianity shapes the family and the community, it cannot really shape the state.[100] This does not mean that Christian ethics has nothing to say to the state—Schleiermacher charges, for instance, that the death penalty is wrong— but the alternative structures developed in the church are not allowed to shape the world in a deeper sense.[101] The most that Christianity can do, according to Schleiermacher, is to shape human community, rather than the state; the task is to "penetrate" (*durchdringen*) this community with the Christian Spirit.[102]

When Schleiermacher addresses the relationship to what he calls "uncivilized peoples," another aspect of his anticolonial tendencies reemerges (*CS* 289). He rejects the use of force, even at the level of the state. Since the condition of the modern middle class (*der bürgerliche Zustand*) is a blessing for humanity, it is a duty to enable those who have not yet encountered this middle class to live in similar ways. Nevertheless, this cannot be achieved by force, only by peaceful means. Recall that Schleiermacher's Christ, too, works by attraction rather than by coercion. Where force is used to spread the condition of the middle class, people will feel oppressed, and this leads to resentment; in his opposition to the Spanish conquest, the earlier Las Casas came to similar conclusions. This use of force is the main reason, according to Schleiermacher, that despite centuries of contact between Christian and non-Christian peoples, no desire (*Neigung*) for Christianity has developed. Not that non-Christian peoples would have no interest at all in Christianity, but through the use of force Christianity has inspired hate. Without the use of force, Schleiermacher maintains, the "benign tribes" to which "one came in the fifteenth century" would have become Christians, and this is "a disgrace for the Christian peoples."[103] This position is not atypical for German sensitivities in the nineteenth century: there was a feeling that colonialism had done a lot of harm, and the problems were not just with the Spanish conquest. Even the later colonial powers had used force inappropriately and had oppressed people. The later Schleiermacher seems to have moved beyond his earlier admiration of British and Dutch colonialism. Here, his Christology shows some anticolonial sentiment, even if it does not go much beyond the common opinion of his time. In the contemporary United States, the aggressive foreign politics of the Bush administration might have learned from Schleiermacher's critique. A softer approach both in Iraq and Afghanistan would probably have been more successful, given the obvious failures of war—although even this approach would of course not necessarily have put us outside the confines of the colonial mentality.

Schleiermacher's approach could thus potentially result in placing restraints on colonialist activism and expansionism. Purifying action is connected to a second step, which he calls broadening action. Christian action is not self-empowered activism and expansionism but based in Christ's own actions; Christ is the source of Christian action. What moves is the Spirit (of Christ).[104] The "quality of the redeemer" combines two aspects: his being without sin and his power to confer it upon others.[105] Patterned after Christ's power, which works through attraction rather than sheer force, Schleiermacher identifies a Christian desire to act in broadening ways on the one hand and, on the other, a desire to receive, manifest in those who do not yet know Christ.[106] This and nothing else is the basis for Christian mission: he rejects "an institution, like in the [Roman] Catholic Church, which is called 'Mission,'" because Christianity spreads quite naturally through colonial expansion and other connections based on "worldly interest." There is simply no need for Christian expansionism. Christian missionary activities are required only to the degree that colonialism is unable to contribute to the spread of Christianity.[107] Schleiermacher goes one step further and connects the subject of mission to the idea of progress within the church as well: just as mission ultimately grows out of the strength of the personal conviction of individual Christians, so each member of the church should have "freedom of judgment, freedom of communication even of those things which might look like a deviation," because such freedom might lead to progress within the church.[108] When those in whom the Spirit is at work are at a point where they can be considered to be "of age" religiously, they, too, earn the right to contribute to the progress of the church. In this way, the church is like a school that continuously educates itself "in and through" its members in whom it seeks to infuse its basic principles (*CS* 388–89). In this context, Schleiermacher even compares the church to a language, in which and "into which" everyone has to form his own thinking but that is still open to being perfected.[109] Depending on how this moment of integration into a language is interpreted and on how one is to understand the "coming of age" of the neophytes, Schleiermacher's approach contains some real potential for resistance. Due to his emphasis on the openness and perfectibility of Christianity and Christian language, he is more open than contemporary cultural-linguistic approaches in theology.[110] Authority is rooted, not surprisingly, in the level of people's education and the comprehensiveness of their consciousness, but also in the "diversity of experience."[111] The latter category is of special interest in the resistance to empire and colonialism; it potentially pushes toward a greater sensitivity for the colonial other who, forced to live a hybrid existence that pulls together the reality of colonizer and colonized, might well display the greatest diversity of experience of all.[112]

This trajectory needs to be connected with Schleiermacher's resistance not only to the more obvious forms of slavery but also to the particular forms of slavery endured for instance by Prussian workers, introduced by capitalist modes of production. People are enslaved, he says, when they are inserted into a "mechanism" in which they lose the ability to experience a free spiritual existence. At this point, it seems, idealism and materialism meet in dialectical fashion; while the recognition of material challenges to the spirit is one of the key insights of the later Karl Marx, Schleiermacher seems to have a premonition of the problem. Schleiermacher's rejection of the industrial enslavement of the spirit is clear, and it is based on his christological logic: no one who is capable of communication with Christ—and this includes all of humanity—should be turned into a "living machine." Here, he clearly advances beyond the earlier position of Las Casas, who was content to let the Native Americans work in peace, in both fields and mines (see previous chapter). Although Schleiermacher's protest against the emerging capitalism of his time is brief, the christological surplus on which this challenge is based must not be overlooked; this challenge also includes a rejection of the ethics of the ancient world (which Schleiermacher otherwise greatly admires), because it found slavery to be "always very good and convenient" (*CS* 466).

Finally, in his comments on representational action Schleiermacher displays the basic principles on which his Christian ethics rest. Most importantly, Christ's divinity guarantees the "essential equality" of all members of the church, since what matters is the relation of individual Christians to him who is absolutely superior.[113] Even the non-Christians are included in this vision, since the difference is only temporal: some have the Holy Spirit already, others not yet (*CS* 514). The democratizing tendencies that we have seen earlier are also visible in worship: no worship service should be without elements in which the "productivity of all" can find expression. Furthermore, and not insignificantly, Schleiermacher rejects the suggestion that there should be separate worship services for the lower and the upper classes. It is not that he challenges the distinction of classes as such; it is simply that the "religious" is not the place for this distinction (*CS* 556, 568). But perhaps something can be learned from this religious equality after all. Modern theology might have shaped up differently if Schleiermacher would have pursued these impulses further and openly addressed the power differentials in the church between the upper and the lower classes, as well as between the colonizers and the colonized. A mere insistence on equality that does not also seek to overturn the basic presuppositions that undergird the unequal distribution of power is not enough.[114]

Schleiermacher concludes his *Christliche Sitte* by returning to his particular notion of "feeling," and thus to the core of his theology; feeling, rather than knowing or doing, brings together self and other and enables understanding. In its ultimate form, as "feeling of absolute dependence," feeling brings together humanity and God.[115] Communication with those who are different cannot happen without "greatest toleration" (*grösste Duldung*) and "the most determined respect for the modifications of feeling in other people"; no one can contribute to the "purification and perfection" of others except those who are able to put themselves into the feelings of the other. This brings us back to where we started—the growing sense that modern theology and hermeneutics are inextricably connected to the encounter with the colonial other. Schleiermacher's focus, however, is here not negative but positive: he is not searching for the shortcomings of the others but for their achievements; the one who is pure, he says, will be able to identify what is pure in others as well (*CS* 666–67). Here is real potential for overcoming some of the more blatant colonialist enterprises, yet we need to keep in mind that Schleiermacher still operates from a position of superiority. Thus, the colonial situation is ultimately not challenged.

The surplus of Schleiermacher's position can perhaps best be seen in contrast with other intellectuals of his day. Johann Gottfried Herder, for instance, another enlightened thinker with ties to the earliest Romantic movement, also rejects slavery. He begins his *Reflections on the Philosophy of the History of Mankind* with the statement that "notwithstanding the varieties of the human form, there is but one and the same species of man throughout the whole of our earth."[116] But while Herder emphasizes common humanity, he also shows clear prejudices that appear to be stronger than Schleiermacher's. Africans, Herder argues based on anatomy, are not made for "finer spirituality." His views of anatomy lead him to a more positive view of Native Americans. Their "savagery, passivity, and weakness" are not innate but caused by the Spaniards who destroyed their culture. These Native Americans can be compared to the Europeans at an earlier time.[117] Herder's observations were put down in 1784. After 1790 theories of race gained even more prominence, a development related to a Germanic sense of weakness and fragmentation.[118] While Schleiermacher is not free from racist influences, as his descriptions of the Australian Aborigines show, he does not resonate with the stronger forms of racism of his day.

Under the heading of representational action Schleiermacher finally emphasizes the notion of love. Love is at the basis of Christ's attractive power, and James Brandt has highlighted this emphasis on love as key to Schleiermacher's concern for the transformation of society.[119] We must indeed acknowledge that Schleiermacher broadens the notion of Christian love so that it includes all of humanity (*CS* 514). Yet, as Zantop reminds us, love was also a favorite metaphor in eighteenth-century colonial discourse: love could establish natural boundaries, improve the races that need improving, and even let the colonial enterprise appear in the light of "legitimacy and mutuality." One of the prominent colonial fantasies of love was the patriarchal relation between father and child on which education was based.[120] The notion of love as such does therefore not necessarily overcome the colonial system. Yet we have seen a surplus in Schleiermacher, and there is a sense in which his categories can provide resistance to other incarnations of colonialism in his day and perhaps in ours as well, and this is true not least of all for the notion of love. As heirs of modern theology we need to pursue this trajectory further.

Notes

1. Friedrich Schleiermacher, *The Christian Faith,* ed. H. R. Mackintosh and J. S. Stewart (Edinburgh: T.&T. Clark, 1986), 427 (henceforward *CF*). The German term, *"anziehende Kraft"* can be found in Friedrich Schleiermacher, *Der christliche Glaube nach den Grundsätzen der evangelischen Kirche im Zusammenhang dargestellt,* vol. 2 (Berlin: Georg Reimer, 1884), 91.

2. James M. Brandt is correct that Schleiermacher's Christ resembles H. Richard Niebuhr's notion of "Christ transforming culture," rather than being the "Christ of culture," as

Niebuhr assumed. *All Things New: Reform of Church and Society in Schleiermacher's Christian Ethics* (Louisville: Westminster John Knox, 2001), 4, 130. This Christ does not surrender "distinctive Christian identity." At the same time, however, we will have to see how much of a challenge Christ will pose to culture and how Christian identity challenges culture.

3. See, for instance, the work of R. S. Sugirtharajah, Kwok Pui-lan, and Catherine Keller.

4. Yorick Spiegel was the pioneer, in his *Theologie der bürgerlichen Gesellschaft: Sozialphilosophie und Glaubenslehre bei Friederich Schleiermacher* (Munich: Chr. Kaiser, 1968); see also Frederick Herzog, "Schleiermacher and the Problem of Power," in his book *Justice Church: The New Function of the Church in North American Christianity* (Maryknoll, N.Y.: Orbis, 1980), chap. 3; and Dieter Schellong, *Bürgertum und christliche Religion: Anpassungsprobleme der Theologie seit Schleiermacher*, Theologische Existenz heute, 187 (Munich: Kaiser, 1975). See also Joerg Rieger, *God and the Excluded: Visions and Blindspots in Contemporary Theology* (Minneapolis: Fortress Press, 2001), chap. 1.

5. Kwok Pui-lan has addressed some of the colonial connotations of Schleiermacher's work in her book *Postcolonial Imagination and Feminist Theology* (Louisville: Westminster John Knox, 2005).

6. Brandt tracks Schleiermacher's involvement in political matters; Schleiermacher was not always supportive of the political powers of his day and dared to critique the government of Prussia's King Friedrich Wilhelm III, which almost cost him his position. *All Things New*, 109–34. Schleiermacher was interested in a *Volksmonarchie*, a constitutional monarchy that would grant more of a political role to the middle class; see Kurt Nowak, *Schleiermacher: Leben, Werk und Wirkung* (Göttingen: Vandenhoeck & Ruprecht, 2001), 380. Schleiermacher was even active in the resistance against the French, undertaking secret missions in 1808. See Theodore Vial, "Schleiermacher and the State," in *The Cambridge Companion to Friedrich Schleiermacher*, ed. Jacqueline Mariña (Cambridge: Cambridge University Press, 2005), 275.

7. In the late seventeenth century, Prussia briefly established forts on the coast of West Africa and leased part of the West Indian island of St. Thomas from Denmark. In 1751, Frederick the Great established the unsuccessful Asiatic-Chinese Merchant Society. See the introduction to *The Imperialist Imagination: German Colonialism and Its Legacy*, ed. Sara Friedrichsmeyer, Sara Lennox, and Susanne Zantop (Ann Arbor: University of Michigan Press, 1998), 9. Unfortunately, colonialism in German history has not received much sustained attention yet.

8. See Susanne Zantop, *Colonial Fantasies: Conquest, Family, and Nation in Precolonial Germany, 1770–1870* (Durham, N.C.: Duke University Press, 1997), 22, 29.

9. Tillich notes that "the bourgeois wants to analyze and transform the whole of reality in order to control it." *Perspectives on 19th and 20th Century Protestant Theology* (New York: Harper & Row, 1967), 46. The bourgeois middle class assumes that God has made the world, but does not interfere any longer—humanity is now in charge; ibid., 47. Yet Tillich seeks to overcome this separation of God and world by claiming—with Schleiermacher—a fundamental "identity" between humanity and God; ibid., 94. We approach the divine from within the human: "Without having the universe in ourselves we would never understand it"; ibid., 101. The question we need to raise, however, is, Whose humanity is affirmed here?

10. Karl Barth, *Protestant Theology in the Nineteenth Century: Its Background and History* (Valley Forge, Pa.: Judson, 1973), 82.

11. Barth, *Protestant Theology*, 38–39.

12. See Zantop, *Colonial Fantasies*, 122.

13. Barth, *Protestant Theology*, 38.

14. Between 1770 and 1800, the production of travelogues increased five times in Europe, and German readers consumed the most. Zantop, *Colonial Fantasies*, 32.

15. Günter Meckenstock calls it *gewichtig*; Friedrich Daniel Ernst Schleiermacher, *Schriften aus der Berliner Zeit 1800-1802*, ed. Günter Meckenstock, Kritische Gesamtausgabe, ed. Hans-Joachim Birkner et al., Abt. 1, vol. 3 (Berlin: Walter de Gruyter, 1988), LXXXV.

16. Edward Said observes that German scholarship about the Orient and other non-European places was based on materials gathered firsthand by imperial Britain and France. *Orientalism* (New York: Random House, 1979), 19.

17. This helps us better understand scholars such as Friedrich Max Müller, who in the second half of the eighteenth century became one of the top authorities on Indian language and religion without ever traveling to India. Interestingly enough, Müller is still appreciated in India today because, due to his German origins, he could be seen as an "outsider" rather than as a representative of the British colonial powers. See Peter van der Veer, *Imperial Encounters: Religion and Modernity in India and Britain* (Princeton, N.J.: Princeton University Press, 2001), 106.

18. For the term *colonial fantasies* and an interpretation of particular German colonial fantasies see Susanne Zantop, *Colonial Fantasies*. Zantop notes that the term *fantasy* links "the individual subconscious and the political subconscious of a society"; ibid., 4. See also my own reference to Jacques Lacan's use of the term *fantasy* in the context of romanticizing women as a repressive move. Joerg Rieger, *Remember the Poor: The Challenge to Theology in the Twenty-First Century* (Harrisburg, Pa.: Trinity Press International, 1998), 79-83.

19. Zantop, *Colonial Fantasies*, 41, and 38–40.

20. Friedrich Daniel Ernst Schleiermacher, "Letter of March 1, 1799," in *Briefwechsel 1799–1800*, ed. Andreas Arndt and Wolfgang Virmond, *Kritische Gesamtausgabe*, ed. Hans-Joachim Birkner, et al., Abt. 5, vol. 3 (Berlin: Walter de Gruyter, 1992), 24.

21. Friedrich Daniel Ernst Schleiermacher, "Materialien zur Siedlungsgeschichte Neuhollands (Australiens)," in *Schriften aus der Berliner Zeit 1800–1802*, ed. Günter Meckenstock, *Kritische Gesamtausgabe*, ed. Hans-Joachim Birkner, et al., Abt. 1, vol. 3 (Berlin: Walter de Gruyter, 1988), 251; these insights are from his translation of a 1789 report by Arthur Phillip, "The voyage of Governor Phillip to Botany Bay."

22. Ibid., 252, from Schleiermacher's translation of Phillip.

23. Walter Mignolo talks about Occidentalism as the approach that, having had its beginnings in the sixteenth century, had a significant impact in shaping Europe, preceding the eighteenth- and nineteenth-century developments of Orientalism. *Local Histories/Global Designs: Coloniality, Subaltern Knowledges, and Border Thinking* (Princeton: Princeton University Press, 2000), 18–21. See also Zantop, who coins the phrase "German Occidentalism" in contrast to Said's notion of Orientalism. *Colonial Fantasies*, 10.

24. Schleiermacher, "Zur Siedlungsgeschichte Neuhollands (Australiens)," in *Schriften aus der Berliner Zeit: 1800–1802*, 269.

25. Ibid., 271.

26. Schleiermacher, "Materialien zur Siedlungsgeschichte Neuhollands," 253. Tench's book is titled *A narrative of the expedition to Botany Bay*.

27. Schleiermacher, "Zur Siedlungsgeschichte," 271.

28. Ibid., 270.

29. "*Ohne die eigenthümlichen widrigen Gesichtszüge des Negers*"; see ibid., 271.

30. Ibid., 278.

31. Ibid., 279.

32. Said, *Orientalism*, 117.

33. See Hans Peter Herrmann, Hans-Martin Blitz, Susanna Mossmann, *Machtphantasie Deutschland: Nationalismus, Männlichkeit und Fremdenhass im Vaterlandsdiskurs deutscher Schriftsteller des 18. Jahrhunderts* (Frankfurt: Suhrkamp, 1996), 125–27.

34. Zantop, *Colonial Fantasies*, 7.

35. "Only by recourse to colonized peoples, to men and women of color, whom they displaced or desired, could white European males define themselves as the White European Male, predestined by biology to a position of physical and cultural dominance"; ibid., 5.

36. See ibid., 8.

37. Mary Louise Pratt, *Imperial Eyes: Travel Writing and Transculturation* (London and New York: Routledge, 1992), 115. Humboldt reinvented South America as a place of natural phenomena that "dwarfs humans, commands their being, arouses their passions, defies the powers of perception"; ibid., 120. In Humboldt's case, the fact that he was independently wealthy allowed him to pursue his own visions. Mary Louise Pratt notes an increase in interest and even travel after von Humboldt; ibid., 146–47. From the 1820s, small European communities were forming in South American capitals, tied to capitalist economic ventures; America's "backwardness" legitimated the capitalist interventions; ibid., 152. Pratt notes that "Westerners are accustomed to thinking of romantic projects of liberty, individualism, and liberalism as emanating *from* Europe *to* the colonial periphery, but less accustomed to thinking about emanations *from* the contact zones *back* into Europe"; ibid., 138. Pratt's point is that the tensions, starting in the 1780s with Amerindian uprisings in the Andes, revolts in South Africa, rebellion in Brazil, and revolution in Santo Domingo, also had impacts on the European imagination.

38. Stephen Prickett, "Coleridge, Schlegel and Schleiermacher: England, Germany (and Australia) in 1798," in *1798: The Year of the Lyrical Ballads*, ed. Richard Cronin (London: Macmillan/New York: St. Martin's, 1998), 181–82. Prickett is mistaken, however, when he claims that the challenge was to include the Aboriginals "within the fold of Christianity." Schleiermacher's notion of religion was broader. Most recently, this argument has been picked up by Terry Eagleton: "Schleiermacher was concerned about how we could understand the beliefs of this people even though they seemed desperately alien to us. It was from a colonial encounter that the art of interpretation was born." *After Theory* (New York: Basic, 2003), 23.

39. *CF* 31; he explicitly rejects the view that "Christian religion (piety) should adopt towards at least most other forms of piety the attitude of the true towards the false."

40. For a discussion of the concept of the panopticon, first suggested by Jeremy Bentham, see Michel Foucault, *Discipline and Punish: The Birth of the Prison*, trans. Alan Sheridan (New York: Pantheon, 1977), 195-228. David Spurr notes as many as twelve different strategies of empire in colonial discourse; surveillance is one of them. *The Rhetoric of Empire: Colonial Discourse in Journalism, Travel Writing, and Imperial Administration* (Durham and London: Duke University Press, 1993), chap. 1.

41. This role of language and the connection to Foucault's thought is noted by Gunther Pakendorf, "Mission as Gewalt. Die Missionsordnung im 19. Jahrhundert" in *Mission und Gewalt: Der Umgang christlicher Missionen mit Gewalt und die*

Ausbreitung des Christentums in Afrika und Asien in der Zeit von 1792-1918/19, ed. Ulrich van der Heyden and Jürgen Becher (Stuttgart: Franz Steiner Verlag, 2000), 240: "The means which the church primarily employs in its missionary work, *i.e.*, the word and language, becomes the primary instrument of violence."

42. Homi Bhabha, *The Location of Culture* (New York: Routledge, 1994), 111.

43. The common charge that Schleiermacher's approach is the paradigm for liberal theology is too simplistic. Schleiermacher struggles with both Enlightenment Christology on the one hand and ultra-orthodox Christology on the other. In his major work, *The Christian Faith*, Schleiermacher distinguishes between what he calls a "magical" and an "empirical" view. The latter, the position of various Enlightenment thinkers, understands the redemptive activity of Christ as producing an increasing perfection of the Christian self through his teachings and example; ibid., 430. In this view, Christ's work is reduced to the natural level of "ordinary daily experience"; ibid., 434. Christology becomes a function of human subjectivity. Here the modern turn to the self is complete. Conversely, the premodern "magical" position understands Christ's redemptive activity as a supernatural act that is independent of any natural mediation, even the mediation of the Christian community. Some see Scripture as a means of mediation; others do not; ibid., 430. This view is related to a premodern "objective" view of the work of Christ. What counts is not the personal relationship to Christ but "the punishment which Christ suffered"; ibid., 435. For Schleiermacher neither position is viable. While his critique of the orthodox misunderstanding is well known (Protestant Orthodoxy did nothing but repeat the old doctrines), his critique of Enlightenment modernity is equally important.

44. See also Brandt, *All Things New*, 119, in reference to Schleiermacher's *Christian Ethics*. Brandt records Schleiermacher's opposition to wars of aggression, the death penalty, violent revolution, divorce, dehumanizing labor, and other manifestations of crude power in his context; ibid., 118–24.

45. As Said has pointed out: "Nearly every nineteenth-century writer (and the same is true enough of writers in earlier periods) was extraordinarily well aware of the fact of empire." *Orientalism*, 14.

46. Said: "orientalism . . . has less to do with the Orient than it does with 'our' world"; ibid., 12. The Orient helps to define the West; ibid., 1.

47. Ibid., 3.

48. Ibid., 20–21; for the notion of the *real* as that which is created in situations of repression see the introductory chapter, above, and Rieger, *Remember the Poor*, chap. 3.

49. Schleiermacher notes that the three offices display "new and intensified forms of those through which in the old covenant the divine government was revealed." *CF* 439.

50. Friederich Schleiermacher, *On Religion: Speeches to Its Cultured Despisers*, trans. and ed. Richard Crouter (New York: Cambridge University Press, 1996), 239. Nevertheless, Schleiermacher considers it basically dead; ibid., 238. Judaism is a matter of the past. As a childlike religion, "it could only work on a narrow scene, without complications, where the whole being simple the natural consequences of actions would not be disturbed or hindered"; ibid., 240.

51. *CF* 37. Still, the trajectory of Schleiermacher's argument is the same as the more polite language of the *Speeches*.

52. Friedrich Schleiermacher, *Briefe bei Gelegenheit der politisch theologischen Aufgabe und des Sendschreibens jüdischer Hausväter. Von einem Prediger außerhalb Berlin* (Berlin: Friedrich Franke, 1799), 12-13, quoted in Jonathan M. Hess, *Germans, Jews and the Claims of Modernity* (Hew Haven: Yale University Press, 2002), 186.

53. See Kurt Nowak, *Schleiermacher: Leben, Werk und Wirkung*, 2nd ed. (Göttingen: Vandenhoeck & Ruprecht, 2002), 95–97.

54. Schleiermacher, *Briefe bei Gelegenheit*, 15, once again quoted in Hess, *Germans, Jews, and the Claims of Modernity*, 188.

55. *CF* 440; in this case "harmony between the old covenant and the new."

56. Schleiermacher leaves open the possibility that there will be new natural or historical epochs, "so long as they are not in the sphere of religion" that "could still be announced by miracles." But this needs to be judged by natural science and not by theology; *CF* 449.

57. See Schleiermacher's typology of religion, which takes for granted states of religious development, with Protestant Christianity being at the very top; *CF* 31–52.

58. Ernst Troeltsch, "The Significance of the Historical Existence of Jesus for Faith," in Ernst Troeltsch, *Writings on Theology and Religion*, ed. and trans. Robert Morgan and Michael Pie (Atlanta: John Knox, 1977), 204. Troeltsch affirms the turn to social psychology.

59. *CF* 460; suffering is also dubbed "sympathy with misery," *CF* 436. For the position of the church fathers on this issue see above, chap. 2.

60. In his *Speeches*, Schleiermacher tells the Prussians: "You alone are capable, as well as worthy, of having awakened in you the sense for holy and divine things." Following common sensitivities of his day, he is quite critical of other European Christians, including the British, French, and Greek. Schleiermacher, *Speeches*, 9ff., 23 n.3.

61. *CF* 469. We must, however, not overlook the critical edge of this approach. Schleiermacher critiques both traditional theocracy, which subordinates civil society to religion and a form of civil religion where religion is animated by the spirit of society; *CF* 473.

62. *CF* 363: "But there is given to us, instead of His personal influence, only that of His fellowship, in so far as even the picture of Him which is found in the Bible also originated in the community and is perpetuated by it."

63. *CF* 473: "The stronger and the more extensive His Kingdom becomes, the more definite becomes the severance between Church and State."

64. Even when Christian missions "had almost gone to sleep," Schleiermacher trusts the dynamic element of religion to move to higher stages; *Speeches*, 257. Spiegel notes that in the royal office of Christ the foundational role of faith for society is expressed most explicitly. See *Theologie der bürgerlichen Gesellschaft*, 253. Once again Spiegel: "At the same time the work of Christ retains the task to impact both nature and the masses, in order to subdue everything to the Spirit and its rule"; ibid., 250. All this happens without brutal force.

65. Schleiermacher supports the spread of "civilization." See Brandt, *All Things New*, 121, reference to Schleiermacher's *Christian Ethics*, 288.

66. Von Arnim followed Schleiermacher as editor of the newspaper *Der Preussische Correspondent*. Von Arnim's circle blamed the Jews for what they saw as the maladies of modern capitalism and proposed a nationalist ethos that rejected modernity, liberalism, and capitalism. While violence against Jews was declared un-Christian, threats and warnings were not uncommon in this situation. See Hans Peter Herrmann, et al., *Machtphantasie Deutschland*, 123–59.

67. Jonathan Hess has put a similar insight in terms of the following comparison, arguing that Schleiermacher assumed that "European Christians are familiar with and can even appreciate the Jews' 'Oriental' tradition in much the same way as educated Germans know and speak French. Like the French, however, Jews are completely unacquainted with the language, culture and religion they are threatening to dominate." Hess, *Germans, Jews, and the Claims of Modernity*, 189.

68. *Speeches*, 241.

69. In *The Christian Faith* Schleiermacher argues early on that the self is less in danger of ideological distortion than the concern for God or the world; *CF* 126. See also Rieger, *God and the Excluded*, chap. 1.

70. Cf. Schellong, *Bürgertum und christliche Religion*, 33–35. Schellong points out that the struggle for universals was an important part of the modern middle class coming to power.

71. *CF* 450; see above.

72. *CF* 64; clarified at ibid., 400. Not the "capacity," only the "possibility" is innate.

73. *CF* 368. Schleiermacher denies the two opposing positions that sin is inevitable or that it is "decreasing of itself"; *CF* 355. Neither does he agree with the view that sin is a necessary or even "wholesome" reality; *CF* 367.

74. This relates to Schleiermacher's critiques of theological conservatism and liberalism; one group is exclusively focusing on the magical and supernatural, the other on the empirical and natural. See *CF* 429–31, 434–36.

75. Schleiermacher suggests a new understanding of the divinity of Christ. Christ's divinity is no longer an abstract metaphysical entity but inextricably related to humanity. Schleiermacher cautiously avoids two traditional expressions, that of "divine nature" in Christ and that of the "duality of natures in the same Person." The basic point, as far as Christ's divinity is concerned, is simply that in Christ the God-consciousness "was absolutely clear and determined each moment"; *CF* 397. In this way, Schleiermacher feels he has circumvented the two major christological heresies, Ebionite (Christ as mainly a human being) and docetic (Christ as being not really human), the former implied by Aulén's charges, the latter by David Friedrich Strauss, *The Christ of Faith and the Jesus of History: A Critique of Schleiermacher's* Life of Jesus (Philadelphia: Fortress Press, 1977). There is only one thing that distinguishes Christ from other human beings. In Christ, God-consciousness manifests itself in its pure form, an initial supernatural divine activity becoming a "natural fact of history"; *CF* 365; see also 367, 387. Christ is necessary in order to turn the general God-consciousness of humanity into the actual presence of God in human nature.

76. *CF* 433. Schleiermacher calls this the "mystical" perspective as opposed to a magical and empirical one; *CF* 434.

77. "In our view, the suffering of Christ has nothing to say," states Schleiermacher; *CF* 435. At best, it is "an element of secondary importance"; *CF* 436.

78. *CF* 558–59. This ambivalence is even stronger in the statement that "all other religious fellowships are destined to lose themselves in Christianity"; *CF* 564.

79. *CF* 560. Schleiermacher argues that "only that part of the world which is united to the Christian Church is for us the place of attained perfection, or of the good, and–relatively to quiescent self-consciousness—the place of blessedness"; *CF* 527.

80. *Speeches*, 242–44. "Bad religion" and "false morality" need to be exposed, although "behind all distortions and degradations" there is hidden "the heavenly germ of religion."

81. Ibid., 251.

82. Ibid., 245.

83. Ibid., 236–37.

84. Ibid., 251.

85. Ibid., 252.

86. Christian doctrine, he notes, consists of the two fields: *Sittenlehre* and *Glaubenslehre*. Schleiermacher, *Die Christliche Sitte nach den Grundsätzen der evangelischen Kirche im Zusammenhang dargestellt* (Waltrop: Spenner, 1999), 3 (hereafter *CS*). The two fields are not separate, because ethics is also theology, and theology is also ethics, *CS* 12. Both are focused on God; the difference is that theology deals with human interest (*Interesse*) in the relation to God and ethics deals with the motivation that grows out of our relation to God (*Antrieb, impetus*); *CS* 22 and 23.

87. *CS* 32. Schleiermacher distinguishes the community of God and Christ as original and perfect and the community of God and humanity as in progress; *CS* 38.

88. *CS* 11: "Our main proposition is, after all, that Christ is the redeemer of humanity."

89. Schleiermacher talks about "the principles of the development of Christian action," *CS* 70.

90. *CS* 94–95.

91. This relation of the awareness of the human other and awareness of the divine Other is at the core of my book *God and the Excluded*.

92. The first two forms of action are further combined under the rubric "effective action" (*wirksames Handeln*).

93. *CS* 135–36; see also his discussion of national and racial differences; *CS* 453–54. Schleiermacher even affirms the freedom to unite with other nations and races in particular cases but sees no necessity to abolish nation and race. Of course, while Schleiermacher affirms human difference he assumes that the religious essence is the same.

94. Schleiermacher notes, for instance, that while children have some connection to the Spirit, they are not agents of purifying actions; *CS* 221. The only ethical action for children is obedience; *CS* 232.

95. *CS* 129, 132–33; this restriction applies not only to civil society but also to the church.

96. *CS* 659; England, on the other hand, would have to fear less than Germany.

97. *CS* 128. Schleiermacher is willing to consider the possibility that in civil community individuals can have some limited impact on the whole, but does not consider this a significant issue; *CS* 129: "Consequently, in this case the conditions are strictly separate."

98. Zantop, *Colonial Fantasies*, 14, 105, 114–15. Nevertheless, there are also parallels between the approaches. The "perfectibility of *all* humans" is a core belief of both Campe and Schleiermacher.

99. Neither world trade nor sea power are the primary goal of Germany, but "the cultivation of natural peoples and natural territories"; ibid., 199, quoting Heinrich Hübbe-Schleiden.

100. *CS* 241. Elsewhere, Schleiermacher identifies people (*Volk*) and state (*Staat*): state is simply the "form" that the people gives itself; *CS* 455. One of the horrors of Schleiermacher is action that would lead to the dissolution of the state; *CS* 266, 284. Schleiermacher analyzes purifying action within the state in terms of whether Christians can agree with it or not, but the focal point of this analysis is the individual Christian; this focus on the individual is demonstrated in that he offers two perspectives, one for those who are part of the governing authority and one for the subjects; *CS* 241–43.

101. *Christliche Sitte* makes a contribution in terms of the death penalty, for instance. Schleiermacher holds that the Christian in positions of government authority cannot level a punishment that he could not apply to himself; since it is prohibited to kill oneself, the death penalty is ethically wrong; *CS* 248. At the same time, he sternly repudiates the fact that Quakers and Mennonites reject military service and killing in war; *CS* 282. While he clearly rejects wars of aggression (*CS* 278, 454), he provides a justification of killing in war, since killing of soldiers is not the intention of killing in war, only "that one takes possession of that which constitutes the power [of the enemy], that is, land and people"; *CS* 281.

102. *CS* 640–41. Human community, too, is older than the Christian community; *CS* 620, 640. Human community and the state are not the same thing—the latter is the form of the former.

103. *CS* 288–90. In these passages, Schleiermacher uses the terms "situation of the middle class" (*bürgerlicher Zustand*), "state" (*Staat*), and "Christianity" (*Christenthum*) almost interchangeably.

104. *CS* 91–92. The basis is God's grace; *CS* 317. Since Schleiermacher identifies a relation between the Holy Spirit and the human spirit, he is able to appreciate human achievements. At the same time, the Holy Spirit is clearly a higher form of the human spirit; *CS* 313.

105. *CS* 365. The goal is clear: the perfection of humanity in Christ; *CS* 330.

106. *CS* 370–71. The Christians experience a "religious desire" (*religiöse Lust)* and the non-Christians desire to receive "the true object of their desire" (*den wahren Gegenstand ihres Verlangens)*.

107. *CS* 382, from the earlier lectures of 1824–25. In the final edition, Schleiermacher declares that Christian missions should be related to points where the civilizing mission is already at work; *CS* 381.

108. *CS* 383. Once again, this argument is developed in contrast to the Roman Catholic Church, because it assumes that the church is already perfected; *CS* 384.

109. *CS* 394. This proves wrong George Lindbeck's claim that Schleiermacher is an experiential expressivist; Schleiermacher is much closer to Lindbeck's own "cultural linguistic" approach. See Lindbeck, *The Nature of Doctrine: Religion and Theology in a Postliberal Age* (Philadelphia: Westminster, 1984).

110. For a critique of Lindbeck along those lines, see Rieger, *God and the Excluded*, chap. 3.

111. *CS* 396, the terms are *Geistesbildung, Vollständigkeit seines Bewusstseins,* and "*Vielseitigkeit seiner Erfahrung.*"

112. For the notion of hybridity, see Bhabha, *Location of Culture* (and the reference to Bhabha in the previous chapter). Bhabha would agree that the hybridized embody the greatest diversity of experience and the broader horizons.

113. *CS* 518. This is another example where the Protestant and Roman Catholic churches differ (*CS* 519); the latter does not assume this basic equality.

114. Brandt underscores Schleiermacher's emphasis on "mutuality and equality" as one of the crucial goals of Christian transformation of the world, but he is unaware of the problems that remain tied to these notions in a colonial context in which power differentials are at the core. *All Things New*, 129.

115. For a brief discussion of Schleiermacher's notion of "feeling of absolute dependence," see Rieger, *God and the Excluded*, 21–23.

116. Johann Gottfried von Herder, *Reflections on the Philosophy of the History of Mankind*, abridged and with an introduction by Frank E. Manuel (Chicago: The University of Chicago Press, 1968), 3.

117. See Zantop, *Colonial Fantasies*, 75–77, reference to Herder's *Reflections on the Philosophy of History of Mankind*, 1784. Later, Herder also challenges the colonial practices of other European nations; while the Spanish were cruel, the British were greedy and the Dutch cold. See ibid., 94.

118. See ibid., 81–97.

119. Brandt, *All Things New*, 129.

120. Zantop, *Colonial Fantasies*, 100–01.

6

Resisting and Reframing
Christus Victor

Christology and Neocolonialism

S WEDISH THEOLOGIAN GUSTAF AULÉN (1879–1977) has made famous the notion of *Christus Victor*, the victorious Christ, in theological circles. It is this motif that makes him so intriguing for our investigation of Christ and empire, as well as his claim that this ideal recaptures older traditional images of Christ's resistance to evil. Nevertheless, this notion, too, is ambivalent if one considers the global constellations of power at the beginning of the twentieth century. Asserting Christ as *Christus Victor* can provide resistance to empire; yet this assertion might also need to be resisted and reframed in the struggle against empire.

Aulén's argument for the victory of Christ has become one of the classics of modern theology. The importance of his work is widely acknowledged and his book *Christus Victor* is still in use today. It broke new ground in a theological debate that was preoccupied by a narrow opposition of "liberal" and "conservative" concerns. Aulén's work also struck a chord with the neoorthodox tendencies of the twentieth century. In 1968, more than three decades after its publication, Jaroslav Pelikan called Aulén's *Christus Victor* a "modern classic,"[1] based on its considerable impact in the English-speaking world since World War II. At present, it is being claimed for diverging theological interests—conservatives have referenced Aulén off and on, but there are other voices as well. In 2001, a Swedish theologian pointed out the usefulness of Aulén's approach in the Christian struggle against violence to women.[2]

The assertion of Christ's victory over sin, death, and the devil pursues themes that have to do with liberation. Nevertheless, even those themes can be used in support of empire. Consideration of the following questions will help locate the resistance factor of Aulén's approach: What are the causes of sin and death? Who are the forces of darkness that Aulén describes as the devil? If the forces of evil are not specified, *Christus Victor* can be quite useful for empire builders who often refer to notions of evil in order to blame the victims of empire. Blaming the victims in a neocolonial or postcolonial situation, especially where such blame transcends moral categories and a mere assignment of guilt, is often related to efforts to promote new kinds of control (for instance, intellectual and economic) over former colonial territories. Nevertheless, by refusing to cooperate with mainline liberal and conservative models, Aulén's model does create a christological surplus that can be genuinely inspiring and that pushes us beyond the limits of empire Christology in our own time.

The historical context of Aulén's Christology is closer to our own than that of the previous chapters. What might be its contributions to Christian resistance to empire today? Without considering our close historical neighbors in the twentieth century, constructive theology and Christology in the twenty-first century cannot develop the alternative perspectives and visions needed so desperately.

Theology between Colonialism and Neocolonialism

After the shock of World War I, which led to a reshuffling of colonial relations, and with the subsequent end of the great colonial empires after World War II, many strands of explicit empire theology also came to an end. This does not mean, however, that the colonialist mind-set and empire theology disappeared altogether. Pushed underground, it returned in more covert ways, in the political and cultural unconscious; the term *neocolonial* refers to these transformations. On the surface, most European theology after World War II was no longer colonial empire theology; the end of World War II is often seen as the point of transition from colonialist to neocolonialist mentalities. Some European theologians can be understood only when seen to be resisting the most glaring fallacies of colonialist modernity, the corresponding optimism that would often undergird global expansions, and its theology. Modern colonial theology manifested itself, for instance, in an overly optimistic belief in modern humanity's autonomy and power and in the neglect of a solid doctrine of sin. The work of the German-speaking dialectical theologians of the 1920s and 1930s, by contrast, opposes such optimism; unlike most of the other European powers who lost their colonies after World War II, Germany lost its colonies after World War I. Karl Barth, one of the more radical representatives of this group, even made the occasional explicit allusion to the colonialist tendencies of modernity and criticized its theological forms. In the United States, the so-called neoorthodox movement picked up similar theological concerns, such as the challenge to human autonomy and a more substantial understanding of sin, and developed them in its own ways. In the United States, however, anticolonialist references are less frequent and mostly suppressed in favor of critiques of communism, fascism, and secular humanism.[3]

The early work of Gustaf Aulén, often classified as belonging to the Swedish Lundensian school of theology, represented by Anders Nygren and Ragnar Bring, among others, shows some parallels to both German-speaking dialectical theology and U.S. neoorthodox theology, particularly in its basic critique of theological liberalism and humanism and in its interest in classical church doctrine. Common to these theologies is a distinct disillusionment about liberal optimism in the time after World War I. Disappointed with continental liberal theology and its narrow historicism and moralism that failed to transcend the sphere of the modern self, Aulén is one of those theologians who pursues a different theological path. Hope, for Aulén, does not come from the powers of modern humanity and its civilizations, but from God alone. This view of God emphasizes God's revelation and rejects the liberal tendency toward anthropocentrism, which he feels shapes God in the image of humanity and focuses primarily on innerworldly issues.[4] Another problem with the theological liberalism of the nineteenth and early twentieth century, according to Aulén, is that it was liturgically and musically impoverished, due to a lack of attention to the traditions of the church and to the "original, ideal liturgy." As a result, he judges, the "full sonority of the Christian message" had been lost.[5] Aulén's concern is, therefore, for "continuity stretching right back to the first beginnings of the Christian Church." He finds this concern also in "all contemporary efforts of liturgical renewal, in whichever church communion they occur," as they are "prompted by biblical or early church impulses."[6] At the same time—and here is another parallel to Barth that has often been overlooked—Aulén rejects not only the liberal approaches but also the conservative ones, especially approaches that might be classified as fundamentalist and foundationalist. The problems with the latter have to do with a narrow rationalism that limits the radical nature of the Christian faith.[7]

Common to the theologies represented by Aulén and Barth is, therefore, an emphasis on the power and autonomy of God, often coupled with an insight that

God's work is radically different from human standard morality.[8] Despite their differences, a theocentric approach that somehow operates "from the top down" is the most important link between Aulén's and Barth's work.[9] This approach, potentially resisting an identification of the powers that be with God's power, creates some space for theological independence from empire and occupies an important place in our ongoing investigation of the relationship of Christ and empire. My choice ultimately fell on Aulén rather than Barth, due to the motif of Christ's victory and its strong emphasis of the top-down movement of Christ; Aulén also expands our analysis of empire into an area of Europe that is not often considered in those terms.[10] Christian thought about Christ no doubt will shape up differently in this context.

Naturally, these theological approaches have received their own share of critique. Critics have noted, for instance, the lack of confidence in humanity if not an anthropological pessimism. Critics have also argued that there is too much emphasis on the work of God and not enough on humanity's contribution. But there have been virtually no critiques that have focused on the connections of any of these approaches with empire, whether in colonial or neocolonial form. An exception to this rule is the recent work of Catherine Keller, who has raised the question of the connection between a strong doctrine of God that emphasizes God's omnipotence and the omnipotence of empire. Keller argues that any reference to God's omnipotence, even if it is initially developed as resistance to empire, will end up supporting the unilateral power of empire.[11] Yet Keller's argument is not developed directly in dialogue with theological approaches that share family resemblances with Aulén's. A closer look is necessary to determine whether this critique applies here and what the underlying issues are that might be repressed in this mode of theology.

At first sight, there is little indication that Aulén's work would have anything to do with colonial or neocolonial developments, which makes him so interesting for our investigation. Sweden was not one of the prominent colonial powers; it had lost its territories in Finland and Aland to Russia in 1809; and after 1878, when it sold its only remaining non-European possession, Saint Bartholemy in the Caribbean, to France, the country was no longer a colonial power in the strict sense of the word. In 1905, Norway declared itself independent of the Swedish king. Nevertheless, Sweden was not completely isolated from the European high imperial era of the 1880s through the 1920s. In the words of one interpreter of Swedish developments, "International flows of capital, goods and people skyrocketed and for the first time their scale was global." These developments were connected to the missionary work of the church: "The missionary movement with its dependence on international religious, cultural, and personal networks, and its purpose to connect the world can be seen as social, cultural, and religious concomitant—not merely a response."[12] Even though the time after World War I was economically difficult, Swedish capital moved in neocolonial directions by inventing and pioneering multinational companies[13] and thus contributed in its own way to the push toward neocolonialism. Multinational companies embody one of the key differences between colonialist and neocolonialist systems, based on a different organization of power: while colonial powers maintain direct political control over another territory, neocolonial powers maintain power through economic, cultural, and other less visible networks, often long after official colonial control has been given up. Such neocolonialist developments were aided by modern methods of communication through telephones and telegraphs, which provided new possibilities for the development of international relations.[14]

All of this had implications for the church in Sweden as well. As Gustav Sjoblom has pointed out, "the missionary movement widened the horizon from Lutheran parochialism to global universalism."[15] This broadening of horizons can be seen as an important event in Swedish history with significant implications for Swedish Christianity. Initially, Swedish missionaries, due to the small number of Swedish colonial ventures, worked closely with the colonial enterprises of the British and others. In a case study of the official missions of the Swedish church with the Zulu nation from 1885-1895, Gustav Sjoblom observes some tensions between the Swedish missionaries and the British colonial powers but concludes that "there was never any doubt that the British were the main instrument chosen to execute the divine punishment and uplifting. Colonial law and judicial authority were the providentially appointed instruments to break the power of the chiefs. And there was never any doubt that the Swedish mission and the Swedish people were part of the enterprise."[16] In other words, mission and colonialism went hand in hand at that time. Several years later, P. P. Waldenström, elected president of the Mission Covenant Church of Sweden in 1904 (an independent church in the Lutheran tradition), did not want to rule out "the possibility of shared interest of Swedish missions and Swedish industry abroad,"[17] a move that points ahead to neocolonialist tendencies. But even where the missionary programs did not go to such extremes, they supported modernization, understood as "the introduction in traditional societies of new institutions and values in order to improve social and human living conditions."[18] The basic assumption, and one of the key assumptions of a neocolonialist mind-set that came to replace more drastic colonialist attitudes, was that Western values would be beneficial for the people; the churches' thinking about Christ would not be far removed from such attitudes.

Many of these developments took shape during the early years of Aulén's life and continued throughout his life. The Swedish Student Christian Movement in which Aulén was involved as a leader also showed lively interests in mission. Nevertheless, the major publications of Aulén take little note of these developments, and herein lies the problem. There is virtually no reflection on the broader political and economic contexts of theology, and even mission is addressed only in general and abstract terms. Aulén argues, for instance, that Christian missionary efforts should avoid the two extremes—absolute rejection of other religions and syncretism that tries to mingle religious insights—but this is as far as his comments go. His theological point is that Christianity is unique in its emphasis on God's revelation in Jesus Christ and that this should be the norm for any other revelation, although "the Christian faith is broad in so far as it does not set any limits to the possibilities of revelation."[19] But what does this mean for the shape of actual missionary enterprises, and what are the implications for the neocolonial tendencies of the missionary work of that time? By not addressing actual missionary and other practices of his time, Aulén is unable to challenge neocolonialism and thus ends up endorsing it by default.

Even though Aulén cannot be described as an adamant supporter of colonial movements, the fact must be taken into account that his theological work does not address the dangers of well-meaning and forward-looking economic expansionism—one of the trademarks of neocolonialism, which was characteristic of his time. The 1920s, the time when Aulén developed the basic ideas of his *Christus Victor* and the beginning of neocolonialist tendencies in Sweden,[20] were times of great changes even within the country of Sweden itself. Industrialization and internationalization were two of the key marks of these changes. The conflicts related to industrialization were so strong that in 1917 the country seemed to be on the verge of a revolution not unlike the Russian revolution; this led the Swedish king and the economic leaders to accept democratic reform, and power was handed over to a cabinet of Liberals and Social Democrats.[21] Nothing of these issues shows in Aulén's writings. Neither is there much of a sense of the strong social concerns developed by the Church of Sweden, which in the 1930s even led to various collaborations with the labor movement.[22]

It must be noted, however, that Aulén joined the resistance against the expansion of German National Socialism and that he understood some of the problems produced by this overt form of aggression that resembles the old colonial era. Early on in 1934, for instance, he helped defeat a German effort to have German Nazi Reichsbischof Ludwig Müller consecrated by the Swedish Church. For his ongoing resistance to National Socialism, his life was threatened; fortunately, four representatives of the German secret police were arrested before they could carry out their plans to silence him.[23] As bishop in Strängnäs, his house became a center of resistance, providing space for secret communications with the German-occupied countries of Norway (the birthplace of his wife) and Denmark. It might be added here, in order to grasp Aulén's context and not in order to diminish his achievements, that the fascist groups in Sweden were not as strong as the ones in Norway and Denmark and neither was the Swedish Church pressured to the same degree. A Scandinavian commission of church historians, writing in the 1970s, puts it thus: "The church opinion in Sweden could never be described as lending [*sic*] towards pro-fascist support."[24]

Stig Ekman identifies two paradigms of resistance in the Swedish struggle against Nazi Germany. The "realist paradigm" practiced a "flexible neutrality policy" that was mainly aimed at keeping Sweden out of World War II. The "moral and ideological paradigm," on the other hand, went beyond the official government's position of neutrality, strongly opposing any adaptation to Nazi Germany. This paradigm included support for people in occupied Denmark and Norway and support for the Allied cause.[25] Aulén definitely belongs in this latter category, stressing moral values. Indeed, in retrospect he interprets the situation as a "moral catastrophe" that violated "even the most elementary claims of justice."[26]

In regard to Nazi colonialism, Aulén identified the church's task as being watchful, as being the conscience of the world.[27] Nevertheless, it is quite telling that he identifies the basic theological problem with a fall away from Christianity rather than with a fundamental distortion within Christianity itself.[28] His critique ushers in a lament about "a long decline of the sense of righteousness,"[29] of which Nazi Germany was only the tip of the iceberg, and which was also seen in other movements that showed "open hostility against Christianity and the Church," such as the French and the Russian revolutions and, more generally, the "secularized world."[30] Again and again, Aulén warns of societies in which "the state maintains principles contrary to Christianity."[31] But this does not appear to present much of a challenge to the church in Sweden, and it seems as unimaginable to Aulén as to many of us now that the Nazis and other empire builders were indeed not all that hostile to Christianity but tried to embody Christendom in their own ways. Aulén is as optimistic about Christianity as he is pessimistic about the "world," arguing that "the people who belong to Christendom" have been subject to positive values "since the day Christianity came to them."[32]

When Aulén addresses the failure of the churches, this failure simply has to do with "how the Church—naturally enough against her own will—may have co-operated in the dissolution of the idea of justice."[33] Ultimately, the "principal reason for the passivity of the Church is to be found in her individualistic interpretation of Christianity"; Aulén's point is that this individualism led the church to dispense "private charity," according to the "Law of love," but at the same time allowed it to forget the "Law of justice," whereby "the brutal power of mammonism must be fought not only by charity but also and foremost by creating a better order of justice in the life of Society."[34] One might wish that the leaders of the church today would dare to say as much, but this is still not enough. Aulén's concern about the failure of the church leads him to call for renewal,[35] but notions of renewal usually show little concern for deeper distortions or for the possibility that there are distortions that go deeper than the level of the "will," into the unconscious; Aulén's call for renewal is no different. While Aulén's theology is open to "the world,"[36] we need to wonder whose world we are talking about, and how we will reach into those distortions of the world that, by and large, remain invisible especially in a neocolonial situation that is less clear-cut than a colonial one. And what are we to make of the fact that the Nazis really did present themselves as preserving and building on the Christian heritage, particularly Luther's German Reformation, going all the way back to Jesus who was seen as the first and greatest Aryan?[37]

An interesting footnote: in 1909 Aulén, who occasionally also composed music, wrote the music for a nationalistic Christian hymn propagated by the Young Church Movement and written by Bishop John Alfred Eklund. This hymn, we are told, became "practically a religious national anthem." And, although Aulén did not write the text, we need to take note of the fact that it was accepted in the 1937 edition of the Swedish hymnbook at a time when Aulén was bishop in Strängnäs.[38] Its text announces a struggle against evil in which king and people are united. Christ is said in the hymn to have "accompanied" Sweden's struggles, and for this reason the cross is inscribed on the Swedish flag: "The struggle earned peace for God's Church."[39] Aulén's notion of *Christus Victor* will need to be seen in this light as well.

One of the leaders of the Swedish Church with a broader view than Eklund was Einar Billing, one of Aulén's theology professors at Uppsala. According to Gustaf Wingren, Aulén is the one Swedish theologian who has made the greatest contributions to preserving Billing's contribution. Most important for our discussion is the concept of the primacy of God's action, which both Billing and Aulén share.[40] Billing positioned the Young Church Movement against tendencies to separate church and world, emphasizing that the Christian God is the God of Israel, who battles destructive forces in the world, rather than the Greek god who is static and does not intervene in the world.[41] In this context, according to Stephen Mitchell and Alf Tergel, the concern for mission provides a new impulse, because it can be seen as an antidote to self-centered nationalist efforts: mission is first of all the work of Godself. In addition, World War I also helped to push the Young Church Movement out of its nationalistic shell and toward international relationships. As a result, the Swedish Church came to be understood not as serving "popular egoism and national pride" but as "a tool by which people were turned into servants in the world of nations."[42] While this is a significant move, it does not immediately contradict the neocolonialist dynamics that also push beyond national boundaries and seek to shape the world of nations.

In all this, Sweden's place as a powerful nation in northern Europe must be taken into account. There is a significant difference between the feelings of national chosenness of those in power and those who lack power. One interpreter, Knut Aukrust, finds this exemplified in the difference between Sweden and Norway, the latter occupying a more peripheral place: Sweden's idea of chosenness was conservative, he argues, trying to shore up the traditionally privileged powers of the nation in a time of transition; Norway's idea of chosenness was progressive and introduced a radical push in both church and politics, supporting the positions of the peasants and the working class.[43]

According to Aulén, the lessons the church learned from World War II and the threat of German National Socialism were, among other things, the importance of "supernationalism" and of the "unity and universality" of the church.[44] Despite certain nationalistic tendencies and blind spots for the deeper and unconscious distortions of the church, Aulén thus cannot be seen as a colonialist or as an explicit supporter of empire. In this respect, his work parallels that of Schleiermacher. Aulén's reflections on the ecumenical unity of the church reject the monochromatic tendencies so common to the church and include a positive appreciation of difference: "Multiplicity in and of itself is a great asset; it bears witness to the tremendous, creative power of the gospel in manifold human situations." Aulén anticipates that this multiplicity will grow as the church grows in places like India, China, Japan, and Africa.[45] In ecumenical encounters, he notes, it is important to be clear about one's position but to remain open.[46] Nevertheless, Aulén's appreciation for difference may not be quite strong and pointed enough to overcome the structures of neocolonialism that have become rather refined in the twentieth century, and that are now more often than not at work invisibly, below the surface; in fact, neocolonialism itself has developed some taste for difference. After all, appreciation of difference has become useful in a neocolonial project that needs to expand its markets both into other parts of the globe and to minorities at home.[47] Here lies the challenge for any contemporary theology, even if it considers itself "postcolonial" (see next chapter).

Christus Victor of the Winners

In his book *Christus Victor*, Aulén develops what he calls the "classic" position of the atonement of Christ in contradistinction to two other models that dominated theology at the time. One is what he calls the "Latin model," and the other is the Enlightenment model. According to Aulén, theology has been a struggle between those two models, one traditional, and the other modernist.[48] In terms of colonialism and empire, one might identify these positions with various stages of empire formation, but this question is of no concern to Aulén. Aulén is most concerned about the influence of modern liberal theology and the Enlightenment. His focus is on the anthropocentrism of these intellectual developments without noticing the connection to empire. But he is also worried that traditional theology (he calls it the "Latin model") has forgotten its roots in the Bible and in patristic theology. This traditional model of theology, which has come to be accepted as orthodox by much of the West, and which has experienced a recent revival in the movie *The Passion of the Christ* by Mel Gibson, champions the cause of what many see as "classical theology" and an "objective" understanding of doctrine. Nevertheless, Aulén suspects that even the traditional model foreshadows the modern turn to the self. When the theology of this model talks about salvation and atonement, it talks about a collaboration of Christ and humanity that reflects a certain legalism and rationalism that, in Aulén's assessment, is part of both the medieval approach (here Anselm of Canterbury is the central figure)[49] and of the later Protestant Orthodoxy of the sixteenth and seventeenth centuries (in the wake of Philip Melanchthon).[50] Here, reason and law impose restrictions on

God's work in Christ and lead to an overemphasis on human participation in the atonement. Aulén suspects that even the Lutheran emphasis on the *communicatio idiomatum,* which states that both Christ's human and divine nature interact in salvation, is putting too much emphasis on the work of Christ's human nature, so that it becomes all important.[51] Aulén is thus extremely concerned about anthropocentrism but not about the implications for empire and domination inherent in this approach.

The modern liberal Enlightenment model (Aulén includes Schleiermacher's work in this category) is formulated in opposition to the traditional "Latin theory."[52] It is characterized by an even stronger concern for the subjective side of Christology and the atonement. Starting as far back as Abelard in the Middle Ages, Christ is understood mainly as an example for humanity,[53] and thus the whole approach depends on the moral powers of the human self and its ability to follow Christ's example. In this model, sin is made relative. Consequently, reconciliation, like atonement, is a process that plays down the role of God and "takes place in man." Schleiermacher, according to Aulén, is one of the prime representatives of this approach, and even though Aulén acknowledges that Schleiermacher tried to deepen Enlightenment theology, he finds that the "humanistic and anthropomorphic outlook" of his theology remains the same.[54]

Suspicious of any form of human participation in salvation, Aulén suggests another theological model—beyond these liberal and the traditional approaches—which he terms the "classical" model. According to this model, God in Christ is the sole actor in salvation. In this respect, Aulén's model is conceived in diametrical opposition to modern liberal theology and its concern for human initiative and participation. The failure of modern theology is substantial, he feels, because any sense of God as acting in salvation appears to be lost. Nevertheless, Aulén also feels that even the traditional orthodox model, which envisioned humanity and God working together in salvation,[55] has failed to preserve this single-minded emphasis on God's work.

Aulén's approach thus focuses on Christ as the one who is victorious over three manifestations of evil that are repeated again and again in *Christus Victor*: sin, death, and the devil.[56] He wants to direct attention away from any contribution that humanity can make in regard to Christ's victory. In fact, he even finds the approach of medieval theologians like Anselm of Canterbury suspect because they grant too much of a role to humanity in salvation. Aulén is convinced that the "classic model," which he claims to have recovered after it had been forgotten by the church for many centuries, offers a way beyond the exclusive alternatives of the modernist "subjective" and the traditionalist "objective" views of the atonement.[57] In opposition to both views, Aulén stresses the exclusivity of God's work in salvation. Everything is God's work. God is not only the One who reconciles but also the One who is reconciled in the atonement.[58]

Aulén's emphasis is on the work of God, on God's action. This is not the static God of orthodoxy who depends on human participation in order to complete the task, nor is it the God of liberal theology who offers mainly moral support and guidance to otherwise self-determined subjects. Aulén's model, emphasizing Christ's victory over the forces of darkness, is dense and rich, redolent with images of liberation. How could Aulén's Christ possibly be the Christ of the winners, that is, of those who end up on top of the modern world, who reap the benefits of empire and neocolonialism?

First of all, Christ's victory over sin, death, and the devil in Aulén's account seems to be a fairly straightforward deal, taking place without much of a struggle. Christ simply overpowers his enemies and then celebrates victory. In this victory, even though it is presented as a "drama"—one of Aulén's favorite terms—there is no real place for suffering, loss, and death—whether on the cross or anywhere else. True to his theological program, Aulén argues for a Christology that starts "from above," with the "movement of God to man,"[59] to a degree that he claims has seldom been achieved in the history of the church. Aulén finds support for this position in the New Testament, the early Fathers, and Luther, who all seem to agree that Christ's divinity is the exclusive source of agency.[60] At first sight, this move resembles the Barthian dialectic in which God operates from above as well, *senkrecht von oben*. In Barth's Christology, however, the line from above is intersected by another line that moves from below. Christ's move from God to us is related to Christ's move from the depths and sufferings of marginalized humanity to God. This second line cannot be found in Aulén. Christ victorious does not seem to get his hands dirty and does not pass through the suffering and defeat of those at the margins. This kind of victory closely resembles the schemes of the powerful—who typically can rest assured that their efforts will pay off without too much of a struggle. Christ's victory has no similarities to the messy victories of the powerless that often move through long, arduous labors, fraught with complications, setbacks, and suffering. The focus on Christ's victory thus acquires a triumphalistic note. Despite Aulén's heavy focus on Luther, Luther's theology of the cross is completely absent in *Christus Victor*.

This approach brings us to the question of omnipotence and Catherine Keller's question of the connection between a doctrine of God that emphasizes God's omnipotence and the doctrine of the omnipotence of empire. Aulén's approach illustrates Keller's concern: power that is not shared does indeed seem to end up supporting the status quo. We might add that since God's power is not portrayed as critiquing the powers of the neocolonial empire, God's power appears to be in sync with the powers of this empire, if only by default.

On the other hand, however, Aulén explicitly rejects notions of omnipotence that talk about "God's all-causality," that imply that "all that happens is thought of as being derived from God's omnipotence."[61] Aulén notes that, except for the book of Revelation, the New Testament does not speak of God as "Almighty." Since God's power is not "all-causality," in the sense that God is the cause of all that exists, Aulén resists the totalitarian notions of omnipotence that often support empire. God's power, therefore, cannot be defined in terms of abstract notions of power. Aulén argues that "God's power shows itself in definite actions in the service of the process of creation and redemption." God is involved in a specific history: "God exercises his power in conflict with the anti-God elements, those who resist him."[62] The problem, however, is that we are never told what the anti-God elements are, and so Aulén's approach is wide open for being co-opted by those who are victorious and successful—they are the ones whose success seems to determine by default what the "anti-God elements" are.

Another way Aulén's Christ ends up the Christ of the winners is by displaying a lack of ambivalence. Aulén presents a clear dualism between good and evil. In this model, a happy ending is always a given; good fights evil and ends up victorious. Furthermore, there is simply no question about what is good and what is evil—Aulén never feels any conflict in determining who is on which side. While his later resistance of Nazi Germany justifies this approach to a certain degree, we need to take a closer look at its shortcomings as well. In Aulén's mind, the problem with the church is not that it is sometimes unclear about good and evil and what is properly Christian and what is not; the problem with the church is that it does not put into praxis what it believes. Aulén's church is *ekklesia militans*, the church engaged in battle with evil, a church that practices its faith, "characterized by the unceasing struggle between the loving will of God and those destructive powers which in this age oppose God's will."[63] Aulén never wonders whether the church as such might be on the wrong track and whether its own beliefs might have been unconsciously influenced by the powers of evil. If the church makes mistakes, it is against its better knowledge and because it consciously adapts to the powers that be.

Nevertheless, christological dualism—the position favored by Aulén that contrasts the work of God and the work of humanity—and a combative church as such do not automatically have to lead to a Christ of the winners. In situations of severe suffering and oppression such as those that occur in colonial empires and that continue under neocolonialism, clear awareness of what the problems are can be helpful in overcoming those problems. Dualism, as I will argue below, is not always oppressive in and of itself.[64] Dualism, however, tends to become oppressive if it becomes a tool of those in power and if it is connected to triumphalistic attitudes. Precisely such an attitude, however, is reflected at times in Aulén's doctrine of the church. This is closely related to a christological triumphalism, according to which Christ single-handedly destroys the forces of evil—completely, and without any sense of ambivalence; an ongoing struggle does not appear to be necessary.[65]

Aulén's Christ also favors the winners due to his failure to reconstruct the self and to provide alternative images. At first sight, Aulén's critique of the anthropocentric dreams of modern liberal theology looks like an effective challenge that has implications for colonialism and empire as well, because it addresses the ethos of the oppressors who see themselves as superior and at the center of the universe. As in Barthian dialectical theology, critiquing the seemingly autonomous human self might indeed present a challenge to those who are in power in the modern world. In this regard, Aulén makes good use of Luther's understanding of faith as that which *rapit nos a nobis et ponit nos extra nos*,[66] that is, that which liberates us from ourselves and puts us outside of ourselves. The problem, however, is that in Aulén's work a deeper engagement with the self is lacking. Thus, he misses the opportunity not just to deconstruct the modern neocolonial self but to reconstruct a theological understanding of the human self. Instead of being reconstructed, the self disappears. Yet the question is whether the self can indeed disappear without a trace or whether it is merely repressed.[67] In this latter case we need to remember Freud's lesson that whatever is repressed is not really overcome; moreover, what is repressed returns through the back door and tends to become more powerful than before by taking its place in the unconscious. Jacques Lacan has expanded Freud's view by showing that these phenomena are not only at work in the individual psyche but also in transpersonal social relationships.[68] What might be the role of this repressed self in colonial relationships?

In Aulén's critique of a self that takes things in its own hands, it is never quite clear what the problem is. What is wrong with humans acting alongside Christ in order to accomplish their salvation? At times it appears as if Aulén's argument has to do more with effectiveness. Christ's work is more effective than human work. But, unlike in Barth, there is no mention of a fundamental distortion of the modern self. In this critique, those who fit the description of the modern neocolonial self—particularly people who are used to taking things into their own hands and who succeed in the world of politics, business, and so forth—are merely told to leave things to Christ. There seems to be nothing wrong with what they are doing, and there is no need to worry about neocolonial tendencies; it is simply that Christ is more effective than they are. Thus, Christ fits the image of the winners; he is not necessarily qualitatively distinct but quantitatively. The modern self is not overcome and neither are its neocolonial efforts.

Even though Aulén fails to reconstruct the image of the human self, Christology could have offered him a wealth of resources, particularly in terms of the image of Christ's humanity. One example is Luther's insight, quoted in *Christus Victor*, that "the Divine Life, the Righteousness and the Blessing of God, is present in power, in 'the despised Man Christ.'"[69] But Aulén does not unpack what this means for an alternative image of the human being. Similar statements can be found in his study of Christian dogmatics, *The Faith of the Christian Church*.[70] Aulén's argument that faith "is not concerned with an idealized humanity" is right on target, but the conclusion that he draws leaves out humanity completely, simply stating one more time that Christian faith is concerned "with the divine, with God." In other words, Aulén's de-idealization of humanity refers to a generic humanity, and thus, paradoxically, ends up with another idealization of humanity; those in charge tend to produce generalizing notions of humanity, if only by default.[71] Certain contemporary postmodern approaches that similarly reject the idealized humanity of modernity might run into analogous troubles.

In his book *The Drama and The Symbols* Aulén admits that his book *Christus Victor* could be criticized for not paying enough attention to Jesus' humanity.[72] But, as he immediately clarifies, giving more attention to Jesus' human side does not amount to a change of view; nor does it seem to make much of a theological difference. Only much later, in the 1970s, does Aulén address this question once again, but even then there is still no significant challenge since faith and the historical Jesus are seen as harmonious.[73] Aulén points out that the historical records verify that besides being the one who reveals, Jesus is the one who liberates. As "liberator and restorer" Jesus "stretches out his hand to the most despised of persons and takes them into his fellowship, he answers his angry accusers by telling them stories which show that *God* acts in just that way. And so he reveals who 'God' is."[74] But this more detailed account of Christ's struggle may simply be too little, too late, and it still does not give much of an image of the particular character of Jesus' humanity.

Finally, Christ might be seen as resisting the winners because of Aulén's substantive understanding of sin. He claims to be even more serious on this issue than Anselm, whose reminder of the gravity of sin has been discussed above in chapter three. Aulén's Christology understands sin as "an objective power standing behind men, and the Atonement as the triumph of God over sin, death, and the devil."[75] The notion of sin covers the whole range of destructive powers. As far as humanity is concerned, Aulén defines sin as "unbelief and egocentricity" and as "perversion of the will," making clear that sin "applies to the whole man."[76] In this context, Aulén even reintroduces the notion of the devil, not frequently found in mainline theology. The devil, as Aulén makes more explicit in his later work, "is an expression of the concerted powers of evil." Sin and death, too, are destructive forces.[77] The "radical nature" of Christianity is to point this out. Sin is not to be taken lightly, and it affects all of humanity, including those at the top.

Yet while Aulén is taking the reality of sin more seriously than Schleiermacher (and Schleiermacher took sin more seriously than the liberal Enlightenment theologians—a fact conveniently overlooked by Aulén), one looks in vain for specifics. Not unlike his discussion of human nature, which was supposed to overcome the idealizing tendency of liberal theology, Aulén's discussion of sin remains on an abstract level. And despite his emphasis on the connection of sin and death, there is not much of an account of the life-and-death struggles of his time. It is not merely that Aulén might have given a more concrete definition of the form that sin took in his day. The problem is that for Aulén apparently there is no need to do so in his christological approach. Christ's victory is a rather generic reality. God's saving activity, the main concern of Aulén's approach, stays at the abstract level of a theological concept. Even Aulén's self-examination of the failure of the church after the Third Reich—truly a matter of life and death—remains general. One of the problems he identifies is that the church has been too passive toward secular values. But then he immediately tells us that "it is not my intention to examine when and how far the Church has failed through passivity and feebleness."[78]

252

As a result, Aulén's Christ remains the Christ of the winners. Failing to draw a connection between the great struggles of the time and the notion of sin and neglecting to identify the details of sin, Aulén directs attention away from the problems that kill and enslave humanity. His notion of sin can thus easily be adopted for the ends of those in power. The vagueness of the concept allows for identifications like President George W. Bush's famous comments about the "axis of evil," which find fault primarily with others but not with the self, and it does not curtail other colonial moves that are based on the colonizers listing the sins of the colonized. There is a parallel all the way back to the time of the great colonial missions. In the words of Gustav Sjoblom: "The central concept for explaining the demise of the Zulu nation was sin."[79] This problem does not arise by accident: Aulén simply does not seem to be worried about the kinds of sins that are specific and that are located outside the realm of abstract metaphysics. The divine drama takes place mainly within Godself and never touches the ground.[80]

This problem continues in his doctrine of salvation. Having emphasized the objective reality of sin, Aulén stresses the objective reality of salvation. Salvation is not just a subjective change that takes place within humanity as the liberal model suggests, spurred by Christ as the perfect example.[81] Salvation is something much more radical. It deals with a real transformation of life, not only with inner change. Salvation is nothing less than God's victory over all the powers of evil, personal and historical. It is ongoing.[82] Yet Aulén leaves open one important question: Once Christ has claimed victory, what happens? Obviously, sin as such does not vanish. But how exactly does the struggle for salvation continue? Where do we find it and what does it look like? Does salvation challenge empire and neocolonialism or does salvation find expression and embodiment in neocolonial empire? Aulén does not feel the need to address this question. Since his notion of sin is not specific, his notion of salvation does not need to be specific either. *Christus Victor*, therefore, results somehow in the confidence that "everything is absolutely all right."[83] Resistance is not so much futile as it is unnecessary. Paradoxically, Aulén seems to help to reinforce the status quo of the neocolonial empire despite his challenges to modernity and the Enlightenment: once evil has been overcome by a divine act, a fairly uncontested place is carved out in which humanity can once more create its own world—and if this world happens to be Christian and influenced by the church, like the neocolonial Sweden of Aulén's day, no further questions are necessary.

Christus Victor of the Marginalized

Aulén's Christology is not one that would display overt colonialist tendencies or support empire openly. Nevertheless, although neocolonial structures of empire are not promoted, they are able to filter in where Aulén refuses to take a position and where he fails to be specific with regard to the nature of God, the life of Jesus, and sin. At the same time, there is a christological surplus that cannot be controlled by empire, and there are a number of places where Aulén's model might help in developing resistance.

Aulén makes an important point in response to various critiques of the existence of God. The question of the existence of God, he notes, cannot be answered without considering the question "Which god do you mean?"[84] More significant than the abstract question of whether God exists is the question of what God we are talking about. Here is an important parallel to various schools of liberation theology that have made similar cases in the resistance against empire. As Gustavo Gutiérrez has pointed out, for instance, this is precisely the question raised by people on the margins, such as the poor in Latin America, and similar questions are asked in other situations of pressure. It seems that this question is asked wherever people suffer under empires that justify themselves in reference to God.[85] The underlying sense is that the God of the masters, the God of empire, is easily proved: God and success go hand in hand in empire theology. Yet this is, of course, also the God who appears to be dead. The God of the neocolonial empire has become a function of the system to such a degree that the existence of this God can be taken for granted and nothing miraculous and mysterious remains. The question of whether God exists is, therefore, less important than the question of whether there are alternatives to the God of empire. What about another God, a God who resists, who does not fit in? With this question, theology and Christology gather new energy and relevance.

An alternative Christ who does not fit in needs to be portrayed as dynamic, as active. This Christ cannot be the Christ who upholds the status quo and guarantees the stability of the powers that be. Aulén, as we have seen, emphasizes God's struggle in Christ: when he uses the notion of "drama," he might have in mind not smooth, predictable action from the top down after all, but action manifest in the midst of tensions and opposition.[86] In the context of the Bible, God is portrayed as living and acting in the midst of the tensions of life. Aulén quotes John Macquarrie who argues that this presentation of Christianity is relevant to an age characterized by a struggle with "vast forces that threaten to enslave or even to engulf mankind."[87]

From here, it seems to be only a short step to a position that resists empire and the powers that be; but the forces that enslave and engulf would have to be named, and this would lead to changes in other details of Aulén's approach. The victorious Christ who resists empire needs to take on more specific form.

Gustaf Wingren, one of the theological heirs of Aulén, has provided this more specific form and developed the theme of Christ's victory further; here the anticolonial implications of Aulén's own position become clearer. Rejecting the conventional distinction of Christology from above and from below, he talks about Jesus' humiliation and victory, arguing that "victory is won in the deepest humiliation."[88] This perspective changes everything and provides a real alternative in a neocolonial world where victory and success are expected to be top-down phenomena. "At the depth of his humiliation," Wingren continues in reference to 1 Corinthians 1:28, Jesus gathers "what is low and despised in the world, even things that are not."[89] Wingren argues (probably against Barth) that the line that goes down is not intersected by a line that goes upward into victory. The line "goes downward without interruption, but victory is found in the utmost depths." Ultimately, this revised view of Christ's victory leads to a revised view of God and thus of anything that can be considered at the heart of empire: "Victory lies at the deepest point of humiliation! And there in the depths Jesus brings it about that God becomes different," requiring of us a new understanding of God.[90] Christ victorious is the Christ of the marginalized.

Going back to the New Testament resources—an important concern of Aulén's project—might point further in this direction if we keep the pressures of the neocolonial empire in mind. Most dramatic, of course, is the fact that the Christ who resists empire ends up on one of the crosses of the empire. At this point Aulén's approach "from above" would have to be rethought, since the reality of Christ on the cross challenges the exclusive movement "from above" and introduces what would appear to be a movement "from below." But in the process, the notions "from above" and "from below" gain new meaning. Gustavo Gutiérrez, taking into account the underside of history in Latin America, realized the paradox over two decades ago: even the liberal approach "from below" (from humanity) really is an approach "from above" (from the powers that be) if it is controlled by the middle class, while the theological approach "from above" (from the triumphant Christ) turns into an approach "from below" (from the Christ engaged in the struggle against sin and evil) if we take seriously that Christ dies in solidarity with the oppressed and in resistance to the Roman Empire.[91]

In other words, Aulén's approach "from above" is not incompatible with a particular kind of Christology "from below" that starts from where Christ himself, divine and human, started: with those who suffer from the tremendous afflictions of the neocolonial world (Aulén's "sin, death, and the devil" spelled out) and who struggle for liberation, suspended between life and death. We now see more clearly that Aulén's approach "from above" (from Christ), does not necessarily have to be wedded to colonial and neocolonial approaches "from above" (from the elites).

Another point made by Aulén is worth remembering in this context: until the thirteenth century Christ on the cross was presented not only as the one who suffers but also as one who through his suffering wins the victory.[92] Here, perspectives from below and from above meet in an unexpected way that has significant implications: a perspective that takes seriously the resistance factor of suffering puts an end to defeatism and to common equations of suffering with passivity and masochism. This approach invites more constructive reflections on suffering that are of particular importance in a culture like our own that tends to repress suffering and equates victory and success.

Following the logic of Aulén's "classic" model, which "is characterised by a whole series of contrasts and opposites, which defy rational systematisation," the deeper problems of the liberal and traditional models are exposed, having to do with the development of rational systems that are based on human concerns. The crucial thing to notice here, though, is that these concerns are not necessarily general human concerns but usually the concerns of the winners. Here is an interesting parallel to the postmodern concern for difference rather than sameness. Aulén's classic model knows that "theology," or Christology for that matter, "lives and has its being in these combinations of seemingly incompatible opposites."[93] In this form, the speculative temptations of objectivizing conceptualism (the problem of the traditional model) or subjectivizing philosophy (the problem of the liberal model) are resisted. Aulén—prefiguring postmodern sentiments and their suspicion of totalitarianism and metanarratives—prefers not to call the classic position a "theory" or a "rounded and finished theological *doctrine*." This move has the potential of bringing his model in closer contact with the messiness of real life and with the suffering that is present everywhere at the underside of the neocolonial empire, a factor that is often missing even in the postmodern critiques of the modern status quo.[94] Unfortunately, however, Aulén does not quite manage to leave the security of the conceptual level when he argues for the preference of terms like "idea," "motif," or "theme." A peculiar type of "idealism" creeps back in, when he states that "it is the idea itself that is primary."[95] Unfortunately, no attention whatsoever is given to the reality and the shape of God's own work in the present, and here Aulén's position is once again easily pulled into the status quo of the neocolonial empire; after all, it is a lot easier to ask "What would Jesus do?" (usually implying: "if he were here, but he is not") than having to face the messiness of God's work in a chaotic present.[96]

In this context, we are in for a surprise that flies in the face of most contemporary progressive theoretical sensitivities: the dualism proposed by Aulén may lead us beyond a typical strategy of the neocolonial empire that uses dualistic patterns to decide who is in and who is out. Dualism here may help to produce resistance to empire because it throws a wrench into neat systems and secure ideas and thus announces a struggle.[97] Recently Darby Ray has picked up this issue in her own way and pointed out that early Christian dualism needs to be seen in terms of its context, as emerging during a time of suffering and pressure in which the world can indeed look bifurcated.[98] Yet this dualism differs from the absolute dualism of empire: it refers to a struggle that is not expected to last forever, and it therefore creates hope and the possibility of resistance.

Aulén's critique of liberal humanism needs to be taken seriously, despite a current political and intellectual climate in the United States best described as backlash against all liberal ideas. Unfortunately, this backlash seems to be part of the reason for the continued popularity of Aulén's *Christus Victor*, especially if it is conveniently overlooked that Aulén also criticizes certain conservative positions. Nonetheless, there are some aspects of the critique of liberalism that need to be taken into account in the struggle against neocolonial imperialism. It is often forgotten that modern liberalism as it developed from the Enlightenment onward has been one of the engines of colonialism.[99] Thus, the optimism and activism of the modern liberal self may ultimately not be the solution to the pressures of empire since this optimism and activism are parasitic on the energies produced by that empire; after all, the modern self developed its powers in relation to the colonial others, as we have seen in the previous chapter. In this perspective, Aulén's point, that we need to build a relationship with a different power, the power of God in Christ, is well taken.

But simply eliminating the modern liberal human self, as Aulén does, is not enough. The self that is the object of Christ's salvation needs to be reconstructed; otherwise any vacuum will be filled quickly by the overbearing presence of empire. This requires us to broaden our thinking about the self. In this context,

Aulén's preference for biblical images in thinking about Christ might be helpful, specifically if it is extended to include the Old Testament. As Jürgen Moltmann has pointed out, the context of the hope for the Messiah in the Old Testament is quite specific. It is not some generic hope for human perfection or the victory over sin and evil in general: it has developed as the hope of the oppressed and marginalized in particular situations of pressure[100] and, we might add, as the hope of those in solidarity with them. What implications do these perspectives of hope of the oppressed and marginalized have for reconstructing the image of the self and the movement of salvation in Christ? Is there another model of the human self emerging from the margins and other places of pressure? Thinking about Christ in light of the hope for the Messiah in the Old Testament might provide a different critique and a more productive reconstruction of the modern neocolonial self.

Even though Aulén's vagueness about the character of sin can open the door to empire, his attempt to direct attention not first of all to the effects and consequences of sin but to sin itself is helpful. We need to deal, after all, not just with symptoms but also with root causes. In Aulén's words: "It is the sin itself that is overcome by Christ, and annihilated; it is from the power of sin itself than man is set free."[101] Sin is more than the sum of individual sins; it is a deeper reality that needs to be taken seriously. But Aulén falls into the other extreme. For him, the symptoms of sin appear to be unimportant. His definition of sin does not need to be informed by a discussion of its symptoms, and thus his identification of the root causes becomes problematic.

From the perspective of Black theology, James Cone commends Aulén for recognizing the radical nature of evil and oppression that was played down in modern liberal theology. This awareness of radical evil makes us realize the power of God's reconciliation upon which the marginalized, those not included in the modern (middle class and patriarchal) idea of the self, depend. But we can now no longer see it as a mere coincidence that Aulén's approach, according to Cone, "limits the contemporary applications of his findings as they might be related to oppressed peoples."[102] This is part of the deeper problem with Aulén's approach.

This problem might be overcome, however, if one includes the perspectives and struggles of oppressed people. The specific descriptions of James Cone, who fills in the gaps and names the "principalities and powers," reclaim Aulén's Christology in a way that resists empire. Cone, writing in the 1970s, refers, for instance, to "the American system" that oppresses the poor and humiliates the weak, to the Pentagon and the "police departments and prison officials" that kill black people.[103] Following Cone's lead in a situation that is now even more clearly defined by the structures of empire than when Cone wrote these lines, Christ's victory must be thought through once more in very specific ways that dare to reconsider and refocus the particularity of both his divinity and humanity. How is Christ's reality tied to the millions of people who starve every year, to those who are forced to work in dehumanizing conditions every day, and to the victims of war, the concentration of capital in fewer and fewer hands, and other contemporary forms of the neocolonial empire? If these questions are raised, Christology becomes an invitation to new theological construction, rethinking both God and the human being as related to an analysis of God's work in specific locations.

Aulén is right: Sin needs to be named in its most damaging forms, as a life-and-death issue. At this point, however, Aulén seems to forget that even Schleiermacher would agree. Schleiermacher critiques Enlightenment theology for abandoning the notion of redemption (as removal of sin).[104] He is worried that if sin is not taken seriously, the question of the reality of salvation—to him the question whether humanity is developing toward a greater perfection—must remain open.[105] It is up to us to pick up the torch and think about the manifestation of sin in the world of neocolonial empire. Only then can we describe the victory that Christ has won and continues to win in nontriumphalistic terms that do not imitate but resist the powers that be. There are no easy answers, but whatever develops from this investigation stands a chance to be more real and push toward resistance.

Despite the limits of his response to German National Socialism, Aulén was perhaps the most outspoken theologian in Sweden. There is an important difference between his approach and the one by the famous Swedish theologian Anders Nygren. While Nygren is concerned about religious implications and whether the church is able to maintain its theological independence, Aulén's horizon is broader and includes a concern for the world. He notes that positions that pursue this broader horizon are often told that "Christianity has nothing to do with politics." However, those who make such statements do not seem to mind when the church supports their own political aims.[106] These voices can be heard again today, in a different time and in a different place. But if God in Christ is concerned with the world and a victory over sin and evil that sets people truly free from all that is oppressive, Aulén's *Christus Victor* can still point us in the right direction.

Notes

1. Jaroslav Pelikan, foreword, in Gustaf Aulén, *Christus Victor: An Historical Study of the Three Main Types of the Idea of the Atonement*, trans. A. G. Herbert (New York: Macmillan, 1969; first published in 1931), xi. How comprehensively *Christus Victor* portrays Aulén's Christology can be seen in comparison with his main theological work, *The Faith of the Christian Church*, trans. Eric H. Wahlstrom (Philadelphia: Muhlenberg, 1960). In this work, even in its latest edition in 1956, published over twenty years after *Christus Victor*, Aulén does not make any claims that would be substantially different from his earlier work.

2. Mikael Mogren emphasizes God's struggle on the side of the marginalized as well as the fact that the atonement is not yet finished. "Gustaf Aulén och kortslutning," *Kyrkans tidning* [Church of Sweden News] 15/16 (2001).

3. Elmer George Homrighausen's *Let the Church Be the Church* (New York: Abingdon, 1940), for instance, is an important text of the neoorthodox movement, encouraging the church to "become genuine" (ibid., 11) in the face of the challenges posed by communism, fascism, and "cultural humanism" (ibid., 18). But this book contains no critique of colonialism.

4. Aulén, *The Faith of the Christian Church*, viii; see also Gottfried Hornig's discussion of Aulén, "Offenbarungstheologie und Motivforschung in Schweden," *Neue Zeitschrift für systematische Theologie und Religionsphilosophie* 16, no. 2 (1974): 169.

5. See Carl-Gustaf Andrén, *Renewal: A Central Concept in Gustaf Aulén's Work with the Liturgy in Theory and Practice* (Lund, Sweden: Publications of the Royal Society of Letters at Lund, 1979), 5–9.

6. Quoted in ibid., 13.

7. Aulén, *The Faith of the Christian Church*, viii. This is also one of the concerns in *Christus Victor*. Aulén picks up this issue again in his book *The Drama and the Symbols* (Philadelphia: Fortress Press, 1970), with a critique of Bultmann's method of "demythologizing" on the one hand and a critique of fundamentalist (and foundationalist) rationalizations on the other. The problem with the former is that it tries to adapt Christianity to the framework of existential philosophy (ibid., 129); the problem with the latter is that it tries to make faith appear rational—as if theological statements were precise metaphysical concepts rather than symbols— and defend it on those grounds (ibid., 133). It is interesting that Aulén defends analytical philosophy, claiming its usefulness for theology because "it seeks to be neutral," without "propounding any attitude to life" (ibid., 135). Barth would have questioned the possibility of such neutrality.

8. Nevertheless, Aulén notes that God's work is described differently. In dialectical theology, God's love is often subordinated to God's wrath, and there is a stronger emphasis on lordship, sovereignty, holiness, and distance. Aulén argues for a stronger emphasis on God's love in Christ. See Hornig, "Offenbarungstheologie,"167.

9. Despite these parallels, the differences must not be overlooked. Unlike dialectical theology in its Barthian shape, Lundensian theology in the 1930s does not reject philosophical insights. Gustaf Wingren adds that historical sources, particularly Luther and Irenaeus, were more important in Aulén's work than in Barth's. "Was geschah eigentlich in Lund in den dreissiger Jahren?" *Theologische Literaturzeitung* 97, no. 12 (1972): 889. According to Wingren, Aulén was the representative of the Lundensian school who was least willing to follow the separation of religion and theology; ibid., 890. Furthermore, the Lundensian interest in *Motivforschung*—trying to identify a few central motifs of the Christian message—also differs from Barth's method and leads to a focus on *agape*/love. See Hornig, "Offenbarungstheologie," 152–53.

10. For Barth's contribution to resistance against the powers that be see chap. 2 of Joerg Rieger, *God and the Excluded: Visions and Blindspots in Contemporary Theology* (Minneapolis: Fortress Press, 2001).

11. Catherine Keller, *God and Power: Counter-Apocalyptic Journeys* (Minneapolis: Fortress Press, 2005).

12. Gustav Sjoblom, "The Missionary Image of Africa: Evidence from Sweden 1885–1895." Henry Martyn Center, http://www.martynmission.cam.ac.uk/CSjoblom.htm (accessed November 13, 2006).

13. See Donald Meyer, *Sex and Power: The Rise of Women in America, Russia, Sweden and Italy* (Middletown, Ct.: Wesleyan University Press, 1987), 54. The most prominent of these companies was Ivar Kreuger's matchstick consortium, which went bankrupt in 1932. See also Lars Magnusson, *An Economic History of Sweden* (New York: Routledge, 2000), 166ff.

14. See Tore Furberg, "The Origins and Early Years of the Church of Sweden Mission," *Swedish Missiological Themes* 88, no. 1 (2000): 59.

15. Sjoblom, "The Missionary Image of Africa."

16. See ibid. For an account of the origins of the official Church of Sweden Mission, see Furberg, "The Origins and Early Years of the Church of Sweden Mission." Carl F. Hallencreutz points out that mission after World War II became more open, more independent from the colonial powers, and tried to "safeguard the supranationality of mission, parallel to that of the Red Cross." "Swedish Missions—An Ecumenical

Perspective," in *Missions from the North: Nordic Missionary Council 50 Years* (Oslo, Norway: Universitetsforlaget, 1974), 103.

17. Carl F. Hallencreutz, "Church-centered Evangelism and Modernization—Emphases in Swedish Missions 1880–1920," in *Missionary Ideologies in the Imperialist Era: 1880–1920* (Denmark: Aros, 1982), 67.

18. Ibid., 71. Following this definition, the next step after modernization would be civilization, which is a more all-inclusive concept.

19. Aulén, *The Faith of the Christian Church*, 30–31.

20. Early manifestations of the idea are already present in his *The Faith of the Christian Church*, first published in 1923. *Christus Victor* was first published in 1931.

21. Since this time, the king's role has been that of a ceremonial head of state.

22. See "Church and Society in the Scandinavian Countries in the Period 1930–45," various authors, in *The Church in a Changing Society: Conflict—Reconciliation Or Adjustment?* Proceedings of the CIHEC Conference in Uppsala August 17–21, 1977 (Uppsala: Swedish Sub-Commission of CIHEC, 1978), 319.

23. See Bernard Erling, "Gustaf Aulén: A Life Well Lived," *Christian Century* (April 19, 1978), 423.

24. "Church and Society in the Scandinavian Countries in the Period 1930–45," 327.

25. Stig Ekman and Klas Åmark, eds., *Sweden's Relations with Nazism, Nazi Germany and the Holocaust: A Survey of Research*, John Toler, ed. for the English version (Stockholm, Sweden: Almqvist & Wiksell, 2003), 12ff.

26. Aulén, *Church, Law and Society* (New York: Charles Scribner's Sons, 1948), 19. Aulén's discussion of justice (ibid., 21 ff.) is interesting: he concedes that the Nazis had their own views on justice, but he wants to suggest a broader, more "universal" notion. The notion of justice that he prefers contains the Christian commandment to love the neighbor but then moves on to "humanitarian" considerations and the values and rights of the individual.

27. See Birger Gerhardsson, *Gustaf Aulén in Memoriam* (Lund: Gleerup, 1979), 8.

28. See, for instance, Aulén, *Church, Law and Society*, 30, where he talks about the "heathenism" and "moral nihilism" of the Nazis and adds that "the theory was that the Church had only to do with other-worldliness, and was not allowed to interfere in temporal questions."

29. Ibid., 36.

30. Ibid., 19f; 25. Aulén worries about both "totalitarian ideologies" and "democratic masks" of immorality; ibid., 27.

31. Aulén, *The Faith of the Christian Church*, 372. "The present time furnishes fearful examples of this." The church must, instead, be the "conscience of the state"; ibid., 377.

32. Ibid., 372. "And this has to a large degree determined their social life." In this context, Aulén critiques the idea of the separation of church and state, arguing that "a closer connection between church and state presupposes that the state recognizes the significance of the work of the church"; ibid., 376. Neutrality of the state is not possible: he assumes either a positive or a negative attitude toward the church.

33. Aulén, *Church, Law and Society*, 27.

34. Ibid., 95.

35. Andrén, *Renewal*, interprets Aulén's work in this light; renewal here includes an interest in "modernizing" the church, making it more contemporary.

36. Gustaf Aulén states his approval of the emphasis on "the church's responsibilities in relation to the world and its manifold problems" as proposed by the Second Vatican Council and the World Council of Churches. *Dag Hammarskjöld's White Book: An Analysis of* Markings (Philadelphia: Fortress Press, 1969), 101.

37. This point that is often overlooked has been argued recently in English language by Richard Steigman-Gall, *The Holy Reich: Nazi Conceptions of Christianity, 1919–1945* (Cambridge: Cambridge University Press, 2003).

38. See Kjell Blückert, *The Church as Nation: A Study in Ecclesiology and Nationhood* (Frankfurt, Germany: Peter Lang, 2000), 226.

39. See ibid., 229; the reference is to the Thirty-Year War.

40. Gustaf Wingren, *An Exodus Theology: Einar Billing and the Development of Modern Swedish Theology*, trans. Eric Wahlstrom (Philadelphia: Fortress Press, 1969), 123–25. Wingren lists four themes that tie together the work of Billing, Aulén, Anders Nygren, Ragnar Bring, Per Erik Persson, and his own work: the doctrine of atonement centered on God's work, the doctrine of the church in which God is the acting subject, the Bible and Luther, and an understanding that Luther is relevant for the church as a whole, not just for Lutherans.

41. See Stephen A. Mitchell and Alf Tergel, "Chosenness, Nationalism, and the Young Church Movement: Sweden 1880–1920," in *Many Are Chosen: Divine Election and Western Nationalism*, Harvard Theological Studies (Minneapolis: Fortress Press, 1994), 239.

42. Ibid., 246f.

43. See Knut Aukrust, "Response," in *Many Are Chosen*, 253ff.

44. Aulén, *Church, Law and Society*, 105.

45. Aulén, *The Faith of the Christian Church*, 381.

46. Aulén rejects both "self-sufficient confessionalism," which does not listen to others, and ecumenical efforts, which uncritically overlook and deny differences. Ibid., 384.

47. The advertisement industry embodies this trend. In order to tap new markets the traits of other cultures are displayed favorably, including their language. In Texas, for instance, beer commercials are often in Spanish. For a more theoretical discussion and critique of neocolonialism, see also Joerg Rieger, "Liberating God-Talk: Postcolonialism and the Challenge of the Margins," in *Postcolonial Theology: Divinity and Empire*, ed. Catherine Keller, Michael Nausner, and Mayra Rivera (St. Louis: Chalice, 2004), 204–20.

48. Aulén, *Christus Victor*, 133.

49. Ibid. Aulén's interpretation of Anselm is, however, problematic.

50. Ibid., 128.

51. Ibid., 131–32.

52. Ibid., 141.

53. Ibid., 99.

54. Ibid., 136.

55. Ibid., 88.

56. Ibid., e.g., 108.

57. Ibid., 102 n.3. In his 1968 preface Aulén argues that the central argument of *Christus Victor* is more important than ever since both models that he had rejected continue to be influential.

58. Aulén finds this model in the classic theological positions of Irenaeus (ibid., 35), Paul (ibid., 67), and Luther (ibid., 108).

59. Ibid., 154.

60. This is how Aulén interprets Luther. See ibid., 108.

61. Aulén, *The Drama and the Symbols*, 131.

62. Ibid., 107.

63. Aulén, *The Faith of the Christian Church*, 369.

64. See also Rieger, "Dualism," in *Encyclopedia of Religion and Nature*, ed. Bron Taylor (New York: Continuum International, 2005), 510–12. A case for the liberative function of dualism is also made by Darby Kathleen Ray, *Deceiving the Devil* (Cleveland: Pilgrim, 1998). Catherine Keller, *God and Power*, also finds some value in dualism.

65. Darby Ray, referring to the work of Sharon Welch, argues that this sort of triumphalism is related to an imperialist notion of God by removing the risk and ambiguity of life. *Deceiving the Devil*, 128.

66. Aulén, *Christus Victor*, 148 n.2.

67. In this repression lies a parallel to the work of Karl Barth; see my discussion of Barth in Rieger, *God and the Excluded*, chap. 2.

68. See my use of Lacan in Rieger, *Remember the Poor*.

69. Aulén, *Christus Victor*, 152.

70. Aulén, *The Faith of the Christian Church*, 193. At this stage of Aulén's work, the "historical Jesus," insofar as he belongs to history, is human and cannot be the basis of faith; faith directs itself only to God. Aulén puts it thus: "Divine revelation cannot be identified with anything historical and human"; ibid., 19. This would "destroy that distance between the divine and the human which is fundamental for faith"; ibid., 50. Here Aulén's position is very different from Barth's: faith and history are diametrically opposed. His position on the historical Jesus changes later in his work, but here the surprising insight is that faith and the historical Jesus are fairly harmonious. See Per Erik Persson, *The Unique Character of Christian Faith* (Lund, Sweden: Publications of the Royal Society of Letters at Lund, 1979), 9.

71. Even when Aulén talks about "the humble circumstances of man," this is generic; ibid., 193.

72. Aulén, *The Drama and The Symbols*, ixf.

73. Gustaf Aulén, *Jesus in Contemporary Historical Research*, trans. Ingalill H. Hjelm (Philadelphia: Fortress Press, 1976), viii, 157f.

74. Ibid., 162: "His revelation is radical. He exposes all kinds of human illusions, hardness of heart, prestige-oriented success, and, not least, the wrong side of piety—self-assurance and superiority. He thereby also reveals the life that is meaningful—the life that consists of mutual care and service."

75. Ibid., 147.

76. Aulén, *The Faith of the Christian Church*, 231ff. See also Aulén, *Christus Victor*, 148 n.2, where he quotes Luther's definition of the sinner as "*incurvatus in se*" (turned in on him- or herself). Likewise, Aulén quotes approvingly the early church father Irenaeus for his strong doctrine of sin; ibid., 23, 34.

77. Aulén, *The Drama and the Symbols*, 155–56.

78. Aulén, *Church, Law and Society*, 38.

79. Gustav Sjoblom, "The Missionary Image of Africa." Sjoblom continues: "Several national sins were identified, but *ind olence, savagery*, and *haughtiness* were by far the most important ones, together with a general *indecency*, which was perhaps more to do with middle-class values than Christian ideals." This is the analysis of the official Church of Sweden Mission.

80. Aulén, *Christus Victor*, 114.

81. Ibid., 151.

82. Both inner change and historical change come together in Christ. "Christ for us" is also "Christ in us," atonement and justification are one; ibid., 150.

83 For many years, this motto was displayed on the billboard of a church in Durham, North Carolina. The theology could have indeed been inspired by *Christus Victor*.

84. Aulén, *The Drama and the Symbols*, 4.

85. See, for instance, the work of Frederick Herzog and Gustavo Gutiérrez, as discussed in Rieger, *Remember the Poor*.

86. "Action versus opposition equals drama"; Aulén, *The Drama and the Symbols*, 144.

87. Ibid., 156.

88. Gustav Wingren, *Credo: The Christian View of Faith and Life*, trans. Edgar M. Carlson (Minneapolis: Augsburg, 1981), 97.

89. Ibid., 99–100.

90. Ibid., 102.

91. Gustavo Gutiérrez, *The Power of the Poor in History,* trans. Robert R. Barr (Maryknoll, N.Y.: Orbis, 1983), 222–33.

92. Aulén, *The Drama and the Symbols*, 168. In the later Middle Ages, there was more and more emphasis on the suffering alone and the sharing with Christ in suffering.

93. Ibid., 155.

94. For reflections on the limits and potential of the postmodern critique from liberation perspectives see the essays in *Opting for the Margins: Postmodernity and Liberation in Christian Theology*, ed. Joerg Rieger, American Academy of Religion, Reflection and Theory in the Study of Religion Series (Oxford: Oxford University Press, 2003).

95. Aulén, *The Drama and the Symbols*, 157–158. Here are the limits of Aulén's method of "motif-research," the attempt to get beyond outward forms and expressions to the underlying motifs.

96. A significant difference between Aulén and Barth is that Aulén sees the subject of theology not as "God himself" but as the "idea of God which is characteristic of Christian faith." Aulén, *The Faith of the Christian Church*, 3. Theology's task is to "elucidate the content and meaning of the Christian faith by the use of all available resources"; ibid., 4.

97. This dualism is emphasized, for instance, in Aulén, *Christus Victor*, 30–31, and 34–35.

98. See Ray, *Deceiving the Devil*, 126–35. Ray performs a "feminist retrieval" of a dualistic patristic model that has its strength in confounding evil, without imposing an absolute dualism, a suprahistorical drama, or an assumption of the final defeat of evil. Dualism can help us value struggle as a theological category.

99. The ongoing relevance of this insight is easily forgotten during the "conservative" rule of Republican President George W. Bush. But Bush is not the founder of the American empire, which has a much longer tradition and, immediately before Bush, made good progress under the presidency of Democrat Bill Clinton.

100. Jürgen Moltmann's book *The Way of Jesus Christ: Christology in Messianic Dimensions*, trans. Margaret Kohl (Minneapolis: Fortress Press, 1993), is an important contribution to Christology, especially in its concern for the Old Testament.

101. Aulén, *Christus Victor*, 148 n.2.

102. James Cone, *God of the Oppressed* (New York: Seabury, 1975), 231–32.

103. Ibid., 232.

104. Friedrich Schleiermacher, *The Christian Faith,* ed. H. R. Mackintosh and J. S. Stewart (Edinburgh: T.&T. Clark, 1986), 431f., see also above, the previous chapter.

105. Ibid., 357.

106. See Martin Lind, "Church and National Socialism in Sweden 1933–1945," in *The Church in a Changing Society,* 305–08.

7

Resisting and Reframing
the Cosmic Christ

⸻⸻⸺⸻⸻

Christology in a Postcolonial Empire

A T THE END OF THE TWENTIETH CENTURY and at the beginning of the twenty-first, the horizons of Christology have been broadened once again by the notion of the cosmic Christ. In the broadening search for the "ever greater Christ," this is about as far as we can get, but the notion of the cosmic Christ also points us back to some early Christian origins since it can be found both in ancient and contemporary thought. Nevertheless, even the cosmic Christ proves to be ambivalent. Talk about the cosmic Christ can provide resistance to empire; it might, however, also need to be resisted and reframed in the struggle against empire.

Statements about the cosmic Christ, when connected, for instance, to the theme of evolution in a framework of social Darwinism, can be used to affirm ideas like the survival of the fittest.[1] In this case, the cosmic Christ matches the status quo of postmodern and postcolonial empires and their celebrations of a (mostly illusory) autonomy according to which people are supposedly able to take their lives into their own hands and to ensure their own success. Nevertheless, even when the cosmic Christ represents a different spirit—that of mutuality and interdependence—empire is not ruled out: emphasizing values like mutuality, interdependence, relationship, and equality in situations of great asymmetry of power can obscure the reality of empire and thus provide an unintended cover-up.

On the other hand, the image of the cosmic Christ might resist postmodern and postcolonial forms of empire where it directs attention to precisely those elements of the cosmos that are most overlooked and that suffer most under the pressures and exploitation of empire. If the cosmic Christ relates for instance to the

269

environment under attack and to people who are forced to labor under inhuman conditions, Christology begins to break out of the status quo.

Interest in the cosmic Christ and the cosmic character of Christianity is spreading. It reaches in diverse forms from Europe (Pierre Teilhard de Chardin, Jürgen Moltmann) to Australia (Paul Collins) to Latin America (Leonardo Boff, Ivone Gebara), to the United States (Sallie McFague, Matthew Fox, and various process theologians). The cosmic perspective provides a broader horizon of the world and counters the narrow rationalism and anthropocentrism of the Euro-American Enlightenment and what is seen as a pernicious dualism that dichotomizes humanity and nature as well as the spiritual and the material. In this chapter we will examine the work of Matthew Fox, who has become an important figure in creation spirituality. Equally important for the selection of Fox is that, living and writing in the United States, his work shapes up in close proximity to one of the major centers of empire at the beginning of the twenty-first century.

Like Bartolomé de Las Casas, Fox might be perceived as one of the theologians struggling against empire from within. Like Las Casas, he is using stronger language than most of his contemporaries, comparing contemporary phenomena to the Holocaust, fascism, and other expressions of empires in the past. Yet while he is deeply suspicious of conservative religious trends and their relation to empire, Fox appears to be less concerned about postmodern workings of empire. In fact, as the "modern era is yielding to the postmodern in religion,"[2] Fox appears to be hopeful that empire is losing force in the wake of postmodern attention to pluralism, ecumenism, interdependence, unity in diversity, and the dispersion of the center.[3] Likewise, while Fox clearly demonstrates problems with fundamentalism, authoritarianism, elitism, modern dualism, and punitive images of God, he seems to assume that less severe images of God are less problematic by default. Fox's critiques are not always consistent—at times he fights on different fronts without a clear sense of the common thread; for instance, how is a strictly hierarchical authoritarian fundamentalism related to a more fluid liberal and modern elitism? Or, how is the dualism of Newtonian science related to the dualism of conservative Christian creationism? Nonetheless, his work deserves serious attention because it has struck a nerve in our own time and represents broad and forward-looking cultural and religious developments. The common charge that Fox promotes "spirituality lite" harbors an arrogance that does not acknowledge the limitations of all theology. Academic theologians need to investigate what it is that captures people's attention in Fox's work.[4]

With this chapter we have arrived at the contemporary manifestations of empire. This does not mean, however, that the connections are easier to see. Indeed, the opposite is the case. Due to our close proximity to empire, it becomes more difficult to see where the forces of empire warp us and, for that reason, where resistance is necessary and how it might be possible.

The focus of this chapter is on progressive Christianity. Progressive Christianity, too, is shaped by the influence of empire, a fact that is often overlooked for two reasons. One reason is that until recently there has been only limited recognition that we are still living under the rule of an empire; the other reason is that there is a serious lack of awareness that the influence of empire affects even those who do not explicitly agree with it. Consequently, the christological surplus of progressive theology is not as clear as it seems at first sight, calling for a more thorough self-critical perspective. To be sure, conservative Christianity is more directly related to current embodiments of empire; if it has not openly applauded empire, it has produced very few critiques.[5] Conservative mainline Christians can be found in the highest positions of the second Bush administration and the imperial agendas of this group[6] have received substantial support from conservative Christianity. While a christological surplus cannot be ruled out even in these positions, a search for it will require careful analysis and might best be done in self-critical fashion by those who represent the conservative approach.[7]

Postcolonial Empire and Relational Theology

Since there is very little historical distance, we need to address the sociopolitical and theological situation with particular care in this section. Empire is always evolving and taking on varying shapes in different periods. The stage for the most recent situation is set by the 1997 statement of principles of the "Project for a New American Century," which foreshadows the policies of President George W. Bush and which was signed by a number of the later top officials of his administration (including Vice President Dick Cheney and then-Secretary of Defense Donald Rumsfeld). One of the principles of this statement is that "we need to accept responsibility for America's unique role in preserving and extending an international order friendly to our security, our prosperity, and our principles." Thus, the special role of the United States in the world is claimed and projected. The final sentence sums things up, leaving no doubt about the determination to put the United States first: "A Reaganite policy of military strength and moral clarity may not be fashionable today. But it is necessary if the United States is to build on the successes of this past century and to ensure our security and our greatness in the next."[8] The spirit of empire speaks for itself, claiming both past and present. What is now often overlooked, though, is that the United States had the traits of an empire long before the members of the Project for the New American Century came to power, and the empire will not automatically end when another government is elected. Change might be around the corner, as the "Bush Doctrine"—which proposes a triad of preemptive strikes, government change, and the battle of good vs. evil—is increasingly questioned, even by conservatives such as Francis Fukuyama, who was among the original signers of the statement of principles for the New American Century.[9] Moreover, President Bush has seen the lowest approval ratings of any U.S. president, reflected in the politically significant takeover of both the Senate and the House of Representatives of the United States by the Democratic Party after the elections in November 2006. Yet that does not mean that the end of empire is in sight. In addition, we need to remember that, while the United States plays a key role, empire at a time that is marked by economic globalization can no longer be limited to one nation alone.

To speak of a postcolonial empire appears as a contradiction in terms, especially if empire is identified with colonialism. How can an empire be postcolonial? Postcolonialism, taken as a historical term, refers to the end of official systems of colonialism; colonialism proper refers to a system in which the colonies are governed and directly influenced by colonialist nations. The term *postcolonial* can thus be understood to mean the time after the colonial era, when mostly European nations owned and governed colonies abroad. Indeed, direct colonial rule has now ceased for the most part, and with it the time of the great colonial empires, of which Great Britain's was no doubt the most prominent.[10]

And yet, even in this postcolonial situation, the process of empire building has not ceased. There are now other ways of construing and exercising power. Direct political rule has given way to economic and cultural influences that frequently operate without overt attention or oversight and also without much detection. Normally, the mainstream news media in the United States do not attend to or report on these flows of power, except at the crudest levels. These powers are hidden so well and have worked so well in the late twentieth century that we have witnessed substantial debates on whether the United States, currently the most powerful nation of the world, should even be considered an empire. Much of this has changed with the presidency of George W. Bush. The United States is now more clearly seen in terms of empire by both critics and supporters alike, and in some quarters there is considerable pride about this fact. Clearly there has been a change in the politics of empire in the transition from the Clinton to the Bush administrations. This does not mean, however, that one administration pursued empire while the other did not. The difference has mostly to do with how the powers of empire are deployed. At the level of military action, we might compare the war in Iraq that began in 2003 with the mostly invisible "low intensity warfare" through which the U.S. military has been involved in Latin America for decades. The war in Iraq is highly visible and tied to strong feelings of patriotism that God will bless America and to notions like the "power of pride"; the "low intensity warfare," on the other hand, has rarely been mentioned in mainstream debates and few are aware that it continues even today through the training of foreign military leaders by the United States and low-key military actions. With the Clinton administration, as David Harvey has put it, "soft power was preferred to hard, and the rest of the world was treated with considerable multicultural tolerance. Politics was conducted in multilateral rather than unilateral terms."[11] Of course, multicultural tolerance and soft power were still in the service of empire. The Bush administration, by contrast, has embraced power more openly and unilaterally. This use of power is much more obvious and has resulted in significant resentment against the United States. Still, Bush is no old-style colonizer and the United States has no plans to colonize other nations like Iraq. Direct U.S. rule in Iraq is not necessary and neither is expropriation if Iraqi property; even the oil resources, often named as one of the key interests of the Bush administration, continue to belong to the nation of Iraq. What the United States acquires are "production sharing agreements" (PSA), according to which the oil remains in the possession of the nation but the fields are operated by U.S. companies, a deal that is more lucrative for the companies.[12] Iraq is supposed to govern itself so that the strings that tie it to the United States will disappear from view again at some point in the future. Despite the more open displays of power now being seen, in the long run the less visible tactics of the postcolonial empire are the more significant ones.

Living in the context of such a postcolonial empire, modeled by the United States but not limited to it, contemporary theology faces new challenges. In the American mind, there are no emperor cults that embody the theological claims of the empire as in the days of the Roman Empire; neither are there any medieval crusades to be blessed (although the Bush administration might have come as close to this old model as any modern government, with the president after September 11, 2001, briefly using the term before he was asked to retract it); there are no direct conquests as with the Spanish, or entire colonies waiting to be Christianized as with the Europeans. Outside the United States, of course, these things are often seen differently, but it is true that the rules of empire have changed.[13] Those who want to discuss contemporary empire in terms of the old strategies can point to certain parallels, but the analogies are limited. In addition, the discussion is complicated by the fact that there is something peculiar about the American lack of awareness of empire and its deeper historical roots and structures. As David Harvey has pointed out, the American empire was acquired not absentmindedly, as the British see it, but "in a state of denial."[14] Imperial actions of the U.S. were not to be discussed. In this context, David Spurr is right: "The first step toward an alternative to colonial discourse, for Western readers at least, has to be a critical understanding of its structures."[15]

Those kinds of theologies that at present support the unreflective patriotism and flag-waving associated with the most recent manifestations of empire are easily spotted. The theologies of blessing and success, for instance, that ground the popular "gospel of prosperity," have little to offer by way of resistance to empire. If God blesses those who are on top, the empire must be the entity most blessed. The doomsday theologies of much of right-wing Christianity fail us here as well because they tell us not only that resistance to empire is futile but that the empire that is threatening us is located elsewhere; in any case, for the doomsday theologians, empire has nothing to do with the politics of the United States today.[16] Nevertheless, some of the more careful scholars who realize that evil is not only on the side of the enemy but affects all of us still fail because, as Mark Lewis Taylor has shown, "they do not carefully examine the line of repression of other nations that runs through U.S. history,"[17] nor do they carefully examine the evil that is perpetuated even by our best intentions.

Equally worrisome, however, are the progressive theologies that fail to pose deeper challenges to empire. This is what concerns us in this chapter and it is the less obvious but therefore more interesting problem. Unfortunately, the current debate over the more obvious demonstrations of the power of empire can keep us from dealing with these deeper challenges. As in my previous work, I am seeking to identify blind spots[18] because it is only here that the deeper problems can be seen more clearly. How do theologies that do not explicitly support empire continue to support it implicitly? While I do not want to play down the clear and public manifestations of empire in any way, attending to the hidden manifestations of empire enables us to locate the roots of power imbalances and oppressions, and may reveal the locations of the most severe and dangerous problems.

One of the most distinctive problems of the postcolonial situation is that official colonialism and its more direct forms of domination and control over other people have been replaced by less visible forms of power. Moreover, those less visible forms of power are often more far reaching. In the current situation, invisible forms of power have created a paradoxical situation: while relations of direct control have been reduced, relations that seem on the surface to be more egalitarian and equal nonetheless perpetuate the powers of empire. Where in the colonial period other people were subdued by colonial governments and their operatives, in a mostly postcolonial world we do not need colonial governments anymore in order to exercise the power of empire. Even direct military action is no longer intended to establish direct political control.[19] As noted above, there were no plans for Iraq to be ruled directly by the United States and even the common observation that the war is about oil needs to be nuanced,[20] as the United States has not sought to claim ownership of Iraqi oil. Military action in Iraq has opened the door to closer business relationships with U.S. corporations, where contracts on the production of oil are worked out in the spirit of a "free" market; buyer and seller thus seem to enjoy a basic equality. In this situation, the hierarchical relationships of empires past seem to give way to egalitarian relationships. All this is possible, of course, because invisible powers are in place that assure the interests of empire and reduce the importance of direct political control.

Similar processes can be observed in the church—most clearly in its attempts at missionary outreach. While under colonial empires missionary enterprises were often synchronized with the exercise of colonial power (even though missionaries at times softened that power and protested against excesses), in a postcolonial situation missionary enterprises often endorse more egalitarian relationships and follow the multicultural paradigms developed at home. Today, missionary activities frequently emphasize relationship and respect for cultural differences. Nevertheless, if drastic differentials of power exist, even the pursuit of relationship can be used for the purpose of furthering empire.[21] Interreligious dialogue may serve as another example. In the colonial context of the nineteenth century, even those scholars of religion who appreciated non-Christian religions ended up reproducing colonial models. Friedrich Schleiermacher, as we have seen in chapter 5, developed an appreciation for other religions but only within a hierarchical framework. Other scholars of the later nineteenth century like Friedrich Max Müller, who spent their lives studying the intricacies of other religions (in this case Hinduism), reconstructed Hindu texts mostly *for* the Hindus rather than *with* the Hindus.[22] In the context of postcolonial empire, proposals for considering other religions have often adopted a more egalitarian outlook, parallel to other postcolonial relationships and a general appreciation of multiculturalism. The cosmic Christology of Matthew Fox, for instance, is in sync with other egalitarian proposals when he encourages Christians not only to take other religions seriously (both the "major world religions" and "the more earth-centered traditions of the native peoples"[23]) but to enter into a dialogue. The problem with egalitarian models, however, is that they often operate on the basis of hidden power structures and build on, replicate, or reinforce them in their own ways. In sum, unless all these seemingly egalitarian relationships—whether they are formed in the areas of religion, culture, politics, or business—begin to deal with the underlying asymmetry of power, the structures of the postcolonial empire remain unchallenged.

The invisibility of economic power structures and their virtually universal reach is one of the key aspects of the postcolonial empire. As Ellen Meiksins Wood has observed, we are witnessing a split between economic power and political power in capitalist societies. Unlike precapitalist societies, where economic power was closely linked with political power,[24] in capitalist societies economic power can develop more independently of political power. "In capitalist societies," Meiksins Wood points out, "it is even possible to have universal suffrage without fundamentally endangering capitalist economic power, because that power does not require a monopoly on political rights."[25] This split between economic and political power is at the heart of the extended reach of the postcolonial empire: "One of the most important consequences of this detachment of economic power from direct coercion is that the economic hegemony of capital can extend far beyond the limits of direct political domination."[26] Today, these broadening economic influences are often talked about in terms of "globalization."

At the same time, this new distribution of power in the postcolonial empire does not mean that other powers, including the political powers of the nation-state, are fading away. Nation-states do not disappear, but they function differently: no longer for the benefit of the nation but for an emerging global power structure.[27] The expansion of economic power needs stable and predictable social arrangements and thus politics has an important role to play.[28] The powers of culture and what is called religion must not be neglected either—which is why the topic of Christ and empire remains so important even in the contemporary situation. Once again, the problem is easily spotted where Christ is used to bless empire, as so often happens in the current climate of "God bless America."

However, even progressive Christian proposals to establish more harmonious relationships with other Christians around the world and with other religions can, unconsciously, become part of the production of stable social arrangements that can be used for the expansion of the economic powers that be.

Despite the significance of these other powers, economic powers do shape much of what is going on in the postcolonial empire. The most powerful manifestations of those economic powers are at work mostly below the surface (or behind closed doors), and thus go unchallenged. When economic powers are challenged today, it is mainly for blatant moral failure, as in the case that led to the collapse of Enron, or for the most outrageous excesses, as in the case of a ninety-eight-million-dollar payout for Exxon Mobil's retiring CEO.[29] Political power is much more likely to be challenged than economic power, particularly when military actions are clearly visible and do not produce rapid, overwhelming success (as in the case of the Iraq war of the new millennium), and when police actions and laws that control people's movements are perceived as oppressive or ineffective (whether they demand free expression or free migration). Unfortunately, the beneficiaries of such political actions are mostly overlooked. It is neither the government nor the military that benefit in the long run from political or military victories; economic interests benefit the most, as the corporations benefiting from the war in Iraq have clearly shown.[30] It might come as a surprise that this pattern holds true even for those activities of political power that are most challenged today and deemed to be the special interests of "big government." Even in matters of welfare and Social Security, for instance, which are still maintained by political power despite tremendous cuts, some of the key beneficiaries are often overlooked. Beneficiaries of welfare and Social Security—assuring basic survival in difficult economic times—are not just the individual recipients but the economic powers that be, which thus have at their disposal a vast "reserve army of labor" whose wages and benefits can be held low since someone else will pick up the tab.[31] In this context, rather than becoming an outdated relic of the past, the political powers of individual nation-states are not fading away but prove to be, in the words of Meiksins Wood, "more useful transmission belts for capitalist imperatives than were the old colonial agents and settlers who originally carried the capitalist market around the world."[32] This insight can be applied to cultural and religious phenomena; they can turn into "transmission belts" as well—most visibly in the advertising industry, which mostly works with cultural registers. Missionary activity, both at home and abroad, might also continue to convey Western culture along with Christian religious indoctrination, and the work of the Christian churches needs to be examined in this light as well; for this reason, we will need to pay closer attention than ever before to the role of Christology in empire.

In the postcolonial empire, the real problems have become more difficult to identify—and in this difficulty lies the challenge to cosmic Christology and its own potential correspondence with empire. While in precapitalist empires the driving forces were clearer, now things are more hidden. In some sense, the forces of culture and religion are more important in what I call the postcolonial empire. As Meiksins Wood has observed, "capitalist imperialism . . . seeks to impose its economic hegemony without direct political domination wherever it can."[33] This lack of visibility of the flow of power in the postcolonial empire is paralleled by the lack of visibility of the flow of power between the classes in the contemporary United States. In contrast, as Meiksins Wood has pointed out, in the Middle Ages "there was nothing particularly opaque about the feudal lords and the peasants."[34] One of the most persistent misconceptions in the United States is that class differences do not matter anymore because most people are members of the middle class. But even where it is noted that there continue to be class differences—and that the gap between the classes is steadily widening—there is little awareness of the differentials of power and of the fact that the wealthy are living at the expense of all others (whose wages have either not seen significant increases over long periods of time or have even gone down if adjusted for inflation, as is true of the minimum wage).[35]

In sum, the postcolonial empire is marked by the fact that the direct exercise of power has given way to more subtly powerful and far-reaching forms of exercising power. Direct political power has given way to economic influences that move according to the seemingly universal, neutral laws of the free market. The same is true in the realm of culture. Direct control of education, for instance, and other intellectual endeavors have given way to the more subtle influences of mass media such as television, the World Wide Web, and other forms of communication. In the realm of religion, direct control over the church, as practiced, for instance, by the various state churches in Europe, has given way to other, more subtle forms of making use of all sorts of religious expression.

This new form of postcolonial empire is evolving through the expansion of many areas of contemporary life that are otherwise celebrated and welcomed. In fact, one sign of a potential problem in this regard is the uncritical celebration of the broadening moves of a globalizing world that celebrates relationship and cultural exchange without realizing the underlying patterns of economic exploitation on which the power differentials of the contemporary empire are based.

The Cosmic Christ of the Postcolonial Mainline

While some of the Christologies discussed in earlier chapters of this book came closer to identifying with empire than others, many did not consciously identify with the empires of their times. Fox goes one step further. He explicitly rejects efforts at building empires. His book *The Coming of the Cosmic Christ* (hereafter *CCC*), written at the very end of the Cold War in 1988, seeks to resist militarism, the exploitation of the poor by the rich, and a general feeling of Western superiority. In his most recent publications, he uses strong language to warn against contemporary manifestations of empire. Yet in spite of Fox's overt resistance, his cosmic Christ at times fails to challenge the more invisible powers of empire.

Fox's notion of the cosmic Christ transcends some of the most common battles in contemporary theology that are waged in the so-called culture wars between liberals and conservatives and thus he provides a breath of fresh air. The basic challenge of our times, according to Fox, is the survival of the earth, an issue that is today increasingly noticed again in light of global warming. Only the cosmic Christ can save us from the predicaments we have created that threaten our destruction (*CCC* 78). On the one hand, Fox affirms a mystical approach to Christ that affirms Christ's presence in the universe, human and nonhuman. This approach has roots in ancient theology and comprises the classical affirmation of Jesus' humanity and divinity. This cosmic Christ provides the frame for an understanding of the historical Jesus. On the other hand, Fox also affirms the historical Jesus because he provides roots for the cosmic Christ: "A theology of the Cosmic Christ must be grounded in the historical Jesus, in his words, in his liberating deeds. . . , in his life and orthopraxis" (*CCC* 79). More specifically, Fox calls for a "Cosmic Christ *with wounds*," a "Cosmic Christ balanced by the suffering of Jesus" (*CCC* 161; emphasis in original). Hidden away in the long and sometimes repetitive prose of his book is a term that sums it up and has potential for future christological debate: Fox talks about the need for a "*historical Christ*" who is "a living Christ who can change history once again and ground that change in a living cosmology" (*CCC* 162; emphasis in original). Fox's cosmic Christ is not a remote historical figure (concealed in the depths of history), nor is he a remote metaphysical figure (distantly sitting at the right hand of God). The cosmic Christ is present and at work.[36]

Consequently, Fox rejects both conservative theology's narrow focus on Christ as well as liberal Enlightenment theology's narrow focus on the historical Jesus. The problem in both cases is identified as "religious dualism" and a lack of balance; balance is a notion that can be found throughout Fox's work. We have produced imbalances everywhere, even in ourselves, for instance by neglecting the right hemisphere of the brain (the place for mystical experience and synthetic and sensual tasks) and favoring the left hemisphere (the place for analytic thinking and verbal expression) (*CCC* 18). The lack of balance of male and female aspects is another example (*CCC* 22). The cosmic Christ helps us restore that balance and reminds us of the "interconnectivity of all things" (*CCC* 19). Of course, one problem with this approach that is not hard to see has to do with a stereotypical understanding of the opposites. The other problem is that the notion of balance hardly addresses the asymmetries of power, as I will argue later.

The basic challenge, according to Fox, is to overcome dualism and the rationalism that goes with it.[37] Dualism splits apart things that ultimately go together, like body and spirit, people and nature, men and women, young and old, Christians and non-Christians, and even rich and poor. The underlying spirit of this dualism, according to Fox, is closely related to modernity, especially to Newtonian physics and to a mechanistic view of the world. It was the Enlightenment, he claims, that banished mysticism and the cosmic Christ (*CCC* 77). The resulting fragmentation must not be taken lightly; it reaches all the way into our daily lives and even affects our most intimate spheres.[38]

There seems little doubt in Fox's narrative that the ultimate culprit is the Enlightenment with its emphasis on the mind, that is, on knowledge and information. Unfortunately, however, he fails to investigate the larger web of problems,[39] beginning with the fact that the Enlightenment itself is tied to economic and political processes that resulted in some of these fragmentations—already Karl Marx noted the alienating powers of capitalism. Having worked our way through the various earlier manifestations of empire, we are finally beginning to realize that we can no longer adequately understand the Enlightenment without its connections to colonialism and the empires of modernity. If fragmentation is indeed a problem, what causes it? A clearer understanding of the roots of a problem helps to develop more adequate responses. Fox appears to be somehow caught in the assumption that the problem can be solved by developing alternative ideas.

But is the problem caused by ideas? It is hard to imagine that ideas of individuals such as Isaac Newton would be the root causes of modernity.

At the same time, there is another front on which Fox battles. While the Enlightenment has fractured the world, the church has turned into a system that is authoritarian, "essentially sado-masochistic," and self-centered. Using even stronger language, Fox notes fascist tendencies in the church's affirmation of a hierarchical structure that holds that the leader is always right (*CCC* 28–29). This church, as he argues in even sharper relief in his most recent book: "worships a Punitive Father and teaches the doctrine of Original Sin. It is patriarchal in nature, links readily to fascist powers of control, and demonizes women, the earth, other species, science, and gays and lesbians. It builds fear and supports empire building."[40] According to Fox, what ties together leaders as diverse as Osama bin Laden, Jerry Falwell, and Pope Benedict XVI is "religious fundamentalism" and that they identify a common enemy in what Pope Benedict XVI has called the "dictatorship of relativism."[41] The struggle with fundamentalism can be traced back to Jesus himself, who challenged the patriarchal religious system of his day. Fox claims that this is what ultimately killed Jesus (*CCC* 31). Jesus' battle against patriarchy was also a battle against fragmentation and dualism, since his goal was to restore compassion, which is "not about pity or feeling sorry for others. It is born of shared interdependence" (*CCC* 32).

Fox deepens these more general notions of disconnect and fragmentation when he clarifies that fragmentation includes "the dispossessed—those least connected, those least established and least part of the connections that 'the establishment' has to offer." He notes that "Jesus offered connections to the dispossessed in particular: to the lepers, women, slaves, sinners, and outcasts of society." Furthermore, Jesus "connected with them not only by conversation and scandalous associations at meals but by undergoing the death of the unconnected, the death of the dispossessed on Golgotha" (*CCC* 135). In this interpretation of Jesus' ministry, Fox's approach differs significantly from other cosmologies that argue for more abstract notions of connection (compare the cosmology of Platonism) and that lack concern for the oppressed. Disconnect and fragmentation are identified at all levels, for instance, in the "unimaginable gulfs between Northern and Southern nations, between rich and poor, between employed and unemployed, between men and women, between heterosexuals and homosexuals." For Fox, these are all expressions of the fact that our civilization lacks coherence, that "it is chaotic" (*CCC* 136).

If this narrative of disconnect and fragmentation is followed, the search for coherence and interconnectedness becomes key. Jesus shows how this might happen when, according to Fox, he "connects the poverty of the materially impoverished with the poverty of the spiritually impoverished" (*CCC* 136). When connections are restored, it is even possible that the disconnected and oppressed make a difference in the lives of those in power; one of the things that the "two-thirds world" can do for us is challenge the meaninglessness of our society, claims Fox (*CCC* 136). The work of the cosmic Christ, in this context, is to bring "together parts which have been scattered and separated" (the theme of Ephesians) and to make peace (*CCC* 136).

While Fox makes a strong argument, the question is whether his cosmic Christ can take us much beyond the status quo of the postcolonial empire. While establishing connections and peace sounds intriguing, especially after four years of U.S.-initiated military action in the Persian Gulf and in the face of an ever-widening gulf between one-third and two-thirds world nations, what kind of peace does he envision? How does the notion of peace address the underlying issues that have caused the separation? The exploitation of the two-thirds world, one of the key symptoms of the postcolonial empire, is caused by economic imbalances of power, from which the one-third world benefits. Any notion of peace that does not address these imbalances only makes things worse. What the two-thirds world would need to do for us to promote peace is not to challenge our feelings of meaninglessness, as Fox assumes, but to challenge the power differentials that have led to the current tensions. The problems of dualism and fragmentation need to be seen in this light as well: what might look like fragmentation (due to the invisibility of power relations) is in reality a particular kind of relationship. The rich and the poor are never disconnected, for instance, even though the rich would like to believe this in order to perpetuate the myth of the self-made man who pulls himself up by his own bootstraps. Instead, the rich use the poor for their own purposes and build their success on the backs of the poor. In this context, *exploitation* would be a better term than *fragmentation* or *disconnect*. There is a sense that the oppressed are not the most fragmented but perhaps the most connected of all, since without them the one-third world could not function. Lamenting fragmentation, therefore, tends to support the status quo and the myth of individualism made up by the elites.

The sort of connection and relationship that is required at this point—and that Christ indeed may bring—is not a response to a lack of connections but a transformation of invisible and distorted connections. Calls for connection and relationship that do not take into account the asymmetries of power might end up reinforcing distorted connections. The problem, then, is not primarily the dualism of Newtonian physics but the kinds of connections that are in place and that are, if people are aware of them, closer to particular readings of the thought of Charles Darwin. Modernity, therefore, might be less about dualism and fragmentation than about the distorted relationality of social Darwinism and its conviction that only the fittest survive. Clearly, we need the cosmic Christ to liberate us from that sort of relational cosmology. Unfortunately, Fox talks about interconnectedness exclusively in positive terms[42] and thus overlooks the problems of distorted relationship that cause the most damage to people and the planet.

In order to address the challenges posed by the deeply embedded and often invisible structures of empire in our own time, a deeper encounter with its tensions and discontents is necessary. Fox gets into some of these issues when he talks about Indigenous people. In order to make a strong case for the protection of Indigenous people and their religions and cultures, he chronicles the decline of Native American populations from eighty million in 1492 to one million in 1600, and he draws a line to the Holocaust of the twentieth century: "What happened at Auschwitz was heralded, and indeed surpassed, on American soil four centuries earlier" (*CCC* 25). Unfortunately, there is no account of the later North American history with Native Americans without which we may not be able to draw the lessons for our own situation. Thus, an otherwise promising start fails to break free from the force field of the mainline.

Fox's main concerns in his relations with Native Americans are constructive. He commends "native people" for "always living out of a cosmology" (*CCC* 25), and considers them allies in his struggle against the Enlightenment. This alliance is based on his assumption that "religions of the native peoples of the Americas, Africa, ancient Europe, Australia, Polynesia, and Asia" arose in matrifocal cultures that showed reverence for the earth and were nondualistic because they would see all creatures as interrelated. Noting that "these are the oldest religions on our planet," older than the world religions of Hinduism, Buddhism, Judaism, Islam, and Christianity, Fox manages to build a considerable level of respect for these religions, a respect that had been lacking in colonial times (*CCC* 24). This respect is not just on paper. Fox has frequently collaborated with Native Americans, and in the 1980s invited a Lakota spiritual teacher (Buck Ghosthorse) to join his institute at Holy Names College.[43] Neither is Fox's interest merely academic.

Common spiritual experiences are key. Fox notes that "praying with native peoples has always been a source of deep spiritual renewal for me" (*CCC* 225).[44]

While Fox thus enters into relation with some of the most repressed people in the United States, a certain tendency to romanticize them must nevertheless be noted. Even though we need to acknowledge that Native American worship can indeed support Fox's efforts to create interrelationships, generalizations like the following are counterproductive: "Native peoples have never lost faith with this essential, core meaning of worship" (*CCC* 213). As Jacques Lacan has pointed out, developing an insight of psychoanalysis, romanticizing the other can amount to a form of oppression. Not only is the other used for one's own purposes, but the romanticized other is coerced to conform to the expectations of the powers that be.[45]

The lessons that Fox has learned from praying with Lakota peoples at a Sun Dance in South Dakota include an appreciation of sacrifice, gratitude, bravery, community, and a sense of the cosmic Christ's presence. Yet some Native American theologians have felt that Fox does not develop the notion of community strongly enough.[46] Moreover, what is absent in his account is the connection to the actual struggles of the community, its land, its politics, and the particular histories of oppression (cf. *CCC* 225–27), the kinds of things most important to Native Americans. We must not forget that the Native American traditional topics of community and relationality are inextricably tied to the struggles of the people and the land.[47] It is no wonder that certain interests in Native American traditions have at times been met with resentment. The comments of feminist theologian Rosemary Radford Ruether, who shares some of Fox's interests, display more sensitivity: "The indigenous peoples of North America have been so alienated and destroyed that I have little right to claim use of their culture. Native American peoples have grown deeply suspicious and hostile to counter-cultural exploitation of their traditions from 'new age people.' Yet I believe that the First Nations peoples hold unique bioregional spiritualities of the Americas, and only by reconciliation with their ways can we heal this land and ourselves. But we must do it not by simply appropriating their artifacts, but by supporting their land and fishing rights. Thereby we may earn the right to enter and learn from their cultures."[48] Fox's commendable efforts to learn from Native Americans fail to resist empire if they do not participate in Native American struggles and enter into deeper awareness of the problem.

Even though Fox broadens the horizon of Christology by paying attention to other religious traditions and other cosmological traditions, he cannot be accused of neglecting Christianity. The cosmic Christ is strongly tied to biblical and traditional Christian sources. There is an Old Testament strand in the wisdom traditions and in the prophets that finds a divine presence in all things and in the suffering of all creation (*CCC* 83–87). The New Testament also provides a wealth of material. Fox points out that in Paul's writings (and ultimately in the Bible as a whole), unlike in many other cosmic mysticisms, the cosmic Christ is grounded in a history, a people, and in the person of a real human being who died on a cross (*CCC* 88–90). The cosmic horizons of Colossians and Ephesians push beyond an anthropocentric definition of the church as the "people of God." In this context, to claim Jesus' lordship means to affirm him as the "ruler of the universe" and also as ruler over the things of this world (*CCC* 90–97). Even though this is mostly overlooked, Fox points out that the Gospels and the book of Acts contain plenty of images of the cosmic Christ, beginning with the infancy narratives, Jesus' baptism and temptation, the transfiguration, and ending in cross and resurrection: it is Christ's resurrection in particular that demonstrates the extension of his power over the "cosmic forces of death" (*CCC* 99–107). In detailed analyses Fox shows how the cosmic Christ is related to each of the major events of Jesus' life.

The two other strands in postbiblical Christian history that help Fox to lay the foundation for the cosmic Christ are the early Greek fathers and the medieval mystics. While Western influence, according to Fox, was mainly individualistic and eventually led to Descartes's rationalism,[49] the Greek fathers preserved a cosmological perspective and were not afraid to incorporate cosmic notions like the "deification" of humanity (although we must add that this term can also be misused in individualistic fashion). This mystical tradition, however, lacks a deeper appreciation for the shape of Jesus' earthly existence, due to an adherence to what Fox calls its "platonic dualisms" (*CCC* 107–09). Fox thus draws his main inspiration from the second strand of postbiblical Christian mysticism, the broadly conceived group of mystics of the medieval West including, among others, Hildegard of Bingen, Francis of Assisi, Thomas Aquinas (whose mystical interests Fox underscores, against scholastic Thomism), Mechthild of Magdeburg, Julian of Norwich, and, perhaps most importantly, Meister Eckhart. Fox uses their resources to bring together the cosmic Christ and the prophetic Jesus. He takes up Eckhart's emphasis on the "radical equality" of all creatures, based on Eckhart's claim that "all creatures are words of God." This means that even animals and children can have an impact on the whole—"an observation" that Fox rightly claims is "as political as it is ecological" (*CCC* 212–22).

Fox's account of mysticism ends with the Middle Ages, which represent "the last time that there was a living cosmology in the West" (*CCC* 128). Later on, he adds a few references to other mystically inclined thinkers, including the Quaker George Fox, the Wesley brothers, John and Charles, and Unitarians in the United States such as Henry David Thoreau and Ralph Waldo Emerson (*CCC* 237). Surprisingly, however, other nineteenth- and early twentieth-century figures are missing, including the Romantics in Europe and related theologians like Friedrich Schleiermacher. Also missing is a reference to the French theologian Piérre Teilhard de Chardin. This oversight has serious consequences for Fox's thinking about the relation of Christology and empire: he completely overlooks the softer imperialisms of nineteenth-and-twentieth-century Europe and is thus unable to give an account of the problems of the less visible structures of the contemporary postcolonial empire. His critique applies mostly to clearly hierarchical and top-down power relations, which include the fifteenth-century conquest of Latin America and the strictly patriarchal forms of the church.

Early modernity and its empires are Fox's main focus in the time frame between the Middle Ages and the present. Accordingly, in *A New Reformation* (hereafter *NR*), Fox poses a virtually unilinear problem: "Conquest—of native peoples and of nature itself—was part of the modern era from the beginning" (*NR* 110). Modernity is synonymous with domination of other people and of nature, considering the wisdom of premodern peoples inferior. At the same time, however, Fox assures us, not all of modernity has to be rejected (*NR* 116–18). Postmodernity, moving beyond the modern but incorporating it, is thus presented as the solution. While modernity focuses on conquest, postmodern consciousness focuses "on our common survival" (*NR* 112). It appears that in the absence of conquest the road to a new relation is open. Many feel that way today about empire, as can be seen, for instance, in the responses to some of the recent wars. Yet this contemporary sentiment that things would go back to normal again if only we could stop open conquests and wars is hardly on target. The more hidden forms of modern empire and neocolonialism are often overlooked by Fox and thus postmodern interests in other people and in the premodern are seen as unambiguously positive: "Postmodernism is pluralistic and honors the wisdom of premodern peoples; it honors the whole body, not equating truth exclusively with patriarchal headiness; it looks for the *whole*, that is, for cosmology."[50]

Several things are overlooked here. Empire is not simply a remnant of early modern conquests but continues in milder modern colonialisms and, in mutant form, in postcolonial postmodernity. Fredric Jameson, for instance, has called the postmodern fascination with the premodern a form of "cannibalism," where the postmodern appropriates what it finds attractive without deeper engagement.[51] As the "cultural logic of late capitalism" (Jameson), the postmodern asserts its own kind of control and its own kind of power over the other. The asymmetrical distribution of power, based in economic structures, obviates the need for political top-down structures that were required to various degrees in order to maintain control. The same is true for some of the postmodern concerns for the whole, which Fox mentions, and globalization might be their poster child. But what makes the processes of globalization possible is the unequal distribution of economic power; and it is this concentration of economic power in a few hands that guarantees successful economic exploitation without too much overt political or military control. Fox's intent should be honored, though. Quoting French philosopher Andreas Huyssen, he points out that we need to reach out to others not in order to steal but in order to learn and to "purify" our own traditions (*NR* 118). In this way he is attempting to incorporate a self-critical element. But postmodern concerns for diversity and relativity,[52] despite offering improvements over early modern models of conquest and forced assimilation, still need to be examined for the ways they can perpetuate postcolonial forms of empire.

An example of how empire is perpetuated in these more hidden ways is provided in Fox's confidence that science will fix our current problems. Fox builds his cosmic Christology on "the holy trinity of science (knowledge of creation), mysticism (experiential union with creation and its unnamable mysteries), and art (expression of our awe at creation)" (*CCC* 78). In these elements lies the foundation for what Fox calls "deep ecumenism": he claims that "the scientific story is today being heard and believed globally," that "art too is transcultural," and that the mystical experience of the cosmic Christ is, like art, "a common language, uttering a common experience" (*CCC* 228–30). In terms of the first element, science, he assumes that scientists are in fundamental agreement.[53] Yet here a metanarrative shapes up of the kind that the postmodernists have taught us to question,[54] an "origin story" (*Creation Spirituality* 28; hereafter *CS*) that may amount to nothing less than a myth of origin that shores up the powers that be. With this uncritical endorsement of science, Fox is closer to empire than he realizes. Obviously, the metanarratives of science are not devoid of the use and abuse of power either and we would need to take a closer look at which powers are supported here. As we have seen, the postcolonial empire does not need to proceed by conquest and explicit political aggression and domination; unifying moves at the levels of the economy and of culture and knowledge where power is hidden are now more effective. Even certain efforts to promote "unity in diversity" can backfire in the presence of significant imbalances of power. Fox does not seem to be aware of this problem.

Yet not all metanarratives support empire by default. Fox introduces another metanarrative, the "preferential option for the poor," and provides a myth of origin for it too. We opt for the poor, Fox argues, "because a creation story instructs us in the fact that in our origins we are all poor" (*CS* 29). Creation spirituality thus "empowers" those who have been forgotten and ignored to become "co-creators of a new historical vision" (*CS* 32). This insight is related to mysticism, which is the second element of the "trinity" mentioned above. Fox envisions a very particular kind of "mystical solidarity" in which the oppressed are "our natural spiritual leaders," an approach that can "promote and sustain political solidarity" (*CCC* 232). This insight is linked to the cosmic Christ: "A preferential option for the poor . . . is far closer to the teaching and spirit of Jesus than is a preferential option for the rich and powerful . . . " (Thesis 20, *NR* 70). Fox's concern for the margins is rooted in his Christology. The goal of this second metanarrative/myth-of-origin complex is self-critique: "a deep ecumenism will critique and attempt to renew one's own roots" (*CCC* 243). This attitude dramatically changes the dynamics of the metanarratives of empire, which are geared toward control and the kind of critique that is not self-critical but seeks to shape the other in one's own image. The function of metanarratives thus changes depending on their relation to power; while metanarratives have shored up empire for centuries, it may well be that we need counter-metanarratives in order to exercise effective self-critique. But Fox does not seem to realize that for his self-critical project to succeed the second metanarrative would need to be allowed to challenge and transform the first. Merely adding them up is not enough.

Every now and then the reader gets the sense that Fox fails to engage the causes of empire at a deep enough level, even though his argument starts out in the right direction. Fox is one of the few theologians writing in the North of the Americas who have made the suggestion that we need to think about the North and South of the Americas in relation.[55] The fact that both Americas have experienced colonialism indeed provides a common bond—one more likely to be seen from the perspective of the colonized than the colonizers. Furthermore, Fox points out that "The United States colonized Latin America, often with the kind of cruelty that a wounded child effects on others when that child becomes a 'killer adult'" (*CS* 117). This is an interesting thought: What happens when the colonized become colonizers? Fox pursues this question along the lines of addiction and wonders "what would happen if the Americas could break the habit of colonialism and of empire building" (*CS* 117). But whether the problem can fruitfully be compared to addiction is questionable, and Fox's use of the category is not convincing. Discussing the three-hundred-billion-dollar debt that Latin America owes to banks in the United States, he wonders, "Why not a breakthrough that will 'get the monkey off' Latin American economies, and thus free them to enter the world economy not as debtors but as partners?" (*CS* 119). Fox wonders out loud why the United States and Canada cannot create a Marshall Plan for Latin America (*CS* 145). This shows that he does not grasp the complexity and seriousness of the problem. There are systemic reasons why there is no breakthrough. The encouragement of the cosmic Christ to "let your compulsion to conquer go. Let your militarism go" (*CCC* 142) does not address the deeper web of power and it is not even likely to help the individual addict. Here, one feels tempted to respond like Anselm to Boso: "You have not yet considered the weight of sin."[56]

Fox's way of addressing the matter of sin has been subject to frequent criticism. His rejection of an Augustinian notion of original sin[57] has been called an "accommodation to modernity," with the result that "creation and redemption are brought so close together in Fox's work that his programs for social transformation are almost inevitably simplistic."[58] What these criticisms often overlook, however, is that Fox's stance has much deeper roots in the Christian tradition; Fox initially encountered the distinction between a fall/redemption spirituality (which affirms original sin) and a creation spirituality (which rejects original sin) in the thought of his mentor, French theologian M. D. Chenu, who identified this pattern in the ancient theologies of the church.[59] The more important question here is whether Fox's approach is simplistic in relation to empire.

Though Fox rejects the doctrine of original sin, he does not reject the doctrine of evil. One problem of the current deterioration of religion, he points out, once again moving in the right direction, is that it "underestimates the human capacity for evil" (*CCC* 8). Inspired by Latin American liberation theology, Fox calls for "historical, sociological, political, and economic analyses" in order to discern the "paths of sin" (*CS* 81). But he immediately reverts to talk about addiction to drugs and other things, which grow out of a failure to control and leads to dishonesty, denial, and perfectionism.[60] But does this move capture the depth of sin and evil in the postcolonial empire? What if there were different kinds of addiction, and if the "addiction to militarism and misuse of the world's resources" (*CS* 87), the kind of addiction that may very well describe the powerful, were different from the addiction to drugs (*CS* 90) that is more typical of the oppressed? If it is true that one of the problems of the middle class in the "overdeveloped world" is that we take things for granted (*CS* 92), we need to take a closer look at the sort of evil that comes in the form of success and progress, including the seemingly positive scientific and spiritual developments that Fox praises. In these cases, "addiction" does not always have to do with a lack of self-esteem, and Fox's concern that reminding people of their participation in evil would inevitably lead to low self-esteem and fear misses the mark.[61] The postcolonial empire does not seem to lack self-esteem, nor does it lack a sense of its own agency. In this context, saying things like "[evil is] a choice that we make as humans . . . and that we can unmake" (*NR* 20) sends the wrong message to those in charge, as if it were within their own powers to take on the empire; at the same time, this might be the right message to the oppressed, because it reminds them of their agency.

In a later book Fox displays a somewhat deeper sense of evil. In the spirit of ancient Christianity he observes a widespread loss of "the drama of a sense of evil and sin—angels, demons, powers, principalities"; instead, he notes, "we have substituted psychology for spirituality."[62] This is an important note, since the psychologization of sin and evil has indeed tended to cover up the deeper problems. A therapeutically oriented culture often tries to solve problems at the level of individual therapy and without going into the deeper causes of psychological disruptions. But this is precisely where Fox's own references to addiction got stuck earlier. Here, Fox seems to have developed a sense, sorely lacking before, that "evil abounds when humanity's capacity for creativity is greatest" (*Sins of the Spirit* 155; hereafter *SS*). Still, when he cites as examples the Holocaust and environmental destruction, he neglects again the deeper roots of evil in the postcolonial empire. Ultimately, the lack of critical reflection on the limits of modern scientific cosmology and the lack of a deeper analysis of the evils of empire combine with the result that evil gets naturalized: "perhaps evil is inevitable in a universe as powerful and creative and full of eating and being eaten, living and dying as ours is. Perhaps evil is to blessing what terror is to beauty" (*SS* 160). But it is far from certain whether the notion made famous by Hobbes of "nature red in tooth and claw" that is probably in the back of Fox's mind should be used in comparison with the atrocities of empire, and we must wonder how "natural" the evil is that contributes to the untimely death of thirty thousand children each day.

In this context, Fox's rejection of the notion of God's judgment makes things worse. While the notion of a "punitive God" does indeed merit critical investigation, Fox gets rid of God as judge altogether. His argument is christological, claiming that Jesus "critiqued images of God that his culture and religion took for granted, images of God as judge and lawgiver versus images of God as generous and compassionate."[63] With this move, Fox joins the mainstream of liberal thinkers who continue to play off images of a punitive and a benevolent God, an attitude recently popularized again by George Lakoff, not a theologian but a cognitive scientist and linguist. Conservatives, Lakoff says, understand God as punitive— "that is, if you sin you are going to hell, and if you don't sin you are going to be rewarded." In conservative Christianity, Jesus gives you credits toward heaven. Liberals, on the other hand, see "God as essentially beneficent, as wanting to help people." Consequently, liberal Christianity is focused on grace and love. In the liberal camp, spiritual experience has to do with connections to other people and the world and with service—all that liberals need to do is unite across the religions and with secular liberals who hold the same values.[64]

Several points need to be made in response to this approach. First of all, it is highly questionable whether Jesus wanted to get rid of images of God as judge ("Woe to you. . . ," pronounces the Jesus of Luke [Luke 6:24-26], and the Gospel of Matthew talks about the "Judgment of the Nations" [Matt. 25:31-46]). The question is, Who is really served by the removal of God's judgment? Those who do not benefit from the current system benefit little from a benevolent God who is unwilling to judge, that is, restore justice.[65] That injustice will be judged is one of the hopes held by the oppressed. There are notions of judgment that are not primarily punitive but restorative, addressing the restoration of justice for those who have experienced injustice. Fox presents us with a false alternative. Thesis 4 of his "95 Theses" is a case in point: "God the punitive Father is not a God worth honoring but a false god and an idol that serves empire-builders. The notion of a punitive, all-male God is contrary to the full nature of the Godhead who is as much female and motherly as it is masculine and fatherly" (*NR* 62). The common gender stereotypes that Fox endorses are perhaps more easily recognized as problematic. But stereotyping God's judgment and God's benevolence is equally problematic, and for this reason striking a "balance" between them does not help us much, unless God's judgment and God's benevolence are allowed to reconstruct each other. Under the conditions of a postcolonial empire a benevolent God can easily be appropriated by the empire builders, especially if that God coddles the perpetrators of injustice.

All this does not mean, however, that Fox's Christology has no concept of redemption. His notions of sin and evil are strong enough that redemption becomes necessary. We cannot save ourselves and cannot simply continue with business as usual. The Greek term *metanoia* ("repentance"; Fox translates it as "change of heart") is mentioned in terms of a "prelude to world peace and justice" and a movement beyond war and militarism (*CCC* 233). This notion is crucial, especially in a postcolonial empire that does not want to be reminded of its shortcomings and that presents itself in terms of progress. Yet in close proximity to this insight Fox quotes Mechthild of Magdeburg: "I have the power to change my ways" (*CCC* 234). This move plays down the rupture required by repentance and the insight that is most sorely lacking with the powerful, namely that while we have plenty of power we may not have the power required to significantly change our ways. Fox forgets that Mechthild's statement sounds different when uttered by a medieval woman mystic who asserts herself, constantly being made aware of her limits, and the beneficiaries of a postcolonial empire whose power is peaking.

These observations throw new light on Fox's efforts to address the top-down mentality of colonialism. One model of social interaction—Fox calls it "Climbing Jacob's Ladder"—is clearly elitist, hierarchical, and competitive. It conceives of God as a "Sky God." This model needs to be replaced, he argues, with what he calls "Dancing Sara's Circle," a model that is "participatory, circular, close to the earth, egalitarian and self-healing, self-motivating and self-organizing, like the universe itself" (*CS* 128). In this context, Fox returns to his concern for the margins, pointing out that "creation spirituality works out of the base to the extent that it awakens those at the bottom . . . to their own leadership potential" (*CS* 128–29). Yet even though this looks, at first sight, like a reversal of the powers that be, Fox's model never quite gets to such a reversal. Once the obvious hierarchies are leveled and relationships are rearranged in a circle, things appear to be back to normal and an egalitarian structure seems to be established. Where real solidarity between the countries might emerge—for instance, in terms of workers who are exploited in North and South—Fox shifts gears and claims egalitarian relations already in place: The "First World" is said to sport a "predominantly middle-class culture," only the "Third World" appears to be still sharply divided between rich and poor (*CS* 129). Yet theology in resistance to empire can no longer afford to overlook the class divides in the First World and the potential for solidarity between First and Third Worlds where the lower classes are exploited.

While Fox is thus not clear enough about the challenges of contemporary empire, he shows more awareness of past empires. We must not forget the past, he reminds us, and need to "ask forgiveness through dialogue and prayer before true 'forgetting' can take place" (*CS* 66). Elsewhere, he also acknowledges that "*some* confession of sin is in order" (*CCC* 232; emphasis mine). He ends his book *The Coming of the Cosmic Christ* with appendices containing three different apologies (by three different church bodies) to Native Americans. It is telling, however, that none of these apologies addresses the deeper systemic entanglements of empire that continue into the present. Support is offered only "in the righting of previous wrongs" (*CCC* 248), and in the Native American "struggle to reclaim cultural traditions" (*CCC* 250) that seem to have been lost before our time. In the documents, furthermore, Native Americans are asked to "walk with us . . . so that our peoples may be blessed" (*CCC* 247) and to accept "a reconciliation that seeks to share your wisdom, truth, and sensitivity" (*CCC* 250). Unfortunately, there is no word in these church documents that oppressive relationships persist and that more is at stake for Native Americans than the reclaiming of religious traditions. Fox's own repentance does not go much beyond that of the official church bodies: "It is time that Western, white, European Christianity apologized publicly to the native peoples of America, Africa, Asia, and Europe and asked for forgiveness. With this reconciliation, we might gather at our altars with power once again" (*CCC* 233). Something is missing here.

The notion of "letting go" is at the heart of what Fox means by repentance. Letting go works both on the smallest and on the largest scale. We cannot "restore balance" to the relationship of "First" and "Third" worlds, he says, without the "First World" "learning to let go."[66] Such letting go seems to come easy, and it does not have to happen in "sackcloth and ashes. Letting go can be done in celebrations and rituals that allow us to grieve and that also inspire us for the next stage of relationship" (*CS* 40–41). Thus, he suggests rituals around letting go of one hundred billion dollars of defense budget. What is lacking, however, is once again a clear acknowledgment of what went wrong in the first place. A deeper engagement of the problem is not called for. Thus, the following statement might be perceived as a slap in the face of the victimized: "We are not here to bemoan our existence, to blame ourselves or others, or to wallow in our sinfulness" (*CS* 37). Also lacking is a sense that repentance and restoration might be related, as the old story of Jesus and Zacchaeus shows; Zacchaeus repaid four times what he took (Luke 19:1-10).

The greatest problem with this approach to the cosmic Christ, however, is that it underestimates the empire. Sin and evil have deeper roots than Fox realizes, and they can be found even in what might look like steps in the right direction. In the postcolonial empire, as we have seen, economics plays a special role. Fox, unlike many other theologians, does not bracket this issue but once again he does not seem to grasp the whole of the challenge. Fox exposes "nondemocratic capitalism," which uses democratic slogans in order to deceive the middle class, and shows that capitalism is always hierarchical; those without capital are squeezed out (*CS* 111). In *A New Reformation*, Fox even observes the rise of multinational global corporations as a problem, since this contributes to the increasing gap between rich and poor (*NR* 13). Yet when it comes to real engagement of the economy, he underestimates the challenge. Realizing that one of the casualties of contemporary economics is work, Fox encourages a "vast effort by the human imagination to *create work*, good work for our vast armies of unemployed adults and youth the world over" (*CCC* 205). What is lacking in the effort to create good work in this account is mainly "the political will and imagination" (*CS* 110). Everybody gets blamed here except the monied interests themselves and there is no clear notion as to what the real problem is. Whose imagination might be lacking? Can the problem be fixed if we only want to? By mustering whose political will? In his book *The Reinvention of Work* (hereafter *RW*) the deepest problem is identified as the "desacralization of work."[67] But how does this happen and who is responsible? Furthermore, consumerism, says Fox, "has become the engine driving our economic world today" as a force of "avarice" that "is not restricted to the ruling classes" (*RW* 7). Consumerism thus seems like another choice or a more harmless sort of addiction that we could simply let go (*RW* 37). There is no word here about the temptations presented by the advertisement industry, which incites the consumer spirit in order to explore new and greater markets. It seems as if all that is lacking is the moral resolve of consumers; again something is missing here. The postcolonial empire is really given the upper hand, though, when Fox encourages workers to hang on and make the best of a bad situation: "Given a deep spirituality, one can turn even a job into work, re-envisioning its place in the whole" (*RW* 6).[68] What more could the postcolonial empire ask for?

The Resisting Christ of the Cosmos

Most theologians are unaware of the connections of Christology and empire. They engage in christological reflection as though Christology could be done in a vacuum, or at least without the powers that be having an impact on it. The common result is that the connection to empire comes in through the back door and makes things worse. Evangelical theologian Millard Erickson, for instance, develops his Christology without any references to the power struggles that shape our lives today. His reflections on the rule of Christ remain so generic that at no point is a connection made as to how Christ poses a challenge to the dominant powers of our own day.[69] Fox's approach does not fall into those traps. He is aware of the fact that religion and empire have worked hand in hand and that empire is legitimized by religion (*NR* 22). Noting the problems of accommodating religion to the powers that be, he asks whether religion can become a force of resistance. Fox hopes that religion, and Christology in particular, can "become an instrument of social awakening and deep social change for and by the masses" (*CCC* 162). The question now is how Fox's cosmic Christ might provide resistance.

As mentioned before, when Fox juxtaposes two Christianities, one is reminded of the limiting paradigm of the culture wars between liberals and conservatives, an arrangement where mostly white, middle-class Americans are locked in a closed system. Is the alternative that Fox proposes able to push beyond this system? While the conservative group worships a "Punitive Father," the alternative group "recognizes the Original Blessing from which all being derives. It recognizes awe, rather than sin and guilt, as the starting point of true religion. It thus marvels at today's scientific findings about the wonders of the fourteen-billion-year journey of the universe. . . . It prefers trust over fear and an understanding of divinity who is source of all things, as much mother as father, as much female as male" (*NR* 19). The postcolonial empire is not necessarily challenged, however, by this alternative. While fear of the other is a problem in the first group, the second group knows that "love drives out fear" ("says John's Epistle," *NR* 59). While Fox is right that fear of the other does indeed contribute to the drive for dominance, we are beginning to realize that "love" does not necessarily guarantee the end of colonialism (see also above, chapter 5). In fact, the postcolonial empire is full of examples of "loving" approaches to the other that invariably end up shaping the other in one's own image.

Nevertheless, Fox has some deeper insights into the dilemma. He rejects the "New Age" label, for instance, because his approach seeks to preserve a sense of "darkness, shadow, and injustice."[70] There is, after all, a sense of the demonic aspect of human power that is "cosmic in scope."[71] These insights nudge him beyond the notorious image of the liberal do-gooder: "Since the pain, suffering, and sin are cosmic—bigger than we can control and far more complex in space and time than we can imagine—the redemption must be cosmic as well." We cannot fix things merely out of the goodness of our own hearts. Christ will have to "disarm cosmic forces" (*CCC* 152). In this context, a description of the members of alternative groups as "mystical activists" (*NR* 55) might open up a new world of resistance: resistance to empire is not primarily middle-class activism but the pursuit of God's own actions.[72] The horizon broadens beyond the typical self-centeredness of the contemporary church. Rather than being church-centered, these groups will be eco-centered, says Fox;[73] put in christological terms, we might say that the alternative is to be centered on the cosmic Christ. The cosmic Christ in this scenario embodies a different kind of activism; action is linked not to being in control but to suffering and resistance—the cosmic Christ is wounded, as we have seen. The grounding of the cosmic Christ in Bible, tradition, and solidarity with those who suffer is crucial. Fox's call for a "historical Christ" is key for the resistance to empire. The question is not primarily "What would Jesus do?" but, to use the words of Frederick Herzog, "What is Jesus doing now?"[74]

Fox also goes deeper than the culture-wars paradigm when he develops a more complex understanding of the problems with conservative ideas. Rather than simply rejecting the notion of sin altogether, as liberals locked in battle with conservatives often do, Fox develops awareness of the problems of an insufficient notion of sin in the conservative camp: "Very often a fall/redemption religious ideology trivializes sin just as it trivializes creation and grace and spirit" (*SS* 157). This, he argues, might be the deeper reason that the "bridge generation between the modern and postmodern worlds has been very reluctant to engage in sin-talk"; perhaps there is such a thing as "cheap guilt" and "many people wisely resist it" (*SS* 157).

This insight goes hand in hand with a deepening of the notion of sin. Fox has never fallen into the trap of privatizing the notion of sin as if sin were only the problem of individuals. Sin includes the disruption of social relationships and social injustice as well as the disruption of our relationship to world and cosmos. In his book *Sins of the Spirit*, however, Fox expands his understanding of sin by talking about the "evolution of sin" (a phrase attributed to David Korten). Sin, he recognizes now more clearly, is not just the disruption of relationship through domination and conquest. The days of imperial nation-states who conquer the world, he notes, may give way to "transnational financiers," "corporate colonialism," and "globalization" (*SS* 156). These sins, we cannot help but note, refer to the kinds of things that are used by the beneficiaries of postcolonial empire to gauge the progress of our world. No matter what the common opinion is of globalization and of the corporations that pursue it, the stock market, retirement benefits, and the future of the empire are all tied up with their success. Naming these things as sin, therefore, introduces a new tone that could introduce not only a major challenge to the status quo but also another broadening of the relevance and field of action of the cosmic Christ.

The two most important aspects that lead us beyond the limited scope of the culture wars are Fox's critique of elitism and his concern for the margins.[75] His guide for these insights is not a particular political preference—neither conservatives nor liberals truly identify with the margins, we might add—but Christ himself: "The Cosmic Christ is present wherever there is pain" (*CCC* 153), explains Fox. Furthermore, suffering connects us with the margins and broadens the self, an insight that is mostly lacking both in conservative and liberal circles: "The compassionate solidarity that Jesus learns comes from the cosmic suffering he undergoes. The same is true of us. We imbibe the healing power of the Cosmos Christ [sic] to the extent that we are emptied of mere personal suffering to experience all suffering as cosmic or shared suffering" (*CCC* 153).

To the degree that Fox's argument allows for the leadership of the margins, he offers a new paradigm. The concerns for the margins displayed by conservatives and liberals have no room for this aspect, as conservatives seek to teach personal responsibility and liberals seek to support the margins through social programs; in each case, the goal is to integrate those on the margins back into the system. Fox's emphasis on the leadership of the margins leads beyond these two positions, but it would need to be developed more fully. Perhaps his own journey will help him in the process. An article in *The Christian Century*, commenting on his departure from the Roman Catholic Church after years of struggle, indicates that he "left the Roman Catholic Church and joined the Episcopal Church as a gesture of solidarity with young people and the environmental movement."[76] Fox praises the Episcopal Church especially for the possibility of leadership from the margins, including the ordination of women, participation of laity, and for keeping bureaucratic structures to a minimum. But this is only a first step at best. Elsewhere, Fox notes that the poor are natural allies of the middle class; the members of the middle class differ from the poor mainly by virtue of their education (*CS* 78). This insight might change fundamentally the current attitude of the middle class, which often feels like it is "reaching out" (if not "reaching down") to the poor, but unfortunately Fox does not offer much clarification of his claim beyond the point that most of the ancestors of European Americans did not come from privileged classes in Europe. Other contemporary thinkers have been clearer about this issue, pointing out that most Americans who consider themselves middle class belong in fact to the working class since they are not in control of their own work (or the means of production).[77] If one of the problems of postcolonial empire is the ever-widening gap between the rich and the poor, which threatens the middle class and pushes it in the direction of the underside, this insight is important. In this context, the goal is not to develop hatred for the rich,[78] but to learn how to relate to each other in new ways and to form solidarity that includes those who have been overlooked (the lower classes, non-whites, etc.) in the world of the culture wars.

The cosmic Christ thus initiates new kinds of relationship that resist the distortion of power under the conditions of empire. As we have seen, the problem with these distorted relationships manifests itself not just in situations of violence and domination but also in situations where love and compassion are promoted. Jesus restores a kind of compassion, says Fox, that is "not about pity or feeling sorry for others. It is born of shared interdependence" (*CCC* 32). In relation to the other, the self is thus not eliminated but becomes more fully human and true to itself: "the true self is the *self-in-relationships to all others*," including relationships to creatures and to the cosmos (*CS* 96).

The reconstruction of relationships under the conditions of the postcolonial empire can also benefit from Fox's helpful point that compassion and altruism are not the same. Jesus never called for altruism, he explains, but for compassion and justice (*SS* 152). Altruism, defined as "self-destructive behavior performed for the benefit of others," differs from Jesus' command to "love others as you love yourself," which does not aim at self-destruction. Interestingly enough, the sort of compassion that is called for turns out not just to be a human trait. Fox refers to a study that not only humans but "animals other than humans go out of their way to assure the survival of others."[79] True compassion does not destroy the postcolonial self but reshapes it.

Sexuality, often demonized by the church, is another area in which true relationships can be formed. Fox refers to the Song of Songs in the Old Testament, which describes an encounter of two lovers. Here is a relationship that is truly mutual, where one is truly seeking the "other" rather than "merely the missing parts of his own soul."[80] Other interpersonal relationships reflect the concern for the margins. Fox arrives at what might be called a "preferential option for the child"; clearly, the situation of children deserves attention, because abuse is common and one of every four children under six lives in poverty in the United States (*CCC* 183), a number that has not significantly changed even today. Once again, Jesus is Fox's guide. He valued children and, as with other marginalized groups in society, he saw them as "spiritual directors and sources of wisdom" (*CCC* 186). In this context, however, romanticizing children does not help, and unfortunately Fox's argument is not entirely free from this. Claiming, for instance, that Jesus turned out so well because Joseph treated him like a child of God[81] can only distract from the deeper issues at stake. At stake in the Gospel passages quoted by Fox (Matt. 11:25-26; Luke 10:21-22; Luke 22:26 [*CCC* 186–87]) is not so much age, as he seems to think, but power: those who are not in positions of exerting power over others have the edge, which may be in part where the advantage of children lies. Fox also supports his concern for children by referring to tradition: the monastic rule of St. Benedict advised listening to the youngest of the community first, since the Holy Spirit was closer to them (*CCC* 190). Fox fails to mention, however, that this rule is not as radical as Jesus when it comes to the matter of power, since the abbot makes the final decision.[82]

In the struggle against empire, liberation cannot just be for the oppressed. The imperialists need to be liberated as well. Fox does not address this question directly, but his concern for the liberation of men provides a model: "Male liberation will constitute the next important chapter in the awakening of women's consciousness, for men too have been victimized by the system that exploits Mother Earth, women, and children" (*CCC* 174). This is a good start because he does not moralize or blame individual men. There is some awareness of systemic issues, and that those in power are controlled by the system too. But since Fox fails to explore the systemic issues, he makes things look as if all are victims of the system, and thus no one is to be challenged. As a result, male liberation seems to be achieved by drumming, dancing, and "entering into the irrational processes that have been native ways of ritual and wisdom for tens of thousands of years" (*CCC* 177). Nothing indicates that men's positions of power need to be addressed. While assigning moral blame is indeed self-defeating because the deeper problems of empire are not to be found in the ill will or consciously immoral actions of oppressors and imperialists, coddling them might make things worse.

The position that Fox develops in response to the Mel Gibson movie *The Passion of the Christ* is more helpful in this regard. In his review he notes that "in many ways the film is a monument to sadomasochism. Gibson makes Jesus a victim rather than a martyr while removing Jesus' passion for justice and substituting the term 'passion' to mean passive victim." Fox more clearly identifies here the problem of empire: "Our culture is deeply engaged in sadomasochism—understood . . . as the haves lording over the have-nots." While most critics of Gibson in one way or another highlighted his one-sided emphasis on suffering, Fox points out the connection between religion and empire. Apparently, during the advertising campaign for the movie, fliers were sent out to churches stating that "Dying was Jesus' Reason For Living." According to Fox, it is difficult to imagine a slogan more contradictory to Jesus' life or his teaching or indeed to that of the Christ who in John's Gospel says: "I have come that you may have life and have it in abundance."[83] In this review, Fox also lists some startling numbers that throw light on the deeper problems of the postcolonial empire—for instance, the fact that the income of the richest 225 people in the world is equal to the income of three billion poor people.[84]

Fox adds the Earth to his list of the marginalized and thus broadens the horizon of resistance to empire: "Is Mother Earth herself not . . . the most neglected of the suffering, voiceless ones today? And along with her, the soil, forests, species, birds, and waters are not being heard where legislators gather, where judges preside, and where believers gather to worship" (*CCC* 17). Almost two decades after this statement the awareness is spreading again that global warming might indeed be a serious issue and that uninhibited pollution and exploitation of the environment cannot continue without dire consequences. Fox may yet be proven right that "the killing of Mother Earth in our time is *the number one ethical, spiritual, and human issue of our planet*" (*CCC* 142; emphasis in original). Once again, however, a romantic view of the marginalized does not help. The following statement reminds us of the tremendous gift that the Earth is, but it blends out the struggle for survival in nature and that at times nature turns deadly: "[The Earth] has blessed us for four and one-half billion years by providing water; separating continents; establishing just the correct amounts of oxygen, hydrogen, and ozone in our atmosphere for us; birthing flowers, plants, animals, fishes, birds to delight us and bless us with their gifts and their work of making air and soil healthy and welcoming to us."[85]

One of the basic reasons why religions have the power to change the world and to "birth global peace and justice" is because they hold collective power that is more in touch with the voiceless than governments or anyone else. This power can help to "motivate governments," Fox asserts (*CCC* 235). Of course, this may not hold true in general, but it points to an opportunity for those religious groups that are learning to pay closer attention to those on the underside of history.

Another place where the idea of the leadership of the margins shines through is Fox's notion of a "democratization of wisdom" (*CCC* 240), since democratization does not mean pluralism, in which different wisdom traditions would merely run on parallel tracks. A closer connection leads to mutual challenges, in which leadership is provided even by those who are most silenced at present: "The power of native religions to regenerate Christianity and to reconnect the old religion with the prophetic Good News of the Gospels has yet to be tapped" (*CCC* 240). One small example of the fruitfulness of this kind of interaction might be seen in Fox's reference to Kabir, a Medieval Indian mystic. Kabir answers his own question, "Who is a holy person?" thus: "A holy person is one who is aware of others' sufferings" (quoted in *CCC* 151). Here, the insight of a non-Christian theologian is harbored to deepen an insight that is at the heart of the Christian message as well but that has been mostly neglected throughout the history of Christianity. It is not hard to see how this insight contributes of the resistance to the postcolonial empire, which strongly depends on not being aware of the causes of other people's suffering, even as it is trying to show benevolence.

Lately, Fox has revived an old Christian notion—the notion of holiness. In recent history, this notion has hardly been claimed in the resistance to empire. Yet the "single greatest difference" between fundamentalism and creation spirituality lies in how we define holiness, claims Fox.[86] The markers of this alternative holiness are: courage to step outside the status quo; creative use of anger; curiosity; the prophetic; and creativity. Creativity, in particular, is described as "being at the edge between order and chaos" and living on the margins.[87] Solidarity and identification with the margins are what provide the strongest kind of resistance in an empire that thrives on the backs of those on the margins but never acknowledges them, thus perpetuating the myth of individualism. Fox's list of what holds us back at present comprises two elements: the elitism of modernity (the elitism of the current postcolonial form of empire may be more hidden but the problem has not gone away) and the presumption that grace is scarce.[88] This notion of scarcity is one of the key assumptions of contemporary economics, which leads to the hoarding of things by some to the detriment of the many.[89]

Fox continues to hold what are often separated: mysticism and prophecy.[90] The combination of those two components leads to a self-critical stance, which is perhaps the thing most lacking in the postcolonial empire. While modernity has promoted the notion of critique (though not self-critique), postmodernity often proceeds under the assumption that critique is no longer necessary. Yet the tensions of empire remind us that both critique and self-critique may be more important than ever, and Jesus is once again guide: "Jesus would not have been crucified had his message and person not been radical and critical" (*CCC* 69). Mystics, too, need critique, and Fox talks about the need for mystics "to let go of projection onto others" and to avoid the "internalization of hatred." The goal of critique and self-critique is not destruction but love: "*It remains for those who have been touched by the power of religious faith to love religion enough to criticize it*" (*CCC* 53; emphasis in original). The christological surplus should be set free and become effective in the process.

In conclusion, we need to note that Fox's cosmic Christ deals with matters that have often received less attention in modern Christologies, including the cross, resurrection, and the second coming.[91] His cosmic Christology does not bracket suffering. It seeks to embrace the mystics' "dark night of the soul" and to understand how "suffering is redemptive."[92] After all, Jesus himself "chose to align himself with those in society for whom darkness and death were an ever-present reality even before he confronted his own intense darkness and death on the cross" (*CCC* 71). In suffering and in the cross, God's own self is present: "The experience of God as integral to human history is the experience of the suffering, the pathos, the anguish, and the anger of God who suffers when innocent victims suffer from injustice."[93] In the postcolonial empire, where suffering is either repressed or sedated, paying attention to suffering is significant. Suffering, in this case, is not passive but constructive. Resistance and a new world grow out of it.[94]

While Fox has less to say about the resurrection, he quotes Otto Rank, a Jewish thinker, who calls the resurrection the "greatest revolutionary idea in human history" (*CCC* 148). The resurrection is so powerful because it helps cut through the fear of mortality, putting to rest anxiety and the need to control. As such, the theme of the resurrection could provide a crucial lesson for those who seek to build empires. If their need to control the world and others could be laid to rest, one of the engines of empire could be shut down.

The topic of the second coming is discussed in unusual length (for about one hundred pages in *The Coming of the Cosmic Christ*). Christ's coming is anticipated in new relations between the sexes, new respect for children, art, worship, and the development of deep ecumenism. In this context, Fox might have talked about one of the key differences between evolutionary and revolutionary thinking: while evolution builds on what is, revolution turns things around. The second coming of Christ is more than the development of what is; it presents challenges and ruptures the status quo. Jürgen Moltmann has developed these matters in helpful ways in his own reflections on the cosmic Christ. The eschatological movement of redemption, according to Moltmann, "runs counter to evolution." In terms of the vectors of time, "it runs from the future to the past, not from the past to the future." In terms of the challenge, it is "the divine tempest of the new creation."[95] Christ is thus not the supreme point of evolution (against Teilhard de Chardin), but relates to the weakest points.[96] In other words, the resisting Christ of the cosmos looks different than the cosmic Christ of evolution, especially when evolution is understood in a social-Darwinist manner. If Christ is not locked into the survival of the fittest, perhaps evolutionary motives can be reconceived so that they emphasize the importance of greater diversity and new models of success might emerge that are not identified with the top echelons of society. But the issue is not just evolution; we might also give thought to a different concept: Christ's revolution. In both cases, there are forces at work that are bigger than the postcolonial empire. Perhaps we can see in Fox's hope in the "great power of the universe, a power of constant generativity" and that humans are "co-creators" in these ways (*CCC* 211).

Notes

1. This is part of Jürgen Moltmann's critique of the work of Pierre Teilhard de Chardin. See Jürgen Moltmann, *The Way of Jesus Christ: Christology in Messianic Dimensions,* trans. Margaret Kohl (Minneapolis: Fortress Press, 1993), 292, 300. Moltmann suggests an understanding of Christ as the "redeemer of evolution," 301–05.

2. As is stated in one of the headlines of Matthew Fox's *Confessions: The Making of a Postdenominational Priest* (San Francisco: HarperSanFrancisco, 1996), 246.

3. Fox notes that "the cosmology of the postmodern era . . . teaches us that *there is no one center of the universe but that the universe is omnicentric*", ibid., 267; emphasis in original.

4. Margaret Goodall and John Reader point out that "academic theology has not taken him seriously enough as yet to launch its deconstruction job." "Why Matthew Fox Fails to Change the World," in *The Earth Beneath: A Critical Guide to Green Theology* (London: SPCK, 1992), 105.

5. While recent efforts to decouple Evangelical Christianity from the Republican Party might be noted (George G. Hunter, *Christian, Evangelical, And—Democrat?*

[Nashville: Abingdon, 2006]), empire today is by and large a bipartisan project, and so this move does not necessarily amount to a critique of empire.

6. These agendas are announced, for instance, in the "Project for the New American Century," which, according to its self-description is a nonprofit educational organization dedicated to a few fundamental propositions: that American leadership is good both for America and for the world; and that such leadership requires military strength, diplomatic energy, and commitment to moral principle. See http://www.newamericancentury.org. (accessed 11/13/06). Several high officials of the Bush administration, including Vice President Dick Cheney and former Secretary of Defense Donald Rumsfeld, are related to this organization. Its aims have helped to produce the war in Iraq, hastened the Central American Free Trade Agreement [CAFTA], and strengthened the global pursuit of U.S. business interests.

7. It should be noted, for instance, that there are more and more efforts in the evangelical camp to address burning issues that have traditionally not been on the radar screen of evangelicals, including issues of global warming and a more progressive stance on politics based on Jesus' own politics. See, for instance, Brian D. McLaren, *The Secret Message of Jesus: Uncovering the Truth That Could Change Everything* (Nashville: W Publishing Group, 2006). Nevertheless, those dissenting voices whose thought might point to a christological surplus are met with heavy criticism from their conservative peers.

8. See http://www.newamericancentury.org/statementofprinciples.htm (accessed 12/16/06). This statement is dated June 3, 1997, and signed by twenty-five high-powered conservatives, including Cheney, Rumsfeld, William Bennett, Jeb Bush, Steve Forbes, Francis Fukuyama, George Weigel, and Paul Wolfowitz.

9. See, for instance, Francis Fukuyama, "Invasion of the Isolationists," op-ed article in *The New York Times* (August 31, 2005), who argues that the Bush empire misses the real potential of the American spirit due to its isolationist tendencies.

10. The time frame during which the various colonies gained their independence covers more than two centuries. The official colonial status of many Latin American countries, for instance, ended in the early 1800s. As is well known, the United States gained its independence from Britain even earlier, in 1776. Most African countries, on the other hand, have achieved postcolonial status only during the last few decades.

11. David Harvey, *The New Imperialism* (Oxford, England: Oxford University Press, 2003), 6.

12. Revenue is first used to pay the company—sometimes at inflated cost—and then split 60/40, 60 percent for the state, 40 percent for the company. The contracts last for

twenty-five to forty years, which is the life expectancy of an oil field; Iraq has the third largest oil reserves in the world, after Saudi Arabia and Canada (*People's Weekly World* [January 7–13, 2006], 13).

13. A report in the *Christian Science Monitor* (September 19, 2001) notes that Europeans cringed at Bush's remark of a "crusade against terrorism," while Americans hardly noticed it. See http://www.csmonitor.com/2001/0919/p12s2-woeu.html (accessed 11/13/06).

14. Harvey, *The New Imperialism*, 6, reference to Michael Ignatieff.

15. David Spurr, *The Rhetoric of Empire: Colonial Discourse in Journalism, Travel Writing, and Imperial Administration* (Durham, N.C.: Duke University Press, 1993), 185.

16. See, for instance, the books by Hal Lindsey, Tim LaHaye, and Jerry B. Jenkins. For an interpretation that pays attention to diverse manifestations of the Christian Right see Mark Lewis Taylor, *Religion, Politics, and the Christian Right: Post-9/11 Powers in American Empire* (Minneapolis: Fortress Press, 2005). Unfortunately, Taylor identifies the problem mostly with the Christian Right and a truncated form of "contractual" liberalism; ibid., 85. Taylor does not consider the systematic problems with the liberal heritage itself: Is it a mere coincidence that liberal values were born in a colonial world (see above, chap. 5)?

17. Taylor, discussing the 2002 statement "What We're Fighting For—A Letter from America," drafted by Jean Bethke Elshtain and signed by sixty others, including theologians Richard J. Mouw, Michael Novak, and Max L. Stackhouse. Ibid., 22.

18. Joerg Rieger, *God and the Excluded: Visions and Blindspots in Contemporary Theology* (Minneapolis: Fortress Press, 2001).

19. In the Roman Empire, for instance, military force was used directly in the expansion of empire and in securing land for private property that was distributed to local aristocracy. See Ellen Meiksins Wood, *The Empire of Capital* (New York: Verso, 2003), 34.

20. See also Harvey, *The New Imperialism*, 18–25; and Naomi Klein, "Baghdad Year Zero: Pillaging Iraq in Pursuit of a Neocon Utopia," *Harper's Magazine* (September 2004), 43–53, available also on the Web at http://www.harpers.org/BaghdadYearZero.html (accessed 12/14/06)

21. This is one of the problems of David Bosch, *Transforming Missions: Paradigm Shifts in Theology of Mission* (Maryknoll, N.Y.: Orbis Books, 1991), who assumes that since modern colonialism is over, we do not have to worry about distortions of power any more and can start over as "postmoderns." For an extended argument on issues of mission see Joerg Rieger, "Theology and Mission in a Postcolonial World," *Mission*

Studies: Journal of the International Association for Mission Studies 21, no. 2 (2004): 201–27.

22. See Kwok Pui-lan, *Postcolonial Imagination and Feminist Theory* (Louisville: Westminster John Knox, 2005), 187, 193–95.

23. Matthew Fox, *The Coming of the Cosmic Christ: The Healing of Mother Earth and the Birth of a Global Renaissance* (San Francisco: HarperSanFrancisco, 1988), 65 (hereafter *CCC*).

24. Even in the precapitalist "Empires of Commerce," extra-economic power was still the basic force. The Arab Muslim, Venetian, and Dutch empires established themselves as "vital economic links among separate markets in dispersed communities and regions," as Ellen Meiksins Wood notes (*Empire of Capital*, 47). The success of trade depended fundamentally on various extra-economic advantages, particularly on military power and less on inner-economic competition in production.

25. Ibid., 10.

26. Ibid., 12. Wood states: "Expansion of capital is possible precisely because it can detach itself from extra-economic power in a way that no other social form can"; ibid., 25. The capitalist empire begins with the British: "As landlords lost their extra-economic powers to an increasingly centralized state . . . their wealth increasingly depended on the productivity and commercial success of their tenants"; ibid., 76. There was a transition from the consideration of land as basis of political power to the land as "income-yielding investment" (R. H. Tawney, quoted in ibid., 77). In this case, economic competition through an increase of labor productivity laid the foundation for a new form of empire, even though it took a long time for economic power to overtake other forms of power. See ibid., 87.

27. Michael Hardt and Antonio Negri, *Multitude: War and Democracy in the Age of Empire* (New York: Penguin, 2004), 163.

28. See Meiksins Wood, *Empire of Capital*, 17; Meiksins Wood charges that Michael Hardt and Antonio Negri in their earlier book *Empire* (Cambridge, Mass.: Harvard University Press, 2000) were not clear enough about the indispensable nature of the state in this arrangement; see Ellen Meiksins Wood, "A Manifesto for Global Capitalism?" in *Debating Empire*, ed. Gopal Balakrishnan (London: Verso, 2003), 61–82.

29. As stated in an Associated Press Report of April 17, 2006, Lee R. Raymond received $69.7 million in compensation and a $98 million pension payout. According to the report, *some* shareholders and economists are asking "How much is enough?" (emphasis mine). The report can be found on the Web at http://www.msnbc.msn.com/id/12356099/from/RSS/ (accessed 11/13/06).

30. The Halliburton Corporation, which was awarded the most lucrative contracts, is only the tip of the iceberg. In the long run, the oil companies who score the new contracts with Iraq will benefit, as will all the other business ventures that flooded into Iraq right after victory was declared; that many of them are now on hold due to the ongoing insurgency does not mean that they will not come back at a later time. See also Naomi Klein, "Baghdad Year Zero: Pillaging in Iraq in Pursuit of a Neocon Utopia."

31. Wal-Mart, for instance, has been accused of failing to provide benefits, with the result that its employees have to fall back on public-welfare benefits. Thus, public welfare and Social Security funds subsidize Wal-Mart's operating costs by supporting employees' health-care needs. This has been documented for instance by the film *Wal-Mart: The High Cost of Low Prices*, directed by Robert Greenwald, 2005.

32. Meiksins Wood, *Empire of Capital*, 23.

33. Ibid., x. In addition, the role of those larger economic forces remains "opaque, because in general it operates not by intervening directly in the relation between capital and labour, or between imperial and subordinate states, but more indirectly, by sustaining the system of economic compulsions, the system of property (and propertylessness) and the operation of markets"; ibid., 4.

34. Ibid., 2.

35. In fact, any effort to increase the minimum wage that does not build in automatic increases related to the cost of living ends up increasing the gap between the classes.

36. In this context, Fox praises the "Trinitarian Christians" who "refuse to lock God up behind our projections." This is "about creation *and the divine presence in it* and about the spirit *and divine presence in it.*" *Confessions*, 154; emphasis in original.

37. See *CCC* 67ff.; Fox repeats over and over again that we are up against dualism: 49–50; 56–57; 6–7; 59.

38. Newtonian fragmentation, Fox explains, even "reigns in our sexual lifestyles and the result is boredom," *CCC* 206.

39. *CCC* 21; the problem seems to be a one-way street that begins with knowledge, since the Enlightenment's emphasis on knowledge and information required a "multibillion dollar industry" be created to "store it all and retrieve it."

40. Matthew Fox, *A New Reformation: Creation Spirituality and the Transformation of Christianity* (Rochester, Vt.: Inner Traditions, 2006), 19 (hereafter *NR*).

41. Still, Fox is aware of differences, for instance that Protestant fundamentalism stresses the authority of the Bible while Roman Catholic fundamentalism stresses the authority of the church. See ibid., 24, 41, 45, 49.

42. "We must get out of the way so that the connections and interdependencies that already exist might emerge." *CCC* 50.

43. Fox, *Confessions*, 139.

44. It is a bit surprising, though, that in a footnote to this confession Fox quotes Otto Rank's unreconstructed statement that "here, too, the primitives disclose to us the deeper sources." *CCC* 225 n.18.

45. See Jacques Lacan, discussed in Joerg Rieger, *Remember the Poor: The Challenge to Theology in the Twenty-First Century* (Harrisburg, Pa.: Trinity Press International, 1998), 79–83.

46. See, for instance, George Tinker, "Spirituality, Native American Personhood, Sovereignty, and Solidarity," in *Native and Christian: Indigenous Voices on Religious Identity in the United States and Canada*, ed. James Treat (New York: Routledge, 1996), 127; although he misjudges Fox somewhat when he charges him with promoting "value-neutral creation theology." His concern for a stronger "theology of community," however, is on target.

47. Vine Deloria puts it this way: "Tribal religions were almost entirely focused on the group. The individual may have done the sun dance or vision quest but the traditional motivation was always to sacrifice for the benefit of the people." *For this Land: Writings on Religion in America* (New York: Routledge, 1999), 282.

48. Rosemary Radford Ruether, "Ecofeminism and Healing Ourselves, Healing the Earth," a lecture in the series "Keeping the Spirit Alive," presented by St. Stephen's College and given in Edmonton and Calgary, Alberta, on June 2 and 3, 1998. Available on the Web at http://www.ualberta.ca/ST.STEPHENS/ss-rueth.htm (accessed 11/13/06).

49. At times, Fox speaks as if things happened because of philosophers like Descartes, who "has influenced 'First World' education and thinking for three centuries." Matthew Fox, *Creation Spirituality: Liberating Gifts for the Peoples of the Earth* (San Francisco: HarperSanFrancisco, 1991), 102 (hereafter *CS*).

50. Fox, *Confessions*, 247.

51. Fredric Jameson, *Postmodernism, or: The Cultural Logic of Late Capitalism* (Durham, N.C:. Duke University Press, 1991). Postmodern architecture is one of his examples.

52. In *NR* 112–13, Fox provides a list of differences between the modern and the postmodern. His insight on relativity is helpful in response to those who worry about relativity: "we do not feel driven to discard all socially constructed realities just because we recognize them as such." *NR* 121.

53. At one point he talks about "scientists agreeing the world over on the basic facts of the new creation story." *CS* 27.

54. See Jean-François Lyotard, *The Postmodern Condition: A Report on Knowledge*, trans. Geoff Bennington and Brian Massumi (Minneapolis: University of Minnesota Press, 1984).

55. See, for instance, *CS*, chap. 8.

56. See above, chap. 3.

57. Captured in Thesis 32, *NR* 76: "Original sin is an ultimate expression of a punitive father God and is not a Biblical teaching. But original blessing (goodness and grace) is biblical."

58. Wayne G. Boulton, "The Thoroughly Modern Mysticism of Matthew Fox," *The Christian Century* (April 25, 1990), 432.

59. Fox, *Confessions*, 69.

60. *CS* 81–87. Margaret Goodall and John Reader have a point when they argue that Fox's efforts to link his work with liberation theology are too superficial. "Why Matthew Fox Fails to Change the World," 108.

61. *NR* 26; the biggest problem, then, is fear; fundamentalism is based on it. *CS* 99.

62. Matthew Fox, *Sins of the Spirit, Blessings of the Flesh* (New York: Harmony, 1999), 154–55 (hereafter *SS*).

63. Matthew Fox, *Creativity: Where the Divine and the Human Meet* (New York: Jeremy P. Tarcher/Putnam, 2002), 104, reference to Marcus Borg.

64. George Lakoff, *Don't Think of An Elephant! Know Your Values and Frame the Debate* (White River Junction, Vt.: Chelsea Green, 2004), 102–03.

65. Justice is more strongly emphasized in another approach to the cosmic Christ in Moltmann, *The Way of Jesus Christ*.

66. *CS* 39; one example is to cut down on meat consumption.

67. Matthew Fox, *The Reinvention of Work: A New Vision of Livelihood for Our Time* (San Francisco: HarperSanFrancisco, 1994), 12 (hereafter *RW*).

68. Rather than being one of the pillars of the postcolonial empire, economics appears to be a fairly harmless affair in Fox's account, only interested in "facile numbers about stocks, bonds, capital, and money." *CS* 112.

69. Millard J. Erickson plays it safe. *Christian Theology*, 2nd ed. (Grand Rapids, Mich.: Baker, 1998). The benefit of Christ's divinity, for instance, is that "we can have real knowledge of God," that "redemption is available to us" and that "God and humanity have been reunited"; ibid., 720. Nowhere is the challenge of Christ's divinity mentioned; not even Christ's Lordship presents a challenge—it only affirms "divinity" in generic fashion; ibid., 707–08. Surely, the readers will fill in the blanks.

70. Fox, *Confessions,* 158.

71. *CCC* 152; at that time in the late 1980s he lists nuclear weapons, power plants, and the nuclear accident in Chernobyl in the former USSR (now Ukraine).

72. Frederick Herzog, in his book *God-Walk: Liberation Shaping Dogmatics* (Maryknoll, N.Y.: Orbis, 1988) talks about Theopraxis, Christopraxis, Spiritpraxis; he never uses the term *orthopraxis* because such a term when used for those in power would fail to lead us beyond the status quo.

73. *NR* 56. The problems are simply too big, notes Fox: "denominations pale in comparison to nature, creation, and creation in peril." *Confessions*, 247.

74. Herzog, *God-Walk*, xxiii.

75. This topic occurs off and on but not always consistently; see *Confessions*, 279, 283.

76. Reported in *The Christian Century* (April 27, 1994), 442.

77. Michael Zweig, *The Working Class Majority: America's Best Kept Secret* (Ithaca, N.Y.: ILR, 2000).

78. This solidarity with the poor does not have to lead to hatred of the rich, as is often mistakenly assumed. In reference to Leonardo Boff and Latin American liberation theology, Fox puts it like this: "The issue is not to fight the persons who are rich, but the socioeconomic mechanisms that make the rich wealthy at the expense of the poor." *CS* 78.

79. *SS* 153. Fox quotes a study by Jeffrey Moussaieff Masson and Susan McCarthy. This research contradicts the findings of biologist Lyall Watson, who claims that "our genes drive us to aggression and adultery alike"; ibid., 149.

80. *CCC* 171, rejecting Freud's "negative view of sex." It seems, however, that Fox misunderstands the problems, including mechanisms of repression.

81. *CCC* 186; reference to Alice Miller.

82. "The Lord often reveals to the younger what is best," says the Benedictine Rule; this rule implies that the community of monks be called together if an important decision is to be made; but Fox does not mention that it is the abbot who collects advice and ultimately makes the decision and that the brethren are encouraged to give advice with deference and humility and not "stubbornly defend their opinions." The text is available on the Web at http://www.osb.org/rb/text/rbejms2.html (accessed 11/13/06).

83. Matthew Fox, "Mel Gibson's Passion and Fascism's Piety of Pain," 2004, on the Web at http://www.matthewfox.org/sys-tmpl/htmlpage7/ (accessed 11/13/06).

84. Fox provides more numbers: "In the 1960s, the overall income of the richest 20 percent of the world's population was thirty times that of the poorest 20 percent. Today, it is 224 times larger. In the 1960s, the richest 20 percent held 70 percent of the world's revenues; in 1999 it was 85 percent. . . . The income of the three richest people in the world is equal to the collective national incomes of the poorest forty-nine countries!

It would take no more than 5 percent of the overall annual sales of arms in the world to feed all the starving children, to protect them from dying of preventable diseases, and to make basic education accessible to all."

85. *CCC* 145; "like Jesus at Golgotha, she is innocent of any crime." The Earth yearns to "take *all* the children—including the adult ones—under her wings of protection." *CCC* 146; emphasis in original.

86. Fox, *Confessions*, 276.

87. "Living *sur la marge*," *Confessions*, 277–79.

88. Fox, *Confessions*, 283.

89. M. Douglas Meeks has elaborated on this fundamental assumption of scarcity. *God the Economist: The Doctrine of God and Political Economy* (Minneapolis: Fortress Press, 1989).

90. This dialectic was announced early on in *CCC* 63.

91. The whole part 5 of *CCC* is dedicated to the matter of the second coming, a topic that is also addressed in Moltmann, *The Way of Jesus Christ*.

92. Reference to Martin L. King, *CCC* 60–61.

93. *CCC* 85. Worship: "*that* we celebrate is directly proportionate to admission of shared suffering"; *CCC* 219. Fox also remarks on the "pitiful positivism" of worship represented by "human-made balloons and homemade smiles"; *CCC* 219.

94. This insight might help address a challenge to Fox from feminists. Joanne Carlson Brown and Rebecca Parker reject the idea that salvation is not from pain but through pain. "For God So Loved the World?" in *Christianity, Patriarchy, and Abuse: A Feminist Critique*, ed. Joanne Carlson Brown and Carole R. Bohn (New York: Pilgrim, 1989), 6–7. But here suffering has a constructive and active character. Nevertheless, at times Fox uses language of sacrifice and talks about the "expiatory value" of Jesus' death; salvation is thus understood as "liberation from bondage"; *CCC* 150; but this language can be problematic, especially if it is not clear why sacrifice is needed in the first place and for what offense expiation needs to take place.

95. Moltmann, *The Way of Jesus Christ*, 303; references to Walter Benjamin.

96. Ibid., 306. At the same time, the eschatological emphasis of Moltmann pays less attention than Fox to what the cosmic Christ is doing at present; ibid., 340. While Moltmann points out that people do not live from traditions alone but also from expectations, he does not develop the mystical experience of the present.

Conclusion

-------⇒●⇐-------

The Truth Shall Make You Free

(John 8:32)

THE THEOLOGICAL THEMES DISCUSSED IN THESE CHAPTERS have been prominent in Christian thought, particularly those of the first millennium represented by Paul, Nicaea, Chalcedon, and Anselm and the loaded concepts of Christ's lordship, divinity, and satisfaction. The problem, however, with unreflected repetitions of such traditional concepts by mainline theology should now be clear: if the relations to empire of each of these ancient approaches go unnoticed, it is more likely than not that the spirit of empire will be perpetuated in our own time. While in the contemporary United States, for instance, images of empire often have overt theological undertones, the problem is not simply the explicit political hijacking of theological ideas or the explicit theological justification of empire. Such moves can be more easily identified.[1] Just as problematic is the unconscious support of empire by those who do not explicitly identify with the theological and political moves of empire. This is perhaps the main challenge of empire in our own time, and it is especially problematic under the conditions of the softer forms of empire that often proceed under the guise of mutual relationship and that appear to value difference, since these softer forms often go unnoticed. Those who want to do "only theology," whether conservative or progressive, and those who seek to be faithful to Christ at the religious level alone will have to face the uncomfortable truth that they might be drawn into the force field of empire unconsciously, without being aware of it. The deep-seated and well-established force fields maintained by empire must not be underestimated. Christian theology that seeks to stay true to the alternative and challenging inspiration of Christ, identified in each of the chapters, will have to find new ways of dealing with the influences of empire.

Christ and Empire

The stakes are high at a time when the empire is claiming more and more of the globe and when alternatives seem to crumble or be crushed easily, or never even materialize due to the sheer weight of the system. There are many parallels to earlier empires, but there are also differences. Strategies change, power mutates, and the rulers now often have term limits and rotate every few years. Since the Roman Empire, empires have become not less but more powerful and more extensive. Already some of the medieval empires, headed by popes and supported by emperors, were larger and more powerful than the Roman Empire. The structures of colonialist modernity, created by various European countries and their rulers, reached farther into remote areas of the globe that were not even known to the medievals. The contemporary postcolonial reality of empire of the twenty-first century is more extensive and global yet, even though the United States has emerged in a leadership role and provides somewhat of a center. Even in this leadership role, however, the United States is not an autonomous entity but is influenced to a significant extent by broader economic interests. While this empire faces growing political resistance that was unimaginable only a few years ago, its structures are all-pervasive to a new degree. For the most part, control is no longer a matter of direct political rule (here is the fundamental difference between colonialism and neocolonialism); economics, technology, and culture, at times supported by military interventions, have proven far more effective in creating an empire than ever before. Not only does this new empire reach farther around the globe, it reaches further into our collective unconscious, and thus into our deepest theological thoughts, than anything previously imaginable.

That many of the most significant moves of Christology have been shaped in relation to the force fields of successive empires is a sobering discovery, and some might see the necessary investigative work of the historian and theologian performed in this book as mainly an effort to put down Christianity. But something else has emerged. We have seen that even where the pressure is greatest, where the empire appears to be so powerful as to swallow up everything else, there remains a certain ambivalence that allows for some room where alternative inspirations can grow. While large parts of the development of Christology beg to be understood in their relation to empire, empire can hardly ever control all of our thinking about Christ, and here lies a very strong reason for hope. Nevertheless, we will only find this inspiring space—tied to ambivalence and the surplus that I have been talking about in each of the chapters—by facing the encroachment of empire into our theologies head-on. In fact, our theologies and the historical perspectives

314

tied up with them will continue to support empire by default unless we look for those particular and often repressed places where we encounter alternatives. In other words, in order to find true christological inspiration and an answer to the now-frequently asked question, "What difference does it make?" we need to face the forces that constantly threaten to hold captive our thinking about Christ.[2] Theologies and Christologies that do not dare to confront their assimilation and bondage to empire stand little chance to push through to new visions of liberation. Perhaps this is why our theological and historical efforts often seem so harmless and irrelevant (of course, they are neither harmless nor irrelevant because they end up supporting the status quo). Here we are back at the methodological problem addressed in the introduction, that of a historical theology that is unfortunately not yet even historical-critical but that needs to move on to what, to use a term coined by Frederick Herzog, might be called a "historico-self-critical" perspective.[3]

Christological Surplus

In this context, the christological surpluses that have been identified in each of the chapters of this book have the potential to make a tremendous difference: fresh inspirations of Christ as the resisting Lord challenge any and all self-proclaimed lords who follow the conventional logic of top-down power and seek to shape the world in their own image (chapter 1). New visions of Christ who embodies the coequality of divinity and humanity radically reshape our images of what is divine and human; neither humanity nor divinity can be defined any longer in the image of those in power but both need to be seen in relation to Christ who literally embodies ("incarnates") solidarity with the outcast (chapter 2). Christ as God-human resists the common trivialization of Christology by confronting head-on the gravity of sin under the ambivalent conditions of empire and by restoring justice in situations where injustice is rampant (chapter 3). The Christ who embarks on a new and unheard-of way pushes us beyond tired notions of equality defined in terms of the status quo of modernity, walking not first of all with the colonizers who are always on the go but with those who walk in less conspicuous ways at the margins, turning the one-way streets of the powerful into two-way streets (chapter 4).

Furthermore, a Christ who blows the lid off conventional images of prophets, priests, and kings shows us a new kind of love that is renouncing its paternalistic baggage by engaging in ever deeper encounters with those who are not like us and who, like Christ, refuse to be assimilated to the agendas of empire (in however benevolent a form they may present themselves) (chapter 5). The image of Christ victorious morphs from a triumphalistic image into an image that creates hope by engaging the messy life-and-death struggles of empire where tremendous numbers of people are perennially struggling for hope and survival (chapter 6). And, finally, the Christ who encompasses the cosmic inspires us in unexpected fashion not by endorsing the "survival of the fittest" but by embodying the challenge of true difference and respect for others throughout his life, all the way to crucifixion, resurrection, and second coming (chapter 7).

In all these ways, both colonizers and colonized, those who benefit from empire and those on whose backs empire is built, are transformed and ultimately liberated. If the churches do not make use of this christological surplus, they will lose much of their inspiration and what keeps them vital, even though the surplus itself can never be completely suppressed; since Christ's work is an expression of God's love for the world (John 3:16), perhaps "the stones [will] shout out" (Luke 19:40) if Christians will not. Of course, many others shout out too and Christ today finds expression in the most unexpected places.

Truth

Empire presents its own claims to truth even if, as in contemporary embodiments of the postcolonial empire, often in hidden fashion. While there are few strong claims to truth in a cultural climate determined by postmodern sensitivities, there are nevertheless commonly accepted truths that support empire and that are never open for discussion or questioning. Recently, some of the truths of empire have been stated more openly by the administration of George W. Bush—for instance, in terms of the self-proclaimed superiority of U.S.-type democracy and U.S.-type capitalism or in terms of a rather limited set of family values (rooted strongly in nineteenth-century models of the middle-class patriarchal family). Yet other truths are still hidden and covered up, especially the question, Who ultimately benefits from the current structures of empire? Why else would so many common people vote for the interests of the wealthiest and most powerful members of society—for instance by endorsing tax cuts for the rich and for limits to the social and ecological accountability of monied interests—and against their own interests, that might better be served by a strong social security net that includes health care for all and a well-funded educational system?

In this context, we need to uncover not only the hidden truth of empire (its real face) but initiate a search for an alternative truth that points to a different reality. Since none of these truths are visible on the surface, we need to move through the netherworld of truth as that which is being repressed by empire and pushed below the surface.[4] Here is where the chapters of this book ultimately converge and where we have found hope and new inspiration; truth—the truth of empire and the alternative truth of Christ—can only be found if we search below the surface of the powers that be and explore the christological surplus manifest between the lines of the status quo. Commonly presupposed and accepted images of Christ can now be seen in a new light.

This move is reminiscent of Jesus Christ's truth found and pronounced in solidarity with those confined to the netherworlds of the empire. Jesus finds truth in unexpected places: "I thank you, Father, Lord of Heaven and earth, because you have hidden these things from the wise and the intelligent and have revealed them to infants" (Matt. 11:25), that is, to one of the many insignificant groups in the Roman Empire (and even today, since the little ones tend to be of least value to the empire). Christ's special connection to the underside of empire is manifest throughout his earthly ministry during which he repeatedly asserts that the last shall be the first and the first shall be the last. Paul carries on this tradition when he reminds the Corinthian Christians that God chose the foolish, the weak, the low and despised in order to shame the wise, the strong, and "to reduce to nothing things that are" (1 Corinthians 1:27-28); and that "none of the rulers of this age" understood God's wisdom (1 Corinthians 2:8). Christ's solidarity with the underside of empire is perhaps symbolized in its most extreme form by his descent into hell, confessed in the traditional versions of the Apostles' Creed—a part of the Christian tradition that has raised more than a few eyebrows and is now often left out of the recitations of the creed altogether. As we have seen in the different chapters of this book, resistance to the truth of the status quo arises precisely in unexpected reversals of Jesus Christ's perennial assimilation by empire and is manifest in the resisting Lord of the New Testament, the resisting coequality of Jesus human and divine, the resisting God-human, the resisting way of Christ, the resisting prophet, priest, and king, the resisting *Christus Victor*, and the resisting cosmic Christ. Thus, the Christ who is lesser at first sight becomes the Christ who is greater.[5]

This unexpected christological dynamic feeds back into the dynamics of an empire that faces its own challenges in matters of truth. The problem here is not so much an intentional cover-up or a conscious lie (although lies and cover-ups are part of the repertoire). The problem is with the fact that the most basic truth about empire is often invisible, only to be found between the lines. The truth about the American empire, for example, is that it took shape not accidentally (the empire was not thrust upon us, as is often assumed[6]) but in a state of denial that did not allow reflection or debate.[7] In this situation, the task is not so much to find someone to blame for empire but to wake up, to realize what is really going on, and to see what difference Christ makes in such a world. Jon Sobrino is right: what we need now is not another demythologization but the "depacification" of the Christ of empire who has aided our denial.[8]

The question of truth thus becomes the question of where we see Christ at work today; even the well-meaning question "What Would Jesus Do?" does not go far enough in depacifying Christ, because it often leaves the reality of Christ in the past. Can we still see Christ in places where the dominant logic of empire does not expect to find him? Resistance to empire is not enough in this situation; in fact, assuming that whatever resists empire is good in and of itself would be reactionary. The deeper question has to do with how we can find our way into the alternative truth of Christ, whose claim is to be "the way, and the truth, and the life" (John 14:6). Resistance needs to be seen in this context—as resistance against whatever limits Christ's reality and against whatever keeps us from following Christ. If Christ is truly God and truly human, for instance, he cannot be simply coterminous with the empire, and it is this surplus of his person and work that will ultimately set us free.

This sort of truth pushes beyond the realm of the epistemological. Awareness of a powerful alternative reality that cannot be captured by empire inspires fresh action and generates new energy.[9] For this reason it is truth that liberates, that makes free, which is the point of the statement by the Johannine Jesus (John 8:32). In this sense, the condition given by Jesus for this liberating truth—namely, that his followers "continue in my word" (John 8:31)—needs to be seen in a horizon that is much wider than "reading the Bible" or an existential connection to Christ, as conservatives and liberals have interpreted this passage respectively. Why not think about "continuing in [Jesus'] word" in terms of participating in Jesus' alternative reality, which includes the realities of the kinds of people on the margins with whom he developed relationships? "If you continue in my word, you are truly my disciples and you will know the truth, and the truth will make you free" (John 8:31-32).

Freedom

One of the paradoxes of empire in our own time is that people often assume that we are now closer to freedom than ever before. Enlightenment and modernity have brought us the freedom to think for ourselves (*sapere aude*—"dare to think"— was Immanuel Kant's famous motto of the Enlightenment[10]). The French and American Revolutions have brought new forms of political freedom—at least to the middle classes. And the so-called victory of capitalism in the 1990s is often credited with having completed these freedoms for the economic realm. Large-scale economic enterprises are seen as producing a sphere of freedom for some that was previously unknown. This sphere of freedom appears to be replicated in individual lives as well: anyone is supposed to be able to make it in the globalizing free-market economy. Even those who do not quite buy into the ideology of the free market—one of the major points that distinguishes "liberals" from "conservatives" in the United States—still assume that "anyone can make it—with some help," and thus they devise social programs geared to bringing people "up to speed." But ultimately this amounts to the same thing: freedom remains tied to the status quo. Riding on the coattails of what we now call the free (and postcolonial) market economy and the political transformations of modernity, the twenty-first century thus appears as the century of freedom. In this climate, who still needs what the Johannine Christ offers us—to be set free?

What has gone wrong, however, in this dominant understanding of freedom is that it is self-centered and lacks an understanding of our relatedness to God and to the world in general, and to Christ and our suffering neighbors in particular. The universalizing tendencies of the French Revolution are built on an individualistic foundation: I can do anything I want, as long as it does not hurt anyone else. This is true for the free market that now defines the empire as well: I can make as much money as I want. Period. With this idea of the free market we have unwittingly moved to the next step beyond the French Revolution: we have dropped the idea that freedom might hurt anyone. In regard to both, however—the freedom propagated by the French Revolution and by the free market—we need to remind ourselves that individualism, often greatly lamented nowadays by ethicists and other people who worry about morals, is itself an illusion of those in power. In the empire we never live as individualistic monads. Those who are successful will, of course, claim that their success is self-made, that they have earned every single penny of their extensive wealth, and that they have pulled themselves up by their own bootstraps. But individualistic monads do not exist in the empire of the twenty-first century: our identity always takes shape in relation to others. This is most clear in our families. Who we are is owed to a large degree to our parents.

Virtually no one would deny that. Often, however, our identity also takes shape in a negative way, that is, on the backs of others who are thus deprived of their freedom. This fact is perhaps most clear in economic relationships. Much wealth these days is produced on the backs of impoverished people all over the world—some of whom live in the midst of our own cities and countries.

Here the biblical uses of the term *freedom* might be helpful. In the Old Testament there is no abstract notion of freedom. Freedom is tied to liberation in specific historical situations of oppression. The Exodus from Egypt is, of course, the prime example. The Psalms, too, show a similar concern for liberation from specific modes of oppression. Freedom is thus usually expressed through verbs rather than nouns. It is not a fixed state. Rather, freedom is an ongoing process, always in flux.[11] The same is true in the Synoptic Gospels: freedom does not appear as noun but as verb. The Gospels do not talk about freedom in general but about liberation from specific forms of oppression,[12] and this brings us back to our christological reflections. Freedom is, ultimately, freedom in Christ and this freedom can never be static or self-centered. Freedom is gained through an ongoing process of liberation in Christ.

From what do we need to be liberated? This question is almost impossible to answer from the top, from a position of power. For those on the very top, liberation hardly ever appears to be an issue. Here, freedom is realized ("the land of the free") and freedom is to be spread to others. It is telling that the constant freedom-talk of the Bush administration has never included a call for the expansion of freedom at home.[13] Only those on the bottom, those who have been repressed into the political unconscious of the powers that be, can tell us where liberation is truly necessary. The relationship between men and women, which is still not on equal footing even in the globalizing empire, might serve as an example. Men rarely understand where their actions oppress women. Just the opposite: most men feel that they respect women, that they admire them. Most of us adore our female contemporaries. But in this process of idealization, repression takes place. We shape women in our own image precisely where we idealize them.[14] The need for liberation only becomes clear from the underside. It is the repressed neighbor who helps us to see the reality and reminds us that we are no longer "master in our own house." Here, christological inspiration can flow more freely than it ever could where it had to fit into the schemes of the masters and where it had to adapt to the logic of the empire. Freedom is thus not only the liberation from oppression but also the grace of a true encounter with Jesus Christ at the margins that is inseparable from true freedom.

Final Reflections

No book on Christology can be considered complete without a word about the resurrection and the *parousia*, the second coming, of Christ. Under the conditions of empire, both the resurrection and the *parousia* have often been painted in triumphalistic colors. Much of Protestant Christianity in the United States, for instance, tends to celebrate Easter in such a triumphalistic spirit, often without much recognition of the fact that the resurrection of Christ cannot be disassociated from his crucifixion and that it is therefore necessary to "read between the lines" of the seeming success story of Easter. A view of both resurrection and *parousia* that ties them back to the crucifixion brings us to a more truthful understanding of Christ that might help resist empire. In the stories of the New Testament Gospels, crucifixion and resurrection are kept together first of all by the women who were the first to encounter the resurrected Christ—that is, by those who were not granted as prominent a place in the later Christian tradition as the apostles; here lies the key.

What makes all the difference is whether we try to grasp the resurrection from the top down (from a perspective of control, however diffuse or hidden) or from the bottom up (from a perspective of solidarity with suffering and oppression). The same is true for the *parousia*. Do we try to see resurrection and *parousia* in the perspective of the history of empire (created by the powers that be and written by the winners), or do we try to see the history of empire in the perspective of resurrection and *parousia*?[15] The former perspective—seeing resurrection and *parousia* in the perspective of history—has been the common approach of empire and, in the more recent development of theology, took shape in various ways. Both the liberal theological projects of "demythologization" and the fundamentalist visions of the end of the world represent extrapolations from the history of empire. In order to say something meaningful and striking about the resurrection and the *parousia*, theologians felt that they had to do so in ways that would be acceptable to those who make and shape history and that would correspond with their methods of shaping history. Thus, the resurrected Christ of liberal demythologization fits in with the modern worldview and does not rock the boat (not even putting a minor scratch on our commonly accepted worldviews), and the yet-to-come Christ of the fundamentalists uses fire and sword and all the other apocalyptic terrors of empire to accomplish his goal.

The other perspective—seeing history in the perspective of the resurrection and of the *parousia* of the crucified Christ who lived and died in solidarity with people on the margins—leads to a different understanding. If the coming Christ remains in solidarity with people on the margins, a challenge is presented to those who are used to making and shaping history, and a new space is carved out that creates room for those who are pushed against the wall in the contemporary structures of empire. It is not hard to figure out which views of the resurrection and of the *parousia* might create more space for Christ to work freely and thus which ones offer more of a surplus and are more inspiring. This new perspective—that was often forced underground but never quite lost in the history of Christology—is what ultimately puts us on the way to another Christology and points toward an entirely different "new world order," an upside-down order that might come as a surprise even to those (theologians among them) who thought they knew what Christ was all about. Our growing awareness that Christ is quite different from how we had envisioned him is in good company with the growing awareness of Jesus' reality by his own disciples as presented in the Synoptic Gospels,[16] and perhaps this is how it ought to be.

Notes

1. See, for instance, Stephen Swecker, *Hard Ball on Holy Ground* (Charleston, S.C.: BookSurge, 2005).

2. Catherine Keller is right that "it is *because* the church is implicated in empire that we can decode and transcode the idolatries of empire." *God and Power: Counter-Apocalyptic Journeys* (Minneapolis: Fortress Press, 2005), 21 (emphasis in original).

3. See Frederick Herzog, *God-Walk: Liberation Shaping Dogmatics* (Maryknoll, N.Y.: Orbis, 1988), 7, and my interpretation of this term in Joerg Rieger, *Remember the Poor: The Challenge to Theology in the Twenty-First Century* (Harrisburg, Pa.: Trinity Press International, 1998), 115–16.

4. These different kinds of truth relate back to the distinction between "reality" and the "real"; see above, the introduction, and Rieger, *Remember the Poor*, 75–77. Postmodern and poststructuralist modes of thinking highlight the connections between traditional claims to a single truth and systems of dominance. Is not talk about "the truth" a sign of the dominant colonial and neocolonial mind-set? In *Remember the Poor*, I suggest a different way to think about truth in relation to a passage from Frantz Fanon, one of the early pioneers of postcolonial theory, that pushes the preferential option for the margins to its very limits: "Now the *fellah*, the unemployed man, the starving native do not lay a claim to the truth; they do not *say* that they represent the truth, for they *are* the truth." Frantz Fanon, *The Wretched of the Earth*, preface by Jean-Paul Sartre, trans. Constance Farrington (New York: Grove, 1968), 49; quoted in ibid., 228. I believe that my argument there is still valid: this sort of truth is not the *a priori* truth or the

foundationalist truth of colonial knowledge. Neither has it anything to do with the Cartesian conception of truth, grounded in a self that is in a position of control. Truth here is not a universal category but a relational event. Located at the margins, it simply points to that which has been repressed and covered up. Truth is that which has been pushed below the surface in specific situations—not in a weak sense that we simply do not happen to see it, but in a strong sense that this is what really matters—this is what really determines who we are and what we want since our desires are bound up with such repressions and with such repressed people. See Rieger, *Remember the Poor*, 83–88; 228. See also my reflections on truth in "Liberating God-Talk: Postcolonialism and the Challenge of the Margins," in *Postcolonial Theology: Divinity and Empire*, ed. Catherine Keller, Michael Nausner, and Mayra Rivera (St. Louis: Chalice, 2004), 214–18.

5. An ancient principle states *deus semper maior*, "God is always greater." Revelation has to do with the inbreaking of new possibilities that cannot be accounted for by the powers that be. See, for instance, Mary Aquin O'Neill, "The Mystery of Being Human Together," in *Freeing Theology: The Essentials of Theology in Feminist Perspective*, ed. Catherine Mowry LaCugna (San Francisco: HarperSanFrancisco, 1993), 147.

6. Even Robert Bellah follows this interpretation when he states that "the Americans . . . have become an empire almost by default, leaving us in no way prepared for imperial responsibilities." "The New American Empire," in *Anxious About Empire: Theological Essays on the New Global Realities*, ed. Wes Avram (Grand Rapids, Mich.: Brazos, 2004), 22.

7. See chap. 7 above and David Harvey, *The New Imperialism* (Oxford: Oxford University Press, 2003), 6.

8. Jon Sobrino, *Jesus the Liberator: A Historical-Theological Reading of Jesus of Nazareth*, trans. Paul Burns and Francis McDonagh (Maryknoll, N.Y.: Orbis, 1993), 50. Sobrino's judgment that the problem is not so much atheism but idolatry is also valid in the contemporary United States; see ibid., 180.

9. These two elements are combined in Rieger, *Remember the Poor*. See also Michael Hardt and Antonio Negri, *Empire* (Cambridge, Mass.: Harvard University Press, 2000), 157: "The poor is a subjugated, exploited figure, but nonetheless a figure of production. This is where the novelty lies."

10. Immanuel Kant, "What is Enlightenment?" in *The Philosophy of Kant: Immanuel Kant's Moral and Political Writings*, ed. and trans. Carl J. Friedrich (New York: The Modern Library, 1977), 132; Friedrich translates: "Have the courage to use your own intelligence."

11. Hans-Werner Bartsch, "Freiheit, Altes Testament," *Theologische Realenyzklopädie*, ed. Gerhard Krause and Gerhard Müller, vol. 11 (Berlin: Walter de Gruyter, 1983), 497.

12. Hans-Werner Bartsch, "Freiheit und Befreiung im Neuen Testament," *Theologische Realenyzklopädie*, vol. 11, 506.

13. The following statement, taken from "The National Security Strategy of the United States of America," published by the White House on September 17, 2002, sums it all up: "The great struggles of the twentieth century between liberty and totalitarianism ended with a decisive victory for the forces of freedom—and a single sustainable model for national success: freedom, democracy, and free enterprise." Further down, the point is made that "the United States will use this moment of opportunity to extend the benefits of freedom across the globe." The document can be found in Avram, ed., *Anxious about Empire;* the quotations are on pp. 187 and 189.

14. For a more detailed account of these dynamics see Rieger, *Remember the Poor*, 78-82.

15. For this reversal of perspectives see also Jürgen Moltmann, *The Way of Jesus Christ: Christology in Messianic Dimensions*, trans. Margaret Kohl (Minneapolis: Fortress Press, 1993), 227.

16. Note that the disciples continue to struggle with their understanding of Jesus throughout the Synoptic Gospels. In the Gospel of Mark, for instance, Peter comes to the realization that Jesus is the Christ rather late, in chap. 8:29; but he keeps wrestling with Christ's identity even then, as demonstrated in a whole set of misunderstandings that immediately follow this passage (9:5-6; 9:32; 9:34; and 10:13-14).

Index

Index

Index

Index

Index

Index